American Mystery
and Detective Novels

Recent Titles in
American Popular Culture

American Mystery and Detective Novels

A Reference Guide

LARRY LANDRUM

American Popular Culture
M. Thomas Inge, Series Editor

GREENWOOD PRESS
Westport, Connecticut • London

Library of Congress Cataloging-in-Publication Data

Landrum, Larry N.
   American mystery and detective novels : a reference guide / by
Larry Landrum.
      p. cm.—(American popular culture, ISSN 0193–6859)
   Includes bibliographical references and index.
   ISBN 0–313–21387–9 (alk. paper)
   1. Detective and mystery stories, American—History and criticism.
   2. Detective and mystery stories, American—Bibliography.
   I. Title. II. Series.
   PS374.D4L34 1999
   813'.087209—dc21   98–22916

British Library Cataloguing in Publication Data is available.

Library of Congress Catalog Card Number: 98–22916
ISBN: 0–313–21387–9
ISSN: 0193–6859

First published in 1999

Greenwood Press, 88 Post Road West, Westport, CT 06881
An imprint of Greenwood Publishing Group, Inc.
www.greenwood.com

Printed in the United States of America

The paper used in this book complies with the
Permanent Paper Standard issued by the National
Information Standards Organization (Z39.48–1984).

10 9 8 7 6 5 4 3 2 1

CONTENTS

ACKNOWLEDGMENTS

Many people have made suggestions and offered kindnesses during the writing of this book. I would like to thank the staff of Special Collections at Michigan State University Library, including Peter Berg, Head of Special Collections, Anne Tracy, and Randall Scott. I would also like to thank Jeannette Fiore, former Head of Special Collections. Jennifer Sams worked with me on the final preparation of the manuscript under the auspices of the Undergraduate Research Opportunity Program. I appreciate the opportunity of working with that fine program under the leadership of Natavia D. Curry. M. Thomas Inge, series editor for the volume, has been patient and encouraging. Finally, I would like to thank my spouse, Nancy Pogel, for her support.

INTRODUCTION

Mystery and detection have been among the most popular fictional genres to emerge in Western literature. The roots of mystery fiction have been traced into antiquity, and arguments have been made for the universality of many of its characteristics. Every Western society has laid claim to early versions of the mystery and to innovative works in its varied past. Likewise, puzzles and narrative riddles necessary to the detective story are found in the folklore of all cultures, and the investigation of wrongdoing and the search for solutions to problems found in detective fiction reaches beyond recorded history. The forms of mystery and detection that such interests take are not universal; they emerge in particular cultures at particular times, pass into and come to dominate appropriate modes of expression, and assimilate imagery found in their parent cultures. American mystery and detective novels emerged in the popular literature of the late nineteenth century and have become a rich source of information about popular art and culture. In recent years a great deal of effort has been put into the study of mystery and detective fiction and related genres, providing many new perspectives on how and when these forms emerged and how they are related to culture.

The modern mystery grew out of the transformation from the alliance of the aristocracy and religion to capitalism and science. While many structural similarities suggest a common origin for gothic and mystery fiction, mysteries clearly reflect the growing influence of rational explanations of

mysterious conditions that marked early nineteenth-century popular literature. The gothic element in many mysteries suggests unexplained factors
or the failure of simple cause-and-effect reasoning. There is often some
sense in which the mystery threatens to escape rational explanation. Such
uncertainty is expressed in other ways: the narrator is vulnerable, caught
in a web of intrigue, or susceptible to the frailties of ordinary people. The
central figure of a mystery is often the narrator, and the weight of suspense
allows little distance between the narrator and the reader. In the early detective story, especially, narrative distance is established by focusing the
reader's attention more or less on detection and often by placing a recorder
of the experience—a Watson figure—between the reader and the detective.
Detective stories are more specific than mysteries. They focus the narrative
more directly on the solution of a puzzle that the solution of a crime poses.
Detective stories demand keen observation, superior reasoning, and the dis-
ciplined imagination of their protagonists. The immediacy of physical danger may require a strong arm, fighting skills, or a quick gun or may be
swept away by the furtive investigations of some frail, elderly sleuth or
even by a child. In any case the narrative must provide suitable challenge
with high enough stakes that the measures taken by the detective seem
appropriate.

As entertainment, detective and mystery fiction attracts a following that
is associated with fame, and it is useful to distinguish between appreciation
and literary criticism. Appreciation centers on authors. Most media attention to authors centers on speculation about their personae as authors and
expresses itself as focus on financial success and intentionality. Appreciation is usually associated with reviewing, where the goal is not so much to
provide analysis but to alert potential readers to opinions and information
about books, authors, and trends and to assess the potential interest of new
publications and those publications readers may have missed. Appreciation
may also be concerned with grouping writers and types of books, with
providing a running commentary on the field and keeping track of a branch
of the writing profession. In the case of fans it may be adulation and its
hierarchies, more or less pure and simple, of the authors and/or the fiction.

This form of appreciation is articulated as criticism when it is combined
with textual discussion. In fandom the extension of the author to the work
and vice versa becomes blurred. Since celebrity is a part of the celebration
of art, it is not necessarily negative in any of its forms, but when it enters
the field of criticism, it does tend to be localized as some version of au-
thorial intention. In some cases this means that writers are drawn into
discussions that they would rather avoid, and fans take on questions that
scholars would not consider significant or answerable. Appreciation tends
toward critical models that can be categorized as Romantic in the sense
that readers are expected to "know" writers through texts and biographical
information. This symbiosis is felt by professional critics as well, of course,

but it has traditionally been reserved for authors whose works have been enshrined in literary canons. What has happened in the last few decades is that canons have expanded, opening literary study to a much larger range of texts and authors. Discussion of individual authors is in the manner, generally, of establishing a corpus and biographical information, evaluation of technical competence, taste, popularity, individual psychology, and so on. On the other hand, criticism within genres often opens larger critical questions regarding the field of mystery and detective fiction. These kinds of studies, which are here simply called criticism, may have little to do with the details of individual authors or works.

Author criticism may well become indistinguishable from work produced by reviewers and fans, while critical studies are more likely to be concerned with the phenomenon of popularity itself. Psychoanalytical or deconstructionist or other kinds of approaches can therefore fall into either category, depending on whether the emphasis is on authors and/or their individual works or on an archive of materials.

Writers, more than most fans and literary scholars, produce direct information about the profession and market. One of the distinguishing features of the professional writer is an acute sense of the marketplace—not only of the publishers available for different kinds of fiction, but of the ways of orienting to them stories that writers want to tell. This knowledge itself constitutes a kind of mystery into which beginning writers hope to be initiated. Writers' advice is therefore invaluable and is made available to the public in a multitude of forms—through workshops, interviews, how-to books, lectures, formal classes, personal correspondence, and example. A good deal of attention in trade newsletters and magazines is on the bellwethers of publishing: the emergence and disappearance of new publishing houses or lines, editorial changes, writers opening new possibilities or tapping new audiences. The information emphasizes opportunities for new writers and possibilities for seasoned writers with materials that may be more appropriate for one market than another. For scholars this information helps distinguish between formal and cultural characteristics of novels, as well as distinctions between marketing push and popular pull.

Of course these categories of commentators are not necessarily separate and distinct, since fans and academics become writers, academics have often been fans, writers may well become academics, and so on. Rather, these may be taken to represent somewhat different perspectives on the texts. Writers are mainly interested in the production and distribution of texts, fans in their collection and consumption, and academics in a text or texts in a critical scheme of things—why people read them, how the reading reflects or affects them, why texts take the particular forms they do, how to identify and explain similarities and differences among texts, and questions bearing on the relationships of texts to social, political, economic, and cultural phenomena or intertextual relations. Fans and authors may also be interested in such questions, of course, but are more likely to address, on the one hand, nuts-and-bolts questions—fans on the who and what, authors on the how. Fans tend to give attention to the two extremes of literary production—the minutiae of the facts of production at one end and the wholly speculative aspects of intention and taste at the other—which support a largely Romantic preoccupation with authors and texts. From Edgar Allan Poe in "The Philosophy of Composition" (1846) through Carolyn Wells (1913) in the early twentieth century to contemporary writers such as Hillary Waugh (1991) and others, writers have often bridged, or attempted to bridge, all these categories.

The book is organized in a way that attempts to account for the literary history and types of novels growing out of mystery novels and their two general kinds of attention. Chapter 1 is a history that sketches a broad outline of mystery and detective novels. The chapter evolves definitions for mystery and detective novels and identifies the emergence of variants, but it leaves further definition of these to chapter 2. Likewise, chapter 1 does not cover all the possible influences on mysteries and their development and diversification but does attempt to identify many cultural as well as literary aspects. It also identifies many key writers and provides a context for the later chapters. Chapter 2 identifies major variants of the novels of mystery and detection. These discussions are not exhaustive, of course, but encourage thinking about relationships among diverse kinds of fiction. These are gothic mystery, gangster, suspense, thriller, courtroom and lawyer novels, police procedurals, and postmodern fiction. Chapter 3 is the longest chapter and is organized according to general critical approaches. It attempts to do justice to the varied production of critical thought that has been devoted to crime fiction. Criticism—as distinct from reviewing, providing plot summaries or appreciations of authors—may originate in any number of questions. In many cases, of course, criticism deals with issues that are not confined to American mystery and detective novels, and these have been truncated. Chapter 4 groups authors and their typical publications into periods. The chapter attempts to acknowledge the contributions many individual writers make to the field, but the sheer number of writers also indicates that their significance is not altogether distinct from the genre in which they work. This chapter is therefore arranged according to a rough chronology in order to more directly link it to the chapters on history and types.[1] The chapter is highly selective, and no attempt has been made to cover all or even most works for each author represented. Rather the information indicates the varied production. The chapter also recognizes that author criticism is by tradition mostly in the manner of appreciation, whether or not it is outrightly appreciative. A special attempt has been made to include minority writers who do not otherwise get mainstream attention. Chapter 5 provides an introduction to the available reference works and manuscript collections regarding mystery and detective fiction in the United States.

NOTE

1. Original publication dates are included in parentheses following work titles, but quotes are identified with the date of the edition cited. This is mainly relevant to articles that were published in journals and later collected in books from which quoted material was drawn.

CHRONOLOGY

1764   Horace Walpole, *The Castle of Otranto* (Br).

1773   *The Newgate Calendar* (Br) crime accounts and memoirs first collected.

1794   William Godwin, *Caleb Williams* (Br).

1799   Charles Brockden Brown, *Edgar Huntly; or, Memoirs of a Sleepwalker*.

1823   Catnach's account of the Thurtell murder trial (Br).

1827   Constable's Miscellany and the Library of Useful Knowledge began the era of "cheap libraries." Thomas De Quincey, "On Murder Considered One of the Fine Arts" (Br); *Richmond: or, Scenes in the Life of a Bow Street Officer* (Br).

1828   Catnach's "Confession and Execution of William Corder" sold 1,166,000 copies (Br); François Eugene Vidocq, *Memoirs de Vidocq* (Fr, 1828–29), fanciful memoirs of the French thief turned thief-catcher, who is mentioned by Poe's character, Auguste Dupin.

1828–32   Board bindings replaced leather bindings.

1836–37   Catnach's "execution papers" on Greenacre-Gale murder sells 1,600,000 copies (Br).

1836–37   Charles Dickens, *The Pickwick Papers* (Br) begins a great vogue of
           fiction in shilling parts. This form of publishing lasted until about
           1880.

1837–38   Charles Dickens, *Oliver Twist* (Br).

1839–40   Literacy rate in England: males 65 percent; females 51 percent.

1840   Increase in weekly newspapers and cheap part-issue fiction in the U.S.

1841   Edgar Allan Poe, "The Murders in the Rue Morgue." Charles Dickens,
           Barnaby Rudge (Br).

1842–43   Edgar Allan Poe, "The Mystery of Marie Rogêt." Charles Dickens,
           Martin Chuzzlewit (Br, 1843–44).

1844   Edgar Allan Poe, "The Purloined Letter."

1850   First story papers are published in the United States. Herman Melville
           publishes *White Jacket*.

1852–53   Charles Dickens, *Bleak House* (Br).

1860   First dime novels appeared in the United States. Wilkie Collins pub-
           lishes *The Woman in White* (Br).

1860–65   American Civil War.

1865   Emile Gaboriau, *L'Affaire Lerouge* serialized (Fr).

1867   Seeley Regester [Mrs. Metta Victoria Fuller Victor], *The Dead Letter*,
           one of the first American novels to feature a detective figure. Emile
           Gaboriau, *Le Crime d'Orcival* and *Le Dossier no. 113* (Fr).

1868   Wilkie Collins, *The Moonstone* (Br); *Illustrated Police News* began
           publishing (Br).

1869   Emile Gaboriau, *Monsieur Lecoq* (Fr).

1870   Charles Dickens dies and leaves *The Mystery of Edwin Drood* unfin-
           ished, but it is published later in the year (Br).

1800s   (Late). English penny dreadfuls were joined by penny reprints.

1872   Harlan Page Halsey, "Old Sleuth, the Detective; or, The Bay Ridge
           Mystery" appears in the *New York Fireside Companion*.

1878   Anna Katharine Green, *The Leavenworth Case*.

1883   The *New York Detective Library* and the *Old Cap Collier Library* had
           become entirely made up of detective stories.

1886   John Russell Coryell, *The Old Detective's Pupil*. Began the Nick Carter
           series.

1886   Arthur Conan Doyle, *A Study in Scarlet* (Br).

1887   Fergus Hume, *The Mystery of a Hansom Cab* (Australian).

1891   *The Nick Carter Weekly* began.

1892   Arthur Conan Doyle, *The Adventures of Sherlock Holmes* (Br), stories collected from *Strand* magazine; beginning of Doyle's popularity in the U.S.; adapts Poe's techniques to magazine serialization and expands characters. First major British influence.

1894   End of the three-volume "library" novel.

1896   Mark Twain, *The Tragedy of Pudd'nhead Wilson*; Harmsworth's *Daily Mail* makes success of daily paper.

1901–2   Pauline E. Hopkins's serial novel, *Hagar's Daughter* (1901–2) featuring Venus Johnson as an African-American detective figure.

1908   Mary Roberts Rinehart, *The Circular Staircase*; John E. Bruce serialized *Black Sleuth* (1908–1909).

1909   Carolyn Wells published *The Clue*.

1913   Earl Derr Biggers, *Seven Keys to Baldpate*, a thriller; Carolyn Wells's study guide, *The Technique of the Mystery Story*.

1920   *The Black Mask* began publication (April 1920–July 1951); Agatha Christie, *The Mysterious Affair at Styles*—her first novel signals the second major British influence.

1922   Carroll John Daly's "The False Burton Combs" appeared in *The Black Mask* magazine.

1924   Harry Stephen Keeler, *The Voice of the Seven Sparrows*.

1925   Earl Derr Biggers's first Charlie Chan novel, *The House without a Key*.

1926   S. S. Van Dine's *The Benson Murder Case* is the first Philo Vance mystery; Agatha Christie publishes *The Murder of Roger Ackroyd* (Br); Joseph T. Shaw begins editing *The Black Mask*.

1927   S. S. Van Dine, *The Canary Murder Case*.

1929   Dashiell Hammett, *Red Harvest*; Ellery Queen, *The Roman Hat Mystery*; W. R. Burnett, *Little Caesar*.

1930   John Dickson Carr, *It Walks by Night*; Dashiell Hammett, *The Maltese Falcon*.

1931   William Faulkner, *Sanctuary*; Dashiell Hammett, *The Glass Key*; Leslie Charteris, *Enter the Saint*.

1932   Rudolph Fisher, *The Conjure Man Dies*; as Maxwell Grant, Walter Gibson created The Shadow for *The Shadow Magazine* (1932–1949).

1933   Erle Stanley Gardner, best-selling Perry Mason novels: *The Case of the Sulky Girl*, *The Case of the Velvet Claws*, *The Case of the Lucky Legs*.

1934   Dashiell Hammett, *The Thin Man*; Rex Stout, *Fer de Lance*.

1935   Leslie Charteris, *The Saint in New York* after beginning in England in
          1928; John P. Marquand, *No Hero* (Mr. Moto); Horace McCoy, *They
          Shoot Horses, Don't They?*

1936–38   Erle Stanley Gardner best-sellers: *The Case of the Stuttering Bishop,
          The Case of the Dangerous Dowager, The Case of the Lame Canary,*
          and *The Case of the Substitute Face.*

1938   Mabel Seeley published *The Listening House.*

1939   Raymond Chandler, *The Big Sleep*; Eric Ambler, *A Coffin for Dimitrios*
          (Br); *Ellery Queen* radio program (1939–48); Pocket Books began pub-
          lishing.

1940   Richard Wright, *Native Son*; Frances and Richard Lockridge, *The
          Norths Meet Murder*; Cornell Woolrich, *The Bride Wore Black.*

1941   *The Ellery Queen Mystery Magazine* (1941–present). Howard Hay-
          craft, *Murder for Pleasure*; Avon began publishing.

1942   Popular Library began publishing.

1943   Marie Rodell, *Mystery Fiction: Theory and Technique*; Vera Caspary,
          Laura; Dell began publishing.

1945   Lawrence Treat, *V as in Victim*; Bantam began publishing.

1946   Geoffrey Homes, *Build My Gallows High*; Kenneth Fearing, *The Big
          Clock*; Chester Himes, *If He Hollers Let Him Go*; Howard Haycraft,
          The Art of the Mystery Story.

1947   Mickey Spillane, *I, the Jury.*

1948   William Faulkner, *Intruder in the Dust*; Graphic began publishing.

1949   Ross Macdonald, *The Moving Target* (Lew Archer); Pyramid, Lion,
          Checker, and New American Library began publishing; *Dragnet* radio
          show (1949–56).

1950   Patricia Highsmith, *Strangers on a Train.*

1951   Charles Williams, *Hill Girl.*

1952   Hillary Waugh, *Last Seen Wearing . . .* ; Jim Thompson, *The Killer In-
          side Me; Dragnet* begins on TV (1952–70 under various titles).

1955   Patricia Highsmith, *The Talented Mr. Ripley.*

1956   Evan Hunter, 87th Precinct series as Ed McBain, *Cop Hater*; Robert
          Wade and Bill Miller writing as Whit Masterson, *Badge of Evil.*

1957   Chester Himes, *For Love of Imabelle.*

1959   Robert Bloch, *Psycho*; Walter Tevis, *The Hustler.*

1960   Dolores Hitchens, *Sleep with Slander*.

1963   Thomas Pynchon, *V.*

1964   John Ball, *In the Heat of the Night*; Carolyn G. Heilbrun writing as Amanda Cross, *In the Last Analysis*; John D. MacDonald, *The Deep-Blue Goodbye*, first Travis McGee.

1966   Patricia Highsmith, *Plotting and Writing Suspense Fiction*.

1968   Dorothy Uhnak, *The Bait*; *The Armchair Detective* begins publication.

1969   Michael Crichton, *The Andromeda Strain*.

1970   Bouchercon (1970–present); Tony Hillerman, *The Blessing Way*; Lawrence Sanders, *The Anderson Tapes*; Ernest Tidyman, *Shaft*.

1971   Donald Goines, *Dopefiend: The Story of a Black Junkie*; Robert Ludlum, *The Scarlatti Inheritance*.

1972   George V. Higgins, *The Friends of Eddie Coyle*; Ishmael Reed, *Mumbo Jumbo*; Paul Erdman, *The Billion Dollar Sure Thing*.

1973   Ross Macdonald, *On Crime Writing*; Robert B. Parker, *The Godwulf Manuscript*.

1975   Joe Gores, *Hammett*; Rex Burns, *The Alvarez Journal*; James Crumley, *The Wrong Case*.

1976   Elmore Leonard, *Swag*.

1977   Thomas Berger, *Who Is Teddy Villanova?*; John Gregory Dunne, *True Confessions*; Marcia Muller, *Edwin of the Iron Shoes*; Stuart Kaminsky, *Bullet for a Star*.

1978   William Hjortsberg, *Falling Angel*.

1979   Stephen Greenleaf, *Grave Error*.

1980   Loren Estleman, *Motor City Blue*; *Clues* begins publication.

1981   Martin Cruz Smith, *Gorky Park*; James Ellroy, *Brown's Requiem*.

1982   Paul Auster, *Squeeze Play*; Sue Grafton, *"A" Is for Alibi*; Sara Paretsky, *Indemnity Only*; Private Eye Writers of America organized.

1984   Jerome Charyn, *The Isaac Quartet*; Norman Mailer, *Tough Guys Don't Dance*; Joyce Carol Oates, *Mysteries of Winterthurn: A Novel*.

1985   Andrew H. Vachss, *Flood*; Jonathan Kellerman, *When the Bough Breaks*.

1986   James Lee Burke, *The Neon Rain*.

1987   Scott Turow, *Presumed Innocent*.

1988   Gar Anthony Haywood, *Fear of the Dark*.

1990   Patricia Daniels Cornwell, *Postmortem*; Walter Mosley, *Devil in a Blue Dress*.

1992   Barbara Neely, *Blanche on the Lam*; John Grisham, *The Firm*; Sue Grafton, ed., *Writing Mysteries: A Handbook*; Louis Owens, *The Sharpest Sight*.

1994   Rita Mae Brown, *Murder at Monticello*.

1995   Susanna Moore, *In the Cut*.

CHAPTER 1

HISTORICAL OUTLINE

Mystery novels in the United States are rooted in a complex network of historical and literary conditions. Narrative fragments drawn into the mystery novel are apparent in medieval morality tales, the Romance, the gothic, the bildungsroman, the picaresque tale, domestic fiction, the adventure tale, and so on.[1] To better understand the threads of this network of story forms is to travel many paths as well as the highways of literary history. The shape of American mystery novels begins to form at the end of the eighteenth century in the gothic romances of Charles Brockden Brown. The focus on the murder and Edgar Allan Poe's addition of the puzzle and the specialized investigator established patterns of the mystery that are familiar today. Detective novels as a more specialized form of the mystery are constructed around a formal investigation—usually of a murdered or vanished person—while mysteries more broadly address the solution to a generally threatening situation.

Charles Brockden Brown's novels articulate some of the tendencies of the mystery novel, along with detective elements, over forty years earlier than Poe. In fact, American literary historian Robert Spiller calls *Edgar Huntly* (1799) America's "first detective novel," although it is more appropriately a mystery, since it gives rational explanations for such gothic devices as spontaneous combustion, disembodied voices, and spiritual possession.[2] Brown adapts the captivity narrative to the gothic formula and generally reworks available materials on a variety of subjects into literary form. The novel certainly involves a figure of a detective who is consciously investigating a murder in order to confirm the circumstances of the deed. The narrator "heard the discharge of the pistol," and on discovering his dying friend, Inglefield, feels that "to forbear inquiry or withhold punishment was to violate my duty to my God and to mankind."[3] Huntly then proceeds to "explore the ground," "scrutinize," "search," and shadow his suspect as he meanders around through the wilderness. Later he questions witnesses and uses his observations and reason to develop scenarios of the motives and events leading to the crime. *Edgar Huntly* is a detective story of sorts, certainly a mystery, but shades into a psychological narrative, with the landscape taking on the flavor of Huntly's bewildered imagination. It anticipates qualities of the suspense novel and the tenor of anxiety found in many mysteries and thrillers. Clearly *Edgar Huntly* demythologizes the gothic tale, uses gothic materials for thrilling effect and exposes gothic discourses to contemporary late eighteenth-century explanations. Further, Brown's style is expressive in a particular kind of way, representing the world outside as an uncanny confession of the fevered sensibility of an excitable person engaged in the investigation of the murder of a friend. That is, it is a narrative suspended between the conditions of the mystery and the detective novel, in which the narrator is entrapped by circumstances not of her or his own making as well as those resulting from pursuit, while at the same time following the detective story, whose conditions depersonalize the investigator or shift his or her engagement to a preoccupation with activities of the investigation. But the fact that Huntly is able to proceed without any apparent conscious method undermines the claim that he represents the first detective (see "Early Writers" in chapter 4 of this book).

Brown's fiction illustrates the problem of identifying the origins and differentiating characteristics of mystery and detective novels. On the one hand the threads of mystery are entangled in many kinds of narrative, but on the other hand mystery and detective stories run to formula. The distinction among mystery and detective novels that sets them apart from other literature appears to be the emphasis placed on the unraveling of a mystery or puzzle involving high stakes. In the detective story focus is on investigative action, reasoned explanation of a chain of clues, discovery of motive, and the progressive elimination of all possible suspects or causes except one. This involves a detective figure who identifies motive, assesses probable cause, and sifts through a mass of information to identify evidence following some method or course of action. The mystery deals in demystification but tends to rely more on the potential of psychological tension and social conflict through devices of suspense than on a methodical solution to a crime. Both kinds of stories involve investigation of one sort or another, but the mystery story can more easily rely on a vulnerable central figure than can a detective story, which culminates in control. This can be seen historically in the way the detective figure has been romanticized as a mental giant, an athletic marvel or someone who can endure a remarkable amount of punishment, in contrast to the mystery's reliance on ingenuity, concealment, and other more modest traits.

One critic notes that "For romanticism, mystery is the condition of the world and all external appearance is merely the hieroglyph of a concealed meaning" (Alewyn, 1974, 74). Between 1794 and 1850 over seventy novels appeared in England carrying the word "mystery" in their titles. The tales of Hoffmann and Poe are "nothing but lateral shoots from this common root" (Alewyn, 1974, 75). William Godwin's *The Adventures of Caleb Williams* (1794) is often cited for its dark portrayal of society and a reverse plot structure. This broader discussion is considerably reduced by focusing on novels produced in the United States, but the shadow of Edgar Allan Poe's short stories overcasts even these. Nevertheless, there were some 4,000 gothic novels published in English from the late eighteenth century to the beginning of the twentieth, and all have varying degrees of mystery.[4] Most make less of the complex use of rational practices than does Brown in that time, but the gothic would continue to divide into two streams during the nineteenth century, one of them emphasizing the supernatural and the other emphasizing rational explanations for disruptive events enveloped in mysterious contexts. Though Brown and many other writers following him would explore the form of the mystery through the use of figures sharing traits with the detective, the detective story has come to be understood as having a set of criteria that places distinct limitations on fiction to be included in its definition. The boundaries of novels are not sharply etched in the late eighteenth and early nineteenth century, but only gradually begin to be so by the mid-nineteenth century. The literary reaction to this differentiation of narrative boundaries include first Romance and then realism, which from the Civil War until the turn of the twentieth century competed with more popular forms of literary production for the interest of readers. These literary traditions differentiated themselves from popular works in part by mirroring economic forms of consumption— hardback/paper-covered or newsprint novels; literary journals/slick magazines/story papers/pulps/digests. By the turn of the twentieth century, both forms were marginalized by the aesthetics of modernism. Current detective and mystery novels claim all this territory—realism, popular formula, and art—and the contemporary novel finds its field of representation and artistic play not bound by past territorial disputes. Today many ethnic groups are represented by authors of detective fiction; all cities of moderate size and many small towns and rural areas are represented. The history of detective and mystery novels is, then, necessarily a history that includes a wide range of considerations. It may be helpful to return to formula.

The puzzle structure of mystery and detective novels grew largely out of the possibilities opened by Poe's short stories, the economic and institutional transformation of industrializing societies, a changing publishing industry, a broadened reading public, and numerous cultural changes. Poe's stories in the 1840s provided a compact investigation of a sensational or potentially sensational mystery, a Romantic detective, and suspense provided by the delayed solution of the investigation. The form of his stories are sharply distinguished from other fiction of the mid-nineteenth century, and the Romance of the rational hero is distinct from the image of law enforcement in newspapers and other sources of discourse. Translating these qualities into a longer form that contextualized the puzzle was a slower process that would take much of the rest of the nineteenth century and would be carried on largely in England and France. The evolution of the detective novel depended as much on parallel developments—in other domestic literature, on fiction imported from other countries, on social, political and economic conditions and other nonliterary factors—as on developments peculiar to Poe or those who adopted his formula or expanded on it.

A major attraction of Poe's short story formulas is that they limit the contextualization of the puzzle and tend to keep the narrative within strict boundaries. The mystery novel has a much less exclusionary history in that it is more a tendency that grows out of and reacts to several kinds of fiction than being identified with a particular kind of investigative situation. The plot of the mystery certainly involves the investigation of an enigma, but the investigation is not formal, and the enigma does not necessarily involve motivated acts of violence that have come to be associated with the detective novel. Although Poe's stories did not necessarily involve murder (the ape kills but is not a murderer, the stolen letter is only the "pre-text" of violence, and so on), they raised the stakes by incorporating violence, high office, and vast treasure.

Most scholars accept several stories by Edgar Allan Poe as having defined detective fiction, though some would point to French, German, or English writers who had claim to the honor. The most influential formulations of the detective story circulate through Poe to the rest of the Western world. In the matter of the detective novel, as distinct from the short story, valid claims must be made for European precedent, but for the invention of the detective as the central figure in a plot concerned above all with the solution of a murder, Poe has no serious rivals. Mystery and detection figure in a number of Poe's stories, but those that are central to the puzzle in detective narratives are "The Murders in the Rue Morgue" (1841), "The Mystery of Marie Rogêt" (1842–43), and "The Purloined Letter" (1844). Most historians of the genre agree that many of the conventions of the classic detective story achieve their earliest coherent form in these tales; the variations discussed in chapter 2 are important to the development and directions of the genre. Poe's stories are celebrations of independent observation and reason in the investigation of the murkier levels of human affairs. In "The Murders in the Rue Morgue," C. Auguste Dupin concludes the narrator's line of thought for him by observing his behavior, connecting the behavioral clues to his associative thought processes, then leaping ahead the chain of associations to conclude the thought. In "The Mystery of Marie Rogêt" Poe frames newspaper accounts of the investigation into the actual death of Marie Rogers as fiction and attempts to solve the crime using only the evidence available to him in the newspapers, and in "The Purloined Letter" Dupin illustrates that imagination is crucial to the solution of problems conceived by intelligent criminals. Poe himself appeared to be inspired in part by the fanciful reminiscences of François Eugene Vidocq, a thief who was hired to catch thieves in Paris and who published his memoirs in 1828–29.[5] Poe considered Vidocq only "a good guesser and a persevering man" who often erred because he failed to see the whole as well as the parts. Numerous writers in subsequent years failed to mark Poe's caution and created a legion of detectives whose solutions relied heavily on luck. Dupin's perspective is both aesthetic and objective—at least on the surface—the product of a gothic sensibility in a material world. Dupin's intellectual grasp of the details of the world outside as reported of him by his companion is razor sharp if somewhat narrow; he solved a puzzle for readers and provided a model for writers to come.

EUROPEAN INFLUENCE

Developments in Europe often appeared in America almost simultaneously through pirated editions and magazine serializations. Dickens's works were eagerly awaited and often pirated within a few days of British publication. *Oliver Twist* (1837–38), *Barnaby Rudge* (1841), *Martin Chuzzlewit* (1843–44), and *Bleak House* (1852–53) all have elements of the detective novel in characterization or plot. The unfinished novel, *The Mystery of Edwin Drood* (1870), appears to have been largely a detective novel complete with gothic devices, but only six installments of the novel were finished before Dickens's death, and in chapter 14 Drood disappears.[6] Dickens's descriptions of low-life intrigues and sharply etched characters in particular, influenced popular writers on both sides of the Atlantic. His friend and sometime collaborator Wilkie Collins seemed especially taken with mystery, and detective figures played important parts in his best work. The first of his novels, *The Woman in White* (1860),[7] finds a young artist called to a remote country house where mysteries begin to build around a beautiful young lady and her sister. In the story told through witnesses' accounts, the young man is disappointed in love, disappears for a time from the narrative, then in Book 3 returns to conduct an investigation that immerses him in old court records and a battle of wits with a master criminal–spy. With *The Moonstone* (1868),[8] Collins incorporated numerous conventions and nuances important to detective fiction. French author Emile Gaboriau's *L'Affaire Lerouge* was serialized in 1865, *Le Crime d'Orcival* in 1867, *Le Dossier no. 113* in 1867, and *Monsieur Lecoq* in 1869, with others following. These were translated into English and published in the United States in the 1880s. Imports prior to the turn of the century that stimulated production in the United States included Arthur Conan Doyle's *A Study in Scarlet* (1886). Historians generally credit the publication of Fergus Hume's *The Mystery of the Hansom Cab* in 1887 for stimulating British readership for the detective novel. Detective fiction began to rise in popularity, and Doyle rode its crest for many years. Apart from Poe, more critical attention has been spent on Doyle than any other mystery writer; certainly over the past century Doyle's Sherlock Holmes has become a ubiquitous figure. His books would become staples in private libraries and for better or worse would have enormous influence on the rise of the detective novel in the twentieth century—in the United States as well as England. The English writer Sax Rohmer (Arthur Henry Sarsfield Ward) created the arch-villain Fu Manchu to capitalize on the interest in China. His thrillers were serialized in slick magazines in the United States from around 1913 and remained popular for many years. Earl Derr Biggers inverted this stereotype in *The House Without a Key* (1925) featuring Charlie Chan, the Honolulu police detective who became a household name.

STORY PAPERS AND DIME NOVELS

Cultural, economic, and political changes in the nineteenth century influenced the production of literature in complex ways that are still not well understood. Certainly the establishment of public education and subsequent spread of literacy by the second quarter of the nineteenth century created conditions for a more broadly fragmented market and the diversification of literary interests. One of the arguments for public education in the 1830s in the United States was social control, particularly in the face of popular opposition from the lower classes. As late as 1839 the *Brother Jonathan Weekly* carried both news and fiction but did not apparently provide mystery and detective material. By 1850 story papers employed the construction materials, layout, convenience, familiarity, and disposability of newspapers to package short fiction, poetry and serialized novels. From 1860 dime novels provided adventure tales and romance in inexpensive formats. Newspaper circulation began to grow and in the 1870s actually doubled as the population grew, commercial support increased, and newspapers increasingly exploited sensation. Various forms of reprints, cheap editions, imports (usually pirated editions), and serial fiction flourished.

The figure of the detective emerged slowly and tentatively in the story papers and dime novels from a vigilante figure of instant justice to a special representative of the government and from the West to the urban East. Many crime novels were one-shot attempts to capture readers, though these are sometimes notable. Seeley Regester [Mrs. Metta Victoria Fuller Victor], who published *The Dead Letter* as a detective novel in 1867, qualifies as the first American woman detective novelist. She wrote most of her work for the dime novel firm of Beadle and Adams. The most famous dime novel figure was Nick Carter. Over 100 Nick Carter novels have been reprinted recently in paperback. The *Nick Carter Weekly* began in 1891, and as late as 1933 there were still 400 paper volumes in print. J. Randolph Cox counted 78 serials and 115 short stories in *Street & Smith's New York Weekly*, 282 issues of the *Nick Carter Detective Library*, 819 issues of the *Nick Carter Weekly*, 160 issues of *Nick Carter Stories*, 127 issues of *Detective Story Magazine*, and 40 issues of *Nick Carter Magazine*, as well as scattered stories elsewhere. The detective's exploits were written by various hands, including those by Frederic Van Rensselaer Dey, who wrote 437 Carter novels, and have emerged in radio, film, and television. Nick Carter was typically represented as upper-class, well-educated, and polished as well as physically strong and tough. In short, he combined attributes of the urban gentleman detective with those of the Western adventure hero.[9] Detective figures were also involved in labor strife as investigators of violence, particularly in the cases of Allan Pinkerton and Arthur Conan Doyle.[10]

In the late 1870s Anna Katharine Green and other writers moved detection away from the romanticized adventure tale toward the tastes of the more genteel middle class. The success of Green's *The Leavenworth Case* (1878) probably stimulated sales of mysteries in England as well as the United States and encouraged publishers to print translations of Emile Gaboriau's more adventurous French detective stories, as noted. Novels employing detective figures, many different settings, and one form or another of investigation proliferated in the late nineteenth century. Many of these were written for juveniles or were adapted directly from story papers, but they also included narratives published by quality houses such as Putnam's, Scribner's, and others.[11] Throughout the last quarter of the nineteenth century the form in which the detective appeared remained relatively open. The detective's investigation tended to merge in most novels with themes from gothic fiction, domestic romance, courtroom exposition, exposés, and adventure stories. Investigation in many of these stories was cursory or in any case unmethodical and lacking the rigor and rigidity such writers as S. S. Van Dine and John Dickson Carr would try to bring to it in their early work. The classic story adopted from the British would attempt to bring the mystery into a more rigorous formula.

REALISM

The popularity of the genre did not escape Mark Twain, who saw possibilities for social exposé as well as for humor and literary parody. Twain openly parodied Sherlock Holmes in "A Double-Barrelled Detective Story" (1902), featuring Fetlock Jones, nephew of Holmes. Twain used the concept of fingerprinting as evidence with his use of a thumbprint as early as *Life on the Mississippi* in 1883 and again to identify switched babies in *Pudd'nhead Wilson* in 1894. His *Tom Sawyer Abroad; Tom Sawyer, Detective; and Other Stories* (1896) included "The Stolen White Elephant," "The Facts Concerning the Recent Carnival of Crime in Connecticut," and other stories and anecdotes. Twain published a number of short stories, mostly humorous, dealing with detection, and left "Simon Wheeler, Detective" unfinished at his death. Twain's social realism and satire were outside the boundaries that were firming up around the detective novel. The direction Doyle took the detective story was precisely that laid out by Poe nearly a half a century earlier: the detective functioned as a Romantic figure within an internally logical and rigorously efficient plot, in spite of any bizarre premises upon which it might be based. Twain's realism and humor provided two directions that went beyond this, toward a critique of social conventions and expectations, and toward literary play on the conventions of the formula. Both of these narrative strategies continue to circulate beneath the surface of detective and mystery fiction.

The dime novels of the nineteenth century often featured the semicharted western United States, while around the turn of the century the detective and mystery story began to turn inward toward locked rooms and more rigid formulas. In this form realistic claims were widely based on the techniques of institutional or private investigations. As the focus of the stories shifted to the details of investigation, the status of the detective figures shifted from government agents or freely moving adventurers to local policemen and employees of large private agencies such as Pinkerton's. This form of realism made use of autobiography (however fantasized), references to actual cases, and descriptions of investigative technologies and practices. That is, Vidocq, Poe, Pinkerton, and others turned the narrative away from the social issues implicit in literary realism and toward the figure of the detective and the authority of institutional investigations of crimes. This practice replaced social realism with the realism of documents and detective biography. The autobiographical style of this documentary realism would also urge the narration into a first-person presentation and lead to novels containing documents in imitation of those produced by police departments, medical examiners, banks, morgues, and various other governmental or corporate agencies and prepare the ground for the emergence of the police procedural in the mid–twentieth century. Poe can be argued to have anticipated this tendency by providing facsimiles of ciphers and samples of writing of unknown origin in such pieces as "The Gold Bug" and *The Narrative of Arthur Gordon Pym*. In any case, literary realism did not make a large impact on crime fiction by the turn of the century, whereas documentary realism continued through the Golden Age of classic detective novels until finally Dennis Wheatley and Joe Links simply published boxes of evidence and documents in *File on Bolitho Blane* (1936) and *File on*

Robert Prentice (1937), dispensing with the written narrative altogether. The tightly plotted "classic" or "British"-style novel came to characterize detective fiction.

TURN-OF-THE-CENTURY VARIETY

The detective figure that appeared throughout the nineteenth century was both a pseudo-factual figure, being connected to the government or feasible private authority such as the private Pinkerton agency, and also a fictional image, the former most often as a policeman or Pinkerton agent and the latter as a creation suitable to a more thrilling pursuit of mystery or exposé of criminous activity. In the decade after *The Leavenworth Case*, new types of crime fiction began to appear and shortly after the turn of the century the mystery branched into a number of more distant narrative types: the puzzle, the suspense story, the action story, the procedural, the spy story. Other narratives expanded possibilities of heroes and settings; still others elaborated investigative strategies—psychological, forensic, profiling, legal, chemical, and so on. The commercially successful mystery, on the other hand, is polished to perfection by Mary Roberts Rinehart. Her novel *The Circular Staircase* (1908), which introduced the "had I but known" formula—a story told in retrospect by a narrator who has survived an ordeal through the solution of mysteries—became a best-seller and led to many imitations.

"CLASSIC" DETECTIVE NOVELS

Poe's stories had suggested a compactly structured investigation that favored isolated murder scenes and a limited number of possible suspects and witnesses. The locked-room mystery developed a highly focused investigation. For several decades after World War I detective fiction flowered as a genre and gained millions of readers. This Golden Age of detective fiction saw considerable experimentation and innovation with characters, situations, plots, and styles. The middle-class dream of productive leisure found in many classic detective stories is apparent in the novels of Willard Huntington Wright, who wrote under the pen name of S. S. Van Dine. His detective, Philo Vance, first appeared in *The Benson Murder Case* in 1926, with the detective as a snobbish, bookish eccentric who carried out investigations that informed psychological interpretations of personality, drawing perhaps on Poe, but also on the popularization of Sigmund Freud and behaviorist John B. Watson. The investigations took place in the midst of conspicuous consumption. Van Dine published a list of rules that attempted, more or less unsuccessfully, to constrain the formula.

Another influential English writer, Agatha Christie, came to dominate British detective fiction and often topped American best-seller lists from the mid-1920s through the 1940s. The American writers who entertained the largest number of readers for classic detective novels during this period wrote as a single detective-author—Ellery Queen. Created by Frederic Dannay and Manfred B. Lee in *The Roman Hat Mystery* (1929) and appearing in some forty novels, "Ellery Queen" wrote about his own cases. Dannay and Lee adopted the "fair play" rule for writers, which holds that readers should be given all the necessary information at some point before the detective reveals the solution. Dannay and Lee consistently topped the bestseller lists in the 1930s with such titles as *The Dutch Shoe Mystery* (1931), *The Egyptian Cross Mystery* (1932), *The Adventures of Ellery Queen* (stories, 1934) and *The Spanish Cape Mystery* (1935). Queen has appeared in numerous versions in film, radio, and television and survives on the title of one of the most successful mystery magazines, *Ellery Queen's Mystery Magazine* (1941–present).

PULP MAGAZINES

Pulp magazines such as *Argosy* and *Blue Book* appeared around 1896, featuring an assortment of story types. These inexpensive magazines were made of paper created through new high-acid wood-pulping processes and bound in slick covers designed to attract the eye on newsstands. In part this innovation was brought about by late nineteenth-century changes in the copyright law, the invention of cheaper wood pulp paper, the rise of yellow journalism, and increased adult literacy. Pulp magazines largely replaced story papers and dime novels, and were designed to be sold on newsstands. Pulp magazines were at first extensions of the content of dime novels, but they soon evolved into specialized magazines that reflected the interests of an increasingly urban population.

Shortly after the turn of the century pulps began to feature types of fiction—romances, westerns, crime, horror—and the crime stories began to move away from puzzles, refined heroes, and isolated settings and toward cities and suburbs. A pattern can be seen emerging in the detective fiction of *The Black Mask* (1920–51), a magazine initially financed as a money-making scheme by George Jean Nathan and H. L. Mencken. The stories of Carroll John Daly, who created the detective Race Williams, began to appear in 1922. Daly's stories owed much to the dime novels but had an unsentimental violence that was rare in dime novels and even in literary naturalism. Within a few years *The Black Mask*, especially under the editorship of Joseph T. Shaw, had attracted a number of writers who refined and fashioned the violence of Prohibition into a style for the 1920s and 1930s. *The Black Mask* paid a top rate of about five cents a word and published some 2,500 stories over thirty years. Pulps such as *Dime Detective*, *Detective Story*, *Detective Fiction Weekly*, and others picked up stories in the hard-boiled style. Other writers and magazines adopted the style, as did journalists and mainstream writers such as Ernest Hemingway. Crippled by paper shortages during World War II, pulp magazines in the late 1940s lost ground to television, censorship, paperbacks, and other forms of direct and indirect competition. By the late 1950s they had effectively disappeared. The one-shot paperback novels were tougher and harder to suppress, TV sanitized scripts and imagery for an undifferentiated mass market, and the few remaining pulps were converted to digest-sized magazines.

HARD-BOILED FICTION

Crime fiction in pulp magazines directly influenced the style and content of crime novels. In the first few decades backgrounds became more detailed, and dialogue began to be less stilted. The fiction was sensitive to effects of Prohibition and the Depression. Exposés of city politics and gangster activities, postwar disillusionment, and literary naturalism made conventional juvenile adventure narratives and upscale wit seem less convincing for many readers. Though the relatively genteel puzzle story reached its greatest popularity during the second quarter of the twentieth century, hard-boiled detective fiction began to deal with the feelings and reactions of men and women who were surviving without benefit of inheritance. In these stories police are not intimidated by the people who meet them at the door. Hard-boiled stories tended to look at the political, economic, and social structure from the bottom up. Speakeasies and other signs of underworld chic that sometimes provided a risqué edge to classic fiction were seen as businesses in hard-boiled fiction.

Although pulps also published classic stories, the rougher street fiction often circumvented the social restrictions of the classic story to touch on the shocking rawness of American materialism. Authenticity seemed to demand a rejection of the social complacency found in the formal story, to require a commitment to a vision that sought social meaning beyond the hermetic social structure of the classic story. The hard-boiled story dealt with power, but more directly with the erosion of the ideals and expectations behind social facades. The underside of the illusion created for public consumption by businessmen, politicians, police, and bureaucrats could be revealed by the investigator if there was one. Often as not the story was one of more or less ordinary people who fell into crime or whose ordinary manner of making a living was considered criminal. In the gangster story the treatment of underlings and competitors by those at the top of the hierarchy was not unlike that of businessmen, although with less gentility and often greater finality. Much more common is the portrayal of strains introduced by the combination of political democracy and capitalist economic practices. Whether the protagonist is a reporter, photographer, lawyer, policeman, drifter, detective, or man in the street, the hard-boiled novel dealt with a different level of manners through a vision not dependent on religious doctrine, social graces, or the rule of law.

Of the two hundred or so writers who made their living exclusively by selling short stories and novels to the pulps, relatively few saw their work in hardcover editions. But some could sell anything they wrote, and a few reached fame as novelists as well as pulp writers. Of the detective novelists who emerged in the pulps, Dashiell Hammett's work is probably most significant. His first short story appeared in 1923, with *Red Harvest* (1929) introducing the Continental Op (based loosely on Hammett's experiences with the Pinkerton Detective Agency) to the novel. In *The Maltese Falcon* (1930) the Op becomes the private detective Sam Spade, and in the mystery *The Glass Key* (1931), Spade in turn becomes the political troubleshooter Ned Beaumont, a figure that allowed Hammett to explore other implications of the hard-boiled crime novel. *The Thin Man* (1934) led to a number of witty husband-and-wife detective teams such as Richard and Frances Lockridge's *The Norths Meet Murder* (1940) and Lenore Glen Offord's *Murder on Russian Hill* (1938).

The rougher style of writing that emerged in the pulps and was adapted to the short novels sold as paperbacks followed the possibilities of a naturalistic, rather than a realistic or mannered formalist style. By the beginning of the 1930s this "tough guy" or private-eye style would provide a stark contrast to the urbane classic novel. The classic detective was most likely an amateur, which meant not only that she or he was not a policeman, but that he or she was not in business as a detective. The British consulting detective, popularized by Doyle's Sherlock Holmes, was first of all a gentleman, usually with links to the gentry. The metaphorical link that evolved in the 1920s for the hard-boiled detective was the contract between an independent detective who charged for his skills and a person willing to pay for them; his actions are bounded on one side by the law and on the other by his business and personal code. Hammett's Sam Spade makes this clear in his comments to Brigid O'Shaughnessy in *The Maltese Falcon*. He is a small capitalist, a fitting persona for popular writers making their living by their wits in a fickle marketplace, but also a representative of those who are or have become vulnerable. The private detective both mirrors the social structure with all its ambiguities and is charged with deconstructing it, of revealing its illusory nature.

Raymond Chandler also wrote stories for *The Black Mask* and other pulps and became the spokesman for the hard-boiled school with "The Simple Art of Murder" (April 15, 1950). Beginning with *The Big Sleep* (1939), Chandler's novels capture almost perfectly the balance between the vulnerable suspense narrator in a predatory milieu and the detective who must impose his will to bring about a solution to the crime. Chandler is at his best in *Farewell, My Lovely* (1940), *The Lady in the Lake* (1943) and *The Long Goodbye* (1954). Other writers created appealing variations. Rex

Stout blends features of the classic story with elements of the hard-boiled story by creating a working-class Archie Goodwin to assist his opulent and retiring Nero Wolfe. Goodwin is a streetwise, updated, and sophisticated Watson figure with investigative skills of his own. Stout's fiction, beginning with *Fer-de-lance* (1934), makes entertaining tales of a mixture of classic and hard-boiled detection. The success of Frances Noyes Hart's *The Bellamy Trial* (1927) had shown how suspense could be drawn out of a trial and opened possibilities for subsequent writers. Erle Stanley Gardner demonstrated with his first Perry Mason novel, *The Case of the Velvet Claws* (1933), that the hard-boiled world could be softened by moving his lawyer in front of his private detective, Paul Drake, and dramatizing Randolph Mason–type uses of the law. So successful were Gardner's narrative strategies and the appeal of his characters that he sold more than a hundred million copies of his novels.

PAPERBACK NOVELS

When the pulps declined in the 1940s, many of the writers, some of whom had already produced film scripts, turned to television. Writers who had read pulps in their youth produced original paperback novels, which after World War II became the leading vehicle for hard-boiled fiction. Paperbacks from 1938 contained about the same number of words as pulps but featured a sustained narrative by a single author or a team of collaborators. Another mass-market production, the earliest paperbacks included reprints of the "classics of pulpdom," including the work of Erle Stanley Gardner and Frederick Faust along with popular British writers such as Agatha Christie (see O'Brien, 1981). From the beginning paperbacks were in direct competition with pulps. Pocket Books was established in 1939, followed in 1941 by Avon Books, Popular Library in 1942, Dell in 1943, Bantam in 1945, and others through the end of the decade. Penguin Books (begun in England) established New American Library in 1939. In 1939 34 titles resulted in sales of a million and a half copies; by 1945 four publishers produced 112 titles with 83 million copies in sales. By 1949 paperback publications totaled that of hardback production and by 1953, with 1,061 titles and 292 million copies, paperback production was about 100 million copies ahead of hardback production. Nearly 20 percent of the total sales of literature was detective and mystery fiction (see O'Brien, 1981). The number of titles multiplied from 112 in 1945 to 353 in 1946, to 866 in 1951, although total sales actually fell. Cover art incorporated aggressive styling, concealing content behind abstract covers until the late 1940s, then tended toward the detailed realism introduced by Signet. Paperbacks were investigated by the House Select Committee on Current Pornographic Materials in 1952, which also investigated risqué magazines and comic books (O'Brien, 1981, 42). Ernest Mandel estimates that since 1945,

10 billion copies of crime stories have been sold. By far the most books are published in the English language; annual French sales are over 30 million, German sales 20–25 million; Japanese crime fiction grew from 14 million in the mid-1960s to 20 million in the mid-1970s. Christie alone has sold 500 million copies; Edgar Wallace, 300 million; Georges Simenon, 300 million; and Mickey Spillane, 150 million.

DEVELOPMENTS AFTER WORLD WAR II

Another direction taken by the hard-boiled story in the 1940s was the dark suspense novel growing out of the work of such writers as Cornell Woolrich, Robert Bloch, and others, who infused the crime novel with horror. This innovation quickly picked up a hard-boiled edge in the crime adventure novels of Horace McCoy, Jim Thompson, and others. Dating from *Nothing More Than Murder* (1949) and *The Killer Inside Me* (1952) through the 1960s, Thompson's novels added the first-person psychopath to suspense. In her Ripley novels Patricia Highsmith develops the sociopath as a figure who operates with reason, but without the moral structure implicit in everyday social interaction. Dashiell Hammett had toyed with these perspectives but finally backed away from them. In some senses the other side of the criminal suspense novel is the vigilante detective novel, which celebrates violence against lawbreakers who have become insidious enemies. If one of the risks of the classic story is that it becomes too mechanistically concerned with plot, a risk of the hard-boiled story is that the detective becomes an extension of the atmosphere rather than ameliorating it. Hammett's Continental Op in *Red Harvest* feels himself afflicted with the epidemic killing in "Poisonville," and Mickey Spillane's Mike Hammer, in *I, the Jury* (1947), is stricken with the disease. Spillane became identified with the excesses and distortions of McCarthyism. If this was the case, his popularity suggests how close the country has flirted with fascism. Hammer did the nasty work the police were prevented by law from doing. From 1947 to 1951 his first seven novels were best-sellers and have since sold over 40 million copies. Mickey Spillane's Mike Hammer is a figure with many of the traits of the villain put in the service of vigilante action: he shoots first, administers pain and disfigurement with death, thinks ethical codes are for weak-kneed liberals, and acts as an assassin for the police and government. His success would signal the rise of no-holds-barred right-wing anti-communist literary extermination of enemies of the state. Spillane himself became a celebrity, appearing as a television personality in beer ads. Many critics saw this formulaic expression of the hard-boiled world as signaling a literary dead end, much as earlier critics had seen the puzzle story as the end of the classic detective story.

Instead of closing, new directions were opening in the late 1950s. The influential Ross Macdonald [Kenneth Millar] developed another variation of the detective novel. His early *Blue City* (1947) is close to the Hammett tradition, but later novels show a turn to greater subtlety in which his detective, Lew Archer, is self-consciously developed as an extension of the author's moral sensibilities. Macdonald compressed much of his violence into metaphor, arguing that the mystery provided an opportunity for the detective novel to achieve a higher aesthetic effect, because the solution could reverberate back through the novel's events. With *For Love of Imabelle* (1957), Chester Himes's detective fiction, first published in France, opened several possibilities not available previously. Detective fiction, with few exceptions, had treated black culture as an extension of the underworld or as the source of servants for white culture. Himes's fiction portrayed the world from within black culture and paid little attention to the conventions of white culture. Harlem police detectives Coffin Ed Johnson and Grave Digger Jones are infused with a picaresque spirit, drawing humor out of raucous circumstances. Second, Himes ignores the markers of realism that Chandler had recently claimed for hard-boiled fiction and introduces a surrealism that tends to undermine the boundaries of the crime novel. Later writers would extend Himes's narrative strategies to break through the transparency of the detective formula.

Finally, another form of the detective novel emerged immediately after World War II. The police procedural eliminated the amateur detective's independence and the private detective's ambiguous status by focusing on police work. Unlike the traditional gentleman investigator often found in the classic story or the police renegade or information source in the hard-boiled story, the lawmen in the procedural are collectively immersed in everyday police work. In *V as in Victim* (1945) Lawrence Treat set a pattern that has been generally followed by subsequent authors, though *Dragnet*, set in Los Angeles when it appeared first on radio (1949–56), television (1952–70), and film (1953), probably created the mass audience for the procedural. Hillary Waugh's *Last Seen Wearing . . .* (1952) moved the procedural to the small town, slowed the pace, developed characters, and significantly varied the genre.

Although virtually all the innovations discussed above continue to the present, they have emerged in new combinations that continue to engage readers. In the 1970s the practice of splitting the novel into perspectives grew in popularity. Frederick Forsyth's thriller *Day of the Jackal* (Br 1971) alternated material from the suspense novel's description of criminal procedures with description of the detection and pursuit by government and police agents. The elements of this kind of novel had been available much earlier, and parallel plotting techniques were standard fare in fiction, but the strategy became widespread after the emergence of the procedural, which characteristically juggled the plotlines of several different kinds of narrative action. All of the perspectives tended to be those of the police or their associates and families. After the early 1970s, however, the perspective of the psychopath is threaded into the narrative.

The pathological figures created by Robert Bloch, Patricia Highsmith, and Jim Thompson evolve into the psychopathic monsters of the 1980s in such novels as Thomas Harris's *The Silence of the Lambs* (1988), featuring Dr. Hannibal Lecter, whose rampaging counterpart, Buffalo Bill, is almost literally a monster in a skin suit. The narrative incorporates a procedural and folds Lecter's expertise into the FBI trainee Clarice Starling's search for Lecter's counterpart. In its contemporary form the sociopath's narrative is likely to be conflated with intimate suspense and the procedural, as in such novels as John Sandford's *Winter Prey* (1993), where the narration of "Iceman" parallels similarly structured narrative views of vulnerable Dr. Weather Karkannin and special deputy Lucas Davenport. This combining and branching of narrative forms of mystery and detective novels continues to intensify action and the density of explanation. The reconstruction of historical crimes and the personification of history through narrative is also popular. Merging perspectives from law, medicine, and such areas of expertise with characters and themes had been used by writers since the turn of the century to capitalize on reader curiosity and to augment the authority of investigators, but in contemporary novels such material is elaborated in far greater detail.

CONTEMPORARY DIVERSITY

One of the most striking aspects of detective and mystery novels has been the expansion of cultural perspectives informing crime fiction. This expansion began to have its major effect in the 1970s with the emergence of women's detective novels. Although this brief history makes obvious the importance of women to the origin and development of mystery and detective novels, the women's movement helped dismantle the barriers between "women's" and "men's" fiction. In the past women such as Leigh Brackett or Dolores Hitchens who wanted to work within the private-eye tradition usually wrote male figures. This has changed so that today not only are women's detective and mystery novels among the highest achievements of art and popularity, but they feature a wide range of central figures. Mary Higgins Clark writes thrillers, Sara Paretsky and Sue Grafton write variations of hard-boiled detective stories, Dorothy Uhnak and Elizabeth Linnington write police procedurals, Patricia Cornwell writes forensic thrillers, and a host of women write cozies. What became apparent was that women could operate in all the areas that had traditionally been considered male domains and by doing so extend them.

In some respects a response to the popular appeal of the feminist detective novel and the growing interest in multicultural literature, the 1980s saw the reemergence of the atmosphere of the classic detective novel from the 1930s and 1940s. This less puzzled form of the classical narrative became known as the "cozy," for its premises regarding a situation in which the murder is an irruption in an otherwise trouble-free world.[12] The novels often emphasize domestic life, pets, humor, and mainstream ethnicity as an attribute of lifestyle (as in Sharyn McCrumb's gentle satire of a convention of Scots in *Highland Laddie Gone*, 1986). The novels tend to emphasize regional characteristics—more rural, small-town, or suburban settings than cities—with themes that play on matters of interest to general readers or mystery fandom. Authors who have contributed variations of the cozy include Lillian Jackson Braun, Marian Babson, Dorothy Cannell, Aaron Elkins, Carolyn G. Hart (whose recent mysteries are set in a bookstore, as in *Death on Demand*, 1987), Joan Hess, Faye Kellerman, Charlotte MacLeod,[13] McCrumb, and others. This rather large and influential aspect of mystery fiction has its own annual convention in Washington, D.C., and publishes newsletters. The novels tend to substitute local color for the puzzle, so that the detective is as much a tour guide as a sleuth.

Crime fiction expanded among minorities as writers became aware of the potential of the markets and distortions introduced through stereotyping, omission, and other forms of representation of minority presences (see Perez and Perez, 1987a and b; Planells, 1987; Slide, 1993; Lock, 1994; and Soitos, 1996, 1997). The realistic potentials of the mainstream detective story have been furthered by such African-American writers as Gar Anthony Haywood, Eleanor Taylor Bland, Barbara Neely, and Walter Mosley, while writers such as Toni Morrison disrupt the complacency of the conventions of the detective and mystery story. Similar possibilities are being explored by Native Americans such as Louis Owens. Hispanic detective and mystery fiction is emerging.

Finally, literary experimentation is currently changing the formal structures and narrative possibilities of detective and mystery novels. Fictional detectives usually do not, as even their nineteenth-century detractors were fond of pointing out, correspond very closely to their real-life counterparts. Much of their art is devoted to concealing their essential relation to reality. Postmodern crime fiction is an exploration of these boundaries of popular genre fiction. In postmodern play on the story form, the detective's investigation is beset by indirection, delay, indeterminacy, multiplicity, and the failure of the problem to achieve clarity. In a sense, these writers bring the detective novel to a full circle, from the unintentional fumbling for a form and content that would exploit Poe's model to the intentional attempt to disrupt its hegemony. But despite postmodern writers' attempts to disrupt the symbiotic relation of formula and reader, the formula dominates the popular market.

NOTES

1. Bruce Cassiday has edited a collection, *Roots of Detection: The Art of Deduction Before Sherlock Holmes* (New York: Ungar, 1983), that includes short stories and excerpts from longer works that illustrate some aspect of detection. Collected in this volume are a selection from Book II of Herodotus's *The Histories* (c. 446 B.C.) on thefts from King Rampoinitus's treasure chamber; the *Apocrypha* section of the *Book of Daniel* (c. 500 B.C.), where ashes are spread to reveal the priests' theft of the tributes to Bal; the story of the three sharpers who compete for their lives by ascertaining truth, from Burton's edition of *The Arabian Nights, Supplement* (1888); the queen's bitch chapter from Voltaire's *Zadig* (1747); an adaptation of E.T.A. Hoffmann's "Mademoiselle de Scudéry" (1821) from Offenbach's *Tales of Hoffman*; the section of Edward Bulwer-Lytton's *Pelham*, in which Pelham incorrectly determines that Glanville has committed murder; a section from Vidocq's first volume of his *Memoirs* (1828); Poe's "The Purloined Letter"; a selection from Alexandre Dumas's *The Man in the Iron Mask* (1848–50); Bucket's summing up with Mme. Hortense from Dickens's *Bleak House* (1853); Wilkie Collins's "The Stolen Letter"; an excerpt from Mrs. Henry Wood's *East Lynne*; an excerpt from *The Notting Hill Mystery* (anon. [Charles Felix?], 1862); and the footprints in the snow episode from Emile Gaboriau's *Monsieur Lecoq* (1869).

2. *Literary History of the United States*, ed. by Robert E. Spiller, Willard Thorp, Thomas H. Johnson, and Henry Seidel Canby (New York: Macmillan, 1953), p. 183.

3. Charles Brockden Brown, *Edgar Huntly* (New Haven: New College and University Press, 1973), p. 33. Further references will be to this edition.

4. For lists of gothic novels see Montague Summers, *A Gothic Bibliography* (1941); and Dan J. McNutt, *The Eighteenth-Century Gothic Novel: An Annotated Bibliography of Criticism and Selected Texts* (1975). Elizabeth MacAndrew in *The Gothic Tradition in Fiction* (1979); Coral Ann Howells in *Love, Mystery, and Misery: Feeling in Gothic Fiction* (1978); Dorothy Scarborough, *The Supernatural in Modern Fiction* (1917); and Summers's *The Gothic Quest: A History of the Gothic Novel* (1938) provide useful information on the gothic novel and its development. Elsa Radcliffe lists nearly 2,000 contemporary gothics in her *Gothic Novels of the Twentieth Century: An Annotated Bibliography* (1979). For earlier American editions, see Lyle Wright, *American Fiction, 1774–1850* (1969), *American Fiction, 1851–1875* (1965) and *American Fiction, 1876–1900* (1966).

5. See *Vidocq: The Personal Memoirs of the First Great Detective*, ed. and trans. by Edwin Gile Rich (Boston: Houghton Mifflin Co., 1935).

6. Numerous suggestions and speculations have surrounded the incomplete novel, and several writers have in fact completed it.

7. Serialized in *Harper's Weekly* in the United States in 1859.

8. Serialized in *Harper's Weekly* in 1868; his collection *After Dark* (1856) contains "A Stolen Letter," a theme borrowed from Poe; and his *The Law and the Lady* (1875), like Poe's "The Mystery of Marie Rogêt," is based on an actual crime. Several other stories and novels made use of mystery and detection.

9. See J. Randolph Cox, "Chapters from the Chronicles of Nick Carter," *Dime*

Novel Roundup, May 1974, 50–55; June 1974, 62–67; and *Nick Carter Weekly*, Bibliographic Listing, *Dime Novel Roundup* Supplement, December 1975.

10. See, for example, Michael Denning's *Mechanic Accents* (1987).

11. Chapter 4 includes a brief list.

12. See Dilys Winn's "From Poe to the Present," *Murder Ink: The Mystery Reader's Companion* (1977), 3–6. Winn's other types are the Paranoid, the Romantic, the Vicious, and the Analytical.

13. See Jane S. Bakerman, "Bloody Balaclava: Charlotte MacLeod's Campus Comedy Mysteries."

CHAPTER 2

RELATED FORMULAS

Time, cultural difference, and the ingenuity of writers have led to a wide range of variations on the mystery story. Some variants such as the gothic novel, of course, preceded the modern mystery story and became well established long before the modern mystery emerged as a recognizable genre. This chapter briefly explores the elements and forms of related narrative formulas to the extent that they are variations on the mystery novel.[1] Marie Rodell (1943) identifies formulas and mixtures that have become exploited by mystery writers. The historical flow of the imagery clusters around what Rodell identifies as mystery and detective novels, horror-mysteries, adventure-mysteries, and experimental mysteries, which appear in various forms with one of the elements predominating. Add in Patricia Highsmith's (1966) description of suspense, John Ball's (1976) identification of the police procedural, Phyllis Whitney's (1976) soft gothic, together with numerous specialized formulas, and mix with cultural tensions accessible by the imagery these types generate.[2] Contemporary mysteries can also be divided into specialization of thematic types, such as medicine (research or experimentation, epidemics, personal crisis, hospital, etc.), law, politics, conspiracy, news, individual and collective violence, corporations, ecology, historical events, and so on (all of which may appear predominantly as procedural, horror, suspense, adventure). This chapter provides a brief introduction.

GOTHICS

Gothic mysteries are an outgrowth of Horace Walpole's *The Castle of Otranto* (1765), Mary Shelley's *Frankenstein* (1818), Charlotte Brontë's *Jane Eyre* (1847), Emily Brontë's *Wuthering Heights* (1847), and others. The gothic branched into three main streams: horror through Poe, Bram Stoker, H. P. Lovecraft, and so on through Stephen King to the present; science fiction from *Frankenstein*, especially; and the residue of gothic imagery within the deconstructive apparatuses of secular mystery. The gothic imagery of mystery, our main concern here, sprouts up in several locations. It appears as signifying imagery in cityscapes, in stories dealing with the ambiguation of reality, and in "cozy" gothic mysteries. Gothic imagery associated with urban life tends to signify decadence, as in Raymond Chandler's description of Geiger's photography setup or General Sternwood's hothouse. This is a thinner, minimalist use of imagery that flourished more expansively in the city exposés of the 1840s—George Lippard's *The Monks of Monk Hall* (1844) in the United States—but is still more robust than, say, similar imagery in Henry James's "The Beast in the Jungle." The gothic in the hard-boiled novel is often used to signify the presence of opium or other mind-altering drugs or of the rotting effect of money or political power. In contemporary fiction this may blend with horror in the portrayal of the lair of the psychopath. The visual effects were translated into film noir.

A second use of gothic material is in the sustaining of an ambiguity between a commonsense or scientifically derived realism and alternative realities as in novels with strong religious themes or those whose purpose is to maintain a degree of ambiguity about reality or, by extension, the possibilities of its representation. The latter use erupts in postmodern fiction, which exploits the spaces and boundaries of writing. This gothic effect is found in James's *The Turn of the Screw* (1898). In his *Modus Operandi* (1982), Robin Winks reduces ways to read *The Turn of the Screw* to three:

1. It is a ghost story (exploited in the 1980s in novels and films about "apparently innocent children who possess the power of unspeakable evil, sexual perversity" and so on by Stephen King). This is also the pattern in such supernatural tales as *Rosemary's Baby* (1967) and *The Exorcist* (1971).

2. It is an "account of the evils done by those who see the world with 'certitude.' An insane woman tells her story."

3. James shows both possibilities and how they interact: "The children do see ghosts, and the governess, who is mad, uses their evil to her own purposes, or is herself driven mad by what she perceives. Both this and the preceding view provide James with a creditable claim to have begun another popular subset within the genre of the thriller: Those interminable stories of young women sent to Gothic mansions high on isolated moors, there to look after mysterious chil-

dren and to be terrorized, last seen running from the turreted house into the fogs of romance" (Winks, 1982, 15).

It is the latter that Phyllis Whitney describes in "Gothic Mysteries" (1976). Whitney observes that it is Daphne du Maurier's *Rebecca* (1938) that is the prototype of the modern gothic mystery. The novel has not been out of print since it was published, and the movie made from the novel is also a classic. Other writers such as Mary Stewart and Victoria Holt have proven the viability of the gothic mystery for contemporary audiences. Whitney says that in modern gothics violence is usually offstage, "and it is more likely to be a *threat* of violence that keeps the reader hanging on every page. The always-fleeing girl is there, but she is a much more liberated woman than her earlier counterparts. True, she may tumble gladly into the hero's arms in a last-minute rescue, but she is quite capable of doing something about her dire situation on her own . . ." (Whitney, 1976, 226). Backgrounds are very important. The action may take place in a castle if the setting is in Spain or Germany, but a "large and brooding house" will be involved in any case. The weather may be anything. Typically the background is exotic, foreign—but it must be believable. Novels begin with the heroine "arriving on the scene—either returning to a place she has not seen for many years" or to a new one. Attention is given to the description of interiors—furniture, bric-a-brac—with fashion touches all through the story. There is always a drawing room. This attention extends to costume, with long, flowing skirts more common than pantsuits. There is always an ancient struggle of good versus evil, "often more psychological than physical. Where men readers want fast action and outward combat, the female reader is often more fascinated by the psychological clash with all its ramifications" (Whitney, 1976, 228). The heroine must be threatened by danger periodically throughout the story, but with minimum carnage or description of the physical effects of violence (Whitney, 1976, 229). "Since these are escape novels, and valued as such, one isn't apt to meet garbage cans and dirty sinks in their pages. . . . Characters are apt to be successful and well-to-do. . . . Only the vulnerable and appealing young heroine may feel uneasy amid wealth and luxury and preserve something of a conscience. She is the tie-in with a reality the reader knows. Often both hero and heroine have an admirable [offstage] concern for the state of the world and are trying to do something about it" (Whitney, 1976, 229). Characters often have some specialized knowledge, as in other mysteries. There is an obligatory chase scene near the climax, a life-or-death struggle that must have some originality. The hero may be blond but must still have a dark and brooding nature a la the Brontës, the stamp of Heathcliff, Mr. Rochester, and Maxim de Winter. No police are involved; detecting is entirely amateur, with little digging for clues. The heroine must not be stupid, but she "must be *forced* into that necessary danger" (Whitney, 1976, 232).

Elizabeth Peters prefers the term "romantic suspense stories" for her work. She contrasts Barbara Michaels's emphasis on "historical suspense and on novels with a supernatural atmosphere" to her own modern settings, in which she prefers an archaeological background. See also Kay Mussell's *Women's Gothic and Romantic Fiction* (1981) for an extensive guide to the genre and Juliann Evans Fleenor, ed., *The Female Gothic* (1983). The standard reference source is *Twentieth-Century Romance and Gothic Writers* (1982).

GANGSTER NOVELS

Gangsters and successful businesspeople have many of the same motivations and often use similar strategies for moving through organizational structures and realizing ambitions of wealth and power, so ambiguities were part of crime fact and fiction from Vidocq's early accounts of the Parisian underworld. The tendencies have been to portray criminal masterminds, organizations, or gangland affiliations, and the most successful, such as Mario Puzo's *The Godfather* (1969), manage to blend all three. These are distinct tendencies, however, leading to several identifiable threads. Gangster novels have traditionally been less likely than criminal thrillers to create sympathy for illegal activity and the possibility of the success of criminal activity. As late as the 1920s criminal activity could be of a glamorous nature—say, jewel theft, or a big caper—and the criminal could be dashing and suave. The spy thriller co-opted these characteristics for its hero, and the gangster tale became more directly cautionary. The gangster novels that emerged during Prohibition were associated with newspaper accounts of gangs and alcohol. W. R. Burnett's classic *Little Caesar* (1929) about the rise and fall of Caesar Enrico "Rico" Bandello paralleled the capitalist success story found in the Horatio Alger novels and other juveniles. William Dean Howells had treated the success story to realism, and Frank Norris and others had treated it to naturalism. The gangster story separates legal and illegal capitalism, paints the latter evil, and cautions that it leads to doom. As a crime story Rico is fated to rise and end in an ironic fall. With *The Asphalt Jungle* (1949), Burnett styles an ironical small-time criminal procedural in counterpart to the emerging emphasis on police procedurals in radio and television. Eleazar Lipsky's *The Kiss of Death* (1947) provides in Vanni Bianco a counterpart to Burnett's Rico, in that he is shown less as an inner-directed figure isolated from society and more a product of a criminal culture. This is carried further in later novels such as Dorothy Salisbury Davis's *The Little Brothers* (1973), which portrays life in an Italian-American street gang and George V. Higgins's *The Friends of Eddie Coyle* (1972), which portrays criminal culture. Another possibility emerged in the 1940s that would become a contemporary obsession. Drawing on the possibilities opened by Robert Bloch and others, Horace Mc-

Coy's *Kiss Tomorrow Goodbye* (1948) is an example of the first-person psychopath novel that Jim Thompson and Patricia Highsmith would develop. Once these parameters—criminal counterparts to legitimate business, criminal procedurals, criminal culture, and psychopaths—are established, permutations and combinations multiply.

Another possibility is the transformation of legitimacy into criminality and its obverse, the transformation of criminality into legitimate business. John Miles's *The Silver Bullet Gang* (1974) is about a law-abiding man who becomes fed up and plans a heist. The gangster story reemerges and expands after World War II into several branches. In the process the inner-directed figure of *Little Caesar* is transformed into the tradition-directed figures of *The Godfather* (1969), just the opposite of David Reisman's description that portrayed a social shift to other-directedness. The ambiguities of the novel blur the distinction between criminality/legitimacy and sympathy/caution. But the figure did move into other-directed behavior as well.

Ernest Mandel (1984) notes that Puzo wrote essays drawing parallels between bourgeois society and criminal organizations. In the Mafia novel individual human passions are always less important than business; murder loses its mystery and becomes an anonymous business for profit. Crime stories featuring the business of crime include William Haggard's *Teleman Touch* (1959), Alistair MacLean's *Sea Witch* (1977), Jeffrey Archer's *Shall We Tell the President?* (1977), Robert McCrum's *A Loss of Heart* (1982), John Gardner's sequel to the James Bond series, *Licence Renewed* (1981), Robin Cook's *Fever* (1982), and John Matthews's *Basikasingo* (1982), which deals with a diamond cartel.

SUSPENSE NOVELS

Suspense novels feature narrative elements that are specific to mystery fiction as well as those more generally found in many kinds of fiction. Roland Barthes's (1974) structuralist account of "delay" is helpful here (see chapter 3). His point is that detective narratives embody devices such as the evasion of the truth, mixtures of truth and evasion, and acknowledgment of insolubility to delay narrative closure. Dennis Porter offers a formalist explanation of delay as "a state of anxiety dependent on a timing device." Suspense "depends on such factors as the length of time elapsed between the initial moves in a sequence and the approach to a conclusion, the sympathy evoked for the characters concerned, the nature of the threat represented by the obstacles, or the desirability of the goal" (Porter, 1981, 329). The key element of suspense is an impediment to the solution of the mystery, since without it the narrative would simply rush to completion and the story would be sacrificed. Without the progression of the story, however, the narrative would simply thrash around in digressions.

Tzvetan Todorov finds these tendencies to be more broadly characteristic of suspense fiction itself. He observes that the structure of the suspense novel develops in the gap between the detective story and the thriller. "It keeps the mystery of the whodunit and also the two stories, that of the past and that of the present; but it refuses to reduce the second to a simple detection of the truth" (Todorov, 1971, 50). The story is oriented to the future (what will happen) as much as to the past. Emphasis on suspense shifts the mystery from the puzzle to events that are on the verge of happening, so that the detective figure is suspended in mystery. Todorov suggests that two types of suspense novel correspond to their two moments of emergence. The "story of the vulnerable detective" appeared at the time between the whodunit and the thriller and coexists with it. This is the story of the Hammett/Chandler detective who "loses his immunity" and must survive the introduction to criminal life (Todorov, 1971, 50). The second form of the suspense novel attempts to remove the criminal subculture and return to the whodunit, but in this case the protagonist is the suspect and must become a detective in order to clear his or her name. The novels of William Irish, Patrick Quentin, and Charles Williams tend to be of this type.

While Todorov is helpful in this definition, he does not mention the most important form of suspense novel—that which creates an intimacy between criminal activity and the protagonist. Here the central figure is not a detective nor the mystery a drive toward the solution to a crime that corrects an injustice, but rather the effect of the further collapse of political, economic, or medical discourse into the crime narrative. This tendency began in the 1930s during the Depression in the novels of James M. Cain and others and was recreated by such writers as Robert Bloch, Horace McCoy, Patricia Highsmith, and Jim Thompson after World War II. Most deal with crimes of situation, opportunity, or compulsion in which a central character is brought under increased tension. Since the crime is "unmotivated" and compulsively repeated, emphasis shifts to the mystery of the construction of crimes anticipated in the future. That is, the central figure is caught between the possibility of past crimes being successfully sleuthed while being drawn into or constructing crimes subject to the vagaries of future chance. The formula was rediscovered again and gained popularity in the 1970s in espionage fiction and then in the psychopath fiction of the 1980s.

Mandel notes that in the pure suspense story "either the murderer, or the victim, but in any case not the detective, is the real hero" (Mandel, 1984, 87). Maurice Richardson in "Simenon and Highsmith" (1978) points out that such writers as Patricia Highsmith write about "men like a spider writing about flies" (Mandel, 1984, 113). Highsmith's *Strangers on a Train* (1950) and *The Talented Mr. Ripley* (1955) "tend to focus on the psychological conflict between two men; "one of them generally acts seemingly on impulse, as if out of character, as if some tiny little cerebral implosion had taken place" (Mandel, 1984, 114).

THRILLERS

What are thrillers? In *The Whodunit* (1982), Stefano Benvenuti and Gianni Rizzoni define the thriller as "a narrative work (although it could also be extended to the theater and film) that centers on some criminal plot and is constructed to build up maximum tension. . . . The novelty lay in the combining of suspense and intrigue with action and excitement" (Benvenuti and Rizzoni, 1982, 57). Stefano Benvenuti and Gianni Rizzoni credit Earl Derr Biggers in the United States and Edgar Wallace's Mr. Reeder detective stories published from 1925 in England for the spread of popularity of the innovation among all classes in the 1920s.

But the police procedural has also been considered a thriller, as have spy and political novels. The common denominator seems to be action, excitement, and tension. That is, in contrast with the suspense story, in which tension is created through the envelopment of a threat, thrillers create tension through aggressive action. This definition is consistent with Rodell's distinction that suspense stories mix gothic elements with mystery, and thrillers mix action. Particularly since Frederick Forsyth's *The Day of the Jackal* (Br 1971) the thriller has employed a plot structure that Gilles Deleuze attributed to D. W. Griffith's film editing of the early twentieth century. Deleuze calls this parallel convergent editing, which parallels binary opposites to create both suspense and action. As the Jackal goes through different disguises and assembles his rifle for the assassination of de Gaulle, the policeman is assembling evidence of these activities and closing the pursuit. Most contemporary thrillers use variations of this pattern, but it is not necessarily a closed form.

Criminal Thrillers[3]

Otto Penzler's "The Great Crooks" (in Ball, 1976) recognizes that criminal stories preceded detective stories and that figures such as Robin Hood, Gil Blas, Dick Turpin, Moll Flanders, Fu Manchu, The Saint, Raffles, Count Dracula, Professor Moriarty, The Lone Wolf, Arsene Lupin, Boston Blackie, and many others have had considerable popularity. Penzler quotes Ellery Queen's definition of a crook story: " 'It must contain a crook who crooks; the crook should be the protagonist; and almost invariably the crook should triumph over the forces of the law, amateur or official. In a phrase, a crook story is 'detection in reverse'." Penzler thinks that "the best suspense novels are those that shift between the criminal and the police as a plan is conceived and developed on the one hand, and steps are taken to discover and prevent it on the other, as with . . . Cornell Woolrich's *The Bride Wore Black* [1940]" (Penzler, in Ball, 1976, 323). W. R. Burnett's *Little Caesar, The Asphalt Jungle,* and *High Sierra* (1940) explore realism and cultural context in their treatment of the criminal. In James M. Cain's novels such as *The Postman Always Rings Twice* (1934) and *Double Indemnity* (1943), for which Raymond Chandler later wrote a screenplay, sex and financial gain are interwoven motives. Richard Stark's [pseud. of Donald E. Westlake] *The Hunter* (1962, aka *Point Blank*) and others are centered on Parker, an isolated criminal. Westlake also writes comic novels about criminals, such as *The Bank Shot* (1972) and *The Hot Rock* (1970).

Spy Thrillers

Ralph Harper's *The World of the Thriller* (1969) defines the thriller as essentially spy fiction, though he lists some hard-boiled detective novels. The three stages of spy fiction are those associated with British writers: John Buchan, Eric Ambler, Graham Greene, and Erskine Childers. People read thrillers because reading them releases tension; each novel has a beginning and end, unlike much everyday life. Evils and perils are set right through *commitment* and *competence*, aided by virtue and luck (Harper, 1969, 9). There are five elements:

1. Poetic justice in the thriller includes poetic justice and the absurd. There must be a simple yet shocking view of the world. A "shocker" is the mass media's "imagination of the absurd" (Harper, 1969, 10), a popular counterpart of existialist philosophy.

2. The thriller includes banality and humor—fear of banality often leads to pert repartee parody (as in Bond). Graham Greene's *Our Man in Havana* (1958) is a parody of Fleming.

3. Both the plausible and implausible are present—the implausible happens all the time and includes the success of the hero. When the fantastic is also absurd (Albert Camus) and the hero is believable (he has endurance, self-reflection, and skill and is fortunate), then the actual and dream worlds meet in "an imagined resolution of anarchy" (Harper, 1969, 13). In this sense the experience of the thriller is like a daydream or fairy tale: it is a vicarious experience that allows for a subjectivity like the hero's. By the 1930s the world began to resemble the thriller.

4. It includes a new mythology—the reader enters the "primary world" (J.R.R. Tolkein's terms) and doesn't need a superfluity of facts or outsize villains. The primary world is made up of a love of adventure, a patriotic struggle against evil, the opportunity for individual heroism, and the prospect for reward by love. Harper judges Childers's *Riddle of the Sands* (Br 1903) to be the archetypal thriller.

5. The novel pits gentlemen against professionals—after World War II the hero becomes a trained professional. Hammett and Chandler developed the style. A gentleman is called or invited (like a self). There is a casual beginning in which adventure occurs by chance. The hero's own peril is always central. The hero is vulnerable and can be hurt.

Other critics find the spy story remarkably simple in its structure and appeal. Bruce Merry says "[t]he fit between the standard pattern of the folktale and the modern spy thriller is a strikingly precise one" (Merry, 1977, 235). For Robin Winks (1982) the spy formula is also very simple: introduce the hero, provide difficulties, resolve difficulties.

Critics such as Julian Symons (1985) include James Fenimore Cooper's *The Spy* (1821), but the field is dominated by British writers. William Le Queux's *England's Peril* (1899) and *The Invasion of 1910* (1910), Erskine Childers's *Riddle of the Sands* (1903), Joseph Conrad's *The Secret Agent* (1907), John Buchan's *The Thirty-Nine Steps* (1915), and "Sapper" 's [Herman Cyril McNeile] *Bulldog Drummond* (1920) are of historical importance. Somerset Maugham's Ashenden stories (1928) and Eric Ambler's pre–World War II novels such as *The Mask of Dimitrios* (1938) provide more sophistication. But the real growth was after World War II, with John Le Carré's *The Spy Who Came In from the Cold* (1963) and Len Deighton's *The Ipcress File* (1963).

Jerry Palmer's *Thrillers* (1979) provides an approach that modifies an ideological critique with discourse theory. The hero is a vehicle for competitive individuality, which is justified by a conspiracy—the fear of revolt by the lower classes. Ideology represses this fear and presents conspiracy as the Other, but since the conspiracy is immediately met by heroic opposition, the conspiracy is a disruption of a known world. The specificity of the thriller grounds it in ideology: "the essence of ideology is not to give false answers to real problems, but to pose problems in such a (false) way that the recommendations one wished to make in the first place appear to correspond to a real problem" (Palmer, 1979, 204). Thus, grounded in ideological developments of the nineteenth century, the thriller mounts a claim for competitive individuality within the context of conspiratorial fear of the dangerous classes, but once it had coalesced, new fears of conspiracy could be adapted to its form as long as the symbiosis of its elements remained intact.

Jon Thompson argues that Kipling's *Kim* (Br 1901) is the model of the heroic spy novel. *Kim* is based on the contradiction that "it is an imperial novel that at the same time denies the Indian experience of colonialism" (Thompson, 1993, 83). It is in this sense typical of English colonial novels: seeing English culture as dominant shapes the novel. Kipling fails to incorporate any of the conflicts or resistances in India and openly supported imperialism as did the general British population. Board games, jigsaw puzzles, entertainments all exalted imperialism. The espionage novel is grounded in the culture of imperialism, in the anxiety of foreign invasion, and from 1900–1915 from the refinement of "surveillance on the domestic population and external enemies" (Thompson, 1993, 85). Espionage novels branch out from adventure and detective novels in their "rejection of conventions of the psychological novel, domesticity and women" (Thompson, 1993, 86). *Kim* and Joseph Conrad's *The Secret Agent* (Br 1907) illustrate the two main paths of the "secret-agent adventure" story (Thompson, 1993, 86). *Kim* is in the romantic and heroic tradition of Buchan, Oppenheim, and Ian Fleming, while *The Secret Agent* anticipates the ironic path taken by Somerset Maugham, Graham Greene, Eric Ambler, and John Le Carré.

Kim has the form of a bildungsroman; Kimball O'Hara is the orphaned son of an Irish soldier and a mother who died in childbirth, taken in by a vagabond lama and recruited by the British military. Kim can "pass" for Indian. He is *chela*, or disciple to the lama, and sees no contradiction between this and spying for the British. Espionage is a game for Kim. The game aspect "effectively displaced questions of ethics and legitimacy to the realm of sportsmanship" (Thompson, 1993, 87). The minor Indian characters' "specific function is to ratify the legitimacy of English rule." *Kim* affirms the lama's "conservative and rather innocent worldview" (Thompson, 1993, 88). The novel tries to suppress the resistance of "races, customs, cast cultures, and languages" (Thompson, 1993, 89). Thompson's approach represents research possibilities in linking genre, text, colonial studies, and the iconology of other cultural features that needs further development.

The spy thriller involves the main enemy of the state, with crimes against the state not limited to espionage, but which spill over to spawn the political thriller involving political coups, threats to the president, and so on. The variants possible in this form lead to ambiguity between politics and criminal activity, as in Cruz Smith's *Gorky Park* (1981). Graham Greene illustrates the shift to ambiguity. He first portrays a conservative British intelligence agent "upholding such reactionary causes as the struggle of the Catholic Church against the Mexican revolution" in *The Power and the Glory* (1940) and the merciful role of the Church in human misery in *The Heart of the Matter* (1948). His fiction shifted to satire of imperialism in *Our Man in Havana* (1958). By the 1960s there were lots of novels, such as Le Carré's *The Spy Who Came In from the Cold* (1963), and Len Deighton's *The Billion Dollar Brain* (1966), *Gorky Park* (1981), and *Marathon Man* (1974). The characters are like Kafka's K, caught between unknown organizations. The best "disintegrative" crime story is Sam Greenlee's *The Spook Who Sat By the Door* (1972), about a black nationalist in the United States who stirs ghetto gangs to get out the proletarians. John G. Cawelti and Bruce A. Rosenberg's *The Spy Story* (1987) expands the discussion.

Reference material includes Donald McCormick and Katy Fletcher's *Spy Fiction: A Connoisseur's Guide* (1990), which contains 253 pages of A–Z author entries, followed by very brief sections on the history of the genre, factual events, treachery, international writing, future directions, writers and the world of intelligence, screen adaptations, and the state of the art. Author entries include pseudonyms, titles, biographical notes, a brief critical note, and indication of adaptations. Myron J. Smith, Jr.'s, *Cloak-and-Dagger Bibliography: An Annotated Guide to Spy Fiction, 1937–1975* (1976) and Donald McCormick's *Who's Who in Spy Fiction* (1977) provide checklists.

Political Thrillers

In his tour of American crime writers, *Into the Badlands* (1991), John Williams cites Boston novelist George V. Higgins as an author who writes "about the people that the general public are perhaps most likely to perceive as dishonest: criminals, of course, but also lawyers, politicians and journalists. These are also the people Higgins knows best" (197). Williams considers Higgins's *A Choice of Enemies* (1984) "by some distance the most acute modern political novel I've read" (Williams, 1991, 204). Higgins has been a journalist, prosecutor, and lawyer, having worked for the Associated Press in Providence, Rhode Island, "a hard town by the sea with a heavy Mafia presence" and covered Mafia trials in Springfield, Massachusetts (Williams, 1991, 198). The activity of the district attorney's office "is the only blood sport that's officially sanctioned," Williams quotes him as saying (Williams, 1991, 198).

The network of people skilled in covert activities feeds into government, criminal, corporate, and political representatives of wealth and power in such novels as Jim Hougan's *Spooks* (1978). Such activities inspired, Mandel maintains, a subgenre that might be called the " 'true' political thriller," such as Robert Ludlum's *The Holcroft Covenant* (1978), Spiro T. Agnew's *The Canfield Decision* (1976), and John Ehrlichmann's *The Company* (1976). More recently John Grisham's *The Pelican Brief* (1992) identifies corporate greed in a plot that involves murder to influence the Supreme Court and presidential politics.

COURTROOM DRAMAS AND LAWYER NOVELS

With the ascendancy of the law over the church in earthly matters in the late seventeenth century, lawyers became interpreters of the mysteries of the legal code in a sense similar to the ministers and priests in their relation to religious codes. The possibilities inherent in the lawyer as protagonist are apparent in much earlier fiction, but the lawyer as investigator emerges in popular fiction most clearly in such novels as Anna Katharine Green's *The Leavenworth Case: A Lawyer's Story* (1878), where Ebenezer Gryce is a lawyer, rather than a detective or policeman. Melville Davisson Post's Randolph Mason, "the skilled, unscrupulous lawyer, . . . a 'mysterious legal misanthrope, having no sense of moral obligation,' " demonstrates that legal features of criminal justice could be worked into short stories (Binyon,

1989, 128). As characters, lawyers can serve as investigative figures in the same way that newspaper reporters, private detectives, police personnel and others function. Courtrooms as dramatic stages or the law as a theme or discourse, however, distinguishes courtroom fiction from detective fiction featuring a lawyer, legal aide, court reporter, judge, and so on.

Undoubtedly the most famous lawyer in crime fiction is Perry Mason, created by Erle Stanley Gardner. It was Gardner's discovery that he could team the figure of the lawyer in Perry Mason with Paul Drake, a semi-hard-boiled investigator, much as Rex Stout combined the figure of the classic detective, Nero Wolfe, with Archie Goodwin, a semi-hard-boiled investigator. This allowed him to move the story along while reserving the courtroom for the most dramatic moments. While Perry Mason also serves other kinds of purposes in the novels, his function illustrates that it is the law office and courtroom settings that distinguish courtroom dramas from stories featuring lawyer-detectives, such as Stephen Greenleaf's Marshall Tanner. Most contemporary novels feature action figures who function as semiamateur detectives as well as attorneys.

John Grisham's blockbusters are unabashed thrillers, once again finding gold in an innovative combination of existing plots and characters. Contemporary lawyers are portrayed in such novels as Kate Wilhelm's *Death Qualified* (1991), with a sequel, *The Best Defense* (1994), Sandra Brown's *The Witness* (1995), Ed McBain's *There Was a Little Girl* (1995), Barbara Parker's *Suspicion of Guilt* (1995), John A. Peak's *Spare Change* (1994), Marissa Piesman's *Close Quarters* (1994), Manuel Ramos's *The Ballad of Gato Guerrero* (1994), Michael A. Kahn's *Firm Ambitions: A Rachel Gold Mystery* (1994), and Stephen Solomita's *Last Chance for Glory* (1994). Scott Turow's *Presumed Innocent* (1987), *The Burden of Proof* (1990), and others are important.[4] A brief introduction to the contemporary fiction is John Grisham's "The Rise of the Legal Thriller: Why Lawyers Are Throwing the Books at Us" (1992). See Richard H. Weisberg's *The Failure of the Word: The Protagonist as Lawyer in Modern Fiction* (1984) and for checklists of earlier novels Jon L. Breen's *Novel Verdicts: A Guide to Courtroom Fiction* (1984) and supplement in *The Armchair Detective* (1987–88).

POLICE PROCEDURALS

The police procedural eliminated the amateur detective's independence and the private detective's ambiguous status by focusing more or less straightforwardly on police work.[5] Unlike the traditional gentleman investigator or fool often found in the classic story or the police renegade or information source in the hard-boiled story, the lawmen in the procedural are collectively immersed in everyday police work, and the novels typically feature several concurrent subplots involving byplay among police, personal problems, and various police activities balanced for their comic relief and dramatic impact. Violence in the procedural is externalized and response to it is placed inside the institution, thus reproducing a hard-boiled atmosphere while reducing detection to procedure and highlighting the pressure and social interaction among those charged with law enforcement. Inevitably the novels lend authority to institutionalized surveillance and criminal justice. It is a form that places the amateur and private detective in the secondary position the police occupied in earlier crime fiction.

In *V as in Victim* (1945) Lawrence Treat set a pattern that has been generally followed by other authors, though *Dragnet*, when it appeared first on radio in 1948 and television in 1952, helped create an audience for the procedural (see Dove, 1982). Hillary Waugh's *Last Seen Wearing . . .* (1952) developed variations on small-town procedurals. Evan Hunter, better known as Ed McBain, author of the 87th Precinct series, exemplifies the big-city procedural, beginning with *Cop Hater, The Mugger,* and *The Pusher* in 1956. Other procedural writers include Elizabeth Linington, *Case Pending* (1960, as Dell Shannon), Rex Burns, beginning with *The Alvarez Journal* (1975), Thomas Chastain in *High Voltage* (1979), Lillian O'Donnell in such novels as *The Phone Calls* (1972), Joseph Wambaugh with *The New Centurions* (1970) and others, Collin Wilcox in such novels as *The Lonely Hunter* (1969), and Dorothy Uhnak, beginning with *The Bait* (1968).

George Dove's *The Police Procedural* (1982) notes that the procedural must have a mystery that is solved by policemen using ordinary police procedures. The procedural has five components: (1) police are ordinary people, competent as cops; (2) they do a job that is not as glorious or exciting as they had expected; (3) police are a tight community that defends itself from superiors and the public; (4) the police depend on luck or breaks; and (5) they have time and legal constraints within which their work must be carried out. Dove says the procedural's structure embodies several myths: (1) they include moral absolutes or good versus evil, though not all writers follow this; (2) they often portray an unwinnable war; and (3) police work is dull and boring and unsolved cases are a problem. While these myths are referenced in the novels, the novels themselves portray excitement and success.

Robert P. Winston and Nancy C. Mellerski's *The Public Eye: Ideology and the Police Procedural* (1992) finds American procedurals too uninteresting for consideration, but their general observations about procedurals are worth noting. They suggest that Dove's *The Police Procedural* deals with "formulaic characteristics rather than identifying the mechanisms through which it enters into ideological debate" (Winston and Mellerski, 1992, 9). Dove's version is an "ahistorical and non-contextual definition of reality," so he can't explain "the ways in which police procedurals mediate and manage social fears and anxieties" or the differences among writers and novels of different cultures (Winston and Mellerski, 1992, 10). Winston and Mellerski point out that foregrounding police defuses and "reshapes the potentially destructive impulses of individualism into successful participation in a corporate structure, the police squad" (Winston and Mellerski, 1992, 2). At the same time the series they examine "generally end on a note of barely controlled chaos rather than restored and validated order" (Winston and Mellerski, 1992, 2). The group of police represents the "human face of state power," so that success gains larger social approval—"cooperation between the police and society" is "the source of reader satisfaction" (Winston and Mellerski, 1992, 7). The "spectre of absolute state control" is raised in order to show that it can't be completely coercive since ordinary people wield its power (Winston and Mellerski, 1992, 7).

In *Hillary Waugh's Guide to Mysteries and Mystery Writing* (1991) Waugh claims that the police procedural was the "[s]econd major change in the nature of the mystery story. The mystery was established by shifting the reader from observer (seeing through Watson's eyes) to participant (standing at the detective's side trying to beat him to the solution). The first shift was the establishment of the private eye, which kept the puzzle but moved "from thought to action" (Waugh, 1991, 119); this figure then became the spy. The procedural followed in which the figure is "thrust into the middle of a working police force, full of rules and regulations" and the story "shows how it operates." The story is not only about policemen, but "the world of the policeman" (Waugh, 1991, 119). It is clear that this moving among, rather than away from, the police is a radical shift. The claim of the procedural is often that it is more realistic than the detective novel, but Waugh points out that in a small town of 10,000, such as that in which his own stories have been set, there would not likely be more than one murder every twelve years (eight per century). Seven would be solved within ten minutes after police arrived. A writer, however, will produce crime-of-the-century stories at a pace of two or three a year. On the other hand there were about 1,500 murders in New York City in 1976, so a writer could never keep up that pace. Writers might be accurate about procedures, dialogue, and humor, but informants solve most cases, and if a writer moves away from this, she or he moves away from reality.

For the procedural, knowledge of a police force's structure, which varies from city to city, is essential. The writer must know procedures, the law, rules of evidence, and so on and must be realistic in other ways—if a person drinks too much, he or she gets sick. Another shift in the procedural is in the balance of power: in the classical and hard-boiled story, the lone detective's opposition was powerful; in the police procedural this is reversed—scores of well-armed men, computers, laboratories, fleets of vehicles, helicopters, and the like are arrayed against criminals who usually have fewer resources, little mobility, and so forth. Waugh tends to make his criminals more interesting by making them smarter than average, giving them middle- or upper-middle-class background, and so on, which tend to make the odds less skewed. After this preparation the narrative is ready for a one-to-one conflict. Waugh feels that this strategy works because readers don't seem to be interested in fairness. Apparently they don't root for the underdog, although this may be because they root so hard for the triumph of good over evil. Instead "the desire [is] to annihilate the enemy, and the more overwhelming the victory, the more satisfying it is" (Waugh, 1991, 30).

See Jo Ann Vicarel's *A Reader's Guide to the Police Procedural* (1995) for brief plot summaries for some 1,115 books by 271 authors, with sections including lists of pseudonyms, creators, and series characters, periods from 1700 to 1992, locations, serial killers, humor, police personnel, agencies, and a list of 100 "Classics of the Genre."

POSTMODERN DETECTIVE NOVELS

In *Mystery and Its Fictions* (1979) David A. Grossvogel argues that the popular detective story is only a closed play form of what might be called the premodern metaphysical mystery. Postmodern forms result from writers such as Alain Robbe-Grillet who broke "the seal closing the traditional detective story" and opened it by bending it back toward mystery (Grossvogel, 1979, 20).

Stefano Tani's *The Doomed Detective: The Contribution of the Detective Novel to Postmodern American and Italian Fiction* (1984) is the first book-length study of the uses of the detective formula in postmodern narrative strategies. After providing a brief history of the genre, in which he separates post–World War II American private-eye novels from their classic British counterparts, Tani suggests that the hard-boiled genre provided the groundwork for the use of detective fiction conventions by postmodern writers. Postmodern writers use this strategy: contentional clues are placed by the writer so that the reader is intentionally misled, so that "conventions are paradoxically functional in the disintegration of the genre" (Tani, 1984, 43). The detective in the anti-detective story "no longer has the detachment of a M. Dupin." He "gets emotionally caught in the net of his detecting effort and is torn apart between the upsurge of feelings and the necessity for rationality" (Tani, 1984, 42). There are three solutions to this enigma. The first is *innovation*, which provides a partially satisfying solution, based in a "social preoccupation . . . totally foreign to the 'British' kind, but is already present in the hard-boiled school," which uses variants of rules; conventions are "twisted but not subverted" (Tani, 1984, 43). Second, *deconstruction* is a strategy that suspends the solution (as in Thomas Pynchon's *The Crying of Lot 49*, 1966) or supplies a mocking solution, as in William Hjortsberg's *Falling Angel* (1978). Crime is "seen as a secret organization ruling or perverting society" that provides the occasion for an existential quest. Finally, *metafiction* initiates a " 'book-consciousness-of-its-bookishness,' " which is like British puzzle detection (Tani, 1984, 43). This is only generally related to detective fiction.

The series detective is like Sisyphus in that he must repeat his action of going back into the past in the next book. The anti-detective chooses not to choose to seek a solution—that's his widest choice. Mythological elements include *mirror, labyrinth,* and *map* (Tani, 1984, 47). The detective is a mapmaker (he seeks a solution); present time is the mirror maker; flowing time (the past) is the labyrinth maker, that is, the source of mystery, or crime. The detective follows an Ariadne's thread (a lead). The mirror is also a prefiguration of the double and also deceives the detective. Pynchon's *The Crying of Lot 49* "disappoints the reader's expectations and 'deconstructs' conventional detective fiction by denying its main characteristics: the denouement, the consequent triumph of justice, the detective's detachment (Oedipa goes as far as questioning her own sanity). The tension between the reader and the novel—namely, the tension from detection to solution—is increased in comparison with traditional detective fiction, since inconsequential clues are often much more tantalizing than the ones which eventually fall neatly into place" (Tani, 1984, 30). "In *The Crying of Lot 49* suspense is obtained by an over-richness of clues leading nowhere and by the interplay between the novel and the Jacobean revenge play [*The Courier's Tragedy*] in the novel" (Tani, 1984, 30). "Oedipa strives to reach a middle choice, to break down these binary either/or, saved/damned alternatives that the four possibilities give her, but, ultimately, she grows to maturity because she cannot reach a middle choice" (Tani, 1984, 30–31). She is a "human detective." At one point Oedipa says she was an "optimistic baby [who] had come on so like the private eye in any long-ago radio drama, believing all you needed was grit, resourcefulness, exemption from hide-bound cops' rules, to solve any great mystery" (qtd. in Tani, 1984, 36).

In his discussion of the transformation of the modernist literary world, *Postmodernist Fiction* (1987), Brian McHale distinguishes between the characteristically ontological predicament of the modernist novel and the epistemological predicament of the detective novel. Although he perhaps underestimates the importance of the detective story form to postmodernism (whose characteristic genre of reference he feels is science fiction) and its struggle between the ontology of its hermetic form and the realist tendencies of its content, McHale distinguishes between the detective story formulation of Faulkner's modernist *Absalom, Absalom!* (1936) and that of Pynchon's postmodernist *The Crying of Lot 49* (1966). Mandel notes that the works of such authors as Vladimir Nabokov (emigré Russian living in the United States and writing in English), Jorge Luís Borges (Argentinian), and Alain Robbe-Grillet (French) "transcend, or even reverse, the classical 'reading' of clues." Their stories offer several possible readings of the clues (Mandel, 1984, 63). While this oversimplifies the problematics of contemporary fiction, it provides a useful distinction: the detective novel moves inevitably toward resolution of its mystery through the agency of its detective, while the postmodern figure's quest is beset by indirection, delay, indeterminacy, multiplicity, and the failure of the problem to achieve clarity.

Other studies follow similar strategies to clarify the uses of formula by writers struggling with the hermeticism and formal rigidity of mystery and detective novels. Larry E. Grimes's "Stepsons of Sam: Re-Visions of the Hard-Boiled Detective Formula in Recent American Fiction" (1983) argues that Richard Brautigan's *Dreaming of Babylon* (1977), Jules Feiffer's *Ackroyd* (1977), and Thomas Berger's *Who Is Teddy Villanova?* (1977) "revision" of hard-boiled detective fiction, drawing on Cawelti's *Adventure, Mystery, and Romance* (1976) for a definition. The hard-boiled novel takes a "turn toward subjectivity" with the substitution of the detective's will for intellect. The solution is no longer resolution. Ackroyd exploits diary entries; Brautigan's C. Card is narcissistic and prone to hallucinations from an old head injury. Card is hired to steal the corpse of a hooker. Thomas Berger's novel is hard-boiled rather than a parody or invention that borrows characters and plots from Hammett and Chandler. Taken together, the novels turn the image of the city from the hard-boiled existential vision to absurdity. Norma Rowen's "The Detective in Search of the Lost Tongue of Adam: Paul Auster's *City of Glass*" (1991) discusses Auster's use of the detective figure in the metaphysical search for linguistic relevance. William Lavender's "The Novel of Critical Engagement: Paul Auster's *City of Glass*" (1993) argues that Auster uses *City of Glass* as a vehicle for examining the assumptions and limitations of fiction, particularly by undermining the expectations about form and formulation. Chris Tysh's "From One Mirror to Another: The Rhetoric of Disaffiliation in *City of Glass*" (1994) discusses the use of a detective fiction structure to explore issues of modernism and postmodernism. Bette B. Roberts's "The Strange Case of *Mary Reilly*" (1993) examines the gothic, detective, psychological, and science fiction elements in Valerie Martin's novel about Dr. Jekyll's maid in Robert Louis Stevenson's novel.

NOTES

1. See also Todorov's discussion of elements that provide alternatives, etc., and other studies that provide cues to generic change and relations ("Typology of Detective Fiction," in *The Poetics of Prose*, trans. Richard Howard [Ithaca, NY: Cornell University Press, 1977]).

2. What is still poorly understood is how changes in the flow of imagery lead the public and how the interests and anxieties of publics influence the flow of imagery.

3. See also Mike Pavett's "From the Golden Age to Mean Streets," in *Crime*

Writers: Reflections on Crime Fiction by Reginald Hill, P. D. James, H.R.F. Keating, Troy Kennedy Martin, Maurice Richardson, Julian Symons, Colin Watson, ed. H.R.F. Keating; additional information by Mike Pavett (London: British Broadcasting Corporation, 1978).

4. Alexander Stille's "Fiction Follows Life in Novels of Turow" (*National Law Journal*, July 9, 1990) emphasizes *The Burden of Proof*.

5. Waugh argues in "The Mystery versus the Novel" that detective stories got further from reality as conventions became accepted and writers had to vary plots. See his essay in John Ball, ed.'s, *The Mystery Story* (San Diego: University of San Diego Extension, 1976).

CHAPTER 3

CRITICISM AND THEORY

This chapter discusses critical attention to detective and mystery novels published in the United States. It is not exhaustive of material published but will consider critical views that have been influential on contemporary work or are representative of critical interests. The chapter provides a brief historical overview of criticism, then focuses on areas of critical interest. Chapter 4 references material related to individual writers.

The critical history of detective and mystery novels is largely a late twentieth-century phenomenon, although threads of criticism began as soon as speculation about this curious form of story took its various shapes. If the form itself began to take shape in the oral tales of outlawry and the pursuit of justice, wrongdoing, and mysteries surrounding social outrages, criticism began in the commentary on the art and artifice of the stories. Unless produced by established authors, mystery and detective novels were considered juveniles, sensation stories, or melodramas until the early twentieth century, when they began to receive more critical attention. Howard Haycraft (1946) traces critical notice to 1883, but of a kind that was little more than publicity. Emerging in a critical climate in which literary realism was peaking and attention to modernism was beginning to form, detective fiction occupied no place of respectability. As aesthetic judgment came to dominate literary attention and to form the basis of modernist criticism, literature that sought its justification in the market was likely to receive scant attention. But by the early decades of the twentieth century the popularity of mystery and detective novels was such that it became increasingly difficult to ignore, even though attention to it could be separated from consideration of art. Commentary appeared in magazine reviews in the late nineteenth century and increasingly in scholarly journals from the first half of the twentieth century. Haycraft and others collected much of the best that was available.

Literary criticism first focused on offenses to taste caused by popular novels and on major writers such as Poe, Dickens, and Collins. With the exception of a very few scholars and intellectuals, mystery and detective novels, especially in their common form of the cheap novel or story paper, remained a subliterature to be enjoyed on the sly and not considered worthy of serious literary attention. It would be left to fans and collectors of nostalgia to do much of the work of keeping the records and paying the genre its due. This is not surprising, since literary scholars and critics in colleges and universities hardly considered American literature worth studying until well into the twentieth century. Attention had first of all been given to the classics of Greeks and Romans, the Bible, and gradually to English literature and selected masterpieces of the continent. A. E. Murch's book typifies the kind of approach that demands tribute to classical literature before moving to what must then be considered a lesser contemporary form. This section provides an introduction to critical work beginning with a sample of authors' writing guides and commentary on the craft, then general studies, and finally schools or tendencies in criticism. It was not until the latter half of the twentieth century that criticism began to deal effectively with broader considerations of literature. Critical studies of detective and mystery novels are now widespread in academic journals, and popular periodicals often feature crime writers. Standard reference works now exist that provide accurate factual information and generally circulated opinion on a wide range of authors and trends. Still at issue are theoretical and critical problems regarding the significance, cultural contexts, and formal characteristics of detective and mystery fiction and the relation of the fiction to other forms of literature.

AUTHORS' GUIDES

Following Poe's example, writers themselves became their own best spokespersons, often collecting stories with prefaces that defended and attempted to explain interest in the genre. Writers have provided numerous articles and books on the craft of writing mystery and detective novels and along with fan organizations provided recognition to the work done in the field.

Carolyn Wells's study guide, *The Technique of the Mystery Story* (1913), for the Home Correspondence School may have begun the tradition of writers' how-to guides to the genre. *The Technique of the Mystery Story* translated the general features of the techniques developed by Wilkie Collins, Arthur Conan Doyle and other writers. It was one of the first attempts to formally articulate the conventions of the mystery for aspiring writers and emphasizes plotting as an outgrowth of interest in riddles and puzzles. Though it pays scant attention to the market of the time, the book is a good index of the writing practices Wells considered successful and which would usher in the Golden Age. Her examples for the most part are a survey of the successful authors of the late nineteenth century, including Henry James, Doyle, Brander Matthews, and others.

Marie F. Rodell's *Mystery Fiction: Theory and Technique* (1943, rev. 1952) gives several possible reasons for writing mysteries: money, entertainment, and/or, anticipating later commentators, "wanting to write and having nothing specific to write about, he [*sic*] finds the amount of 'given' material in the mystery form helpful" (Rodell, 1952, 5). Authors of mysteries "write for money" (Rodell, 1952, 7), as the genre is the "easiest form of fiction for which to find a publisher" because publishers seldom lose money on crime novels (Rodell, 1952, 8); yet writers need to produce steadily and not too slowly—at least two a year—in order to make a living. Writers need to enjoy the fiction and to have a logical mind for plot, since mysteries have remained fairly rigid and *"what happens . . .* [is prior to] *how it happens"* (Rodell, 1952, 9). Rodell argues that writers should first prove themselves by selling short stories. If writers can manage character, dialogue, and style, they can probably learn construction. In order to be successful, writers must be aware of and respect the restraints of the formula. Mysteries, Westerns, romances, fantasies, and historical novels are escape fiction because they divert interest and replace everyday experience with heroes and heroines with whom to identify. In addition, the mystery "has an intellectual attraction" and holds out the possibility that the reader may participate in such a mystery (Rodell, 1952, 13). This escape provided by the mystery also taps the childhood "desire to hurt those who thwart us or anger us" (Rodell, 1952, 14). So readers want the vicarious thrill of the hunt, punishment of the transgressor, identification with hero's traits of bravery, beauty, and cleverness, and the possibility of the experience of a similar adventure. As a writer and editor, Rodell addresses formula types that she calls mystery and detective novels, horror-mysteries, and adventure-mysteries. Rodell was an editor as well as an author, so her experience can be considered informed.

The four types of fiction Rodell identifies are usually found in combination, but with one type dominant; a fifth type is the "so-called experimental or non-formula mystery" that conforms to the above rules but not the "standard techniques for achieving them" (Rodell, 1952, 18). Each type has distinguishing features. The detective story is primarily a puzzle. The horror story aims to arouse kinesthetic responses—the hero is chased and

stakes are raised to greater horrors than murder. The adventure-mystery
(e.g., spy) story is more active and aggressive than horror, less intellectual
than detective stories, and involves some important mission rather than
abstract justice; it may use pursuit, as in the detective novel, but is more
physical or employs the horror story's trap technique. The character or
literary mystery is least rigid in its form and opens more variations; the
basic emphasis is portrayal of a character under emotional stress leading
to the exploration of sociological or psychological themes. Its lowest forms
are the had-I-but-known formula, "week-end party mysteries," and ram-
bling stories of heroines wandering in sinister attics and such, but it also
opens the form up to greater literary possibilities. Rodell is somewhat
dated, but since the detective story is a fairly stable form, much of the nuts-
and-bolts logic of the plotting strategies Rodell identifies can be profitably
read today. If one applies her five-type structure to contemporary mystery
novels and their kin, Rodell's model covers a surprising number of them.

In his sprawling collection of reminiscences, *The Pulp Jungle* (1967),
Frank Gruber lists eleven elements that ought to go into the mystery story:
(1) a colorful hero; (2) a theme (the most important element), which may
often include specialized knowledge; (3) the villain, often with assistants,
strong enough to create formidable odds against the hero; (4) a colorful or
unusual background or one that is made to appear unusual; (5) an unusual
murder method, if possible; (6) one of the many subdivisions of two basic
motives—hate and greed; (7) clues for alert readers and the story's logic;
(8) a trick to snatch victory from defeat for the hero; (9) action with pace
and movement; (10) a grand and smashing climax; and (11) emotion: the
hero must be personally involved, doing more than duty or money dictates.
Gruber wrote a wide range of formula fiction, including Westerns and romances as well as mystery and detective stories. Like Frederick Faust, Erle
Stanley Gardner, and a few others, Gruber's strengths lay as much in his
stamina, perseverance, and mastery of the craft as in literary talent. His
sweeping commentary on the vagaries of the fiction market makes it clear
that boundaries between what at any time is considered literature and mere
entertainment are not well defined.

Patricia Highsmith's *Plotting and Writing Suspense Fiction* (1966, rev.
1972, 1982) defines suspense as "stories with a threat of violent physical
action and danger, or the danger and action itself. Another characteristic
of the suspense story is that it provides entertainment in a lively and usually
superficial sense" (Highsmith, 1966, 1). Highsmith writes a practical guide
but also demonstrates quite clearly the difference between the detective as
a vehicle for reader identification and the figure who emerged in suspense
fiction: "If there must be reader-identification, a term I am rather tired of,
then provide the reader with a lesser character or two (preferably one who
is not murdered by the hero-psychopath) with whom he can identify"
(Highsmith, 1966, 43). The difference between a mystery and a suspense

novel, then, is that "the suspense writer often deals much more closely with the criminal mind, because the criminal is usually known throughout the book, and the writer has to describe what is going on in his head. . . . Sleuth-heroes can be brutal, sexually unscrupulous, kickers of women, and still be popular heroes, because they are chasing something worse than themselves, presumably" (Highsmith, 1966, 51). Highsmith thinks Julian Symons is a good model for mystery and suspense writers. She advises writers to avoid the suspense label, which did her no good; it put her in a category of expectations that may have subconsciously influenced what she wrote. In France and England she is just considered a novelist, gets higher quality reviews there, and sells proportionately more books. Highsmith notes that there are a lot of hacks in the business, and selling has a floor and ceiling—the floor is people who will buy almost anything that smacks of crime, and the ceiling is created by literary snobbism. Highsmith admits to reading little fiction but likes Graham Greene's entertainments, mainly because she's interested in morality. While she reads his novels for pleasure, she wouldn't think of imitating him or being influenced by him "except that I would like to have his talent for *le mot juste*, a gift that can be admired in a Flaubert too" (Highsmith, 1966, 147).

Robin W. Winks states that the purpose of *Colloquium on Crime: Eleven Renowned Mystery Writers Discuss Their Work* (1986) is to explain "why writers of mystery and detective fiction write as they do" (Winks, 1986, 1). Moreover, writers are asked to respond to a set of questions: (1) Why do you write crime fiction? (2) How much of the author is in the narrative? (3) Who were the author's literary influences? (4) Where is the genre going? Is it "inherently conservative" (Winks, 1986, 5)? (5) Is academic study good? Although a professional historian, Winks is also a reviewer and pretends a certain degree of naiveté in presenting the writers. His questions as they emerge in the writers' essays are provocative, apparently designed to enlist them in a skirmish with the Yale deconstructionists in particular and literary critics generally. Winks claims that popular fiction has to do with "favorite writers" rather than art or documentation, so the ground rules are different. This assumed perspective has endeared Winks to fans and others who might feel intimidated by critical scholarship or who are anti-intellectual themselves. Yet Winks says he reads over 200 crime novels per year to find about 70 "about which I have something to say" (Winks, 1986, 1). It is in this arena of taste that Winks places popular fiction, rather than the arena of textual evidence: "Over the years I have discovered how to tell a favorite without undue worry for literary theory" (Winks, 1986, 2). Whether in earlier years literary theory helped him choose favorites or should provide that service is not clear. In any case this allows him to assert that Tony Hillerman provides "perfectly accurate and fascinating ethnology," despite its being highly selective and decontextualized. The authors entertain, instruct (how people speak—K. C. Constantine's ear for the "demotic vulgarity" of U.S. working-class speech [Winks, 1986, 3]), and engage readers, rather than provide escape. There are three elements in a successful story: (1) it must read well, (2) it must have a strong sense of place (evoke the senses and depict language), and (3) it must proceed "according to the methodology of the historian" (Winks, 1986, 4). At the beginning all facts count the same (history is the "most democratic of disciplines") (Winks, 1986, 4).

Rex Burns admires Gabriel García Márquez and Roger Zelazny, but the police story is highly structured, and the reader "expects a rising curve of tension" and onstage, offstage action, whereas real life has only death as its final curtain to an otherwise continuous experience (R. Burns, 1986, 24). The paradox is to "recreate the effect and appearance of contemporary life with its everyday formlessness" (R. Burns, 1986, 24). Often writers simplify motives, but the better ones see greed, envy, and hatred as the surface of deeper problems, such as the spiritual starvation in Dostoevski or self-contempt in Graham Greene; other writers are concerned with social dislocations or economic systems. Burns was drawn to the police procedural because of his "disgust with the clichés" (R. Burns, 1986, 26). The "voice of the narrative" is what should happen; Burns wants the "concreteness of our mutually experienced world" to reveal the "resonant, subjective world beneath" (R. Burns, 1986, 27). The impact of the Miranda case intrigued him, as did the difference between law and justice. His buttoned-up Gabe Wager, ex-marine caught between the Anglo and Chicano worlds, will change little, though readers' pressures and the need for novelty will introduce some changes. For these reasons he expanded the locale of Denver and the rest of Colorado. On criticism Burns says that notice of any kind is better than none in the "highly competitive business of marketing fiction" (R. Burns, 1986, 32). Writers should be compared to literary masters, not to their contemporaries. Few are helped by editors and none to his knowledge by critics; he cites James Joyce's motto of "Secrecy, Silence, Cunning" as advice for survival; Winks also uses the phrase. Critics usually assume there is no merit in popular writing, but otherwise academic criticism is harmless and provides jobs for academics. He says that it is "not very damned likely" that criticism will influence the direction of fiction (Burns, 1986, 36). Burns wanted to achieve Georges Simenon's nuance of setting by an analogous method rather than imitation. He likes Robert Parker's one-liners, Elmore Leonard's "patterns of the spoken word," Hillerman's balance between "an alien way of life" and "a fast-moving story" (R. Burns, 1986, 35), Evan Hunter's skill at juggling story lines, John D. MacDonald's ability to incorporate reflection and commentary, and Lawrence Sanders's use of the "mystery yarn" to probe moral issues. He points out that John Hawkes's The Lime Twig (1961) is a mystery not labeled as such.

In "Writing About Balzic," K. C. Constantine says it is nonsense to distinguish between serious and formula writing. He says Winks's question was "What pleases you or angers you about the current academic discovery of crime fiction?" (Constantine, 1986, 56). Constantine says he didn't know academics had discovered crime fiction and thinks of reviewers as "revcrits." His early revelations—seeing members of his community "forget" how to speak English when confronted with police and discovering that the church service in Russian he hadn't understood as a child was roughly the same as Presbyterian services in English—affect him.

Dorothy Salisbury Davis's "Some of the Truth" (1984) provides a longer perspective. Davis doesn't think reviewers always understand her; she survives on library sales. She does not particularly like Ernest Hemingway but learned from "his artistry in evolving plot out of people, action within dialogue" (Davis, 1986, 68). She wanted to write like Dorothy B. Hughes (*The Fallen Sparrow, The Delicate Ape, Ride the Pink Horse*). Although she likes the Golden Age women and American hard-boiled fiction, it's not her; her writing is more like Cornell Woolrich's atmosphere with Poe in it, and Georges Simenon is her most admired predecessor. Crime novels reflect and are bound to their time—"the mores, the tempo, and the urgent concerns" (Davis, 1986, 72). In her encounter with two police in Franco's Spain, she came to understand how dictators maintain power: they share it. Crime fiction is conservative because the prevailing framework is law and order, and readers are also conservative; writers probably aren't conservative on the whole. In the late 1940s when she began writers were aware of the Depression and death camps, and Charlotte Armstrong, Stanley Ellin, Andrew Garve, Patricia Highsmith, Ross Macdonald, and Margaret Millar were savvy. Current nostalgia for the Golden Age that was constituted of "monuments to class and prejudice says much about the anxiety of our times" (Davis, 1986, 73). She considers herself liberal and doesn't like characters who don't change. She thinks any academic attention is good.

Donald Hamilton, in his essay "Shut Up and Write" (1986) says writing can't be taught but that experienced writers can help with the market, mechanics, and morale. Hamilton advises writers to ignore everyone's advice—including teachers, relatives, friends, agents, and the famous writer passing through—except the one who will buy your manuscript. Editors can help improve work. Agents are very helpful in financial matters but should not be considered writing advisers. He doesn't believe in timeless prose and writes only for entertainment. He had to learn the mechanics of the craft and how to produce work fast.

Joseph Hansen, in "Matters Grave and Gay" (1986), notes that he had to turn his first novel into pornography in order to get it published; then he wrote in a more conventional investigative format. He felt that because of anti-gay biases he had to make Dave Brandstetter's father managing director of Medallion Insurance Company in order to make it believable that his character could be described as working there. Hansen says, wrongly, I think, that most of the other social stereotypes have disappeared, while gays remain fair game. The victim is the "organizing factor" in every traditional mystery plot. Characters need motives for killing and the pursuer "must sort lies from the truth, and keep from being killed himself" (Hansen, 1986, 118). His novels are records of day-to-day matters known to him from "friends and strangers, read about in newspapers and magazines or see[n] on television newscasts" (Hansen, 1986, 119). Hansen draws on the multicultural aspects of Los Angeles. His *Nightwork* (1984) deals with pollution of a lake, and his other novels have social problem themes as well. Hansen considers himself liberal but is skeptical of schemes for organizing society; things mostly depend on "personal decency and honor" and these are rare, so he tries to get them into his hero (Hansen, 1986, 124). But he is not deluded about the influence of mystery fiction: *Ellery Queen's Mystery Magazine* has sales of 245,000 compared to *Reader's Digest*'s sales of more than 18 million. Most hardback mysteries sell fewer than 5,000 copies. Mysteries belong in mainstream English Department courses, but acceptance has been slow.

In "Mystery, Country Boys, and the Big Reservation," Tony Hillerman (1986) says he grew up distinguishing between country boys and city boys (he later discovered this division was between small versus smaller town); he and local Potawatomies and Seminoles were country. The first Navajos he saw crossed in front of his truck in an Enemyway ceremony (Harper and Row titled his first novel dealing with Enemyway, *Blessing Way* [1970], which he says had nothing to do with the content). As a child he would order books through the local library, but what actually came usually bore little resemblance to what he had ordered. He was inspired by Arthur Upfield's outback stories, and also by Eric Ambler, Raymond Chandler, Graham Greene, George V. Higgins, and Ross Macdonald, who he says wrote one book over and over, but with great skill and metaphorical language. He learned economy of prose from E. B. White, the early Hemingway, Joan Didion's journalism, paring down "adverbs, adjectives, complicated sentences, and turgid prose" (Hillerman, 1986, 131). As he wrote his first novel, the anthropologist central character shrank and the tribal policemen grew larger. Hillerman is a university professor.

Robert B. Parker and Anne Ponder's "What I Know about Writing Spenser Novels" (1986) expands on an *Armchair Detective* article. Parker doesn't care what people think of his books as long as they sell. A book now takes him three to four months to write. Work toward his Ph.D. was useful but deserves the fun he makes of it. Hammett's flatness is "a loss, because you don't have to give up minimalism, and precision, and conciseness" (Parker and Ponder, 1986, 191). He doesn't emulate anymore as he did initially and doesn't care if he sounds like some other writer. His titles come from searching—*Catskill Eagle* from "The Tryworks" chapter of

Moby Dick—literary allusions come effortlessly, probably because of his intensive earlier reading for exams. Writing is more visceral than intellectual. He doesn't require much editing; the novel goes from scenario to outline to manuscript. He may rewrite, but the work is essentially one draft. He doesn't know how much Spenser is he and in what way. He is mainly interested in relationships such as parent/child and husband/wife. Spenser is committed to the powerless, whom he sees largely as women and children; there is an "unspoken and inarticulate love relationship between Spenser and Hawk" and less so between Spenser and other characters, including bad guys. Parker says he has lots of experience with men in locker rooms and the like, so that in the books games and sports serve the function of clowns in Shakespeare; sports and games help define Spenser. Sports are self-contained and therefore matter in a random universe. He finds Henry James's "The Art of Fiction" (1884) to be good on filtering experience through imagination. He quotes Robert Warshow's *The Westerner* on the Western hero and compares Spenser to that figure. Spenser is Warshow's "the last gentleman" (Parker and Ponder, 1986, 199); Spenser's significant conflict is " 'when his moral code, without ceasing to be compelling, is seen also to be imperfect' " (Parker and Ponder, 1986, 199). But Parker's own work "exceeds the Western formula" because stories portray women who reflect on Spenser (Parker and Ponder, 1986, 200); they get "progressively more substantial than the relation between Miss Kitty and Matt Dillon in *Gunsmoke*" (Parker and Ponder, 1986, 201). He is as capable of writing about a woman as about a man "within the limits of my not being a woman" (Parker and Ponder, 1986, 201). He can't do a female point of view. He and Faulkner use the history of characters.

Hillary Waugh's *Hillary Waugh's Guide to Mysteries and Mystery Writing* (1991) argues that Poe "spawned" detective fiction, having created a pattern based on the existence of police. The reason Poe is first is that "a crime is solved through the accumulation of evidence which points the finger of guilt at the criminal" (Waugh, 1991, 11), but Poe does not play fair with the reader. Waugh argues that Poe does not set out to invent a new kind of story but tells a story the only way it can be told; any other writer would have had to tell the story in much the same way. Waugh says Poe was responding to *Graham's* request for a story with brains. Mary Roberts Rinehart tells great stories, regardless of the "had-I-but-known" element that portrays the woman figure as "a helpless idiot." The device was rejected by readers before feminism made it necessary to discard it.

Most detectives are not police because writers are saved doing police research and can elevate their heroes above "mundane police work" (Waugh, 55). The differences between "police novels" and police procedurals is that in the latter characters are "attached to a police force, bound by its dictums, shackled by the rules of evidence, the laws of the land, the strictures which impose their restrictions upon everything a real policeman *can* do" (Waugh, 55). Waugh thinks of the period from 1900 to 1920 as a "waiting period," because most publications were short stories and the field was shifting from "reader as ineffectual witness to the storied events, to the reader as competent competitor against the detective hero" (Waugh, 1991, 56–57), as in the shift from the Sherlock Holmes tales to Agatha Christie's novels. In the next decade the contrived puzzle story died and novels shifted to the hard-boiled novel that would tell "stories that had little to do with the puzzle" (Waugh, 1991, 85). It is in discussing the hard-boiled tradition that Waugh warms to his task. Although he appreciates the work of Ellery Queen, he is clearly more interested in Erle Stanley Gardner, Rex Stout, Dashiell Hammett, and Raymond Chandler. His analysis of the Hammett novels focuses on their strengths and weaknesses from a writer's perspective; thus, the plot of *The Maltese Falcon* (1930) is seriously flawed. Captain Jacobi delivers the falcon and dies; the introduction of Gutman's daughter to send Spade on a wild goose chase is a mere prop— who was she? Why is Spade drugged? Why is he given a false address? Hammett needed to get Spade out of the way so that the crowd would be there when he got back. But the story is about Spade, so we forgive plot weaknesses, "irrelevant digressions and all flaws" (Waugh, 1991, 105). At other times Waugh shifts his perspective, noting that "sociologists of the future, if they would understand the past, should read the mystery novels of the era"—because mystery novelists "are merely recording . . . the society in which they live" (Waugh, 1991, 106). The "social milieu" is simply there; it is not the writers' concern "why or how" (Waugh, 1991, 106). Descriptions give "a reporter's uncolored picture" of what things were like at a given time and place. *The Thin Man* (1934) paints New York during Prohibition—"speakeasies, the gangsters, the thugs, the way of life, upper and lower" (Waugh, 1991, 106). Chandler was actually better than his reputation, and Mickey Spillane, who is given a chapter, represents the "denouement" of the hard-boiled mystery novel (Waugh, 1991, 115). Waugh feels that mystery writers disliked Spillane because "his hero was really a villain" (Waugh, 1991, 115), an "Anti-Hero." Spillane could write well, but his plots are bad and stereotyped. His books *shocked*, but this novelty wore off quickly and most readers didn't get beyond the second book; yet among the top ten all-time best-sellers are two or three Spillanes.

In his chapter on the police procedural, Waugh is able to bring in his own writing experience. Charles Boswell's *They All Died Young* (1949) containing ten true cases of murdered young women changed his career. He was moved (and inspired) by the "sense of authenticity" of the descriptions (Waugh, 1991, 117) and shortly after in 1950 wrote his first procedural, which appeared in late 1952. Only later did he find out that Lawrence Treat had beat him to the procedural in 1945 with *V as in Victim*, followed by *Big Shot* (1951), using the same characters. He says the radio program *Dragnet*, by ushering in the second major change in the

form of the mystery story, would have to be called the father of the procedural. The mystery was established by shifting reader from observer (seeing
through Watson's eyes) to participant (standing at detective's side trying to
beat him). The private eye story kept the puzzle but shifted "from thought
to action" (Waugh, 1991, 119) and led to spy fiction. With the police
procedural the detective is "thrust into the middle of a working police force,
full of rules and regulations" and "shows how it operates" (Waugh, 1991,
119). This kind of novel is not only about policemen but also about "the
world of the policeman" (Waugh, 1991, 119). The best of these are found
in the work of Ed McBain, Elizabeth Linington-Dell Shannon-Lesley Egan,
John Creasey's Gideon and the Roger West stories; Maj Sjöwall and the
late Per Wahlöö's Martin Beck and his own small town Chief Fred Fellows.
This narrative shift *toward* rather than away from the police is significant.

Waugh points out that neither the classic nor the hard-boiled story were
realistic, since both concealed the realism of police work—the one behind
the puzzle, the other behind action. But the procedural is also unrealistic
in most important senses. A writer will produce crime-of-the-century stories
at a pace of two or three a year, perhaps being relatively accurate about
procedures, dialogue, and humor. But since informants solve most cases,
writers inevitably move away from reality. Procedurals, however, introduce
the family and social life missing from earlier forms, and provide technical
background (police practices, law, rules of evidence). But the procedural is
still fiction and requires reader interest, so certain elements are fudged.
Waugh argues, contra Robert Parker, that women cannot write male fiction
and vice versa. Women include details from daily life that men would usually not think of—a woman detective "does her laundry, takes baths, de-
cides what dress to wear" (Waugh, 1991, 149). You don't know these
details about men, except for Robert B. Parker's Spenser. Males wouldn't
be able to write the same way; "any perceptive reader could tell—and can
tell—the sex of the author from the way the book is written—its slant,
point of view, everything" (1991, 151); see, for example, the male storyteller in Charlotte Armstrong's *The Black-Eyed Stranger* (1951) who
"thinks like a woman" (Waugh, 1991, 151). Peter O'Donnell's *Modesty
Blaise* (1965) was designed to appeal to males, as her name implies. This
is also true of sexual encounters, because women are "saddled with the
results and men aren't" (1991, 151). There are three reasons: (1) women
writers create women detectives "to promote the idea of sexual equality";
(2) "writing to titillate the male is not only anathema, but totally contrary
to their purpose"; (3) women don't "know how to write male-erotic prose"
(Waugh, 1991, 151). Romances prove women writers can stir women, but
men don't respond to the "same triggers and female writers aren't able to
sense what buttons to push to arouse the male" (Waugh, 1991, 151).

In the second part of the book Waugh folds in practical advice that he
had previously published. His discussion of the difference between the novel

and mystery touches on several aspects of fiction. On the one hand, "anything that involves crime or the threat of crime is eligible" to be called a mystery (Waugh, 1991, 157), but this is too broad. Part of the difference may be length: mysteries range from 185 to 225 pages, or about 60,000–70,000 words; gothics are about 300 pages (about 110,000 words). Anything over 350 pages is something more than a mystery, which happens when the writer begins to explore character or situation. The puzzle story was at the furthest point from the novel, and puzzles were "the essence of the mystery" (Waugh, 1991, 159), its skeleton, which still underlies the form. "The mystery story is to the novel what the sonnet is to poetry" (Waugh, 1991, 160). The skeleton "is nothing more nor less than a series of ironclad rules" (Waugh, 1991, 160), which were necessary to "present the puzzle properly and also in the interests of fair play" (Waugh, 1991, 160). The most important rules are: (1) every clue must be available to both detective and reader, though the author can obfuscate them; (2) the early introduction of murderer; (3) the crime must be significant; (4) there must be detection; (5) the murderer must be among the known suspects, which led to the creation of a closed "universe inhabited solely by victims, suspects, murderer, and detective" (Waugh, 1991, 160)—for example, a story set in a mansion cut off by a storm; (6) the reader *has the right to expect that nothing will be included in the book that does not relate to or in some way bear upon the puzzle*" (Waugh, 1991, 161). Although the rules may be relaxed today, they still distinguish the mystery from the straight novel. Beginning writers can benefit from writing mysteries, because it disciplines them in many aspects of fiction; the rules "structure the whole art of fiction" (Waugh, 1991, 163). But "[o]ne distinction is pure and simple. The mystery novel does not contain the equipment to carry messages. . . . The credo can be expressed as follows: 'If you want to write and have nothing to say, write a mystery.' If you have other ambitions, the mystery form had best be eschewed" (Waugh, 1991, 165). This is because the mystery "is, in actuality, a morality play" (Waugh, 1991, 165). The author of a straight novel doesn't have the story as a goal, but rather presents his case through character; in mystery series characters are not "tempered by experience" (Waugh, 1991, 167). The mystery "writer is a storyteller" (Waugh, 1991, 167) whose purpose is "to confound, puzzle, scare, bewilder, or horrify the reader and, generally speaking, to keep him in a constant state of suspense. This, by definition, has to be what he is up to, otherwise he is not writing a mystery" (Waugh, 1991, 168). The "motive" of the author indicates whether or not the novel will be a mystery. The aim of the game is reader involvement, or suspense, which involves two things: (1) reader doesn't know what will happen next and (2) wants to know.

Other books on writing include Herbert Brean's collection *The Mystery Writers Handbook* (1956), which contains essays on mystery writing by authors and fans and a host of Writer's Digest Books, including Shannon

OCork's *How to Write Mysteries* (1989). Sue Grafton's collection, *Writing Mysteries: A Handbook* (1992), includes essays by Jeremiah Healy, Marilyn Wallace, Dick Lochte, Warren Murphy and Molly Cochran, Faye Kellerman and Jonathan Kellerman, Julie Smith, Rex Burns, Sara Paretsky, Nancy Pickard, Sandra Soppettone, George C. Chesbro, Tony Hillerman, Robert Campbell, Max Byrd, Carolyn Wheat, Aaron Elkins, Phyllis A. Whitney, Bill Granger, P. M. Carlson, Lawrence Block, John Lutz, Mary Shura Craig, Scott Edelstein, Russell Galen, Ruth Cavin, Joan Lowery Nixon, and Ed Hoch on various aspects of writing. Finally, Robert J. Randisi's collection of essays in a similar format, *Writing the Private Eye Novel* (1997), includes short pieces by Parnell Hall, Ed Gorman, Lawrence Block, Sue Grafton, Loren D. Estleman, Randisi, Les Roberts, Jeremiah Healy, William L. DeAndrea, Catherine Dain, Wendi Lee, Jan Grape, Max Allan Collins, Jerry Keneally, Christine Matthews, John Lutz, Parnell Hall, and Michael Seidman. Each of these volumes provides similar information and indicates how far the formulation of stories has filtered down through a large coterie of fans. In addition the same publisher provides specialized books featuring information on procedures, evidence, crime scenes, and other matters of common interest to mystery writers.

GENERAL CRITICISM

In 1921 E. M. Wrong collected British detective stories under the title *Crime and Detection*, and in 1926 the volume was published in the United States. In his introduction Wrong traces the roots of the detective story to ancient texts and identifies some of the salient themes of the classic detective story in his introduction. He admires the action potential of what he calls the Moriarty theme, the villain who fights back, and he is put off by the evasion of social retribution he finds in many novels. Wrong feels that too many stories have the criminal punished by self-imposed or accidental means. He suggests that the rise of an organized police and an attention to external detail were necessary to the emergence of the detective story, an argument that Dorothy L. Sayers picks up in her introduction to *Omnibus of Crime* (1929). Sayers also sees the detective story as a substitute for the romance and the adventure story in a shrinking world and lists numerous subterfuges used by writers to make the relatively closed form work for them. The idea that the detective story had to provide clear rules to be followed by writers was articulated by S. S. Van Dine.

H. Douglas Thomson's *Masters of Mystery* (1931) is best read along with E. F. Bleiler's commentary in the Dover edition (1978). Thomson's analysis is essentially an aesthetic one based on the view that bad writing is about "the matter rather than the form" (1978, 18). Thomson says that moral standards "alone probably of all fiction . . . are not examined or questioned," since the essence of the detective story is a "problem"—"a puzzle to be solved, the plot consisting in a logical deduction of the solution from *the existing data*" (Thomson's italics; 1978, 22, 33). The critic's task is to link "personal feelings of appreciation or of censure" to "the code of rules" implicit in the genre (Thomson, 1978, 52). Bleiler argues that the "fairness" device important in Thomson's discussion was "only an accident," even though R. Austin Freeman and S. S. Van Dine made much of it and even wrote it into a code.[1] Bleiler points out that this implied that the detective narrative had to be a puzzle story and that the author had to deceive the reader. Bleiler notes that Thomson failed to see that the late 1920s and early 1930s were a transition period in which the genre was changing. Thomson considers Sam Spade "an honest-to-goodness, 100 per cent. American detective. There does not appear to be much more than this to commend him" (Thomson, 1978, 261). Thomson provides a history that nods to the ancients before touching on Poe, Collins, and writers of the first decades of the twentieth century. Further chapters focus on Poe, Gaboriau, and Doyle, the "domestic," "realistic," "orthodox," "thriller," and "American" subtypes of the detective novel. These final chapters for the most part deal with British fiction, again consistent with the critical climate that preceded New Criticism, which, incidentally, further marginalized detective fiction while exploiting its formulas for enriching and containing a preoccupation with the self.

Thomson argues that the American detective story failed because of the high standards set by Poe. Anna Katharine Green mixed "melodrama with detective interest" and bad prose, while Arthur B. Reeve created improbable thrillers. S. S. Van Dine, on the other hand, is important because of his extension of Thomas De Quincey's idea of murder as a fine art to the notion that murder is created in thought and has "a technique in the execution, and bears the impress of its author's character" (Thomson, 1978, 263); the detective is a psychological analyst who matches the crime with the perpetrator. (A contemporary version of this might be the psychological profiling Patricia Cornwell elaborates.) Philo Vance, Thomson says, is delightful company who spawns a clone in Ellery Queen.

Howard Haycraft's *Murder for Pleasure* (1941) is an appreciation and history that traces the development of the form from Poe through the late 1930s, though it is partial to the Golden Age from 1918 to 1930. *Murder for Pleasure* is a fan's book that contains a reader's list of best fiction that has been quibbled about and revised countless times, a trivia quiz for careful readers, and a list of principal characters. The checklist of criticism is entitled "Friends and Foes." Haycraft's observations on American writers are generally sound and can be read today as a selective guide to the fiction. In *The Art of the Mystery Story* (1946, rev. ed. 1961) Haycraft also collected some of the best early impressions and critiques of detective fiction. The revised edition updates earlier information but is largely oriented to the classic story form, with one section devoted to rules for writers, including "The Detective Club Oath"; it also contains such gems as E. M. Wrong's and Dorothy L. Sayers's introductions. Other important pieces are Joseph Wood Krutch's "Only a Detective Story," Erle Stanley Gardner's "The Case of the Early Beginning," Raymond Chandler's "The Simple Art of Murder," Anthony Boucher's "Trojan Horse Opera" (on spy novels), James Sandoe's "Dagger of the Mind" (on the thriller), John Dickson Carr's locked room essay, Ellery Queen's brief history of the detective short story, and other useful material. The collection also includes parodies and essays on the differences between fictional and actual practices of detectives and criminals. In short, the book promotes the guidelines and perspectives that many later reviewers and critics will bring to the discussion of detective and mystery novels. A. S. Burack's collection of essays by authors, *Writing Detective and Mystery Fiction* first appeared in 1945 and included several essays also found in Haycraft as well as a potpourri from *The Writer*. This collection was subsequently updated.

Writing about the mystery story proliferated during the 1930s and early 1940s and, as Haycraft's remarks on Dashiell Hammett suggest, by 1930 the hard-boiled genre was generally understood to have staked out new territory. When Raymond Chandler's famous essay "The Simple Art of Murder" appeared in the *Atlantic Monthly* in 1944, he was not defining a new departure, but summarizing the development of the form over the past twenty years. Joseph T. Shaw had begun editing *The Black Mask* in 1926 and within a few years had attracted some of the finest detective fiction available. Nevertheless, Chandler's essay underlined the critical importance of the hard-boiled story.

British writer Sutherland Scott's *Blood in Their Ink* (1953) appeared in the United States in 1973. Scott's view on detective fiction is thoughtful, and though his focus is not on American fiction, his familiarity with it appears to be informed by eclectic reading. David Brion Davis's *Homicide in American Fiction, 1798–1860* (1957) is concerned with the literary canon and stops about when dime novels appeared but it is useful background reading. Alma Murch's *The Development of the Detective Novel* (1958) provides a thorough study of the literary antecedents of many of the conventions of detective fiction, but it gives little indication of the direction of the genre after the 1930s. The Golden Age is extended to the 1950s, but it might as well have ended twenty years earlier. Three-fourths of the history is devoted to a pre–Conan Doyle study of backgrounds. The author is anxious to maintain an aesthetic distance from her subject and in doing so tends to attribute too much importance to major writers and hardly anything to the great popular traditions flourishing in France, England, and the United States.

A similar problem of taste confuses Mary Noel's *Villains Galore* (1954), which does deal directly with American story papers and dime novels. Though coverage of detective fiction and mysteries is limited and the study lacks documentation, this was one of the few critical treatments of American nineteenth-century story paper literature. Quentin Reynolds's *The Fiction Factory* (1955) fills in some of the background but remains too general to more than hint at the needs of most investigators. Albert Johannsen's (1950) great reference work contains a mine of material on authors and series. Ongoing work is published in *Dime Novel Roundup* and fan publications.

The pulps are better covered, primarily through the efforts of publishers and writers themselves. Harold Hersey's *Pulpwood Editor* (1937), an early reminiscence on the pulps by an editor and writer, is representative of the style used by most participants to disclaim any deep commitment to the pulps. Hersey thought his audience unimaginative. Robert Turner's *Some of My Best Friends Are Writers* (1970) is another author's view on the pulps, one that emphasizes the human problems of writing in a disposable medium. It is much easier to see from Turner's observations on writers' agencies that the differences in quality between slick and pulp fiction were not clear and in fact were often whimsical, a generalization that could be extended to hardcovers and original paperbacks. Ron Goulart's *Cheap Thrills* (1972) provides an informal introduction to trends and writers in pulp magazines, which is expanded in *The Dime Detective* (1988).

The publication of David Madden's collection of essays, *Tough Guy Writers of the Thirties* (1968), marked a higher level of seriousness toward crime writing than any available earlier. Here hard-boiled fiction achieved academic respectability. Madden's introduction places the hard-boiled writer directly in the modern sensibility, and the genre is examined from a number of perspectives. Essays by Philip Durham, Robert Edenbaum, Irving Malin, Herbert Ruhm, and George Grella provide especially useful views of hard-boiled novels. Francis Nevins, Jr.'s, collection of essays, *The Mystery Writer's Art* (1971), is much more in the Haycraft tradition of an eclectic group of contributors with a common interest in detective fiction. The twenty-one essays in the volume are organized into "Appreciations," "Taxonomy," and "Speculation and Critique" and are concerned with both classic and hard-boiled fiction, with emphasis on appreciation and description. The section on appreciations includes discussions of Poe, Hammett, Queen, Gardner's Cool and Lam, Hitchcock's *Psycho*, and crime films; the taxonomy section provides Philip Durham on the *Black Mask* school, John Dickson Carr's apologia for the classic school, Jacques Barzun on literary qualities, Frank D. McSherry, Jr., on occult relations to crime fiction, and Donald A. Yates on locked room stories; in the final section Elliot L. Gilbert writes on the detective as metaphor, Ross Macdonald writes on the detective hero, William O. Aydelotte on the detective story's historical material, and McSherry on science fiction crime.

Tage LaCour and Harald Mogensen's *The Murder Book* (1971) made international connections inevitable when their delightfully illustrated and useful introduction to crime fiction appeared in the United States. Stefano Benvenuti and Gianni Rizzoni's *The Whodunit* (in English, 1980; Macmillan, 1982) is a useful introductory history with illustrations; like LaCour and Mogensen, they cover crime fiction on an international scale. In 1972 Erik Routley published *The Puritan Pleasures of the Detective Story* in England, with a highly critical chapter on American detective fiction. The year 1973 might be said to be a watershed year for detective and mystery criticism. The Bouchercon published Robert Briney and Francis Nevins's collection of Anthony Boucher's critical essays, *Multiplying Villainies*; William Vivian Butler published *The Durable Desperadoes*, a history of the gentleman outlaw in popular fiction, primarily in England from the mid-1920s through the 1930s; Ross Macdonald's influential *On Crime Writing* was published; and the first American edition of Julian Symons's *Mortal Consequences* appeared.

Symons's *Mortal Consequences* (1985) is part history, part appreciation, and part analysis, a thoughtful attempt to bring the history of detective fiction into the 1970s. As both novelist and reviewer of detective fiction, Symons has a critical appreciation and broad familiarity with the genre. His observations are usually fresh and perceptive, even of his own fiction. Through the first half of his study, beginning with a chapter on why we read detective fiction and a chapter on Poe, Symons supplements discussion of developments in England and the United States with asides on the major writers of other countries. The second half, which is less systematic, includes reviews of books, writers, and topics relating to several countries, resulting in something of a patchwork of insights on numerous topics. Aside from the quirkiness of Symons's preferences and tastes, the observations are some of the best available on the work of many writers.

One of the first studies that attempted to account for the widespread popularity of hard-boiled detective fiction was William Ruehlmann's *Saint with a Gun* (1974), which links the private detective tradition to a broad American longing for vigilante justice. This is a provocative investigation of the relationship between fiction and the disparate violence that has marked modern American history, one that argues for a direct link between this type of fiction and a broad cross-section of the reading public.

Larry Landrum, Pat Browne, and Ray B. Browne's *Dimensions of Detective Fiction* (1976) is divided into sections on the genre, styles, and variations. The section on genres collects essays on myth and the detective story, George Grella on the formal story, Geraldine Pederson-Krag's psychoanalytic essay, William O. Aydelotte on the detective story as historical source, and Edward Margolies on social aspects; the section on styles includes D. F. Rauber on Rex Stout, Allen B. Crider on Race Williams, both Kay Weibel and R. Jeff Banks on Spillane, Darwin T. Turner on John B. West, R. Gordon Kelly on John D. MacDonald, Raymond Nelson on Chester Himes, Elmer Pry on Ross Macdonald, and Sam L. Grogg, Jr.'s, interview with Macdonald; related genres include essays on the Mafia story, the FBI in fiction, Faulkner's crime stories, and Ishmael Reed's creative use of the genre. Also in 1976 John Ball's *The Mystery Story* was published, containing essays by Aaron Marc Stein on "The Mystery Story in Cultural Perspective," Hillary Waugh on "The Mystery Versus the Novel" and "The Police Procedural," Otto Penzler on "The Amateur Detectives" and "The Great Crooks," James Sandoe on "The Private Eye," Michele Slung on "Women in Detective Fiction," John Ball on "The Ethnic Detective," Donald Yates on "Locked Rooms and Puzzles," Michael Gilbert on "The Spy in Fact and Fiction," Phyllis A. Whitney on "Gothic Mysteries," Robert E. Briney on science fiction crime, Allen J. Hubin on series characters, Francis M. Nevins on pseudonyms, and E. T. Guymon, Jr., on readers. In his "Patterns in Mystery Fiction: The Durable Series Character" (also in this volume), Allen J. Hubin notes that the signals publishers and writers send identify the kinds of stories their readers should expect:

1. Publishers' imprints, such as Mystery League, Mystery House, Crime Club; subimprints; and colophons.

2. Authors often change their byline for different genres, thereby signaling different personas.

3. Titles use key words and phrases: colors, "The Case of . . ."; "The . . . Murder Case"; "Operation . . ." and so on.

4. Plot patterns or "formulas," such as (a) Gothic—heroine-walking-blithely-into-danger or (b) Golden Age (classic) story—"initial murder, preferably in a 'closed' setting (such as a country house party), the lengthy questioning of suspects, the final gathering to hear the detective's exposition and identification of the guilty" (Hubin, 1976, 295).

5. Series characters allow for depth of characterization and are often encouraged by readers who like the character.

H.R.F. Keating is among those who have consistently attempted to cover the perspectives of the writer, fan, and reviewer. As Anthony Boucher, Dorothy B. Hughes and many others have done in this country, Keating reviews crime books for a newspaper, in this case *The Times* of London. In addition he has written his own detective fiction and an excellent study of detective stories of the 1920s and 1930s. In *Murder Must Appetize* (1981) Keating self-consciously crosses the line from reviewer to academic critic when he declares, "I don't care if I am giving it away" (Keating, 1981, 8). But generally, unlike the formidable Julian Symons, Keating remains more a reviewer than a literary critic or historian. In *Whodunit?* (1982) Keating supplies a good introductory anthology of brief descriptions of categories of detective and mystery fiction. Keating himself discusses Poe and Doyle; Julian Symons writes on the rise of the American hard-boiled story in the pulp magazines; Hillary Waugh traces the police procedural from the 1940s and points out the influence of the radio program *Dragnet* (1949–1956; television, 1952–1970), and the procedural's tendencies. Eleanor Sullivan discusses the shift from 1894 to 1907 in the "whodunit" short story to the "howdunit" through the medical and scientific detection of R. Austin Freeman's Dr. Thorndyke and others, considering also Melville Davisson Post's Randolph Mason, Mary Roberts Rinehart's "had-I-but-known" formula, the hard-boiled story, and suspense and psychological stories to the present. Jessica Mann indicates how the suspense novel is structured to exploit certain features of the crime story; Jerry Palmer illustrates the way the action thriller's essential features have changed since the turn of the century. Finally in *Whodunit* John Gardner re-creates the ground of the espionage novel from the 1890s through the 1970s and provides a set of rules.

Gavin Lambert's *The Dangerous Edge* (1976) is interesting for its background information on British fiction and its chapter on Raymond Chandler. Nadya Aisenberg ties the motifs of detective fiction to those found in the literary tradition in *A Common Spring* (1979) and argues that this form of story reflects the fears of its audience. Hugh Eames's *Sleuths, Inc.* (1980) appeared with chapters on Hammett and Chandler. R. F. Stewart's *And Always a Detective* (1980) provides useful information on nineteenth-century detective fiction and has occasional remarks on twentieth-century American detective novels. Patricia Craig and Mary Cadogan's *The Lady Investigates* (1981) discusses English and American sleuths from about 1861 to the late 1970s, with chapters on early women sleuths in the United States, women spies in World War I, women sidekicks, girls' series detective novels, career detectives, detectives' wives, and other topics. Edward Margolies's *Which Way Did He Go?* (1982) discusses the detective in the work of Dashiell Hammett, Raymond Chandler, Chester Himes, and Ross Macdonald and finds the future of the detective novel to be open-ended. A specific study of the dime novel detective is Gary Hoppenstand's *The Dime Novel Detective* (1982). Bill Pronzini's *Gun in Cheek* (1982) is a lively discussion of, in effect, why some call detective fiction a form of subliterature. Robin W. Winks's *Modus Operandi* (1982) covers a broad spectrum of crime and espionage fiction with some shrewd insights, but no particular overview. Robert Sampson's two volumes on series characters in the early pulps, *Yesterday's Faces* (1983, 1984), discuss Nick Carter, the devices used to create villains, and numerous detective adventure heroes. The volumes provide a good account of the emergence of detectives in the early pulps, along with the history of pulp magazine story conventions.

Ian A. Bell and Graham Daldry's critical anthology, *Watching the Detectives: Essays on Crime Fiction* (1990) features British critical views on mostly American writers and issues. Ian A. Bell deals with Patricia Highsmith, Simon Dentith with William McIlvanney, Graham Daldry with George V. Higgins, Ffrangcon C. Lewis with Poe, Maldwyn Mills with

Chandler; there are additional essays on Agatha Christie, Marcel Allain and Pierre Souvestre (*Fantômas*, 1911), and John Le Carré. Also included are topical essays by Lyn Pykett on the female sleuth after feminism, John Simons on real detectives and fictional criminals, and Stephen Knight on radical thrillers. Pykett's essay is international in scope, including Amanda Cross and Barbara Wilson in the discussion, and adding weight to the view that a feminist intervention in the genre has made a difference. Simons deals with biographies and memoirs of pathologists to determine their function as texts occupying the same economic and critical space as crime fiction; the texts are effective with audiences to the extent that they conceal the authority they would have as documentary texts. Contrary to Mandel, Knight argues that the thriller (the "spy" model from Childers on) contains radical elements because of its "dialectical character" (Bell and Daldry, 1990, 173). The thriller has a "formal radicalism," acquired when it consciously reversed conventional patterns; the three "basic texts" are Godwin's *Caleb Williams* (1794), Poe's Dupin stories, and Emile Gaboriau's Parisian novels of the 1870s. These texts are grounded in the radicalism of Godwin's *Political Justice*, Poe's "reason that goes beyond utilitarian mathematics, and on a perception that breaches the unknowable," along with Gaboriau's accounts of the crimes of the aristocracy (Knight, 1990, 174). The discussion then shifts to the radical attention to domestic detail in Christie's "thrillers" and reversals in the works of other writers.

Geoffrey O'Brien's *Hardboiled America: The Lurid Years of Paperbacks* (1981) sketches the relation of paperbacks to social issues, politics, and ideology from the first appearance of Pocket Books on June 19, 1939. Pocket Books was a quality product, but Avon appeared as a poorly bound book using pulp paper. The number of titles grew from 112 in 1945 to 353 in 1946, to 866 in 1951, but sales dropped after World War II. Smashmouth action and violence increased from 1951, but outrage from rightwing politicians and religious leaders led to investigations by the House Select Committee on Current Pornographic Materials in 1952. In part the change in content was due to the shift from abstract cover art to realism around 1948, which occurred first with Signet, then with Popular Library and others. O'Brien's discussion of the hard-boiled novelists is useful, but it is his discussion of the cover art that is most fresh. He also discusses the thematic and stylistic relationship between film noir and crime paperbacks. Mysteries and detective paperbacks were gradually replaced, O'Brien says, by the Jim Thompson–style "paperback novel," which emphasized tough violence and sex (or its promise) and was written in streamlined prose designed for reading in a single sitting.

Woody Haut's *Pulp Culture* (1995) locates the beginning of pulp culture with Hammett's *Red Harvest* (1929) and Spillane's *Kiss Me, Deadly* (1952). Haut provides a no-nonsense commentary on Hammett before the

McCarthy hearings on anti-communism. A "tedious" mainstream criticism has largely ignored hard-boiled fiction (1995, 3). By the early 1950s sales slumped because of the impact of TV, which led to "more liquid formats," and paperbacks were attacked as pornography—perhaps because "ordinary people were reading books once thought the province of an educated middle class" (1995, 5), or they feared ordinary people would "create their own literary genre" (1995, 5). Hard-boiled writing "became associated with the paperback industry" only after World War II (Haut, 1995, 6). Mystery novels dropped from 50 percent of the market in 1945 to 26 percent in 1950 to 13 percent in 1955. The term "pulp culture denotes an era dominated by the excesses of disposability, and marks the relationship between pulp fiction and a historical period that begins with the 6 August 1945 bombing of Japan" (Haut, 1995, 6) and culminates between 1960 and 1963. Haut cites eight novels published soon after August 6, 1945: [Kenneth Fearing]'s *The Big Clock* (1946); David Goodis's *Dark Passage* (1946); William Lindsay Gresham's *Nightmare Alley* (1947); Geoffrey Homes's *Build My Gallows High* (1946); Dorothy B. Hughes's *Ride the Pink Horse* (1946); Paul Cain's *Seven Slayers* (stories, 1947); Chester Himes's *If He Hollers Let Him Go* (1946); and Jim Thompson's *Heed the Thunder* (1946). Three were published during the "transition": Chester Himes's *The Heat's On* (1961), Walter Tevis's *The Hustler* (1959), and Charles Willeford's *The Woman Chaser* (1960). Compare Haut with William F. Nolan's remarks in his introduction to *The Black Mask Boys*, which makes a more or less direct connection between sensational news of crime and corruption and the *Black Mask* writers who "wrote it as it happened" (Haut, 1995, 13). Nolan's brief history of *The Black Mask* is useful as a precursor to Haut's less direct analogy. Haut's argument is that as the hard-boiled fiction became more dissociated from the puzzle story, it assimilated more of the ambiences of the culture; narratives then lose their individuality to an undifferentiated pulp culture. This culture can be reconstructed by discussing "the era's most interesting and energetic writers and texts." All of this is open to further discussion, of course, since parameters are lost and the argument depends on a general set of relationships among a large and undifferentiated body of texts. The analysis proceeds largely through biographical criticism and a consideration of "dark paranoid worlds" created by Goodis, Himes, and Thompson, PI politics, the portrayal of women's negotiations of this male genre in Leigh Brackett's *The Tiger Among Us* (1957), Dorothy B. Hughes's *In a Lonely Place* (1947), and Dolores Hitchens's *Sleep with Strangers* (1955). Additionally, Haut considers the crime novel as social critique through examination of William McGivern's *Odds Against Tomorrow* (1957) and *Death Runs Faster* (1948), Gil Brewer's *13 French Street* (1951), and Lionel White's *The Killing* (1956; first pub. as *Clean Break*, 1955) and *The Big Caper* (1955) and discusses the end of the Cold War era in Charles Williams's *The Big Bite* (1956), Charles Willeford's *Pick-Up* (1955) and *The Woman Chaser* (1960).

J. Kenneth Van Dover's *Murder in the Millions: Erle Stanley Gardner, Mickey Spillane, Ian Fleming* (1984) deals with the "superseller," three of the most commercially successful writers in history. Van Dover identifies the stereotypes and notes the moral, social, and political prejudices found in their work in order to understand "the art of the superseller" (Van Dover, 1984, x). He says that while many will be offended by or disagree with the stereotypes in the fiction, he is not offended and will not disclose his disagreements. The strategy is to move chronologically through the novels of each author, with emphasis on the first and later divergences. Bruno Bettelheim's *The Uses of Enchantment* (1975) provides a link between the superseller and fairy tales. Gardner avoids nuances to the point of creating snapshot texts in which there is little depth. His analogy for fiction was baseball, whose rules remain the same while the combination of events vary each time. Spillane embodies an "ethical solipsism" in place of Gardner's legal ethics and Fleming "practices . . . statecraft and principles of epicureanism" (Van Dover, 1994, 152).

John J. Winkler's *Auctor and Actor* (1985) treats Apuleius's *The Golden Ass* as a text that can be accessed as a detective story, "as an unsolved crime that may be unraveled by a somewhat unorthodox procedure in order to learn *quis ille?* ('Whodunit?')" (Winkler, 1985, 59). Winkler draws on American and British detective novels for his analogies.

LeRoy Lad Panek's *An Introduction to the Detective Story* (1987) provides a general history and discussion of the development of the detective story. The large part of his discussion is on British fiction, including chapters on Godwin and George Bulwer Lytton, Dickens, Collins, and Doyle. There are also chapters on Poe and Gaboriau, as well as one each on writers at the turn of the century, the Golden Age (largely British), the hard-boiled story, the police procedural, and contemporary variations. Panek was awarded an MWA Edgar for the book. Another book by Panek, *Probable Cause: Crime Fiction in America* (1990), expands the American ground, but without British material. Here Panek covers fictional periods from Poe to 1890, 1890 to World War I, and from World War I to the late 1980s, alternating surveys of social history (digest information on population growth, monopoly capitalism, criminal activity, police) with discussion of specific texts. The early texts, beginning with one each from Seeley Register [*sic*], Old Sleuth, Allan Pinkerton, Anna Katharine Green, and Julian Hawthorne, are "noxious books, incompetent in style, characterization, setting and plot" whose only virtue is that they "are early." They did not connect with the "real world of crime and violence in America," and did not "create a literary form which would allow the detective to become an actual hero" (Panek, 1990, 40). Throughout it is not clear in what ways the digest information is related to the fiction. The argument that the shift from professional fiction writers ("hacks") to journalists shortly after the turn of the century was "a created phenomenon" dictated by the desires of publishers would seem to raise unanswered questions. Panek concludes that the shift accounted for a greater presence of journalists as characters and the scientific theme of many stories. The discussion includes many stories and novels that are not widely known and provides a wide variety of detail.

Cynthia S. Hamilton's *Western and Hard-boiled Formula Fiction in America: From High Noon to Midnight* (1987) deals with 1890–1940, which allows Hamilton to compare the fiction to "attitudes, preoccupations, and worries" that enter into the fiction of the period due to "historical and institutional pressures" (Hamilton, 1987, 2). This is a sufficiently narrow range within which to develop a new "methodological framework for the study of popular literature" (Hamilton, 1987, 5). The book is divided into two parts dealing with methodological relationships and studies of individual authors. The first part provides a historical framework, discusses the layering of generic patterns and invokes the marketplace; the second part devotes chapters to Zane Grey, Frederick Faust, Dashiell Hammett, and Raymond Chandler. Like Porter (1981), Hamilton sees competitive individualism as a key to capitalist ideology that is taken up by fiction. It is the premise from which the individualism of the hard-boiled narrative is unable to escape. As this is woven into the adventure story, exemplified by Owen Wister and Zane Grey, it is adopted by the hard-boiled story along with the mystery alternative to the classic story's puzzle.

Gary C. Hoppenstand's *In Search of the Paper Tiger: A Sociological Perspective of Myth, Formula and the Mystery Genre in the Entertainment Print Mass Medium* (1987) also attempts to come to grips with formula, but through categorization of pyramidal layers consisting of a base of motifs, upon which is a layer of motif-complexes, then subformulas, then formulas, with genre sitting on the top like a "pyramid, that most solid of structures" (Hoppenstand, 1987, 34). However, in the second chapter formulas are treated as "biological," "not static," but "flex and flow" as authors "arrange the various blocks of motif complexes to build a subformula story" (Hoppenstand, 1987, 34). Drawing on Peter L. Berger and Thomas Luckman's model of the social construction of reality, Hoppenstand argues that the mystery genre is "those collections of formulas and sub-formulas that linearly traverse moral explorations of the human death crisis" through entertaining "rituals of socialization that reinforce institutions," thus being "a social device for myth making" (Hoppenstand, 1987, 32–33). Mystery formulas are solid entities arranged along a "linear spectrum" from the most irrational "supernatural story" (dark fantasy, Gothic nature-as-fate, anthropomorphic beings, psycho-killer subformulas) → "noir formula" (Nature is Fate and "Fate is symbolized by urban society itself," where both individual and social system are evil; light-angel sub-

formula is rescue, while dark-angel subformula features a persecuting figure) → "gangster" (good/bad subformulas) → "thief formula" (good/bad
subformulas) → "thrillers" ("political adventures" of "charismatic"/"dark"
spy subformulas) → "detective formula" (life and death as puzzle; classic/
police/hard-boiled subformulas). Hoppenstand illustrates this apparatus
with numerous examples (1987, 50–51).

Martin Green's *Seven Types of Adventure Tale: An Etiology of a Major
Genre* (1991) includes a chapter on "The Hunted Man Story," which distinguishes a "conservative" version in the manner of John Buchan's British
thriller and a "liberal" version associated with Raymond Chandler. One of
the elements that characterizes the hunted man story is the protagonist's
"anti-romantic" wish for ordinariness while embodying an unusual capac-
ity for action. Both versions give an unusual amount of attention to the
enemy, embodying a conspiracy with which the hero grapples.

Glenwood Irons's critical anthology, *Gender, Language and Myth: Essays on Popular Narrative* (1992), includes essays on romances, Westerns,
detective and espionage fiction, science fiction and fantasy, and horror fiction. Of interest for the present purpose is "New Women Detectives: G Is
for Gender-Bending," in which Irons discusses ways in which Amanda
Cross, P. D. James, Sue Grafton, and Sara Paretsky are independent of
males and earlier models, bring the community of women to the genre,
appropriate male gestures to female detectives (as with Kinsey Millhone),
and undermine phallocentric society. Scott Christianson's "Tough Talk and
Wisecracks: Language as Power in American Detective Fiction" (1989) discusses the hard-boiled fiction of Chandler, Hammett, Ross Macdonald,
Robert B. Parker, Rex Stout and others. His discussion of the exchange of
racial slurs in Parker's *A Catskill Eagle* covers several perspectives. Christianson distinguishes between wisecracks (which need an audience) and the
hard-boiled conceit employing figures of speech that do not. The effect is
not simply a stylistic feature but functions like similar language in "serious"
literature that attempts to make meaning. The hard-boiled novel's language
undermines detective fiction's "control and closure" (Christianson, 1989,
154). Carol J. Clover's "Her Body, Himself: Gender in the Slasher Film"
deals with hybrid genres of horror/crime/pornography. Clover's is one of
the best essays on this important form that mixes several formulaic and
social themes to produce a new form of "bodily sensations" (1989, 286).

Brian Docherty's *American Crime Fiction: Studies in the Genre* (1988)
includes essays on Poe, Hammett, and Chandler, 1930s realism, James M.
Cain, Mickey Spillane, George V. Higgins, and Jerome Charyn. Contributors are Gary Day, Christopher Rollason, Peter Humm, Christopher Bentley, Stephen Knight, Richard Bradbury, Odette L'Henry Evans, Michael J.
Hayes, and Mike Woolf. Rollason's essay on Poe emphasizes doubling,
particularly in "Murders in the Rue Morgue" and "The Purloined Letter."
Humm's essay emphasizes camera consciousness of the photodocumentar-

ies of the 1930s and their relation to the crime prose of Graham Greene, Faulkner, Hammett, and Chandler. Day's essay on the Continental Op concludes that rather than detection there is an open chain of signifiers and "the act of revelation involves hiding the false logic on which that revelation depends" (Docherty, 1988, 52). Bentley does not find the roots of Hammett's anti-capitalism in *Red Harvest* nor the Op short stories. Stephen Knight suggests that Chandler's *Playback* is underrated because it lacks Marlowe and a Los Angeles setting. Chandler's influence came through "cultural media, opinion-makers" rather than his general popularity. His high status and "relatively small sales" (Docherty, 1988, 76) converge in a key audience through the hero and his relationships to effeminate men, doctors, women, police, gangsters, and the rich (no class or race to speak of). The novels contain a critique of power, especially of gangsters, but opposition is individualized rather than collective. Double plots include an outer plot concerning corruption, which fades behind an inner plot of an individual killer (a betrayer) who is a woman—for example, Velma in *Farewell, My Lovely* (Chandler and Edmund Wilson thought this novel his best). The crime of murder replaces theft and dishonor as individualism rises. Marlowe expresses no social or collective sense but is suspicious of closeness. The plots ramble and the characters are stereotypes, but there is an "authentic presentation of a real feeling people have had and still have, itself a response to real conditions of living" (Docherty, 1988, 86). Bradbury notes that Cain's contribution to the "criminal perspective," borrowed by Albert Camus for *The Stranger* (1942), is from *The Postman Always Rings Twice* (1934). Bradbury also considers *Double Indemnity* (1943) and *The Butterfly* (1947, where all figures die) in the relation between money and sexuality. Nineteen-thirties crime fiction suggests, contra Freud, that money motivates, an idea borrowed from earlier "naturalist writers" (Docherty, 1988, 90). All Cain's novels feature violence, sex, and first-person narration. *Mildred Pierce* (1941) is the weakest because it doesn't use these elements. The narrator is "semi-articulate" and only rudimentarily capable of self-analysis (Docherty, 1988, 95), and the women are sexually aggressive, leading the narrator to perversity or a "passive web" in which males trap themselves. Cain seems indebted to Drieser's *An American Tragedy* (1925). In any case, Cain refuses an analytic framework, allowing readers to be voyeurs, and withholds "the paradigms of explication upon which so much other detective fiction rests" (Docherty, 1988, 96). The Great Depression and the rise of Freudianism wreaked havoc on rational explanation of individual consciousness, and this shifts the focus to events. *Double Indemnity* breaks out of Depression California into the nightmare world of Poe and Samuel Taylor Coleridge ("Rime of the Ancient Mariner") and returns to a confessional model.

Odette L'Henry Evans draws on A. J. Griemas and Barthes to diagram the semiological structure of Spillane's Mike Hammer and Tiger Mann novels in order to affirm the readings' sameness and plurality. Michael J. Hayes's discussion of George V. Higgins draws on Jacques Derrida and Geoffrey Hartman. Eighty-five percent of Higgins's early novels are dialogue, with about two-thirds of the "he said" variety. The novels are noted for their realism, but the style employs semantic and syntactic features to signal authenticity. Devices include disruption of the expected flow of utterances (". . . to get half a bath in the, where the pantry was, . . .") or omitted prepositions ("you go the bank"); in later novels these function more as indexes of characters. "Higgins explores the ways in which people arrive at objectives within different groups" (Docherty, 1988, 125), and moves toward politics because it is more directly concerned with the "manipulation of discourses" (Docherty, 1988, 126). The books finally use discursive situations to heal. Mike Woolf's discussion of Jerome Charyn introduces the notion of "exploding genre" to argue that the potential for representing the texture of American experience is much greater than the English "nostalgic and elegaic" form (Docherty, 1988, 132). The detective must be a "failed figure" because his or her struggle is a more prevailing reality than it is criminal (Docherty, 1988, 132). Charyn's fiction does this in the course of eighteen books. Cities in the United States are tribal territories of races and ethnic groups, and Charyn's work is richly regional.

T. J. Binyon's *Murder Will Out: The Detective in Fiction* (1989) begins with the assumption that investigations of types of detective stories are motivated by a desire to lend credibility to the formula. He is convinced that it is the protagonist rather than the story type that is important in the detective novel, because unique to crime fiction the character is the source of the genre and "again uniquely, the character has so often overshadowed and become detached from the author" (Binyon, 1989, 1). Dupin is the prototype for the formula. Binyon notes the five stories usually mentioned, with "Thou Art the Man" providing "the least likely character as murderer, the planting of false clues, the use of ballistic evidence, and the extortion of a confession through a sudden psychological shock" (Binyon, 1989, 5). Dupin is prototype for the amateur half of the detective, with Emile Gaboriau's Lecoq as the prototype for the professional half. Lecoq is the "first modern police detective"—he uses science, reasons logically, and deploys the "machinery and organization of the police force" (Binyon, 1989, 5).[2]

Holmes is half amateur (from Poe) and half professional (from Lecoq), a "consulting detective," a "professional amateur" (Binyon, 1989, 6). A logical classification follows from this, with (1) amateur amateur (dilettante), represented by Dupin and Dorothy L. Sayers's Lord Peter Wimsey; (2) professional amateur (private detective), such as Sherlock Holmes (Doyle) and Hercule Poirot (Christie); (3) the professional (policeman) of two types, the (3a) professional professional (only a policeman), as with Lecoq and Freeman Wills Crofts's Inspector French, and (3b) the amateur professional (not only a policeman) such as Ngaio Marsh's Roderick Allyn and P. D. James's Adam Dalgliesh.

Actual nineteenth-century detectives characteristically handled divorce cases, and the point has often been made that fiction did not; making the detective wealthy was one way of avoiding an actual practice. Binyon provides chapters on comic and historical detectives, and crooks. Conan Doyle's *A Study in Scarlet* led to serial publication in magazines, like the series of stories he did for the new *Strand Magazine* beginning in 1891. Detective fiction emerged into the magazine era from about 1890 through World War I. Binyon also links law, medicine, journalism, insurance and accounting to detection, then breaks private investigators down into private eyes (U.S., 1922–present), private investigators (British, 1920–present), and police. The private detective is largely an English development that appeared about 1920 and runs to the present. Amateurs whose expertise comes from the author's profession are rising, as in Jonathan Kellerman's consulting psychologist, Alex Delaware.

Robert S. Paul's common-sensical view in *Whatever Happened to Sherlock Holmes?* (1991) is that popular writing "*must* largely reflect public opinion" because writers are responsive to sales. To Paul this means that detective "novels reflect the society to which they are addressed, and in a way that the public must generally approve as a true picture of that society, its ethics, its values, and its basic rationality" (Paul, 1991, 7). While detective novels can't be expected to directly articulate theological referencing, Paul argues that seven points are shared by theology and detective fiction: (1) there is a created order in which everything can be rationally explained; (2) " 'truth' is real" and can be discovered by weighing evidence; (3) if all facts are "known, we can discover the meaning of them"; (4) there is a real distinction between right and wrong; (5) human life is "very great, even of supreme value"; (6) people have innate evil, though capable of goodness; and (7) it is important to society to strive for justice (Paul, 1991, 14). American authors who used the "classic puzzler within new-world settings include Erle Stanley Gardner's Perry Mason and Rex Stout's Nero Wolfe; Frederic Dannay and Manfred Lee's Ellery Queen, along with women authors such as Anna Katharine Green, Mary Roberts Rinehart, and Mignon G. Eberhart. Elizabeth Daly's bibliophile detective Henry Gamadge has been called the American Peter Wimsey.

William David Spencer's *Mysterium and Mystery: The Clerical Crime Novel* (1989) directly addresses the religious issue of secular mysteries: "At the end of the quest each honest detective finds the murderer's bloody hands are his or her own. . . . No amount of good work" will change this (Spencer, 1989, 1). With this premise Spencer launches his "quest for the primal mysterium in the mystery" (Spencer, 1991, 1). Spencer's "theory is that the modern mystery novel is a secularized form structured on the ancient mysterium or revelation of God's judgment and grace" (Spencer,

1991, 11). Not surprisingly, the word "mystery" is traced from its Greek roots to its contemporary usage and the mystery story is traced from the Apocrypha. Clerical crime novels are divided into three types: "saintly side-kicks," those in which clergy commit crimes and those "solved primarily by the cleric," which latter is the focus of the study (Spencer, 1991, 13). Spencer is interested in the classical story, rather than the other kind. His discussion ranges from Bel and the Dragon and Susanna to Rabbi Small, Umberto Eco, E.M.A. Allison's *Through the Valley of Death* (1983), Father Brown, H. H. Holmes's (William Anthony Parker White) Sister Ursula in *Nine Times Nine* (1945) and *Rocket to the Morgue* (1942), Margaret Ann Hubbard's Sister Simon, Leonard Holton's Father Bredder, Ralph Mc-Inerny's Father Dowling, "Monica Quill's" Sister Mary Teresa, Dorothy Gilman's *A Nun in the Closet* (1975), Sister O'Marie's Sister Mary Helen, William X. Kienzle's Father Koesler, Andrew M. Greeley's Blackie Ryan series, Victor Whitechurch's Vicar Westerham, C. A. Alington's Archdea-cons, Margaret Scherf's Martin Buell, Stephen Chance's Septimus, Barbara Ninde Byfield's Father Bede, Isabelle Holland's Reverend Claire Aldington, Matthew Head's Dr. Mary Finny, Charles Merrill Smith's Reverend Ran-dollph, and James L. Johnson's Code Name Sebastian series.

Martin Priestman's *Detective Fiction and Literature: The Figure on the Carpet* (1991), which has one of the choicest titles discussed here, examines the "relationship between detective fiction and established literature" (Priestman, 1991, xi). The study is a "direct comparison," of literature and formula; Priestman is interested in a "broader exploration of themes and contexts common to both," but mainly in treating those in detective fiction " 'as if' they were literary ones" (Priestman, 1991, xi). Chapter 1 surveys the genre and its relation to "scandal and shock" and other literary and social conditions. Chapter 2 investigates *Oedipus the King* and *The Moon-stone* for structural and psychological issues. Chapters 3 and 4 deal with Poe and Gaboriau and their use of short story and melodrama. Chapters 5–9 deal roughly with the period from 1890 to 1914, with emphasis on Holmes and modernism; Chapter 5 emphasizes Conan Doyle's creation of the series detective; Chapter 6 covers the Holmes myth, *Valley of Fear*, and subsequent English and American works with themes of crime and capi-talism; Chapter 7 covers the intellectual and social debate in four contem-poraries; Chapter 8 is on how and maybe why modernist experiments are related to genre; Chapter 9 deals with Golden Age detective fiction. Chapter 10 is on Chandler and the U.S. hard-boiled form and its influence on recent British fiction.

Priestman sees *Moll Flanders* (1722), Henry Fielding's *The Life of Mr. Jonathan Wild* (1743), and De Quincey (1827) as registering a "rising scan-dal" leading to the split in circulated information of scandal into reportage in the popular press and literary treatment of it. Poe's "Murders in the Rue Morgue" and "The Mystery of Marie Rogêt" show that crime reportage takes away the necessity for including sordid details so that the literary text invokes a "collage technique" to enable "a fascination with 'real' crime to coexist with a fantasy of infallible detection." Thus a "schizophrenic formula is born as sordid crime is brought under control and introduces a scandal of indifference" (Priestman, 1991, 6).

In "The Philosophy of Composition" (1846) Poe explicates "The Raven" by arguing that "William Godwin's Ur-detective novel *Caleb Williams* was written, roughly speaking, backwards," in that Godwin kept the end in mind. Tales of ratiocination aim at truth, while other tales may aim at "terror, or passion, or horror, or a multitude of other such points," and poetry attempts to achieve beauty (Priestman, 1991, 36). In this sense truth is "highly specialized and relative" (Priestman, 1991, 37). The detective story is born out of Poe's attempt to achieve the specialized effect required by magazines; it expects us to be able to relate fragments (clues) to wholes and moves from difference to difference. The dominance of metonymy in detective fiction makes the genre hostile to metaphor (moving from similarity to similarity). An example is Poe's mind-reading episode, where the narrator's chain of metaphors is analyzed by Dupin's metonymic chain. Dupin is "almost inhumanly resolvent" in his dispassionate picking over the bodies for clues as the ape unemotionally destroys the women. "The Murders in the Rue Morgue" operates on two levels: the first creates many parallels between the criminal and the detective that evolve into a "richly metaphorical psychodrama" similar to Gothic tales; and a second level where for this pattern is substituted an array of "disparate fragments" lying on the surface. This new genre therefore "replaces one kind of formal unity with another," in that "synchronic uncovering of a unified meaning operating throughout the text becomes a diachronic juxtaposition of fragments" that link contexts (Priestman, 1991, 50, 51).

If Poe created the detective short story, Emile Gaboriau (1833–73) created the detective *novel*. Priestman says that most critics have not actually read Gaboriau—he mentions Murch and Tani—and tend to confuse basic details. Gaboriau influenced Collins's "multifaceted mixture of narrative approaches" (Priestman, 1991, 56). He also influenced hard-boiled "self-doubting confrontations with money and power," post-Freudian texts such as Ross Macdonald's family themes, and the police procedural's concern for extracting confession (Priestman, 1991, 56). The "single-viewpoint detection and omniscient historical or psychological narration" of the detective novel make it awkward "for serious novelistic purposes" (Priestman, 1991, 57). But detective and mystery novels are able to include a broad range of content that expands the story beyond pure formula.

I will include a brief summary of Priestman's discussion of Doyle, since Doyle's Holmes had such an important effect on American, as well as English, detective and mystery novels. There are two patterns in the Holmes stories: (1) the biographical "tongue-in-cheek" investigation of minor inconsistencies about dates and names (largest) and (2) the archetypal Holmes formula, focusing either on " 'methods' or on the romantic-scientific blend which accounts for Holmes' overall appeal as a 'personality' " (Priestman, 1991, 74). Doyle is much less interested in philosophical problems than in action, and he plays up sexism and racism more prominently than Poe and Gaboriau while borrowing freely from their work. His real contribution was the series short story; while exploitation of this possibility was present in Poe and suggested in Gaboriau, Doyle is really the first to draw out its potential. In Doyle's work "all deduction depends on the syllogism," as in the example of the hat in "The Blue Carbuncle"— "the unbrushed hat's owner has a wife; all loving wives brush their husband's hats; therefore this wife is not loving" (Priestman, 1991, 91–92). Priestman notes that "wherever these deductions touch on matters of social relationship there are always some very large-scale assumptions about unbreakable social rules implicit in them" (Priestman, 1991, 92).

In Doyle's *The Valley of Fear* (1915) the part of the narrative structure that Todorov called the first story attempts to foreclose a series, but this is frustrated by shuffling the chronology of the stories, so that the appearance of the stories has an indeterminate relation to story chronology, "a permanent adolescence of non-development" like "the retardation of Watson's learning faculties" (Priestman, 1991, 93). Doyle's source was probably "Allan J. Pinkerton's ghosted but purportedly factual *The Molly Maguires and the Detectives* (1877)," which recounted the infiltration of the Maguires by Pinkerton agent McParlan, whose testimony led to the execution of the leaders. Doyle is clearly pro-boss. It is useful to compare *The Valley of Fear* with Hammett's *Red Harvest* (1928); Hammett's radicalism was in part due to his experience in mining communities. Doyle's style in describing the confrontation of manager and miners "already seem[s] to display hard-boiled characteristics teetering on the edge of self-consciousness" (Priestman, 1991, 100), but Doyle adds moralizing lines that undercut this effect.

Early modernism includes such writers shortly before the 1890s as Oscar Wilde, Henry James ("The Figure in the Carpet" in 1896), and Joseph Conrad (*The Heart of Darkness* in 1899). The symbolist phase of early modernism depends "on an intensification of metaphor wherein the referent or tenor—the thing the metaphor is meant to evoke—can theoretically never be given" (Priestman, 1991, 136).[3]

James's metaphor of the figure in the carpet, for example, is a "supreme anti-detective story: deliberately teasing us with an intellectual quest-structure which implies a solution" (Priestman, 1991, 136). Conrad points out that the direction of *The Heart of Darkness* is outward; it presents conflicting versions like a detective story. Wilde's "The Portrait of Mr. W. H." (1889) is like James's "Figure," in that it can be seen as a deliberately designed anti-detective tale; a man does a critical biography from sonnets to find the relationship with the young man to whom they refer;

the story shows the impoverishment of chains of evidence. All of these texts, including "The Critic as Artist," seem repeatedly to assert two positions: (1) the paradoxical need for intersubjective consciousness and its impossibility and (2) the idea that connection may be made through literary figuration if "meaning" is not explicit. Detective fiction proceeds in a similar way to distinguish consciousnesses, and the "central mystery is relayed through a layering of consciousnesses corresponding to a similar layering of narratives" (Priestman, 1991, 145). This common narrative practice in modernism and detective fiction identifies a "common preoccupation" with Self and Other. The sense of this is a "community in isolation" in which meanings are passed through a chain that is not quite an hierarchy, but neither is it a "fully interactive community." Importantly quests "are not quests for direct communal or person-to-person contact, the possibility of which seems denied, but quests to find the Self reflected in the Other" (Priestman, 1991, 145). The "towering central figures" of modernism create a dominant chain as does detective fiction, but while in modernism an endless chain of Selves and Others is created, in detective fiction the Other (the criminal) "recedes into insignificance" (Priestman, 1991, 146). The detective then offers a Self that is a "bourgeois ideal of the free-standing, destiny-creating individual" (146; in this Priestman agrees with Cawelti, Palmer, Knight, et al.). Both forms of literature can be related to a "crisis of confidence in the individual consciousness" (Priestman, 1991, 146).

Priestman argues that what myth and depth psychology were to modernism, "the detective story is to postmodernism" (1991, 151). In detective fiction what appears as metaphor in other fiction may be a clue. The social circle is "upper-middle class, and one of the subliminal effects of the crime is to focus our attention exclusively on this particular group" (Priestman, 1991, 154). Outsiders (including servants) are always red herrings. On the other hand, American hard-boiled narratives are versions of William Empson's "formula for pastoral: 'putting the complex into the simple' " that is different from the British version. A world is evoked in which control seems impossible, largely because boundaries are transgressed: there is often a coverup of crimes and the detective gets sexually involved with suspects and fights his client and the police. These are "the only two legitimate sources of his authority" (Priestman, 1991, 171). Cawelti has analyzed the "dread of dependence" as other-directedness; Fredric Jameson argues that Chandler catches the "tangential" nature of modern urban experience in which "much of what we perceive is perceived instrumentally, en route to something else" (Priestman, 1991, 172). Priestman analyzes two early stories, "Killer in the Rain" and "Curtain," that were cannibalized for *The Big Sleep* in order to explore this richness of tangents. In the novel the short stories are placed end-to-end, and the plot remains "unfocused until the Geiger plot is over" (Priestman, 1991, 174). Priestman agrees with Stephen Knight's deconstruction of Marlowe as an "alienated intellectual" who dislikes touching people; the central criminal in his novels is usually a woman (Priestman, 1991, 175). Priestman is interested in Knight's assertion that an outer plot dealing with "corrupt links between respectable and criminal worlds" collapses into "an 'inner' purely private plot where a woman threatens Marlowe" then kills an alter ego (Priestman, 1991, 176). This shift can be related to a wide range of fiction. Julian Symons's observation that since the heyday of hard-boiled fiction the genre has become the "crime-thriller, presented through the eyes of the criminal without recourse to the moral safety-net of detection" can be seen in Elmore Leonard's splitting of narrative between criminal and cop. Leonard and other writers feed the anti-liberalism of the United States, "whereby the ills of an increasingly acquisitive society are no longer to be accounted for in terms of its structure but of inherent human evil" (Priestman, 1991, 178). This represents a breakdown of the quest for connections and is frequently the starting point of the postmodern. Unless hard-boiled detective fiction turns postmodern, it is limited in what it can do. Finally, despite the marginalization of detective fiction in the mainstream literary/critical world, literature "needs detective fiction as its other" (Priestman, 1991, 194).

IMAGES

In *The Middle East in Crime Fiction* (1989) Reeva S. Simon notes that thrillers, spy novels, and mysteries account for about 25 percent of all fiction books. Simon includes all these as crime fiction. Her study is "not a work of literary criticism" but is concerned with "how the Middle East is perceived through the medium of [crime] fiction" (Simon, 1989, x). Chapter 1 defines the genre and differences among the three subtypes, and "components" such as "suspense, authenticity for heroes and villains, and apocalyptic conspiracy" (Simon, 1989, x). Chapters 2 and 3 provide a history and trends, with attention to differences between British and American writers. Chapter 4 discusses plots and their relationships to "yesterday's news" (Simon, 1989, xi). Chapters 5, 6, and 7 deal with heroes, villains, and the Arab-Israeli conflict, respectively. Simon accepts Dilys Winn's (1977) story categories—cozy, analytical, romantic, paranoid, and vicious—as useful to her purposes. The cozy and analytical types correspond to the classic mystery and detective story and are associated primarily with that period. The romantic type corresponds to "the gothic romance suspense novel" featuring a chase through an exotic locale as noted by Phyllis Whitney. In the paranoid type, villains are the key. Novelists such as Jack Higgins and Robert Ludlum specialize in these. Finally, from the late 1960s a type emphasizing elemental vengeance and violence began to emerge, which describes most of the fiction relating to the Middle East since the mid-1960s. Devices include "plot, suspense, a simplistic hero-villain confrontation" whether or not spies are involved (Simon, 1989, 18). Suspense is maintained by working against a set time of disaster, by constructing the plot like an inverted pyramid with exposition featured in the beginning with ever-shortening episodes of action toward the end; like "peeling an onion" the hero uncovers layer after layer of deceit until no one can be trusted. In the paranoid and vicious books the climax is "a ritual cleansing of fire and blood" either in a direct shootout or as a result of the cataclysm planned for someone else. Following Ralph Harper, Simon believes "people read spy novels and thrillers to escape the mundane duties of quotidian life" and that the thriller appeals to the market values of gadgetry and sex. Readers may also find educational value, since the novels are filled with technical and topographical description. Heroism and vengeance are harder appeals to pin down, and Simon draws on psychoanalysis to argue that readers identify with heroes who attack the vicarious stereotype of the readers' frustrations. It was not until "real events and subconscious historical stereotypes coincided . . . after the 1973 oil crisis" that Arabs became popular as stereotypical villains (Simon, 1989, 139).

H. Bruce Franklin, in *Prison Literature in America: The Victim as Criminal and Artist* (1989) argues that the prison experience produces a unique fiction, but one that is not divorced from crime fiction. Chester Himes's detective fiction came directly from his prison experiences, and Dashiell Hammett produced the prototype of a new, raw form. Himes read Hammett's *Black Mask* stories while in prison.[4] The detective narrative, Franklin argues, "appears only after the consolidation of bourgeois power." The business establishment, "having emerged from its origin as an illegitimate, even outlaw, class, now begins to view the question of crime and criminals from the point of view of the establishment of law and order" (Franklin, 1989, 232). The word "detective" first appears in English in 1843 (*OED*, compact edition, 1971). A number of events prepared for a transformation in fiction, mainly the Russian Revolution, the great crash, the Depression, the rise of fascism, and the crises to the bourgeois order that comes with World War II.

STORY AS GAME

In order to understand where the detective story stands in relation to the larger project of literary criticism, it is perhaps useful to see how the game is played. Here are three different approaches to the detective story as game with which to begin. Roger Caillois in a 1941 essay republished in 1984 as *The Mystery Novel* observed that when the thinking detective (Caillois seems unaware of any hard-boiled fiction) replaced the detective of physical pursuit, his purpose became to evolve a gamelike way of exposing the murderer. The detective novel essentially became an intellectual puzzle that would dispense with the elements of the novel altogether if it were possible. The game qualities are often overt in such novels as S. S. Van Dine's *The*

"Canary" Murder Case (1927), where Philo Vance draws suspects into a poker game. In such stories everyone lies, but the detective must uncover the person who had nothing to hide as terrible as the crime. "Hypotheses" are laid out and rejected until one emerges that fits all the facts. In this puzzle formula the reader's pleasure is "not that of listening to a story, but rather that of watching a 'magic' trick which the magician immediately explains" (Caillois, 1984, 6). Such a literary practice leads to many embellishments—new ways of killing, new schemes. The political crime or espionage (spy) story "works much better in the adventure novel, since it tempts the author to lead us into byways which are impenetrably mysterious by nature" (1984, 6). These complicities continually alter the "original version of the problem," so that the solution can be produced at any opportune time in the narrative (1984, 6).

In these kinds of stories, Caillois notes, the use of "scientific marvels" or "madness" tends to destroy the conditions for "rigorous foresight and proper deduction," unless they are a mask of the murderer (1984, 11). Caillois cites S. S. Van Dine's *The Bishop Murder Case* (1929), where the circumstances of the murders are analogous with known nursery rhymes; Ellery Queen's *The Chinese Orange Mystery* (1934) conceals the fact that the victim is a clergyman; the murderer in Agatha Christie's *The ABC Murders* (1935) throws off the investigation by killing a series of people in towns whose names correspond to the name of a random victim in order to conceal the coincidence of the real victim's name and town. Real madness, then, is not employed. "The culprit's discovery must shock and satisfy simultaneously" (1984, 11), which leads authors into a wide exploration of unusual conditions: Agatha Christie's *The Murder of Roger Ackroyd* (1926) has the murderer as the detective, even though he has narrated the story; this seems excessive to Caillois, who also believes that the reader does not like more than one murderer per story, although multiple murderer combinations have of course been exploited. Caillois sees the classic puzzle story as essentially an intellectual problem whose "true nature at the end of its evolution" is a box of clues with which the reader can reconstruct the crime, as in Dennis Wheatley's and J. G. Links's *Murder off Miami* (1936). "It is not a tale but a game, not a story but a problem. This is why just at the moment when the *novel* is freeing itself from all rules, the *detective novel* keeps inventing stricter ones" (Caillois, 1984, 11). The story becomes more original as it imposes more stringent rules. Setting, psychology, and passion are all plot devices in a narrative form that would, if it could, "dispense with humanity altogether." Unfortunately for the game structure and its calculations the genre "is obliged to give us flesh-and-blood people" (Caillois, 1984, 11).

Bernard Suits's "The Detective Story: A Case Study of Games in Literature" (1985) argues that there are four possible games—the reader plays, the reader views, the author plays, the author makes. The author plays the game using tactics such as misdirection, so that the author both plays and makes. It is a two-move game in which the puzzle is either placed before everything or is subordinated to everything else (Aristotle versus the Romantics and those following). Readers may be solving puzzles or are curious or are looking for a surprise (readers' views). Aristotle's model argues for probability in incidents and outcome of drama, but for the detective story this should be evident retrospectively. Readers who are curious or who want a surprise will be happy if the surprise element is surprising and retrospective probability is high. Audience response features two different kinds of viewing: if the viewed game is between characters, then it is "an *imitation* of a game" rather than a game, for example, like viewing a sporting event played according to a script (Suits, 1985, 210). Writers must construct the two different narratives in radically different ways. For example, the culprit can be revealed at the beginning, as in R. Austin Freeman's novels or the *Columbo* TV series. This type is not a literary game.

John T. Irwin's *The Mystery to a Solution: Poe, Borges, and the Analytic Detective Story* (1994) grew out of the author's recognition that F. Scott Fitzgerald, Stephen Crane, Poe, and Borges share an "engagement with Platonic idealism," especially in the treatment of the allegory of the cave as an image of a womb "that translated the notion of origin (and thus of the self) from a physical to a mental plane and their further understanding that this fantasized return to origin could be assimilated to another structure governing the relationship to art: that sense of the male artist's ability (personified in the muse) to conceive and give birth to the work, the artist's identification with the muse as mother" (Irwin, 1994, xv–xvi). Poe invented a genre appropriate to and dominating an age of technology and science where mental work is largely analysis and created "the most appealing format and the most glamorous mask" for this work and its worker (Irwin, 1994, xvii). Frankenstein and Dupin are alike except that Dupin is "his own monster," the "first great characterless character, the name for a mental position in an entirely plot-driven scenario, the image of a man for whom one could remark that what he does is the sum total of what he is" (Irwin, 1994, xvii). Poe makes it clear that the project of the Dupin series is "the analysis of self-consciousness" (Irwin, 1994, xvii). "No image of the self can achieve absolute closure," since self-consciousness for Poe is "infinitely reflexive" (Irwin, 1994, xvii). Irwin says that like his *American Hieroglyphics* this book is concerned with ontotheology (a "metaphysical quest for the Absolute" [Irwin, 1994, xvii]). Borges and Poe transform this quest into an epistemological question of "*figuring* the absolute," which is an impossible task (Irwin, 1994, xvii). What Irwin sees himself doing is a "history of the critique of figuration" (Irwin, 1994, xvii). Irwin's book "combines history, literary history, biography, psychoanalysis, and practical and speculative criticism" in pursuing Poe into the "history of mathematics, classical mythology, handedness, the three/four oscillation, the double-mirror structure of self-consciousness, the mythography of Evans and Frazer, the structure of chess, automata, the mind-body problem, the etymology of 'labyrinth', and scores of other topics" (Irwin, 1994, xviii) while structuring the book as a detective story.

The analytic detective story is different from the Chandler-style story, which is more concerned with character. Irwin begins by looking at "The Purloined Letter" through Jacques Lacan's "Seminar on 'The Purloined Letter' " (1966), Derrida's "The Purveyor of Truth" (1975), and Barbara Johnson's "The Frame of Reference: Poe, Lacan, Derrida" (1978), then looks at Borges's doubling of Poe's Dupin trilogy with his own series of three stories. From 1957 through 1977–78 each of the essays treats the story as a pretext. For Irwin the thread that runs through all three is the position with regard to "the numerical/geometrical structure of the story" (Irwin, 1994, 3). Johnson notes that Derrida uses the opportunity of Lacan's essay to do exactly what Dupin did to the Minister, because as with the Minister's " 'evil turn,' " Lacan had slighted Derrida (Irwin, 1994, 4). Derrida points out that Lacan collapses what is actually a four-sided structure (which he derives from adding the narrator to positions occupied by Dupin, the Minister, and the Queen) into a three-sided narration in order to leave only triangles that allow him to read the story as an Oedipal triangle. Johnson then points out that it is problematic whether Derrida achieves his quadrangular structure by adding "one to three or by doubling two" (Irwin, 1994, 5). Derrida says that in reducing the structure to an Oedipal triangle, psychoanalytical approaches "attempt to dismiss or absorb the uncanny effects of doubling," which he says are present throughout the tale. Irwin notes that "doubling is almost always splitting and doubling," as involving four because the double "externally duplicates an internal division in the protagonist's self" (Irwin, 1994, 5). Barbara Johnson "doubles Derrida's own insights back upon themselves to make them problematic" (Irwin, 1994, 6). Johnson says Lacan and Derrida are playing the game of even and odd; there is an " 'oscillation' between the former's 'unequivocal statements of undecidability' and the latter's 'ambiguous assertions of decidability' " (Irwin, 1994, 6). Johnson thus dispenses with Lacan and Derrida in order to get away from numbers. This is a game that inevitably leads one to a position in which one is one up, but then the next player leaves one one down, since each move involves attributing a thought process to one's opponent. Irwin says this leaves Johnson's essay in a "disconcerting level of self-consciousness" (Irwin, 1994, 7). He attributes this to Johnson's indebtedness to Paul de Man and his ultimate undecidability, leaving her essay characterized by rhetorical ambushes of grammar—a statement that "says one thing grammatically and means its opposite rhetorically" (Irwin, 1994, 9). This leads Irwin into a discussion of self-reflexive paradoxes such as " 'All statements containing seven words are false,' " so that if the statement is true it is false or if it is false it is false (a paradox of self-inclusion). The only difference Johnson demonstrates is her "complete awareness" of playing out the game of even and odd. "In its translation from fiction to criticism, the project of analyzing the act of analysis becomes in effect the program of being infinitely self-conscious about self-consciousness," which means that the only insight available in this kind of critical game is the pointing out that one is already aware of the implications of one's own position (Irwin, 1994, 11). Irwin says this ultimately produces "a kind of intellectual vertigo" and that Poe more than anybody else enjoyed this sort of "dizzying, self-dissolving effect of thought about thought" (Irwin, 1994, 11). Lewis Carroll and Borges raise the possibility of a map of original size that reveals the paradox that if thinking and the content of thought are distinguishable and thought is able to "represent itself to itself, able to take itself as its own object—then the attempt to analyze the act of analysis, to include wholly the act of thinking within the content of thought, will be a progression of the order $n + 1$ to infinity" (Irwin, 1994, 12).

This paradox of "analytic self-inclusion" is "one of Borges' recurring themes" (Irwin, 1994, 13). "It is fair to say that in the last twenty-five years, the current of critical discussion initiated by Lacan's essay has been the most powerful interpretive tradition for Poe's detective stories in this country and has significantly raised the level of critical discourse about Poe's work as a whole, with the result that Poe's corpus has become a (if not the) principal site for psychoanalytic, structuralist, and poststructuralist readings in American literature" (Irwin, 1994, 442). Irwin observes that there is a good deal of circumstantial evidence that Borges's story influenced Lacan, primarily through Roger Caillois. Poe's story led to Borges's "reading/rewriting," which in turn anticipated Lacan's triad, among other things, and may have caused his anxiety in several utterances, including the curious footnote at the beginning of *Ecrits* (Irwin, 1994, 446). Irwin says Lacan's acknowledgment may take the form of "a footnote or at the foot of a page" (Irwin, 1994, 447). (One could also say in keeping with the spirit of Dupin's stroll with the narrator, underfoot.) Irwin notes that Lacan uses the "doubling of two triangles" to illustrate his "dialectic of intersubjectivity" in the mirror stage where the child realizes his separateness, and this double triangle is essentially the one Borges uses in "Death and the Compass" to illustrate "the encounter [between] two men 'whose minds work in the same way' and who 'may be the same man'" (Irwin, 1994, 447). Poe's "The Purloined Letter" is doubled by Borges's "Death and the Compass," and his "The Murders in the Rue Morgue" is doubled by "The Garden of Forking Paths." Borges's "Ibn Hakkan al-Bokhari," which doubles "The Mystery of Marie Rogêt," also doubles its weakness: "by functioning solely as newspaper readers of the crime they end up intellectually distanced from and emotionally uninvolved in the events, as emblemized by the tales' anticlimactic ending" (Irwin, 1994, 450). Borges had to "create a mixed genre in order to double Poe" (Irwin, 1994, 450). Irwin admits that he has inevitably added a fifth side by adjusting an "infinite progression of interpretations," but he has also included Israel Zangwill's *The Big Bow Mystery* (1892) between "Death and the Compass" and "The Purloined Letter," between Borges and Zangwill, H. G. Wells's "The Plattner Story" (1897), and between Zangwill and Poe he added Lewis Carroll's *Through the Looking Glass* (1872). He ends up finally at Johnson's position, where "there is always another interpreter ready to add one more point or to subdivide the field of inquiry one more time" (Irwin, 1994, 451).

Peter Swirski's "Literary Studies and Literary Pragmatics: The Case of 'The Purloined Letter' " (1996) applies game theory to demonstrate the pragmatics of the author-reader interaction in relation to the story. The zero-sum two-person marble-guessing game is not a model for the more complex author-reader game. The author-reader game is rather a cooperative undertaking, the degree of cooperation of which game theory helps to understand.

MYTH CRITICISM

Academic interest in detective fiction became widespread by the 1970s with the rise of the study of popular culture generally and as the implications of European structuralism began to be influential in the humanities. A series of discoveries and rediscoveries led to renewed interest in the formal structure of texts, such as that put forward by Russian Formalists in the 1920s and more recently Northrop Frye and Tzvetan Todorov. Meanwhile the relation of texts to features of the broader culture was opened by structuralism's linguistic determination, by poststructural indetermination and interest in discourse, and by Lacanian psychoanalysis and reader-response theory. Prior to these developments, however, theories of genre have had much to say about the way we understand the phenomenon of detective stories. Several perspectives have been suggested for the structure and development of genres, with two poles receiving the most attention. At one pole is the idea that genres are self-perpetuating and mutating structures that require little or no human intervention after an initial start or result from a structural symbiosis with the mind. At the other pole is the view that genres are ideologically intertwined with dominant social, economic, and political institutions. While the former emphasizes permanent structural features, the latter tends to emphasize changing features and/or details of the text that myth and formalist criticism would consider filler.

One form of the first argument follows Northrop Frye's general line of thought, argued, for example, in *The Anatomy of Criticism* (1957). Frye's *mythos* is based on the Blakeian notion that incorporates Romance, Tragedy, Comedy, and Irony as forms "logically prior" to literary genres. In Frye's notion, *Comedy* is the mythos of spring; *Romance* is the mythos of summer; *Tragedy* is the mythos of fall; and *Irony* is the mythos of winter. But these mythoi interpenetrate, resulting in generic· tendencies. Romance and Comedy represent wish fulfillment and regeneration; Irony and satire often parody Romance and adapt it to a realistic content that reveals unexpected results. Frye argues that genres result from wish fulfillment or the lack of it, which suggests a similarity to Carl Jung and Sir James Frazer. Frye's schema is fruitfully adapted to the study of detective fiction by George Grella, who uses Frye's notion of mythic archetypes to examine the classic and hard-boiled stories. Grella agrees with W. H. Auden that "the detective novel's true appeal is literary," and in the case of the classic novel this form remains one of the last outposts of the comedy of manners (Grella, 1976, 41). Figures adapted to the detective story include the tricky slave, the benevolent elf, and the Prospero figure, with such detectives as Philo Vance and Ellery Queen as dandies and Nero Wolfe and Sir Henry Merrivale as wizards (John Dickson Carr's Dr. Gideon Fell has the benevolence and Falstaffian gusto of Jung's Wise Old Man). Grella uses Frye's *mythos* of comedy to identify three features of the story: settings, characters, and plots that are conventional features of the classic story.

Hanna Charney's *The Detective Novel of Manners* (1981) is concerned with that quality of (particularly classic) detective fiction identified by Grella in his ground-breaking essay on the comedy of manners (Landrum, Browne, and Browne, 1976, or Winks, 1980). Charney carries the idea into the surface realism of narratives, detective figures, and other areas. However, Rick A. Eden's "Detective Fiction as Satire" (1983) argues that Grella is wrong to attribute the classic detective story to the comedy of manners and the hard-boiled story to romance, since both exhibit only degrees of satire from the Horatian to the Juvenalian: "What engages us is the satiric action of the detective exposing the real, sordid nature of the meretricious society in which the murder occurred" (Eden, 1981, 279). Eden prefers the term *alazon* or impostor and *eiron* or comic hero (who in satire "are almost always outsiders in some sense"; often they are actually from another region, country or social class), with Grella's *blocking figure* as a form of alazon, so that in satire alazons function as impostors who hide their true natures behind conventional behavior. The romantic subplot Grella notes is not necessary to such works as Ellery Queen's *The French Powder Mystery* (1930). Frye's cena, or symposium form, is common to Horatian satire, as in S. S. Van Dine's *The Green Murder Case* (1928), where alazons are presumptuous—while detectives (eirons) are unassuming but attack imposture through wit. Alazons may be fools (like the sidekick) or scoundrels (like the murderer). Readers don't identify with the detective as much as compete with her; they try to become eiron but reach only alazon.

In 1976 John Cawelti's *Adventure, Mystery, and Romance* became the most important contribution to the understanding of the phenomenon of popular American genres to date. *Adventure, Mystery, and Romance* provides a critical framework for explaining the popularity of three broad generic formulas. This work is an important contribution to the understanding of popular American fiction, engaging as it does the broad arena of popular narrative. Cawelti examines the structure of both classic and hard-boiled fiction and the relationships between the creator and the reader and relates these to other genres and to the social milieu. Following Cawelti and Grella, whose work drew on the literary theory of Northrop Frye, numerous critics explored a wide range of approaches to the genre.

FORMALISM AND STRUCTURALISM

Other developments in the 1970s occurred in structuralist thought, which has forced the humanities and social sciences to rethink ideas and methods central to their disciplines. Frank Kermode's "Novel and Narrative" (1974) sees the detective story as a narrative that remains stable while the form of the novel has changed radically. Kermode argues that "the old assumption that a novel must be concerned with social and ethical systems that transcend it—what may be called the derygmatic assumption—is strongly questioned. The consequence is a recognizable estrangement from what used to be known as reality; and a further consequence, which can equally be defended as having beneficent possibilities, is that the use of fiction as an instrument of research into the nature of fiction, though certainly not new, is much more widely recognized" (Kermode, 1983, 176). The differences in older and newer novelistic structures, "as metacritics often allege, . . . are to be attributed to a major shift in our structures of thought; but although this may be an efficient cause of the mutation of interests it does not appear that the object of those interests—narrative—imitates the shift" (Kermode, 1983, 176–177).

In his "Whodunit and Other Questions: Metaphysical Detective Stories in Postwar Fiction" (1971), Michael Holquist makes two related points: "what the structural and philosophical presuppositions of myth and depth psychology were to modernism (Thomas Mann, James Joyce, Virginia Woolf, and so forth), the detective story is to postmodernism (Robbe-Grillet, Borges, Nabokov, and so on); secondly, if such is the case, we will have to establish a relationship between two levels of culture, kitsch and the avant-garde, often thought to be mutually exclusive" (Holquist, 1983, 150). Popular culture is "the skeleton in our academic closets." Holquist will draw on the "clichés" associated with the artistic tradition and popular art; the models of learning demonstrated by the courses described in college catalogs "are to college graduates what the oral tradition is to the savage" (Holquist, 1983, 151). Anything not mentioned in these courses will be below the canon (kitsch), and anything beyond it is the avant-garde. The unity of art and culture "broke down somewhere at the end of the seventeenth, beginning of the eighteenth century," kitsch springs "not from artists or craftsmen but from the machine" (Holquist, 1983, 151). Holquist sees things in primary terms: "art is difficult, kitsch is easy"; "Kitsch seems to appropriate art by robbing it of the demonic, not just its 'aura' as Walter Benjamin has argued, but its dangers" (Holquist, 1983, 152). Kitsch has all sorts of problems with uniformity and being difficult; this assumed, one can "differentiate between various genres of literary kitsch by focusing on the particular pattern of reassurance each provides" (Holquist, 1983, 152–153). Holquist argues that "it is clear that much recent spy fiction is aimed at allaying fears aroused by" science and diplomacy. The pattern of spy thrillers shifts after Hiroshima from "elegant, patriotic heroes" to "amoral supermen" (Holquist, 1983, 153). Holquist wants to focus on stories "of pure puzzle, pure ratiocination," excluding "Gothic romances, psychological studies of criminals, and hard-boiled thrillers" (Holquist, 1983, 154). Poe's stories result from his "powerful impulse toward the irrational." Dupin the detective is "the essential metaphor for order," the "instrument of pure logic" (Holquist, 1983, 156). Holquist wants to lay the groundwork for an attack on postmodernist novelists who substitute things for people in their fiction and commit other literary offenses. He is particularly interested in the rearrangement that Alain Robbe-Grillet, Nabokov, and Borges make of the classic detective story, creating, rather than filling voids as does modernism.

Tzvetan Todorov's 1966 essay "Typology of Detective Fiction," collected in *The Poetics of Prose* (1977), is the most important formalist contribution to date. His conclusions, though often couched in different terms or carried out in different ways, are implicated in many approaches that either see detective and mystery stories as subliterature or as a form of literature that lends itself without resistance to ideological appropriation. Narratological and formalist approaches follow Todorov's practice of reducing narrative to its simplest mechanisms, which allows theorists and critics to construct more controlled and stable models. Todorov notes that genres were devalued by Romantic criticism, which was in revolt against the classics.

Todorov bases his study on the classic whodunit, which enjoyed brief vogue between World Wars I and II. Van Dine tried to define it with his twenty rules, and the best attempt is Michel Butor, who, in his own novel, *Passing Time* (*L'emploi du temps*, 1960), defined the genre as having two murders—that committed by the murderer and the detective's victimization of the murderer—with two "temporal series," two corresponding stories of the crime and investigation that do not intersect because "the story of the crime ends before the story of the investigation begins" (Todorov, 1977, 44). The second story is more or less devoid of action because the characters learn rather than act. In fact, Todorov argues, the rules of the genre stipulate that the detective remain out of harm's way. Instead the reader and the detective serve "a slow apprenticeship" (Todorov, 1977, 45).[5] The narrator is often a sidekick who actually says he is writing a book, while the first (the story of the crime) never mentions the book. It could be said that the first story is "what really happened," and the second story "explains 'how the reader . . . has come to know about it' " (Todorov, 1977, 45).

The Russian formalists "distinguished, in fact, the fable (the story) from the subject (the plot) of a narrative: the story is what has happened in life, the plot is the way the author presents it to us. . . . These two notions . . . are two points of view about the same thing." Todorov says the story of the crime is in fact the story of an absence: its most accurate characteristic is that it cannot be immediately present in the book. In other words, the narrator cannot transmit directly the conversations of the characters who are implicated, nor describe their actions: to do so he must necessarily "employ the intermediary of another (or the same) character who will report, in the second story, the words heard or the actions observed" (Todorov, 1977, 45). This style has to be straightforward, simple, and clearly articulated. The author cannot be omniscient, so what we have then are "temporal inversions and individual 'points of view': the tenor of each piece of information is determined by the person who transmits it, no observation exists without an observer" (Todorov, 1977, 46).

The hard-boiled narrative (Todorov's thriller) originated, Todorov says, in the United States just prior to World War II and intensified after it.[6] The thriller is an offshoot of the whodunit that develops an element that was unnecessary to the whodunit. In other words, genres do not follow logical structural descriptions, but rather emergent genres follow from an element in an old one that was extraneous, leading to different coding for the two forms. "The contemporary thriller has been constituted not around a method of presentation but around the milieu represented, around specific characters and behavior"; that is, it is based on "themes" (Todorov, 1977, 48).[7] In the thriller the first story is sacrificed for the sake of the second, which features violence, amorality, and sordidness. Although it shares such elements as "danger, pursuit, combat" with the adventure story, the thriller also differs from it. The adventure story itself has been effaced by the spy novel in which the influence of the thriller's affinity for the "marvelous and exotic" leads it toward the travel narrative and toward science fiction. All this results from the thriller's "tendency to description" that the detective narrative avoids (Todorov, 1977, 48).

The suspense novel develops between the whodunit and thriller. Todorov says he can't tell whether these forms evolve in a particular sequence or are synchronic. Because such writers as Arthur Conan Doyle and Maurice Leblanc wrote several types of this kind of fiction, the "rule of the genre is perceived as a constraint once it becomes pure form and is no longer justified by the structure of the whole." In the novels of Hammett and Chandler, mystery had become a pretext; so the thriller got rid of the mystery in order to exploit suspense and describe a milieu. When the suspense novel appeared, it dispensed with the milieu, while reclaiming the plot and the mystery. "Novels which have tried to do without both mystery and the milieu proper to the thriller—for example, Patricia Highsmith's *The Talented Mr. Ripley* [1955]—are too few to be considered a separate genre." These two novels are considered by readers as "an intermediary form between detective fiction and the novel itself." This form can become "the germ of a new genre of detective fiction." For Todorov, then, crime fiction does have a definable set of structures that are dependent on unnecessary elements in an existing form rather than on an a priori logical construct. The resulting forms have "a different complex of properties, not by necessity logically harmonious with the first form" (Todorov, 1977, 52).

Because of the importance of Todorov's work in literary theory and especially in genre studies, it may be appropriate to point out several cautions that might be observed in applying it. As is apparent in the summary, Todorov takes his cues for constructing the model from Butor and Van Dine and also brings in readers as a general experiential category. That is, the sample for constructing the model of production of genres is extremely limited considering that the output of crime fiction is so large and diverse. The consumption of the texts is not really theorized, or if it is it is done so in an extremely limited manner. The theoretical model, then, is confined almost exclusively to the text, which leaves both the cause(s) and effect(s) of the text external to the model yet dependent on it. Second, the texts themselves are not likely to be quite as reductive as Todorov considers them to be. Because of the episodic nature of most detective novels within this formal structure, murder very often intrudes a second, third, fourth, or more times in the course of the book, and the detective can in fact be threatened.

Robert Champigny's *What Will Have Happened: A Philosophical and Technical Essay on Mystery Stories* (1977) is not fundamentally about mystery novels, but about the way fiction operates to construct the illusion of a comprehensible reality. Mystery novels provide a means and opportunity for discussing a phenomenology of literary forms. The book continues the author's concern with ontology of narratives. Because Champigny believes that narrative logic introduces misconceptions, he avoids this form for his own presentation in favor of disconnected "patterns of conceptual understanding" in which he examines various motifs and the representation of categories of such matters as justice, adventure, viewpoint, legend, atmosphere, destiny, cryptograms, and clues (Champigny, 1977, 9). Like Todorov, Champigny bases his analysis on the classic puzzle story produced by such writers as John Dickson Carr. He excludes from consideration "social, political, cultural [and] ideological backgrounds, since such embroidery amounts to providing a character or a bunch of characters with an appropriately tailored setting" (Champigny, 1977, 9). This conception excludes the work of such writers as Ross Macdonald, who has argued that "the surprise with which a detective novel concludes should set up tragic vibrations which run backward through the entire structure." Nevertheless, Champigny provides an extensive inventory of narrative devices.

Roland Barthes, the French philosopher, literary critic and semiotician, bridged two major critical perspectives through his work in structuralism and poststructuralism. In *S/Z* (1974) Barthes notes that the structure of formulas such as detective and mystery stories is built around a paradox in the narrative. In the detective story, "the hermeneutic terms structure the enigma according to the expectation and desire for its solution. The dynamics of the text (since it implies a truth to be deciphered) is thus paradoxical"; on the one hand the unfolding of the text moves it along toward closure (solution of the mystery), while the hermeneutic code introduces "*delays* (obstacles, stoppages, deviations) in the flow of the discourse. . . . [B]etween question and answer there is a whole dilatory area whose emblem might be named 'reticence,' the rhetorical figure which interrupts the sentence, suspends it, turns it aside." Between the question and answer there are dilatory morphemes such as "the *snare* (a kind of deliberate evasion of the truth), the *equivocation* (a mixture of truth and snare which frequently, while focusing on the enigma, helps to thicken it), and *jamming* (acknowledgment of insolubility)" (Barthes, 1983, 119). The detective narrative withholds and promises truth "at the end of expectation" (1983, 120). In straight narratives, the structure is like the subject and predicate of a sentence, but in hermeneutic narratives such as the detective story in which "truth predicates an incomplete subject," closure is withheld (1983, 120).

Timothy Steele's "Matter and Mystery: Neglected Works and Background Materials of Detective Fiction" (1983) argues that while the structure of the detective story is consistent with Aristotle's drama and verse in the *Poetics*, eighteenth-century aesthetic theory has also influenced it. Poe acquired his aesthetics through Coleridge and August Wilhelm von Schlegel, who systematized it. A common denominator in the various strands of German Idealism is the idea "that art is an autonomous enterprise and that the individual work of art is to be considered fundamentally in its own terms" (Steele, 1983, 559–560). For Poe taste was "concerned with proportion and harmony" apart from the Intellect and Moral Sense; art is "exclusively concerned with the beautiful," and is self-sufficient (Steele, 1983, 560). Art produced for its own sake can only be discussed "in terms of its formal properties," and Poe talks about composition as a mathematical problem (Steele, 1983, 561). Poe's stories "are characterized by sensational mechanical effects and a paucity of emotional substance" (Steele, 1983, 562). Practitioners after Poe valued his contribution to plot almost exclusively; as Sayers said, "[i]t is better to err in the direction of too little feeling than too much" (Steele, 1983, 563). The "rules" formulated by Willard Huntington Wright and Ronald Knox are directly attributed to Poe's influence, but not everyone lauded the formula.

Anthony Hilfer's *The Crime Novel: A Deviant Genre* (1990) discusses what he calls the crime novel as a formula that "extends, inverts, and generally plays off against the conventions of" the detective novel (Hilfer, 1990, xi). Hilfer's approach is to identify types, particularly "in terms of character type and theme," and more particularly the "themes of madness, alienation, sexual passion, and justice, showing a certain logic of possibilities for what writers can do with these themes" (Hilfer, 1990, xi). Thus he explores rather than denies conventionality. He cites Alastair Fowler, Claudio Guillén, and Italo Calvino, whose "literature machine" is a good model for the "combinatorial games" that produce "unexpected meanings" in the crime novel. His approach is synchronic—he is interested in thematic possibilities, rather than historical ones. Writers tended to keep "reinventing what could be done in a novel whose protagonist is not a detective" (Hilfer, 1990, xii). They don't know each other's work as well as they know the detective novel's conventions. The national differences between U.S. and British fiction arise because each responds to its national form of detective fiction. Doubling, repetition, and revenge are common to many types, together with incest in some (Freudian themes).

Hilfer explores "permutational possibilities of the types within the genre" (Hilfer, 1990, xiii). He draws on "Fowler on genre, Cawelti and Grella on the detective novel, Freud on the uncanny, Merleau-Ponty on the phenomenology of perception, and so on" (Hilfer, 1990, xiii). He employed these "after the fact" rather than "constructed a critical approach and used works of literature to illustrate it" (Hilfer, 1990, xiii). I don't believe Hilfer mentions what criteria he actually did use for selection. He notes that "character psychology and implicative setting are frequently essential in the crime novel whereas an ingenious puzzle may be dispensed with altogether"; the reverse is true of detective novels (Hilfer, 1990, 2). Hilfer observes that the social attitude is conservative and traditionalist in the detective novel, while the opposite is true in the crime novel, but while Julian Symons slots Hammett, Chandler, and Macdonald as crime novelists in *Bloody Murder* (1985), Hilfer sees them as detective novelists. Of prime importance in detective fiction is the solution of a mystery, while in the crime novel this information is often known from the beginning (as in P. D. James's fiction); the crime novel is often concerned with the effect of the crime on the murderer.

What is crucial for Hilfer is that in the crime novel "*self and world, guilt and innocence are problematic. The world of the crime novel is constituted by what is problematic in it*" (Hilfer's italics, 1990, 2). In this sense it differs from other popular art, which serves to create the world as we wish it to be. Hilfer shifts to a reader-response perspective to suggest that rather than absolving guilt in the reader, the crime novel maneuvers complicity. In the crime novel the detective may "prove useful as a threat to the main character and/or as an agent for plot closure but can be the protagonist only when doubling in the role of killer or falsely suspected, since the traditional detective hero would prematurely foreclose the anxiety and guilt central to the crime novel. The protagonist . . . will be the murderer (*The Talented Mr. Ripley*), a guilty bystander (*The Lodger*), a falsely suspected person (common to Cornell Woolrich's fiction), or the victim (*Before the Fact*)" (Hilfer, 1990, 3). This narrative strategy subverts reassurances of the detective story, often by featuring the killer as protagonist, whereas the detective story transforms guilt "from the realm of psychology into that of logic" (Hilfer, 1990, 3).[8] The crime novel collapses the distance.

There are not many examples of the guilty-bystander-as-protagonist; in this type readers are like witnesses and "become accomplices after the fact" by reading. In the falsely-suspected-as-protagonist narrative, as Todorov notes, the character is at the same time the detective, assumed culprit, and potential victim. The protagonist often confuses these roles, thus enhancing paranoia and reader's difficulties. A variation is like the "vanishing lady" described by James Sandoe: a woman and daughter arrive at a hotel and the woman vanishes without a trace; the daughter is unable to find a clue, so that the woman's social existence, memory, and maybe personal identity are questioned. This kind of story deals with structural (organizational) paranoia. The narrative in which the victim is the protagonist is also rare; here the reader is forced to contemplate her or his own murder. Partial complicity is more common; Hilfer identifies victimology as an area of knowledge related to this—for example, 70 percent of victims are usually complicit in some way with the crime perpetrated on them (Hilfer includes failing to lock doors as complicity).

All crime novels include some variation or combination of themes. Selected themes discussed include these: U.S. crime fiction constructs a pathological world that requires fatal passion as a response. British narratives (e.g., P. D. James) are concerned with justice. Both countries produce crime narratives that feature doubling and schizophrenia. The British detective novel confirms rationality, while the U.S. hard-boiled detective "validate[s] the American myth of personal integrity, absolute individualism, and stoic self-control" (Hilfer, 1990, 7). The British novel raises threat of "unexplainable world, the synechdoche for which is an unsolved crime" (Hilfer, 1990, 7). The U.S. threat is of "entrapment of self, its loss of control. The function of the femme fatale is to *fail* to sway the hero, thus highlighting his control over the self and, in a qualified way, the world" (Hilfer, 1990, 7). In the crime novel the protagonist "will give all to love *or destroy himself by not so doing*, shatter into schizophrenia, and confront a world either stubbornly enigmatic or too corrupt to be borne" (Hilfer, 1990, 8).

Marty Roth's *Foul and Fair Play: Reading Genre in Classic Detective*

Fiction (1995) is primarily concerned with "classic" detective fiction. He models his approach on Todorov's work. Roth's "controlling assumption is that in detective fiction gender is genre and genre is male," which means that all women writers are controlled by male structures (Roth, 1995, 5). It should be pointed out that this is a contested area. Roth's view accords with those of Klein and others, but not, for example, of Maureen Reddy (1988). Freud is incorporated to explain the schoolboy experience of British writers. The introduction contains discussions of taste and art in the detective narrative, detective fiction as "a literature in which repression writes itself" (Roth, 1995, 8). Chapter 2 discusses the fiction's lack of realism. Chapters 3 to 5 deal with conventions surrounding the detective and his investigations. Chapter 6 deals with women as a sexual threat, 7 with the crime and its conventions, 8 with the conventions of the solution. Chapters 9 and 10 deal with conventions of the clue as sign, and chapter 11 discusses myths of the frontier and underworld, which form the basis of the structure.

Peter Hühn's "The Detective as Reader: Narrativity and Reading Concepts in Detective Fiction" (1987) argues that the classic detective novel is constructed to lead the reader through an awareness of the artificiality of the narrative, while the hard-boiled novel assumes a greater immediacy on the part of the reader. The shift in narrative practice suggests a shift in the reader's experiential world.

PSYCHOANALYSIS

Psychoanalytic and psychological studies of mystery and detective narratives have a long and varied history. Poe, the writer and historical figure, as well as his work has been subject to close psychoanalytic scrutiny. The following studies focus primarily on texts, but also either implicitly or explicitly on textual relations to a reader or readers.

W. O. Aydelotte, in "The Detective Story as a Historical Source" (1949), argues that the popularity of the detective story is due to its conventions. By studying this literature, one can describe the readers it is intended for in terms of their unsatisfied desires. The detective story presents life as agreeable, reassuring, simple, understandable, meaningful, and secure. The problems are simple, with simple solutions. They glamorize the everyday, for example, the city. They portray a secure universe, subject to fixed laws. The detective always wins. By showing death they minimize the fear of it. Occasionally the victim's death is all for the best. The solution releases everyone from guilt. Drawing on current Freudian theory, Aydelotte argues that the reader is passive—as indeed is everyone in the story except the detective. The villain could be anyone; that is, there is expressed a paranoid suspicion. The detective simplifies life and attributes meaning to it. For the most part he is strong and conservative, but a dictator, a superman.

Geraldine Pederson-Krag's "Detective Stories and the Primal Scene"

(1949) notes, following Haycraft, that about one-fourth of the 1,200 or so volumes of fiction published in the United States in the late 1940s was detective fiction, and about one-third to one-half of the programs on two major radio networks of the time deal with detection. Pederson-Krag argues that the detective story "is less interesting for specific details than because the gratification lies in certain basic elements which are always present (Pederson-Krag, 1976, 58). In this kind of narrative (1) some wrongdoing between two people is revealed when one turns up murdered, but the criminal is hidden by respectability, (2) the detective has acute perception, unlimited knowledge, great perseverance, and usually a sidekick, and (3) the story contains a series of trivial, commonplace, and apparently unconnected observations. These continuities do not explain audience interest.

Psychiatrists have previously argued that narratives are constructed so that "anxieties are built up to be released at the height of tension" (Pederson-Krag, 1976, 58). An element of uncanniness recreates the reader's infantile belief in the omnipotence of his thought, which may involve Oedipal anxieties that are worked through. The reader or viewer may indulge aggressive fantasies by identifying with the criminal, while identity with the detective strokes the "mighty, blameless superego" (Pederson-Krag, 1976, 59). This process allows readers to acquire the detective's intellectual capacities without having to earn them. Victim identification may allow the indulgence of masochistic fantasies. Pederson-Krag says these explanations are too simple, that such effects can be the result of experiencing any kind of fiction, and the murder is usually committed offstage. Furthermore, detective fiction is difficult for readers to identify with because of its conventions: aggression is better satisfied by an adventure story. The quaint qualities of many detectives would not make them easy to identify with, and the victim is also poorly designed for identification, being "cruel, boorish, or miserly" (Pederson-Krag, 1976, 59).

Pederson-Krag argues that the intense curiosity aroused by the detective story is analogous to the primal scene. In this view "the first element of the detective story [is] the secret crime," where the parent (for whom the child had negative Oedipal feelings) is represented by the victim (Pederson-Krag, 1976, 60). The innocuous details represent the child's "growing awareness of the details it never understood" (Pederson-Krag, 1976, 60). The murderer is the other parent "toward whom the child's positive Oedipal feelings were directed, the one whom the child wished least of all to imagine participating in a secret crime." In this sense the detective story is a sadistic return to the primal scene. The detective story "satisfies the voyeurs who . . . gazed with strained attention at the scene of parental coitus" (Pederson-Krag, 1976, 62). The Watson character provides an alternate ego in case the superego threatens guilt. "In the complete knowledge of the crime, achieved by the detective, the ego may participate as either or both parents in the primal scene," since knowledge may be the equivalent of either male or female sexuality (Pederson-Krag, 1976, 63). Pederson-Krag feels that in the largely illiterate sixteenth, seventeenth, and eighteenth centuries "witch hunting took the place of mystery stories" (Pederson-Krag, 1976, 60).

Jacques Lacan, in "Seminar on 'The Purloined Letter' " (1966), plays on the ambiguity of the word "letter" in Poe's "The Purloined Letter," both as a letter in the alphabet and as a correspondence between individuals; this latter leads to a discussion of intersubjectivity of the principles in the plot through the idea of *exchange*. The story involves two scenes, the primal act in the Queen's boudoir and the second act in the Minister's office. In the Queen's boudoir, we are told that an exalted personage would jeopardize her honor and safety, though the King is nearby. The intersubjectivity corresponds with the three logical moments and three places it assigns to the subjects forced to choose. Also three glances—(1) that which sees nothing (police and king), (2) that which sees that the above see nothing and deludes itself about secrecy, and (3) that which sees that the first two glances leave what should be hidden exposed. To understand these relationships, it is important to remember that *"the unconscious is the discourse of the Other"* (Lacan's italics, 1983, 28). The relationships are triggered by the "pure signifier," the purloined letter, the act of deceit (Lacan, 1983, 29). In addition, "the dialogues themselves, in the opposite use they make of the powers of speech, take on a tension which makes of them a different drama, one which our vocabulary will distinguish from the first as persisting in the symbolic order" (Lacan, 1983, 30). The first scene is told through several "filters," thereby sifting out the linguistic content, but the second becomes symbolic through its being told as dialogue. Through this dialogue Poe becomes the "magician" who reveals the key words. Dupin's jibes at the Prelate (he derides him) is for calling the thief a little mad because he is a poet and for overlooking what is "a little *too* self-evident," a phrase for which Lacan says the French have no easy translation, so he calls the relations *singuliers* because they are fixed in place by the signifier. The meaning of the letter is in the nature of the signifier, in that the signifier is "by nature symbol only of an absence" (Lacan, 1983, 37). "It can *literally* be said that something is missing from its place only of what can change it: the symbolic" (Lacan, 1956, 38).

In Poe's story, for Lacan, "the displacement of the signifier determines the subjects in their acts, in their destiny, in their blindnesses, in their end and in their fate" (Lacan, 1983, 43). The thief fails to see the "symbolic situation which he himself was so well able to see and in which he is now seen seeing himself not being seen" (Lacan, 1983, 43). The letter transforms the minister into a likeness of the first loser of the letter until he gives it up as she does. The letter in his possession changes from a red seal to a black, and from a masculine script to feminine. When Dupin comes into possession of the letter, he forms the third figure in the triad of possessors. Thus, it is that "what the 'purloined letter' nay, the 'letter of sufferance' means is that a letter always arrives at its destination" (Lacan, 1983, 54).

In his "Literature High and Low: The Case of the Mystery Story" (1975) Geoffrey H. Hartman promotes a psychoanalytical interpretation of the detective story. He notes that "the formula dominating [the detective story] began to emerge with the first instance of the genre, Horace Walpole's *Castle of Otranto* (1764)" (Hartman, 1983, 217). He takes Aristotle's *tò pathos*, the scene of suffering, which for Aristotle was "a destructive or painful action, such as death on the stage, bodily agony, wounds and the like," to be Freud's primal scene and argues that though modern writers and filmmakers "may remove the scene of pathos, our eyes nervously inspect all those graphic details which continue to evoke the detective story's lust for evidence" (Hartman, 1983, 212). Modernist writers such as Robbe-Grillet, Henry James, André Gide, William Faulkner, and Albert Camus, as well as films such as Alain Resnais's *Last Year in Marienbad*, Michelangelo Antonioni's *Blow Up* and *L'Aventura*, Ingmar Bergman's *A Passion*, and Norman Mailer's *Maidstone* weaken the scene, in contrast to the detective formula, which intensifies it. The primal scene "resembles, first of all, a highly condensed, supersemantic event like riddle, oracle, or mime. Whether or not the power of such scenes is linked to our stumbling as innocents on sexual secrets—on seeing or overhearing that riddling mime— it is clear that life is always in some way too fast for us, that it is a spectacle we can't interpret or a dumbshow difficult to articulate; the "word . . . 'mystery' means that something is happening too fast to be spotted. We are made to experience a consciousness (like Oedipa's in Thomas Pynchon's *The Crying of Lot 49*) always behind and running" (215). Hartman asks, "What is a clue, for instance, but a symbolic or condensed corpse, a living trace or materialized shadow?" The detective story "allows *place* to turn the tables on *time* by means of its decisive visual reanimations" (Hartman, 1983, 216).

MARXISM

Ernst Kaemmel's "Literature Under the Table: The Detective Novel and Its Social Mission" (1962) notes that the article (disputed elsewhere) on mystery stories in the 1946 edition of the *Encyclopedia Britannica* states that about 1,300 different detective novels appeared from 1841 to 1920 and about 8,000 from 1920 to 1940; from a *Publisher's Weekly* report he cites 15,000 to 16,000 from 1940–60. Printings are often very large. From this Kaemmel concludes that although detective fiction is not literature, it is nevertheless socially significant. Kaemmel argues that the great popularity of detective novels indicates a social "problem." "Under the conditions of decaying imperialism" in the United States, detective fiction "has sunk" to the hard-boiled novel and film. Those who argue that the detective story originated with riddle tales overlook the fact that the riddle refers to areas of life beyond belles lettres.[9] Kaemmel believes that murder is always committed for economic motives and asserts that an assistant to the detective is necessary.

Kaemmel points out that circumstances of crime are arbitrarily drawn by the author, so that conclusions fit them. He says that Doyle's readers were largely lower and middle class and were drawn to mysteries by their portrayals of "polite society" and their identification with the "acuity and superiority" of the detective, who they expected would see that the "violated order ... be reconstituted" (Kaemmel, 1983, 59). Kaemmel believes that "the decline of detective literature began when, instead of Sherlock Holmes, Nick Carter and the tribe of the Carters appeared on a lower level in cheap magazines" (Kaemmel, 1983, 60). These latter contain "coarser" figures whose activities don't tax the mind. It was the dead end of plot variations that gave rise to hard-boiled stories. Such detective fiction would not appear in socialist countries. Kaemmel says that an author using the devices of the detective novel might produce a socialist form that exposes criminal offenses against society in a literary plot: he cites novels of Wolfgang Schreyer and Friedrich Karl Kaul.[10]

In "The Origin of the Detective Novel" (1974), Richard Alewyn calls detective novels a "pestilence" that is read and often commented on by "representatives of politics and business, of literature and theology" (Alewyn, 1983, 63). Alewyn notes that apologists have claimed that "there can only be detective novels once there are detectives," but he disagrees (Alewyn, 1983, 65). What is being glorified here, he argues, is the individual, so it makes "more sense to think of the liberalistic spirit of self-help which has been so impressively developed in the Anglo-Saxon countries and which has often enough not been especially pious towards the state" (Alewyn, 1983, 67). The detectives are outsiders. Consider: (1) the murderer is a character known to the reader from the beginning; this means isolation of the characters, (2) the world is deterministic, (3) the rarity of murder in everyday life, especially the ingenuity of the murderers, contrasts with the fictional need for variety by writers; the unusual is there from the beginning in Poe, (4) clues are details that appear to be unimportant, and the least likely suspect is the murderer. This strategy creates a doubt about the nature of the world and the validity of the senses; rather than creating trust in reason and science, it undermines it. Alewyn argues that such stories as E.T.A. Hoffmann's "Das Fräulein von Scuderi" (1818) contain murder (a series), a solution at the end, an innocent suspect and an unsuspected criminal, detection by an outsider, an old maid poet, and a locked room element. Another story, retold by Petaval, "Marquise de la Pivardière" contains everything but the detective, as do many of his stories. The German novel of this period, moreover, is built around mysteries and their solutions. The characters in their wanderings encounter clues that "say nothing to others but in which they recognize signs and messages" (Alewyn, 1983, 74). All these novelists were Romantics who also wrote gothic horror stories, and gothic horror was popular because of the boredom with rationalism and bourgeois security. Between 1794 and 1850 over seventy novels appeared in England carrying the word "mystery" in their titles. The tales of Hoffmann and Poe are "nothing but lateral shoots from this common root" (Alewyn, 1983, 75). "The detective story is distinguished from the horror story by its locale," but Eugène Sue's *The Mysteries of Paris* (1842–43) had already moved the gothic into the city, influencing not only hoards of writers in Europe and England, but also Honoré de Balzac and Dickens. This suggests that Romanticism saw "the trivial surface of the world . . . [as] deceptive, . . . with abysses of mystery and danger underneath" (Alewyn, 1983, 75). Two kinds of characters correspond to these two levels of reality: the Romantics' Philistine, constituting those whose belief "in the rational order of the world and in the reliability of common sense, and who consequently are blind to the unusual and not up to dealing with the improbable" (Alewyn, 1983, 76), and those eccentrics and outsiders to whom E.T.A. Hoffmann says "the power to recognize the wonders of our life is given like a special sense," which Romanticism calls artists. Dupin and his progeny are in this latter category.

In "Rules of the Game of the Crime Novel" (1963) Helmut Heissenbüttel distinguishes between two opposite kinds of detectives: those who beat on people until they find out the guilty party and those who observe and think their way through to a solution. Poe brings Dupin's "positivistic bent" against "the quintessence of horror and inhumanity" (Heissenbüttel, 1983, 80). Holmes has Dupin's bent, but G. K. Chesterton's Father Brown's liberal Christianity retards the detective's "compulsion to disclose." Subsequent writers produce detective characters who become more and more "sociological stereotypes" and who, compared to Poe's and Doyle's, "wear a conventional bourgeois mask." In contrast, "hard-boiled" detectives derive in part from the stories of Bret Harte, Mark Twain, and Ambrose Bierce. The form is usually traced to Hammett and to Raymond Chandler's Philip Marlowe, but James Hadley Chase developed the most original variants, for his fiction takes seriously the "intermediate position between justice and injustice."[11] Chester Himes's Gravedigger Jones and Coffin Ed Johnson are an "impressive, grotesque variant" (Heissenbüttel, 1983, 81). Heissenbüttel cites Mary Hottinger on the difference between the focus of trial reports on the accused and the detective story on the detective.[12] The arrangement of the story is such that the realistic elements must be encoded and decoded into games with patterns. This leaves two possibilities for stylization: abnormality (Poe's orangutan) and reduction (the turning over of previously provided play counters, rather than the straight novel's interest in "representation of characters and the exploration of their motives in reflection and action" (Heissenbüttel, 1983, 82).

The variability possible from this schematism produces "ever new approximation to real scenes and milieus" that turn out to be anchored in topography. Agatha Christie's novels are remarkable for their "betweenness of places" such as the inside of an airplane, sleeping car, or middle deck of a Nile steamer. These places describe bits and pieces of landscape that "acquire the character of interiors as they are treated like rooms." In detective novels, sites are not transformed into language as in the straight novel but occur as a "summarizing of facts into a physiognomy of the scene of the crime" (Heissenbüttel, 1983, 86). Reconstruction of the trace of the unnarrated is carried out in this milieu of "typologically imprinted living space" by the detective, who like the corpse is a "superhuman being. He is immortal and has a higher knowledge, omnipotence" that should not be confused with the author's ego or exaggerated subjectivism. It should be taken literally—"The detective knows from the beginning where his path will take him. The difficulties he has concern the path on which he must go." As with Kafka, "There is a goal, but no path; what we call path is delay" (Heissenbüttel, 1983, 87).

Heissenbüttel rejects the detective as a kind of religious figure (as argued by Chesterton and Sayers). The trace is sociological, in that the characters have some emotional, familial, and economic ties to the victim (the gangster is a more recent development). That is, the "molecular affinities which structure late bourgeois society" constitute the "last sociological cement between the individual persons in a situation in which class divisions no longer exist and despotic methods are not yet binding enough.... This constitution of the group is purchased at the expense of the victim's death" (Heissenbüttel, 1983, 88). The model works for pre-1945 or 1950 detective novels but shifts with Georges Simenon's Inspector Maigret; rather than being a representative of the state, Maigret must—most clearly in *Maigret and the Killer* (Fr 1969)—battle with his deputies (Heissenbüttel, 1983, 88). The detective is usually disguised in some way as an oddity or fool, more like the group including the murderer than in the past. The reconstruction of the trace in these novels "becomes a self-unmasking" (Heissenbüttel, 1983, 91). The internal bonds in these cases become more arbitrary, the topographical anchoring no longer uniquely referential, and the corpse "loses its conclusiveness," becomes unreal (Heissenbüttel, 1983, 91). While in earlier forms the corpse served to bring attention to the value of the molecular bonds of the group, the newer forms tend to make the narrative "clearer and more aware of itself," to become more a game (Heissenbüttel, 1983, 92). The crime novel has its own linguistic and stylistic criteria appropriate to allegorical narrative.

Steven Marcus's "Dashiell Hammett" (1974) focuses on the Flitcraft aside in *The Maltese Falcon*. Flitcraft changed his name to Charles Pierce (compare Charles Sanders Peirce, 1839–1914, the philosopher, semiotician). "What the passage ... is all about among other things is the ethical irrationality of existence, the ethical unintelligibility of the world. For Flit-craft the falling beam 'had taken the lid off life and let him look at the works.' The works are that life is inscrutable, opaque, irresponsible, and arbitrary—that human existence does not correspond in its actuality to the way we live it. For most of us live as if existence itself were ordered, ethical, and rational" (Marcus, 1983, 200). During Hammett's writing career of twelve years, the Op seeks to "stir things up," and Hammett seemed ob-sessed by "the notion of organized crime or gangs taking over an entire society and running it as if it were an ordinary society doing business as usual" (Marcus, 1983, 204). Hammett juxtaposes the fictional world with social fictions of respectability. The world of crime is reproduced in the respectable world and the Maltese Falcon "turns out to be and contains within itself the history of capitalism. It is originally a piece of plunder, part of what Marx called the 'primitive accumulation'; when its gold en-crusted with gems is painted over, it becomes a mystified object, a com-modity itself. The falcon is a piece of property that belongs to no one—whoever possesses it does not really own it. At the same time it is another fiction, a representation or work of art—which turns out itself to be a fake, since it is made of lead" (205–206).

John M. Reilly, in "Beneficient Roguery: The Detective in the Capitalist City" (1976), showed, in his study of the biographies, biographical fiction, and memoirs of police detectives and heads of private agencies writing from the 1870s through the early twentieth century in the United States how the fictional detective grew out of the institutional extensions of state and pri-vate power.

Fredric R. Jameson's "On Raymond Chandler" (1970) attempts to ac-count for the evasion of realism. Jameson points out that Raymond Chan-dler published his first and best novel, *The Big Sleep* (1939), when he was fifty years old. The personal tone of his books derives from his move from the United States at age eight to be educated in English public schools and from his work in Los Angeles for fifteen years as an oil company executive. These experiences gave him, like Nabokov, a distance on the American language, so that "words have become objects for him" (Jameson, 1983, 124). Unlike more traditional or less formalist Marxists, Jameson argues that the detective story is "a form without ideological content, without any overt political or social or philosophical point." This kind of narrative structure permits stylistic experimentation. Other advantages are that the "empty, decorative event of the murder" allows the "real content" of an "almost scenic" landscape, as in "the kind of second wave of the modernist and formalistic impulse" found in Robbe-Grillet's *Le Voyeur* and *La Mai-son de Rendezvous* or Nabokov's *Lolita* and *Pale Fire* (Jameson, 1983, 124). Chandler's description of places "is in its very structure dependent on chance and anonymity; . . . its very essence is to be inessential" (Jame-son, 1983, 125). In great literature, such descriptions may be epiphanies, but in the detective novel they create anticipation of meaning. In both the classic English story and the hard-boiled American story "the moment of violence, apparently central, is nothing but a diversion"; in the classic story it is an interruption that allows daily life to be felt more strongly, while in the American story it serves to "allow [life] to be experienced backwards, in pure thought, without risks, as a contemplative spectacle which gives not so much the illusion of life as the illusion that life has already been lived," as "archaic sources of experience" (Jameson, 1983, 126).

The last great period of American literature, roughly from 1920 to 1945, defined America in geographical terms as the "sum of separate localisms"; but since World War II regionalism has been obliterated by standardization, abstracted by the closed lives of individual family units, the breakdown of cities, and the dehumanization of transportation and the media (Jameson, 1983, 127). Chandler fits "somewhere between these two literary situations" (Jameson, 1983, 127). In the United States there is no longer any "privileged experience" (such as in the nineteenth-century Parisian apartment house of Émile Zola's *Pot-Bouille*) from which the whole of social structure can be grasped. Marlowe visits "either those places you don't look at or those you can't look at: the anonymous or the wealthy and secretive" (Jameson, 1983, 130). Chandler's sentimentalism comes from a sensitivity to "the resistance of things" and is strongest in *The Long Goodbye*, where it is a "compensation" for "the rule of naked force and money" (Jameson, 1983, 131, 130).

Jameson observes that the detective's narrative "is episodic because of the fragmentary, atomistic nature of the society he moves through." The "most characteristic leitmotif of Chandler's books is the figure standing, looking out of one world, peering vaguely or attentively across into another" (Jameson, 1983, 131). This externality is also artistically motivated, as when speech is "external, indicative of types, objective, remarks bounced across to strangers" (Jameson, 1983, 132). This is seen in the kind of emotional tone—"a kind of outgoing belligerence, or hostility, or the amusement of the native, or bantering, helpful indifference." This style was based on a "social schematism" of "fixed social types and categories" based on a shared "coherence and peculiar organization" of the time that disappeared after World War II (Jameson, 1983, 133).

The appeal of Chandler's books is nostalgia; they're camp; they're like "Humphrey Bogart movies, certain comic books, hard-boiled detective stories, and monster movies" (Jameson, 1983, 134). Pop art "is the principle [*sic*] contemporary manifestation of this nostalgic interest"; it has two levels: "a simplified outer expression" and "an inner period atmosphere which is its object" (Jameson, 1983, 134–135). It is a form of art with a content made up of "already formed ideological artifacts." Pop art chose the 1930s as the source of this nostalgia. The atmosphere of a given period is crystallized in its objects, but our nostalgia for the period is mediated through

"industrialism, market capitalism, mass production," while being somewhat simpler than the original representation (Jameson, 1983, 135). Part
of the fascination is simply to note the passage of time, to experience a
historicity. In this time products had stable identifiable signs, but after
World War II change is the order of the day. The "cause" of this constant
change is the diversification and wealth of production, as well as "the in-
creasing autonomy of advertising" (Jameson, 1983, 137). The life problems
created by this lived world are a struggle "not against things and relatively
solid systems of power, but against ideological fantasms, bits and pieces of
spiritualized matter" that leaves people "unable to find a footing in the
reality of things" (Jameson, 1983, 137–138). Chandler describes the artifacts from the outside, without any reference to their utility value.

As an image, Humphrey Bogart is related to Marlowe and coincides with
him in *The Big Sleep*. He is like the earlier Hemingway hero. "Thus, the
perception of the products with which the world around us is furnished
precedes our perception of things-in-themselves and forms it" (Jameson,
1983, 140). In the films of the period, the narrator's voice-over "works in
counterpoint to the things seen, heightening them subjectively . . . through
the poetry his comparisons lend them," after which his "deadpan humor
. . . disavows what it has just maintained" so that they recede into the
sordid reality (Jameson, 1983, 141). Novels have to work against this material to highlight it through individual reference. Chandler's novels have
two forms: "the rigid external structure of the detective story" and Chandler's unique personal "rhythms of events" (Jameson, 1983, 142). Chandler's formula is to invent "a principle for the construction of the plot
itself": Chandler would contrive a "reasonably honest and effective way of
fooling the reader" in a way that results in a form more spatial than temporal (Jameson, 1983, 143).[13] The novels are "descriptions of searches";
this places the detective outside of pure thought, propelled instead into a
sequence of social realities. This headlong plunge results in unexpected violence in which the detective is the catalyst "as though [murders and beat-
ings] already existed in a latent state" (Jameson, 1983, 144). But since these
matters are false scents, the characters are vivid because we will never see
them again. The events and situations, then, are not so much realistic as
legendary as if they were newspaper reports or anecdotes. This leads the
end of the novel back to the beginning; Chandler's novels tend to be variations on the idea that someone introduced at the beginning is involved in
the guilt.

But the novels have two centers: the murder and the search. These combine to form a complex gestalt in which the murder tends to leave us thinking the rest is furniture, while focusing on the search demystifies violent
death. In the classical story, everything is related to the central murder, but
in Chandler's novels "murder comes to seem moreover in its very essence
accidental and without meaning" (Jameson, 1983, 147). The crime is al-

ways old before the book begins. Then at the end when all that depressing dissolution sinks in, we are brought up short "without warning, against the reality of death itself" (Jameson, 1983, 148).

Jerry Palmer's influential *Thrillers* (1978) marks a different emphasis, in that he is concerned with the contemporary ideological implications of the texts of thriller (largely spy) fiction. Palmer argues that ideology in the form of the thriller is a "combination of mystery, in the form of criminal conspiracy, and competitive individualism" as these were reflected in British society in the nineteenth century (Palmer, 1979, 144). The fear by the middle and upper classes of a revolt by the lower against the conditions imposed upon them constitutes a significant condition for the popularity of thrillers. Competitive individualism necessary to the operation of capitalism fragmented populations, creating mistrust and fear among all classes. "The conspiracy that is the motor of the thriller is essentially an inner corruption, a canker, as we have seen: someone trusted is untrustworthy. No more striking incarnation of this reversal could be found than the treachery of one's lover. The association of sexuality and trust is derived from outside the thriller; again it is the commonplace definition of sexuality that allows the dominant procedure of the thriller to incorporate it into this new framework" (Palmer, 1979, 145). Thrillers assimilate elements from narratives that portray different worlds, such as the gothic, to new effects. Palmer draws on Vladimir Propp's concept of formula to argue that "the meaning of any individual function is given entirely by the matrix of the tale as a whole; in my version of the thriller meaning comes from both the context of the thriller and from outside it, from what it is time to call by its proper name: the field of ideology within which the text is situated" (Palmer, 1979, 148). The fear of conspiracy articulated the fear of political combination and widespread theft by the working class. Competitive individualism—the conception of the relationship between the individual and "his social surroundings" emerges through Thomas Hobbes and the social Darwinists and intensifies as the factory system emerges, since "insofar as skill is abandoned, labour becomes more competitive" (Palmer, 1979, 171). Eugène Sue developed this form of hero in the 1830s and 1840s, but the thriller needed a further impetus to emerge at the end of the nineteenth century: fear and conspiracy—the relationship between the legal order and illegalities. Palmer argues that in addition to economic developments there was a legal blurring in the nineteenth century of the distinctions between *mala in se* (things evil in themselves) and *mala prohibita* (evil merely prohibited)—between public and private wrongs—the middle and upper classes could better justify installing "systematic permanent surveillance of the working class" in response to what they saw as a "permanent threat" by midcentury (Palmer, 1979, 200). Parts of the thriller can be found in ideology, but the combination is unique; it can't be "directly rooted in any social process in the way that competitive individualism and the fear of conspiracy can" (Palmer, 1979, 202). But the presence and the specific combination of elements has an ideological basis. The hero represents the existing social order, so his antagonist must come from another, but since it doesn't, its source is "in, but not of" the social order, that is, the pathological—hence the mystery (Palmer, 1979, 203). The combination of the two justifies them: the hero's competitive individuality is justified by the conspiracy, and since the conspiracy is immediately met by heroic opposition, the conspiracy is a disruption of a known world. The specificity of the thriller grounds it in ideology: "the essence of ideology is not to give false answers to real problems, but to pose problems in such a (false) way that the recommendations one wished to make in the first place appear to correspond to a real problem" (Palmer, 1979, 204). Thus, grounded in ideological developments of the nineteenth century, the thriller mounts a claim for competitive individuality within the context of conspiratorial fear of the dangerous classes, but once it had coalesced, new fears of conspiracy could be adapted to its form as long as the symbiosis of its elements remained intact.

Stephen Knight's *Form and Ideology in Crime Fiction* (1981) provides chapters on Poe, *The Adventures of Sherlock Holmes*, Christie, Chandler, and Ed McBain in order to discover fissures revealing the ideological content of fiction. The book has been widely cited for its productive readings of crime fiction. Focusing on a few well-chosen works, Knight argues, has the advantage of "detailed, largely isolated treatment" to establish "implicit meaning" and to avoid implying a continuous history from work to work, insulated from society and history (Knight, 1980, 2). Sociology of literature approaches have emphasized "class, age, attitudes and finances" of authors and readers on the one hand, and textual analysis, as Knight's study does, on the other. Either without the other leads to somewhat tentative results, but it is necessary to make some speculations about audiences based on texts. Pierre Macherey and Roland Barthes treat texts as questions posed to console audiences while being expressions of the dominant ideology, so that selections and omissions of content can be determined by reference to plot. In this sense texts "create and justify" hegemony, but "form is crucial." Form also produces ideology through its system of epistemology and its ontology. Finally, Knight argues that "each work discussed here has a special formal way of presenting the world to us" that is embedded in its "overall structure," "textual language, the presentation of incidents, characters and motives" (Knight, 1980, 5). Lack of unity among these elements or their conflict reveals "strains or 'fissures' " that ideology works to repair and conceal. However content is important in its setting, crimes, criminals and detective's traits.

In his first chapter Knight discusses the formulation of society in relation to crime in *The Newgate Calendar* stories, Godwin's *Caleb Williams*, and Vidocq's *Memoirs*. Chapter 2 discusses Poe's "Murders in the Rue Morgue." Here Dupin "translates the mystifying into the lucid, a peculiarly attractive message for an audience valuing intellectualism yet fearful of and baffled by the complexities of real life" (Knight, 1980, 47), but by "The Mystery of Marie Rogêt" the weaknesses of the method were obvious, and with "The Purloined Letter" it became psychologized in the Lacanian theme of the subject emerging out of language. Doyle substituted a casual chain of events interpreted by a single mind for the often coincidental nature of the solutions offered by contemporary detective stories, while Christie became more suspicious of this narrative strategy and in her late work began to generalize detection, relying more on plotting. Both Doyle and Christie employed an "organic" structure that responds to bourgeois notions of personal effort applied through time leading to moral and physical improvement. Though on a much more modest scale, Raymond Chandler has "considerable sales," "reasonable wealth" (Knight, 1980, 138, 165) and the respect of a literary elite. He was at least as influenced by Erle Stanley Gardner as by Hammett and cannot be codified as merging Romance and Hammett's tough-guy tone, since he is selective about the elements of Romance and exchanges Hammett's objectivity for the disengaged and disgusted persona. *Farewell, My Lovely* is a "mixture of apparent modernism and actual romantic individualism," in which "the scene dominates the structure," as in Chandler's other work (Knight, 1980, 149). Chandler's episodic and often haphazard plots are not organic, but feature the virtues of a hero who is involved only negatively in casual social interaction. Police procedurals have "a more realistic base" (Knight, 1980, 167), with McBain's employing documents (not used as clues) and a duality of moralism and an "objectified urban world-view" (Knight, 1980, 177). This latter is so oppressive that fiction rejects it as a master code and falsifies it with the "image of humane individualism" that is also produced by bourgeois capitalism (Knight, 1980, 177). The result is that the appalling conditions of slums and other urban conditions are acausal. Police procedurals have a consumerist objectification that is set up to be controlled subjectively.

Bethany Ogdon's "Hard-boiled Ideology" (1992) compares the "realistic" description in Chandler, John D. MacDonald, Charles Willeford, Elmore Leonard, Robert B. Parker, and Andrew Vachss to German interwar *Freikorps* literature, particularly in the description of women, people from the lower classes, and immigrants. The fiction creates a subject position in which the contrast between self and other places the reader "comfortably within the dominating 'norm' " (Ogdon, 1992, 84). In contrast to Jameson's fiction without an ideology, Ogdon's view is that hard-boiled fiction is based on "a pre-existing colluding perspective" (Ogdon, 1992, 84).

Ernest Mandel's *Delightful Murder: A Social History of the Crime Story* (1984) traces the origins of the detective story to the bandit story of medieval times. While the bandit story expressed a populist revolt against the feudal order rather than a bourgeois revolt, the tradition of social protest and rebellion against tyranny was incorporated even into aristocratic literature. The middle class was represented by Miguel de Cervantes, Henry Fielding, Daniel Defoe, Friedrich von Schiller, Lord Byron, and Percy Bysshe Shelley, but at the same time a literary activity of much wider appeal arose: broadsheets were read and sold at markets; the famous *Images d'Epanel* emerged; popular chronicles like the *Newgate Calendar* appeared; and melodramas were formulated. These differ from bandit stories in that they reflect a precapitalist society based on petty commodity production. Ideology is still semifeudal, with the unspoken model being an integrated Christian society in which, as Knight (1980) has pointed out, wrongdoers are outcasts who refuse to do honest labor in an honest community; they could be redeemed if they embraced fundamental Christian values.

At the end of the eighteenth century, the traditional Newgate stories were beginning to deviate from the rules, and by the nineteenth century many of the most popular melodramas were concerned with crime. The poverty of displacement was everywhere. Balzac estimated that during the Restoration about 10 percent of the population were criminals who faced a military garrison of about the same size. Professional criminals emerge with the rise of capitalism and its consequent unemployment. De Quincey's "On Murder Considered as One of the Fine Arts" appeared in 1827, with a postscript in 1854; De Quincey insisted on deletation with murder in speculation about whodunit among amateurs and dilettantes. He had been editor of the *Westmoreland Gazette* in 1818 and 1819 and had filled his columns with commentary about murders and murder trials. Mandel says he paved the way for Poe. Honoré de Balzac, Victor Hugo, Dickens, Alexandre Dumas, and even Feodor Dostoevsky were moved by genuine social concerns and ideological motives, but murder topics were also financially very lucrative.

Mandel argues that it is important to understand that this popular form of literature did not stop at the transitional phase with the transformation of the noble bandit into the evil criminal. Klaus Inderthal, German literary historian, says popular literature functions as a distraction, that it is necessary because of the growing anxiety, monotony, and standardization of labor and consumption in bourgeois society. Second, the form speaks to a distinction between biological impulses and social constraints that bourgeois society has not solved. These conditions are manifest in feelings of boredom and anxiety, which are contradictory, leading to Walter Benjamin's remark that a traveler reading a detective story on a train is temporarily suppressing one anxiety with another. A story expresses a basic conflict between individual impulses and social restraint, but because that individualization is criminalized, the weight of the story is on the side of social restraint. At a particular time in the development of capitalism, pauperism, criminality, and primitive social revolt coalesced against bourgeois society. Marx noted that the criminal produces criminal law as well as crimes. The criminal renders a service to society, according to Mandel, by arousing the moral and aesthetic feelings of the public. This makes the monotony of the everyday security of bourgeois life tolerable and keeps it from stagnating; the production of the image of criminality "gives rise to an uneasy tension and agility without which even the spur of competition would be blunted" (Mandel, 1985, 11). It actually stimulates productive forces.

After World War I, Western petit bourgeois were "consumed by nostalgia" (Mandel, 1985, 30). Classic stories are characterized by extremely formalized and conventionalized plots, a unity of time, place, and action, and a small number of characters who often remain throughout the investigation. The criminal is a single individual, often marked by a simple motive (greed—most often—revenge, jealousy, or frustrated love or hatred), who is unmasked by the detective. The puzzle story is "intended to satisfy subjective needs, thus performing an objective function: to reconcile the upset, bored and anxious individual member of the middle class with the inevitability and permanence of bourgeois society" (Mandel, 1985, 29). During the 1920s and 1930s the syndicate marked the coming of age of modern crime in bourgeois society, which led to the decline of the classical story; mass consciousness of crime would pave the way to this awareness with interest in the pulp magazines in the 1920s. Chandler is an outgrowth of this tradition, but his ideological slant "is only the *local*, never the national, power structure," which is also the case with John D. MacDonald's novels (Mandel, 1985, 36).

Since accidental death has replaced other forms of dying in bourgeois society, the crime story draws on this particular fear: "Obsession with death seen as an accident leads to obsession with violent death, and hence to obsession with murder, with crime" (Mandel, 1985, 41). This leads to the polarization of good and bad, which is also depersonalized, resulting in a battle of wits rather than a battle of wills or passions. The pattern is similar to that of the marketplace. Bourgeois rationalism contains the irrational, and this becomes more irrational over time. "That is why the detective story, while placing analytical intelligence and scientific clue-gathering at the heart of crime detection, often resorts to blind passions, crazy plots, and references to magic, if not clinical madness, in order to 'explain' why criminals commit crimes" (Mandel, 1985, 43).[14] Development of the classic novel in England and the United States is tied to the lack of social rebellion in the nineteenth century, so that "it was natural for [the ruling class] to assimilate revolt against the social order into criminal activity, to identify the rebellious proletariat with the 'criminal classes' (an expression that crops up repeatedly in popular Anglo-Saxon detective stories)" (Mandel, 1985, 44). The law enforcement establishment grew enormously during the 1930s, a trend reflected in the growth of the policeman in place of the private detective in the late 1930s and early 1940s with the appearance of such transitional figures as Charlie Chan, Inspector

Maigret, and Ellery Queen. This shift was the result of a change in bourgeois values reflected in the fiction in which police came to be seen as good.

Real massification of the detective novel occurred with the paperback revolution triggered by Penguin Books. The change in sales from the 1930s through the 1950s seems to be based on social pressures, with a shift from "actually practised violence in favour of vicariously experienced violence" (Mandel, 1985, 68). Detective and mystery novels, then, provide an "[o]pium of the 'new' middle classes" in that the novels "realize distraction in a purely passive way, without any effort or sacrifice," and "titillate the nerves in a particular, deliciously naughty way" (Mandel, 1985, 70–71). "Craved security" is accompanied by "a vicarious insecurity," Mandel argues, citing Leo Kofler and Dr. Edmund Bergler. Finally, following Ernst Bloch and Bertolt Brecht, Mandel argues that capitalist society operates as a mystery: " 'History is written *after* catastrophes.' This basic situation, in which intellectuals feel that they are objects and not subjects of history, moulds the thought which they can display for enjoyment in the crime story" (Mandel, 1985, 73). The "decline of pure intellect" reflects the decline of bourgeois rationalism and confidence in capitalist economics' Rational Man. Monopoly capitalism produces an ideology that lags about two generations behind reality, so the emergence of monopoly capitalism in 1885–90 led to the emergence of the thriller and the pure suspense novel, in which "either the murderer, or the victim, but in any case not the detective, is the real hero" in the 1930s (Mandel, 1985, 87). The first includes those produced by Patricia Highsmith, such as *Strangers on a Train* (1949) and *The Talented Mr. Ripley* (1955), while the second includes novels by William Irish, including *The Phantom Lady* (1942) and *The Black Angel* (1943) and many others.

MULTICULTURAL CRITICISM

Patricia Craig and Mary Cadogan's *The Lady Investigates: Women Detectives and Spies in Fiction* (1981) provides a history and detailed survey of women detectives in England and the United States from 1861, with the publication of Mrs. Paschal's [W. S. Hayward] *The Revelations of a Lady Detective* in England, through the date of publication. Women enter into detective fiction because of "novelty," dramatic effect, to justify unorthodox investigative strategies, the fanciful possibilities, to add whimsy or comic effects, and because "nosiness . . . is often considered a feminine trait" (Craig and Cadogan, 1981, 13). Also included are wives and helpers, and some spies. Chapter 1 is devoted to English novels, with the second chapter covering the U.S. period from *The Leavenworth Case* through Hugh C. Weir's *Miss Madelyn Mack, Detective* (1914) (whose device of the "confidante narrator" the authors attribute to Doyle) through the 1920s; U.S. detectives were young, while the English were more likely old.

The chapter on spies (largely British) discusses how writers negotiated the narrative's need for action and suspense, the figure's promiscuity (often based on legendary persons such as Mata Hari), and publishing constraints. Wives such as Nora Charles were complements to their detective husbands. The discussion of professional detectives from the 1920s through the 1960s includes Erle Stanley Gardner's (writing as A. A. Fair) Bertha Cool and Mignon Eberhart's Sarah Keate among others. Teen detectives such as Nancy Drew and Judy Bolton are archetypal because of their "productive eccentricity and independence," which emerge at just the time when optimism about women's independence and capabilities surge; other glamour detectives such as Cherry Ames, Vicki Barr, Connie Blair, and Beverley Gray lack substance (Craig and Cadogan, 1981, 163). Women detectives embody "the power of action and practical intelligence" denied women in the past, although even these figures have not altered the conservatism of the genre (Craig and Cadogan, 1981, 246, 232).

Kathleen Gregory Klein, in *The Woman Detective: Gender & Genre* (1988), is interested in how women authors' gender affects genre and representation "in order to reinforce a nostalgic mythology of women's position" (Klein, 1995, 2) and to discover whether women are able to affect the restraints of formula and conventional portrayals of women. This concern is worked into a framework of social and literary history. The women detectives are compared with the three models identified with Sherlock Holmes, Sam Spade, and figures such as Robert B. Parker's Spenser, who represents contemporary variations of the hard-boiled detective. Covering over seventy detectives, Klein distinguishes between white middle-class women's characteristics and characteristics of the detectives. Klein argues that the scripts of woman and detective are in conflict throughout most fiction from 1854 to the present. Moreover, the figures seem to fail as woman or detective because of the inherent reactionary values of authors and readers. It is only in the 1970s that some progress is made in "challenging the sexist boundaries" of the fiction (Klein, 1995, 5). Klein's focus is on "the paid, professional woman detective who is the protagonist," unlike Michele Slung's *Crime on Her Mind* and Craig and Cadogan's *The Lady Investigates*. The amateur in her view lacks credentials and police are tied to bureaucracy. The study does not rely on reviews because detective novels are often ignored by the mainstream press, and fans are against revealing solutions. Klein includes chapters on British author Andrew Forrester's *The Female Detective* (1864), the U.S. dime novel, the British turn-of-the-century "lady detective," her U.S. counterpart, the Golden Age, hard-boiled detectives 1928–63, detectives from 1972–84, contemporary variations, and partnerships.

Frankie Y. Bailey's *Out of the Woodpile: Black Characters in Crime and Detective Fiction* (1991) discusses an extensive range of imagery of African Americans in crime fiction. Bailey's book is a "sociohistorical study of the evolution of black detectives and other black characters" in crime fiction. The book also contains the views of fourteen writers and "a selective directory of relevant works of fiction, film, and television" (Bailey, 1991, xii). Bailey argues that the presence and portrayal of black characters have been shaped by two generic stereotypes, "1) the plantation slave/rural sharecropper and 2) the urban slum dweller," and that counterimages also derive from these basic stereotypes. Stereotypes and "crime scripts" about victim and offender affect "their encounter with the criminal justice system" and are perpetuated in mass media and popular literature. Bailey draws on Dan Nimmo and James E. Combs's (1980) account of cultural myth as the mediation or "representation of perceived realities that people accept as permanent fixed knowledge of reality."[15] Race mythologies are part of the larger Euro-American mythology that perceived "indigenous and other immigrant populations—'Indians,' blacks, Mexicans, and later Chinese,—as the 'shape of the Devil.' " The "manifest destiny" of the Europeans and their Christian fervor led them to solidify two themes—"the savagery and sexuality of non-whites" that were perceived to be inferior to Europeans. Since the "hero or heroine must be able to probe into the lives of the people involved in the criminal event . . . psychological and physical boundaries" prevented African American access (Bailey, 1991, xii). In spite of these conditions, black detectives did eventually begin to appear.

Bailey shows that Poe (1809–49) supported slavery in his work. In Mark Twain's (1835–1910) *The Tragedy of Pudd'nhead Wilson* (1894), an investigation leads to Roxanna, a mulatto woman. In the popular literature of the nineteenth century, mulattoes were portrayed as conflicted and unhappy. Compare James Fenimore Cooper's Cora Munro, a mixed-blood the author kills off when she is torn between choosing between an Indian and white soldier. Leslie Fiedler in *Love and Death in the American Novel* (1960) talks of a "Dark Lady," who is "typically Catholic or Jew, Latin or Oriental or Negro" (Bailey, 1991, 7). Twain's Roxanna substitutes her son for the "white" baby, leading to his emergence as a scoundrel, and the "white" Chambers becomes miserable as a white after shuffling around as a slave all his life. Twain leaves the nature/nurture question open in Tom's case. In an unfinished story, "Which Way Was It?" (1902), Jasper, a free mulatto who was cheated after purchasing his freedom from his father and was further cheated, seeks revenge and becomes angry and dangerous. This literary heritage was incorporated into crime fiction. Writers such as Melville Davisson Post may have allowed black characters some dignity, but they remained servants. In *Too Many Cooks* (1938) Rex Stout has Nero Wolfe give a lecture on justice and the social contract that persuades a black waiter to tell what he saw—a white man in blackface. Bailey identifies Rudolph Fisher's *The Conjure Man Dies* (1932) as "the first classic detective novel set in an urban black community and featuring black protagonists" (Bailey, 1991, 54). Fisher's book was well received by major reviewers.

Richard Wright's *Native Son* (1940) adapted the Nixon and Hicks case, which occurred as Wright was working on the novel, from Chicago news stories. Bailey notes that Chester Himes's series of nine novels beginning with *A Rage in Harlem* (1957) were written in France, where Himes was living after encountering racism in the United States. The novels are set in Harlem, although Himes spent little time there. The novels feature Grave-digger Jones and Coffin Ed Johnson and focus on the intensity of violence. There are three generations of black police officers: (1) postwar "pride of their race" characters; (2) Civil Rights–era characters led by Virgil Tibbs who demanded recognition as professionals; (3) 1970s and 1980s cops, who still deal with race issues but are concerned with the breakdown of social control. African Americans in post–World War II fiction still tended to be represented as servants, but they "showed signs of autonomy," and the servant role was sometimes an entry into sleuthing (Bailey, 1991, 87).

The emergence of a black elite is represented in some postwar novels, such as Bart Spicer's *Blues for the Prince* (1950) and Dorothy Hughes's *The Expendable Man* (1963). In Rex Stout's *A Right to Die* (1964) a black man who aided Nero Wolfe in *Too Many Cooks* (1938) is now a middle-aged professor of anthropology whose son is involved with a white upper-class woman about whom he has reservations. The woman is killed. Emma Lathen's *Death Shall Overcome* (1966) sees black Ed Parry proposed for a seat on the stock exchange. The novel satirizes black civil rights activists and white liberals. Blacks jeopardize middle-class status because they are unwilling or unable to adapt to rules of the dominant culture. George Baxt's *A Queer Kind of Death* (1966) features Pharoah Love, a black gay detective who investigates a murder in the New York City gay scene. In Joseph Hansen's *Stranger to Himself* (1968) a black playwright named Steve Archer becomes a suspect when his partner Coy Randol is murdered. Joe L. Hensley, a trial judge, wrote *The Color of Hate* (1960) about the trial of a black man for murder and rape in a small Southern town. Hensley then revised and republished the novel as *Color Him Guilty* in 1987 in order to update the perspective. Hensley has published other novels with a similar theme. Such novels do not really attempt to portray the black urban experience, which is better dealt with in more recent novels. None deal with the hope/despair cycle for blacks in cities in which African Americans migrating out of the South were trapped in ghettos for generations. Black male writers have not always created favorable women characters, repro-ducing stereotypes "along a continuum from nurturing Earth Mothers to mean and bitter bitches." Black women, according to the stereotypes, are "constantly 'in heat' " or they function as "natural servants" (Bailey, 1991, 102).

Often cited as having a double advantage, Bailey says, black women actually have a double problem. In crime fiction they rarely appear in continuing roles, except at times as partners. Lesley Grant-Adamson (Br) portrays Holly Chase as an assistant to Rain Morgan, a newspaper columnist, and women can traditionally be secretaries for private eyes. Women can occasionally be investigators. Dolores Komo's *Clio Browne: Private Investigator* (1988) features "the first private investigator in St. Louis" (Bailey, 1991, 111). Susan Moody's *Penny Post* (1985) features British Penny Wanawake (black, six feet tall, daughter of an African diplomat), whose exploits continue in *Penny Royal* (1987) and *Penny Wise* (1989). More often women are exotics, as in Maurice Proctor's *The Spearhead of Death* (1960), or revolutionaries and terrorists, as in Tim Heald's *Blue Blood Will Out* (1974), Patricia Moyes's *The Coconut Killings* (1977), and John Wyllie's *Death Is a Dream . . . Beating Forever* (1977). A variation is black women as prostitutes, and like white prostitutes they are usually either redeemable or lost.

Stereotypes such as Mammy (nurturing and fierce in turn), Uncle Tom (deferential, bowing, scraping before whites), and Sambo (comic and ignorant) became archetypes in the course of American popular literature. However, it should not be assumed that what appears to be obvious stereotyping is such—the "environment, personality, and situation" need to be considered as well. Utterances from villains or fools differ from the same words attributed to positive characters; all speech occurs in context. Writers who deal in complexity handle race best: "they are not always 'card carrying liberals.' " What is needed is "a cross-section of characters" (Bailey, 1991, 118). The promising signs are that "white characters (and by implication their creators) are much less sure of themselves than in the past." There are "more positive images of blacks" than in the past, but "black character 'types' still predominate. Badmen, prostitutes, pimps, addicts, and street people are still more common than black housewives, pharmacists, factory workers, waitresses, and computer programmers." This is partly because the genre-detectives come across as more lowlife and criminal, but "the fact that they do ignore these other aspects of black life is indicative of the status of blacks in American life." Charles W. Chesnutt noted in a symposium that "a Pullman porter who performs wonderful feats in the detection of crime has great possibilities" (Bailey, 1991, 119). In 1926 the NAACP journal, *The Crisis*, solicited questions about black characters from seven well-known writers. Bailey's Symposium on Writers' Views on Creating Black Characters provides perspectives on the difficulties of representation. Comments are provided by Gar Anthony Haywood, Dolores Komo, Michael Avallone, Kenn Davis, Percy Spurlark Parker, Robert B. Parker, Margaret Maron, Sara Paretsky, Nancy Pickard, Joseph Hansen, Susan Moody, Michael Jahn, and Les Roberts.

Joe Weixlmann's "Culture Clash, Survival, and Trans-Formation: A

Study of Some Innovative Afro-American Novels of Detection" (1984–85), shows that recent attempts to reshape the Afro-American novel away from realism and naturalism have encountered W.E.B. Du Bois's problem of double-consciousness.[16] Most have moved toward surrealism and the appropriation of popular culture, especially detective fiction. Weixlmann discusses Ishmael Reed's *Mumbo Jumbo* (1972), Toni Morrison's *Song of Solomon* (1977), and Clarence Major's *Reflex and Bone Structure* (1975). The novelists "have tricked" the detective novel through parody and irony to bear black messages. Morrison refuses closure, and Major suggests that fiction should not attempt to "capture life's realities in an undistorted, mirror-image manner" (Bailey, 1991, 30).

Helen Lock's *A Case of Mis-Taken Identity: Detective Undercurrents in Recent African American Fiction* (1994) begins with the observation that many African-American stories center on mystery, often involving a crime such as murder, but diverge from the conventions of the European-American detective narrative. Rather than having affinities with the story of Oedipus, these stories were more likely to be structured along the lines of the Osiris tale in which "the protagonist in whom truth is located is here the victim of the crime; the reconstruction is of the victim himself, through a communal effort that enables him to activate his own power and regenerate himself" (Lock, 1994, xiii). This narrative strategy opens up the mystery story to numerous possibilities, which are exploited by such writers as Ishmael Reed, Toni Morrison, and Ralph Ellison.

Stephen F. Soitos's *The Blues Detective: A Study of African American Detective Fiction* (1996) takes its title from Houston Baker, Jr.'s, remark that the study of African-American literature should seek "the historical, mythic, or blues force of the narrative" (Soitos, 1996, 9). The study examines narrative strategies of African-American writers playing on an essentially European-American form. Like Lock's, the approach is refreshing in its use of theory growing out of African-American literary and critical traditions, particularly that growing out of Ralph Ellison's *Shadow and Act* (1964). Soitos argues that African-American writers do make a difference in their uses of the formulas, reinventing them and reconstructing their value structures. The effects can be seen in four "figures of thought"—the detective persona, double-consciousness, black vernaculars, and hoodoo—along with black nationalism and "race pride." These operate to subvert mainstream ideology and contribute to the view that African-American culture is distinct from the dominant Eurocentric American culture. Soitos provides close readings of Pauline Hopkins's *Hagar's Daughter*, J. E. Bruce's *Black Sleuth*, Rudolph Fisher's *Conjure Man Dies*, Chester Himes's Harlem detective novels and short stories, Ishmael Reed's *Mumbo Jumbo*, and Clarence Major's *Reflex and Bone Structure*. The first chapter provides background and sketches an ideological perspective in the detective formula, and the second elaborates the four tropes Soitos sees as central to the analysis of narrative. Chapter 3 deals largely with Hopkins and Bruce, with the following chapters devoted to the contributions of Fisher and the Harlem Renaissance, Chester Himes, Ishmael Reed, and Clarence Major.

INFORMATION THEORY

James Guetti's "Aggressive Reading: Detective Fiction and Realistic Narrative" (1982) argues that Hammett uses "itemization" to accumulate detail that information theory suggests is "proportional to the 'resistance' of that situation" that readers want to homogenize (Guetti, 1982, 134). This activity is akin to that of the detective's work. The reader's growing tension is denied release in Hammett's fiction precisely as it is accommodated in Spillane's, where violence releases tension. The strangeness of *The Maltese Falcon* results from the details being "laid out in pieces," forcing the reader to read the text "aggressively, as a puzzle to be solved, whose pieces are its clues" (Guetti, 1982, 137). Chandler also uses this strategy, and Ross Macdonald adds empathy that forces Lew Archer into "the borders of a psychological and emotional hell" (Guetti, 1982, 143). Thomas Pynchon's *V* (1963) and Theodore Weesner's *The Car Thief* (1972) use similar strategies, with Weesner's novel accumulating detail but failing to do more. *V* decomposes solutions as well as assumptions readers may have about reading. Assertive reading is appropriate to some kinds of texts but not others; realistic fiction, for example, motivates aggressive reading but rarely provides "some ultimate solution or significance" (Guetti, 1982, 153). To assume that the reader should occupy the position of an aggressive reader is to narrow the experience of literature.

BRITISH CULTURAL STUDIES

Michel Foucault's suggestive remarks about the institutional context of crime discourses are elaborated in Dennis Porter's *The Pursuit of Crime* (1981). Porter would agree with Palmer that popular narratives reflect the anxieties of the time but finds in detective fiction a somewhat more complex matrix of ideological play among various schools and writers. Porter draws on Pierre Macherey, particularly for the notion of the transparency of texts, that is, that the texts of popular genres utilize rhetorical conventions that are "familiar to the point of transparency" so that they adapt themselves "easily to the changing objects of popular anxiety" (Porter, 1981, 115, 127). For example, Agatha Christie's *Mysterious Affair at Styles* (1920) and Dashiell Hammett's *Red Harvest* (1929) reflect different class assumptions through the stylistic devices used.

Jon Thompson's *Fiction, Crime and Empire: Clues to Modernity and Postmodernism* (1993) covers both British and American detective fiction, with emphasis on British. My discussion will focus primarily on the theoretical perspective and coverage of American materials. The study illustrates one approach possible through British cultural studies, which draws to some extent on Marxist thought, primarily through the work of Raymond Williams, though it is much more wide-ranging and intellectually imaginative than orthodox Marxism allows. For Thompson, " 'crime fiction' is used to denote all the genres and subgenres that concern themselves with violation and the law, whether or not this violation actually took place, and whether or not this violation is sanctioned by the novelist" (Thompson, 1993, 3). He points out that the notion that detective fiction is escapist is a cliché that ignores the fact that detective fiction "dramatizes the contradictory experience of modernity," so it is "not escapist but hermeneutic; it explores what it means to be caught up in the maelstrom of modernity" (Thompson, 1993, 8). The study is neither comprehensive nor a literary history of crime fiction but is intended as an intervention in contemporary literary debates in which crime fiction opens on three issues: (1) the reconsideration of realism, modernism, and postmodernism; (2) "articulation of the relationships between fiction and the dominant ideological values" of empire (first half of nineteenth through second half of twentieth century); and (3) "exploration of the possibilities and limitations of fiction itself as a type of social praxis" (Thompson, 1993, 8).

So Thompson draws mainly on Raymond Williams, Mikhail Bakhtin, Antonio Gramsci, and poststructuralist thinking, with a general indebtedness to Foucault. Chapter 2 employs poststructuralist theory, and chapter 8 provides a critique of it. Thompson's larger project is to "develop a historical poetics of fiction" that will help explain how "culture practices, such as crime fiction interacts with what Gramsci calls hegemonic values." Thompson sees hegemony as "one of the crucial arenas for the resistance, acceptance, or incorporation of hegemonic values," a position that allows ideology to be understood as "impure" (Thompson, 1993, 6).

Modernism is taken to be "the *institutionally* and culturally dominant field of literary practices" (Thompson, 1993, 9), which includes residual realist elements as well as emergent postmodern elements; so what Thompson examines is a "porously modernist" textual field. Analysis begins late in Marshall Berman's period of modernity during the emergence of mass culture; in the United States this was during the early nineteenth century with the emergence of mass circulation magazines, while in England it occurred during the last half of the nineteenth century.[17] Chapter 3 deals with Conan Doyle's detective fiction with respect to imperialism and mass culture, chapters 4 and 5 deal with the emerging spy novel; *Kim* valorizes empire while Conrad's *The Secret Agent* (1907) is more critical in reflecting back on English society. The second moment of modernity (high modernism after World War I) is dealt with in chapter 1; it is a "response to the experience of the metropolis" (Thompson, 1993, 9); the chapter looks at ways critics have tried to define it by distancing it from popular culture;

the discussion prepares for the broader theory of modernism in chapter 6 ("structural, conventional, and epistemological similarities between modernism and detective fiction" [Thompson, 1993, 9]). Chapter 7 analyzes the hard-boiled school and formal English novel of detection.

Poe is appreciated for his formal accomplishments in establishing genres and subgenres (locked room, "armchair detection" in "The Mystery of Marie Rogêt" and code story in "The Gold Bug"), but this implicitly distances them from the historical conditions in which they "embody a specific vision of knowledge structurally similar but ultimately antithetical to the dominant mode of knowledge," a condition that is embodied in subsequent detective fiction. In practical terms this means that the nineteenth-century culture of knowledge was part of the disciplinary society Foucault identified and is implicated in Poe's detective fiction. For example, the figure of the omniscient Dupin "is comparable to that of a panopticon" (Thompson, 1993, 44). This is a shift from the omniscient narrator of the classic realist novel and also incorporates a structural shift in that the sidekick becomes the narrator. Poe's story, then, articulates Foucault's notion of a "desire for a complete form of knowledge" that "changes with the transformations of the genre" (Thompson, 1993, 45). Poe's stories reject empiricism as democratic and establish a rationalism associated with the aristocracy. While Poe was dominated by a society with values different from his, Dupin dominates by virtue of his aristocratic title as well as his intellect.

Thompson draws on Fredric Jameson's notion of repression to discuss Poe's detective fiction in the sense that it evokes fantasy from formal structures that control them. What "is incompletely repressed is the 'unrealizable' desire to be rid of society as an affective experience." This is a "reversal of the conventions of the classical realist novel" (Thompson, 1993, 50) such as *Madame Bovary, Middlemarch*, and *Sons and Lovers*. Dupin dominates society rather than society dominating him, unlike Poe's own experience. Experience and emotion become abstract, a state that is continued in Sayers, Marjorie Allingham, and Christie, where the power of knowledge is associated with a "lack of interest in the interaction between the individual and society" (Thompson, 1993, 51). In Poe's horror stories there is tension between reason (or intellect) and feeling, which reflects the attempt in the nineteenth century to synthesize them. Victorian literature finally sees "ratiocinative genius . . . as sterile and lifeless" as in Dickens's Gradgrind and George Eliot's Cassaubon. Poe avoided realism because it would entail "social disruption" and adopted a "protomodernism that constantly refers back to the enlarged consciousness of the alienated individual in which external reality is dissolved into intensified or even hyperactive mental states" (Thompson, 1993, 53). Furthermore, there is a tension between Poe's patrician tastes and the newly emerging middle-class audience and volatile publishing conditions that included centralized urban publishing centers, a disparate national audience, a volatile market, and scarce venture capital. Publishers relied mainly on reprints of English authors and classics that were royalty free. Poe did not gain a large audience, but the conditions of the literary marketplace are reflected in the exchange of a check for the letter in "Purloined Letter." Poe's gothic tastes were of a previous generation, rather than the "love-adventure-sentiment" fiction of the 1840s. Dupin's aristocratic character and the representation of Parisian society articulates a "class-based" perception of superiority. This legacy persists in the "analysis of manners" found in the work of Sayers, Christie, Allingham, and Ngaio Marsh, but the form is also rich enough to be reworked by such diverse writers as Hammett, Chandler, and Ross Macdonald.

Conan Doyle developed the conditions for the Holmes myth between *A Study in Scarlet* (1888) and *Strand Magazine* stories from July 1891 to June 1892 which gives Holmes greater stature than his author. The stories doubled the magazine's circulation (200,000–400,000). Doyle articulated a realistic style of "vivid, precise detail" that, among other things, "largely" created the "image of a timeless, fog-shrouded London." The success of the enterprise was based on "formal innovation and ideological statement" (Thompson, 1993, 62). The background of popular interest in crime was largely created as a result of the press coverage of two 1861 murders—the "Northumberland Street affair" and the Vidil case, which resulted in public speculation about guilt and innocence and shifted fictional focus from the fantastic (gothic) to the familiar; sensational literature moved from penny papers to the "respectable classes." Doyle's detective fiction incorporates the sensation story, the detective story, and the adventure story. Sensation → "terror, horror, or surprise"; detection → "ratiocinative element"; adventure → "fast-paced action" (Thompson, 1993, 65). Doyle yoked "popular elements from lower-class culture to middle-class empiricism. The "formal structure of these texts articulates an adherence to a particular ideology of empiricism" (Thompson, 1993, 66). Thompson says that Holmes is the "quintessential empiricist" in that "social and emotive characteristics" are reduced to puzzle pieces; Holmes does not lack compassion, but he does not show interest in social problems. Doyle's fiction is representative of the narrowing of social vision of late Victorian authors (1880s–1890s) who had to eliminate rising aspirations of women, class tensions, and imperialist experience. Doyle does, however, bridge the class gap by failing to make detective fiction "an ugly social problem; it is a world in which urban squalor makes a quaint contrast to the elegance of London hansom cabs and gas street lamps" (Thompson, 1993, 77).

RATIONALISM

In his "The Detective Novel and Scientific Method" (1982) Joseph Agassi explains the relationship between detective fiction and science practices to suggest that they share an "ambivalence about the nature of reason," an ambivalence that is "both the source and the dynamics of the tension in the problem-solving novel" (Agassi, 1982, 107).

J. Kenneth Van Dover's *You Know My Method: The Science of the Detective* (1994) argues that "identifying with the detective helps salve the anxieties of readers troubled by the changes—ideological and physical— caused by the triumph of the scientific method in the nineteenth century" (Van Dover, 1994, iii). Chapters feature Poe, Gaboriau, Allan Pinkerton, Anna Katharine Green, Doyle, Arthur Morrison, Jacques Futrelle, Gaston Leroux, R. Austin Freeman, and Arthur Reeve. Van Dover's thesis is not new, but the chapters contain detailed discussions of many authors not often considered elsewhere.

DISCOURSE THEORY

In literary studies poststructuralism has included examining the exclusion of categories of texts and writers from classrooms and research projects. As a result, the concern with how and why genres remained popular over long periods of time and with diverse audiences has become of greater interest. While previous perspectives had attempted to make cultural connections for the detective and mystery novel largely through myth and allegory, from the 1970s these were supplemented by studies that brought in political and discursive dimensions. Foucault's work on discourses, particularly his *Discipline and Punish* (1975), stimulated analytical strategies that competed with more traditional forms of literary investigation that privileged myth, economic determinism, and other means of establishing relations between literature and culture.

Foucault argued that prior to penal reform crime stories were about the exploits of criminals. Published in broadsides and pamphlets, such stories portrayed criminals as heroes of the people, but when reform was instituted, public executions were abolished and the public was distanced from the process of investigation, apprehension, trial and punishment, so that attention was focussed on the state and its anti-crime practices. This development led to a competing hero representing the state, and the fiction became a game of wits between the criminal and this representative figure. Foucault argued that crime stories "moved from the exposition of the facts or the confession to the slow process of discovery; from the execution to the investigation; from the physical confrontation to the intellectual struggle between criminal and investigator" (Foucault, 1979, 69). The result of the shift to mildness, of this concealing of the brutal reprisal of the state, was the emergence of constant state surveillance in the form of organized police.

Martin A. Kayman's *From Bow Street to Baker Street* (1992) finds detective novels to be historical and rhetorical texts that have social significance. The approach "account[s] for the formal and functional continuities" of "narrative discourses" found in literature and science as well as "forensic, diagnostic, theoretical and critical discourses." Kayman emphasizes nineteenth-century detective and mystery fiction and the monstrous. Popular fiction was displaced by realism, then by modernism, both of which claimed greater truth and art. Detective fiction was also derided for its valorization of science. Finally, it is often attacked "for being the slave of a legalistic, policial mentality," but the fiction actually takes a critical stance.

So detective fiction stands in relation to the institutional discourses of religion, science, and law. Along with the secularization of science, the "rise of Law is perhaps the most important single aspect of the secularization of mystery." As the codings of medicine and psychology displace religious codes in defining humans, "the social and ethical subject becomes rewritten by modern Law as the privileged paradigm for the achievement of secular justice and truth." Detective and other popular fiction, however, deal with "natural, social and psychological pathologies" that constitute, "like the genres which narrate it, a field constructed by exclusion" (Kayman, 1992, 8–9). The Others are described as outside "normal" human behavior, which "justifies control [of] the poor, the unemployed, the migrant, the factory worker, the criminal, the insane, the sick, the female, the juvenile, and the savage." Victorian rationality, then, comes at the "price of social and personal repression," which produces a formulated "underworld" of horror and detection (Kayman, 1992, 9). The genres of detection and horror, then, are best understood against the horizon of narrative strategies of realism, law, and science.

Kayman deals mainly with the forty years from Dupin to Holmes during a time of "fragmentation, conflict and coherence of codes" (Kayman, 1992, 17)." He is attentive to law and medicine, with their conflicts and relation to narrative fiction as well as the rivalry between "the novel and the so-called 'sub-genres' " (Kayman, 1992, 17). Kayman's book deals first with the replacement of a "providential narrative order by the development of a model of mastery by 'police,' " in which the detective inherits a failed "Reform model of management" (Kayman, 1992, 17). It then traces the history of detective literature and popular literature, which directly celebrated the rise of the police detective, then looks at mysteries that revenge themselves on police—"the monstrous beings, women and secrets of horror and sensation fiction" (Kayman, 1992, 17–18). The book concludes by arguing that Holmes does not so much culminate a tradition and serve as a model for Freud as invent a new tradition.

Poe's influence, in Kayman's view, is through his introduction of the monster into the realist model. Kayman argues that since the victims in "Murders in the Rue Morgue" were killed by an animal, there is no murder, strictly speaking, and no motive. Dupin's methodology, therefore, is "designed to deal with precisely that which disrupts the surface of realism;

the extra-ordinary. Hobbes's *Leviathan* is a predecessor to crime fiction because it postulates a condition where society "itself is presented as intrinsically monstrous." The monster violates Fielding's "rules of possibility and probability in fiction," which signifies a threat to "legal, scientific and literary" validity (Kayman, 1992, 142). The superiority of Dupin's method is that it is based on difference. Dupin's clues are deviations from the ordinary; they are "seemingly irrelevant" (Kayman, 1992, 166). In such areas as police, law, and journalism "the paradigm of the 'ordinary' " is in symmetry with "the 'mass,' " so that the "theoretical assumptions" are shared by "both writer and reader" (Kayman, 1992, 168). Poe's Dupin effects a transformation of realist sympathy to that which "cannot be embraced by a 'common' discourse" and "denounces the communality of the 'mass' and its police discourses." This monstrous image is marginalized or excluded by realism, with two effects: the writing has to be idiosyncratic, and the "master's . . . *theoretical position has to be present as part of the narrative*" (Kayman's italics, 1992, 168–169). In Poe's story the "theoretical 'eye' is made visible to the reader, . . . if not to the opponent" (Kayman, 1992, 169). Poe could only accomplish this transformation within the network of existing discourses, as in his wagering game, or in discussing the persuasive impact of testimony.

The phrase "detective story" appeared about 1862 in England, about when Wilkie Collins began to expose the fictional apparatus. In the mystery novel "much of the suspense and mystery results from the gaps which are a consequence of the frames imposed by the narrators' or detectives' ideological, theoretical or personal positions," which in reading may "begin to constitute . . . a 'discursive' counter-plot" (Kayman, 1992, 175). Such practices affect stereotypes into which women and others are forced by the viewpoint character.

The quest for sensation that characterized reportage on both sides of the Atlantic and entered the detective novel included newspaper reports of crime, in which opinion followed the fashion from "melioration," to a reactionary reading of Darwin and biological determinism (Kayman, 1992, 176). Interest in nervous disorders and the collapse of a clear line between sanity and insanity led to shifts in legal defenses. There was fear that the lower-class sensation novel would contaminate the middle-class reader. Such novels as Anna Katharine Green's *The Leavenworth Case* (1878) incorporated a detective as a kind of voyeur on women, while policemen learn to restrict themselves to the position of servants "and to leave the question of middle-class family crime" to amateur detectives (Kayman, 1992, 193). Doyle's fiction defuses sexuality in the story and its hero and resolves the anxieties of the middle-class detective in upper-class homes. While Holmes is often given credit for incorporating "scientific rationalism, . . . the intellectual and scientific bases of his practice have nothing to do with the ferment of epistemological ideas generated by the revolutions in physics from the 1880s" but are associated with "older, more stable science" (Kayman, 1992, 216). The "concealment and timely revelation of clues and pieces of knowledge unknown to the reader is the fundamental dynamic of these tales, with Watson collaborating in distracting our attention." Our role "is to trust and to admire. . . . Holmes is not the site for theory but for mastery itself, mastery in a very particular sense." The structure of stories involves "an important displacement, in which the mystery itself is shifted from the crime, its sequel, and even its solution, to the detective's explanation of how he solved it" (Kayman, 1992, 221). "Holmes, very clearly, aims to silence" the "sort of critical narrative of social and personal authority, of discourse, ideology, sexuality, and of science and fiction which has been the monstrous sub-text of the popular literature we have been studying" (Kayman, 1992, 240).

In his *The Aesthetics of Murder: A Study in Romantic Literature and Contemporary Culture* (1991), Joel Black shows how eighteenth- and nineteenth-century thinkers participated in a transformation of the way we experience violence, that it has been shifted from the realm of the real to a vicarious experience acceptable as an aesthetic sublime. Black argues that the appropriation of Immanuel Kant's aesthetic judgment by De Quincey and others resulted in a "customary experience of murder and other forms of violence [that] is primarily aesthetic, rather than moral, physical, natural or whatever term we choose as a synonym for the word *real*. Only the victim knows the brutal 'reality' of murder; the rest of us view it at a distance, often as rapt onlookers who regard its 'reality' as a peak aesthetic experience" (Black, 1991, 3). In addition to the approaches of sociology, criminology, and psychology, which view murder as a problem, it "can be studied in a relatively disinterested mode as a morally neutral phenomenon" (Black, 1991, 6). Crime fiction is a variation of the vicarious experience of violence that has been developed by writers and newspeople. Eighteenth-century European aesthetics from Giovanni Battista Vico onward located the sublime in painful as well as pleasurable experience (Black, 1991, 13). Burke contrasted the beautiful "as a social, civilizing principle of unity, cohesion, and morality, to the sublime rooted in a primal impulse of self-preservation that was intrinsically amoral and antisocial" (Black, 1991, 14). In his *Critique of Judgment* (1790) Kant raised Burke's empirical and psychological account of the sublime and the beautiful to the level of speculative philosophy; henceforth, the critical distinction between the sublime and the beautiful would dominate discussions of aesthetics (Black, 1991, 14). Kant, in contrast to Burke, however, "located the source of the sublime in humanity's moral-rational nature; violent upheavals in physical nature, and especially human acts of violence, are virtually left out of [Kant's] discussion. Such acts do not illustrate the sublime, but rather the 'monstrous' " (Black, 1991, 14). De Quincey, more than Schiller and Coleridge, came to grips with the implications of Kant's moral-rational aesthetics" by relating the "natural sublime" to "the spectacle of murder" (Black, 1991, 15).[18]

Poe turns "the fine art of murder" into "the fine art of detection," thereby appropriating violence into "rational, bourgeois ideology" (Black, 1991, 16).[19] Yet De Quincey's ideas are inherent in the rise of mediation, the fascist aestheticization of politics, and the rise of cinema. Alfred Hitchcock uses film to exploit the "artistic dimension of murder," as do [h]is successors, Martin Scorsese and Brian De Palma. In exposing the pathology of murders, "they call attention to the similarities between their 'artistic' activity as filmmakers and the fantasy-lives of their sociopathic subjects" (Black, 1991, 17). He points out that U.S. society is overexposed to fictional violence and underexposed to U.S.-sponsored political violence. Black points out that the "wars" on pornography, terrorism, and drugs (sensational criminal activities) "have served government and business interests by diverting public attention from any 'violations of the government ethics code,' as white-collar crimes have come to be euphemized" (Black, 1991, 22). This transformation of information in which "violence is routinely sublimated into art" (Black, 1991, 25) is examined primarily through the discussion of films.

In *The American Roman Noir* (1995), William Marling integrates the discourses of the 1920s and 1930s dealing with "economic history and biography, design values and narrative analysis, film scholarship and a theory of technological momentum" into a discussion of the explosion of wealth and its function as an ambivalent fabula—what he calls "prodigality" (Marling, 1995, ix). The first chapter extends the Puritan division of self discussed by Sacvan Bercovitch into the twentieth century, along with the parable of the prodigal. The second examines sources of metonymic figures in technology, design, and the economy, then shifts to discussions of Dashiell Hammett, James M. Cain, and Raymond Chandler as wordsmiths operating in the realm of "copywriter," "journalist," and "executive," respectively. A final chapter discusses the transformation of the imagery into visual form with the emergence of film noir.

NOTES

1. Ronald Knox's rules for writers would seem to be a better choice than Freeman in this case.

2. See *L'Affaire Lerouge* (newspaper serial, 1865; English title, *The Widow Lerouge*, 1887); Gaboriau also published *Le Crime d'Orcival* (1867; *The Mystery of Orcival*, 1887), *Le Dossier No. 113* (1867; *Warrant No. 113*, 1884), and *Monsieur Lecoq* (1869; 1888 in English). *Monsieur Lecoq* is the best.

3. Cites Frank Kermode, *Romantic Image* (London: Routledge and Paul, 1957), p. 46.

4. See esp. 210 and 222–232 on Himes and the origin of the novel in the lives of criminals.

5. Of course it doesn't hold that detectives are not threatened, beaten up, and subject to dangerous innuendo, but it is true that detectives survive the story.

6. Todorov must be thinking of the chronology as beginning with Chandler or reaching a larger public influence about this time, rather than its origination with Hammett or *The Black Mask*.

7. Todorov cites Marcel Tuhamel (1945), who condemned the passions in this type of detective fiction.

8. See Brigid Brophy, *Don't Never Forget* (New York: Holt, 1966) for a "brilliant" distinction between detective and crime stories like his own (and P. D. James's); for P. D. James, see Diana Cooper-Clark, *Designs of Darkness* (1983).

9. Cites Löwnethal's *Golden Gallows* (criminal reportage); Manolescu's *Memoirs of a Confidence Man* (memoir); Fontaine's "Under the Pear-Tree" (criminal story without a detective); Stevenson's *Treasure Island* (adventure novel); Eugène Sue's *The Mysteries of Paris* (thriller); Daphne du Maurier's *Jamaica Inn* (ghost story); and Thomas Mann's *Confessions of Felix Krull, Confidence Man* (picaresque novel) as alternatives to the focus on detection by a detective.

10. This does occur in novels where public lands or the environment are at issue or where the topic is public trust—corrupt politicians and so on; the problem is that issues are always personalized.

11. Heissenbüttel says, curiously, that Sam Spade and Nick Charles were, "like their inventor, mostly small and inconspicuous employees of an agency" (81).

12. See Hottinger's *Mord: Angelsächsische Kriminalgeschichten von Edgar Allan Poe bis Agatha Christie* (Zurich: Diogenes Verlag, 1959). Hottinger was a bookstore owner and fan.

13. Quoted from *Raymond Chandler Speaking*, ed. by Dorothy Gardiner and Katherine Sorley Walker (Boston: Houghton Mifflin, 1977).

14. Mandel cites a Dutch study by S. Dresden and S. Vestdijk, *Marionettenspel met de Dood* (The Hague: M. Nijhoff, 1957), that argues that the classic detective novel moves on two levels simultaneously: concern for exact details and the shrouding of everything in shadow and ambiguity.

15. Quoted from D. Nimmo and J. E. Combs, *Subliminal Politics: Myths and Mythmakers in America* (Englewood Cliffs, NJ: Prentice-Hall, 1980), p. 16.

16. See Dickson D. Bruce's concise definition in *The Oxford Companion to African-American Literature*, ed. by William L. Andrews, Francis S. Foster, and Trudier Harris (New York: Oxford University Press, 1997).

17. Berman defines modernity's three stages as (1) 1500 (approximate date of the emergence of a world market) to 1789 (French Revolution), which is characterized by disorientation of community life; (2) 1790 to the end of the nineteenth century (revolution and emergence of a modern public); (3) twentieth century (modernity becomes problematic because of the necessity of expanding markets resulting in the production of increasingly complex novelty and a paradoxical unity).

18. See also De Quincey's sequel of 1839 and "Postscript" of 1854.

19. See also Dennis Porter's *The Pursuit of Crime: Art and Ideology in Detective Fiction* (New Haven, CT: Yale University Press, 1981).

CHAPTER 4

AUTHORS

This chapter presents information about authors from the nineteenth century to the present and is necessarily highly selective and abbreviated. Unlike standard alphabetical listings, writers in this volume are grouped roughly chronologically according to decade to make it easier to see something of the kinds of work that were being published over a period of time. The information is intended to be consulted along with the history and criticism chapters, and chronological grouping avoids redundancy since authors' names appear in the index.[1]

The working title of this chapter was "Appreciation," which indicates a wide range of relations to the novelists, their work, the reading public, and literary criticism. Authors are included if they are or were widely known or were decidedly prolific or produced even a single work that broke new ground in some way. This selection therefore includes some writers who are not otherwise represented in other sources and omits some writers who are included in other sources. No doubt readers may legitimately quibble with inclusions or exclusions, but relatively small space is devoted to the list, and it must necessarily be selective. A few of the writers discussed below are better known in other countries than they are by the general reading public in the United States, and the fame of some is more localized than it need be. Some of the authors, writing in that relatively ephemeral medium of paperback originals, were uncollected by libraries and forgotten for a time, to be remembered, if at all, by specialized collectors and aficionadoes. This section will also include writers who have received critical attention or have recently come to notice. Bearing in mind that the focus of this book is on novels there is no entry for Edgar Allan Poe even though a good deal of discussion of his work is carried on in the chapter on criticism.

EARLY WRITERS

Charles Brockden Brown's *Edgar Huntly* (1799) provides a transition from the European Gothic to the American mystery by presenting rational explanations for phenomena often regarded as having supernatural origin. The novel is organized around the amateur investigation of a murder and includes early reference to the relation of mental illness to crime.

Louisa May Alcott produced a number of thrillers from 1863 to 1868. See Madeline B. Stern, ed., *A Double Life: Newly Discovered Thrillers of Louisa May Alcott* (1988); Louisa May Alcott, *Louisa May Alcott Unmasked: Collected Thrillers*, edited by and introduction by Madeleine Stern (1995) and *The Lost Stories of Louisa May Alcott*, ed. by Madeleine B. Stern and Daniel Shealy (1995).

Seeley Regester's (Metta Victoria Fuller Victor) *The Dead Letter* (1867, repr. 1979) is one of the first American novels to feature a detective figure. In this sense it could arguably be considered a detective novel. Regester wrote some of the very first dime novels for publishers such as I. P. Beadle, though *Dead Letter* is considered her only detective novel. The novel is sometimes disqualified because the detective is clairvoyant, but this capability seems to be more a device for enhancing status in the manner of Dupin's associative reasoning feat than an unfair aid to detection. See B. J. Raha, "Seeley Regester: America's First Detective Novelist" (1988).

Anna Katharine Green is one of the pioneers of the American detective novel. In *The Leavenworth Case: A Lawyer's Story* (1878) Green domesticates the unruly narrative threads of detection running through legal cases, police memoirs, novels of manners, gothics, domestic novels, and romances. The murder she locks in the library of a dead tycoon is sorted out by a gentlemanly detective whose investigations are duly recorded by the dead man's lawyer. The combination of well-controlled plot, competent writing, suspense, and detection became an immediate hit with readers. Essentially a locked-room murder mystery, the novel is a prototype for many novels to come. Green's *The Leavenworth Case* incorporated no less than three detective figures, including the portly New York police detective Ebenezer Gryce, who soon became well-known on both sides of the Atlantic. Creating a novel of detection more clearly than a mystery or adventure story, Green eliminated many of the extraneous threads of other formulas and focused the action on detection. Gryce would be featured in *A Strange*

Disappearance (1880), *Hand and Ring* (1883), *Behind Closed Doors*
(1888), *A Matter of Millions* (1890), and *The Doctor, His Wife, and the
Clock* (1895). The detective would be joined by Amelia Butterworth, an
older amateur sleuth in *That Affair Next Door* (1897), and they would
continue their investigations in *The Lost Man's Lane* (1898), *The Circular
Study* (1900), *One of My Sons* (1901), *Initials Only* (1911) and *The Mystery of the Hasty Arrow* (1917). Though Green does not surpass the quality
of her first work, she experiments with the form, inventing Butterworth
and a young society woman, Violet Strange, who operates secretly as a
private detective while living with her parents (see *The Golden Slipper and
Other Problems for Violet Strange*, 1915). In the course of more than thirty
novels Green invents devices that become generic and weaves in other narrative elements, shading the detective stories into broader mysteries. Green
continued to write detective fiction through the early 1920s. Although
Green's mysteries were craftily conceived, the stories well plotted and her
writing adequate to nineteenth-century popular audiences, her work eventually fell under the shadow of the more fashionable stylists and storytellers
of the modern period. Among other novels and stories that bear contemporary reading are *The Golden Slipper* (stories, 1915) and *The Step on the
Stair* (1923). Michele Slung, in her introduction to the Dover edition of
The Leavenworth Case observes that Strange is a prototype for Nancy
Drew, and Butterworth is arguably a model for a lineage that runs through
Mary Roberts Rinehart's Rachel Innes, Agatha Christie's Miss Marple, Stu-
art Palmer's Hildegarde Withers, and Patricia Wentworth's Miss Silver.
Later critics complain of the love interest and melodrama, often over-
looking these elements as alternatives to rising violence and intensified ac-
tion. Patricia D. Maida's *Mother of Detective Fiction: The Life and Works
of Anna Katharine Green* (1989) is a biographical study of Green. See also
Barrie Hayne, "Anna Katharine Green" (1981); Cheri L. Ross, "The First
Feminist Detective: Anna Katharine Green's Amelia Butterworth" (1991).
Audrey Peterson's *Victorian Masters of Mystery: From Wilkie Collins to
Conan Doyle* (1984) contains a brief discussion of Green.

Green inspired many other efforts in crime novels, including many in the
burgeoning story papers and dime novels. This variety of novels included
Allan Pinkerton's novels of criminal activities and heroic detectives, such
as *The Model Town and the Detectives, Byron as a Detective* (1876), *The
Gypsies and the Detective* (1879), *Criminal Reminiscences and Detectives*
(1879), *A Double Life and the Detective* (1884); Frank A. Pinkerton's *Dyke
Darrel, the Railroad Detective; or, The Crime of the Midnight Express*
(1886); Judson R. Taylor [pseud. for Harlan Page Halsey] wrote a series
that included *Macon Moore, the Southern Detective* (1881?), *Gipsy Blair,
the Western Detective* (1892) and *Phil Scott, the Indian Detective: A Tale
of Startling Mysteries* (1882); Ernest A. Young's novels written as Harry

Rockwood, included *Abner Ferret, the Lawyer Detective* (1883), *Clarice Dyke, the Female Detective* (1883), *Nat Foster, the Boston Detective: A Thrilling Story of Detective Life* (1883), *Luke Leighton, the Government Detective* (1884), *Fred Danford, the Skillful Detective; or, The Watertown Mystery* (1885) and *Neil Nelson, the Veteran Detective: or, Tracking Mail Robbers* (1885); Emma Murdoch Van Deventer published *The Diamond Coterie*, by Lawrence L. Lynch [pseud.] (1884); "B. and R.," *Helen Elwood, the Female Detective; or, A Celebrated Forger's Fate* (1885); Harry Harper, *File No. 115; or, A Man of Steel* (1886); Symmes M. Jelley, *Shadowed to Europe: A Chicago Detective on Two Continents* by "Le Jemlys" [pseud.] (1885); James Douglas Jerrold Kelley, *A Desperate Chance* (1886); James Milford Merrill's *Tracked to Death; or, Eagle Gray, the Western Detective* by Morris Redwing [pseud.] (1886); Ernest Stark, *Ed Sommer, the Pinkerton Detective; or, The Murdered Miser* (1886); Edmund C. Strong, *Manacle and Bracelet; or, The Dead Man's Secret. A Thrilling Detective Story* (1886?); Nathan Dane Urner, *Link by Link; or, The Chain of Evidence: A Great Detective Story* (1886); Arthur Dudley Vinton, *The Pomfret Mystery: A Novel of Incident* (1886); Jeannette Ritchie Walworth (Hadermann), *The Silent Witness* (1888?); [Harold William], *Silken Threads: A Detective Story*, by George Afterem [pseud.]; Philip Woolf, *Who Is Guilty?* (1886); Francis Farrars's [pseud.] *Jim Cummings; or, The Crime of the 'Frisco Express* (1887); Mary R. Hatch (Platt), *The Bank Tragedy: A Novel* (1890) and *The Strange Disappearance of Eugene Comstocks* (1895); Charles H. Simpson, *Life in the Far West; or, A Detective's Adventures among the Indians and Outlaws of Montana* (1896); Rodrigues Ottolengui, *An Artist in Crime* (1892) and *A Conflict of Evidence* (1893); Edgar Morette, *The Sturgis Wager: A Detective Story* (1899).

Mark Twain included detective material in several novels and short stories. Most directly he structured *The Tragedy of Pudd'nhead Wilson* (1894) around a mystery solved by a fingerprint. Twain's literary realism provided an alternative to the documentary realism that emerged around the turn of the century. See Virginia S. Hale, "Mark Twain, Detective" (1992); John S. Whitley, "Pudd'nhead Wilson: Mark Twain and the Limits of Detection" (1987).

Pauline E. Hopkins's serial novel, *Hagar's Daughter* (1901–1902) features Venus Johnson as an African American detective figure. The novel is included in *The Magazine Novels of Pauline Hopkins* (1988); see Hazel Carby's introduction. See also Soitos (1996).

Mary Roberts Rinehart's *The Circular Staircase* (1908)—put on as a stage play and filmed as *The Bat* (1926) without sound, and as *The Bat*

Whispers (1930) with sound, both filmed by Roland West—became a best-seller and established Rinehart as a mystery writer. Rinehart's short stories in *Munsey's* and the *Saturday Evening Post*, together with numerous well-written novels, made her one of America's highest paid authors. Her "had-I-but-known" device is adapted by contemporary author Paul Auster to open his postmodern detective novel, *City of Glass* (1985). Rinehart's subsequent novels made her one of America's highest paid authors. Rinehart influenced such later writers as Mignon G. Eberhart, Mabel Seeley, and Leslie Ford among others. Rinehart tends to shift focus from police or the detective to the victim or criminal, and her Hilda Adams series (Adams is often called "Miss Pinkerton" by her fictional admirers) is about a nurse who engages in detective work. Other works, including *The Man in the Lower Ten* (1909); *The Case of Jenny Brice* (1913); *The Red Lamp* (1925); *The Door* (1930); *The Album* (1933); *The Wall* (1938); *The Yellow Room* (1945), and others are readable. Rinehart's autobiography is *My Story* (1931, rev. 1948) and Jan Cohn has published a thoughtful biography, *Improbable Fiction* (1980).

John E. Bruce introduced an African-American detective in his *Black Sleuth*, which was serialized in *McGirt's Magazine* (1907–1909). See Soitos (1996).

Jacques Futrelle is best known for his locked-room short story, "The Problem of Cell 13" (1905; collected 1907) but he also wrote several novels that mix romance and the supernatural or science fiction, such as the short novel *The Diamond Master* (1909).

A writer who understood both the craft and business of fiction very well was Carolyn Wells, who wrote over 170 books, including some 75 mystery novels. *The Rest of My Life* (1937) is her autobiography. *The Clue* (1909), the first of her Fleming Stone series, led to a formulaic approach that she outlined in *The Technique of the Mystery Story* (1913). Wells agrees with much of S. S. Van Dine's credo—indeed reprints it in the revised edition of her book and adds to his list of murder clichés, but she questions the wisdom of Van Dine's restriction on love interest. Wells points out that "the last two of Mr. Van Dine's own stories end with the sound of wedding bells or a reminiscent fragrance of orange blossoms" (Wells, 1978, 77). She points out that the models Poe initiated for the detective story narrative were short stories that "had no room for it" (Wells, 1978, 78). Many subsequent mystery and detective story writers would attempt to explain the secret of writing the successful mystery novel. Fleming Stone, a gentleman detective, appeared in over fifty novels from *The Clue* (1909) through *Who Killed Caldwell?* (1942), among which she included mystery series featuring Alan Ford, Pennington Wise, Kenneth Carlisle, and a host of children's books, juveniles, and other novels, together with verse and anthologies of humor. One unappreciative critic calls Stone "a virtual cipher whose activities are somewhat less interesting to watch than an ant making its way across a sheet of blank paper" (Pronzini and Muller, 1986, 826).

Lee Thayer wrote sixty detective novels from *The Mystery of the Thirteenth Floor* (1919) through *Dusty Death* (1966) at the age of ninety-two. Featuring the comic team of Peter Clancy, a wealthy private investigator, and his English valet, Wiggar, the novels range widely in location.

Arthur Reeve, in a series of novels, created professor of chemistry and inventor Craig Kennedy, an American counterpart of the R. Austin Freeman's English scientific detective Dr. Thorndyke. Kennedy has often been compared to Sherlock Holmes, with Walter Jameson his Watson figure, but Reeve was more sophisticated about current science than Doyle. His detective uses devices that make up a catalogue of early twentieth century technological speculation and advanced police procedures. Kennedy appeared in scores of stories and more than a dozen novels as well as in silent film serials. The character was much later revived for a short television series. Among the best works are *The Silent Bullet* (stories, 1912), *The Poisoned Pen* (1913), and *The Clutching Hand* (1934); see also *Guy Garrick* (1916), which features as a detective the figure of the title. For a time Reeve's fiction sold very well in England.

Jack Boyle's famous detective, Boston Blackie, seemingly appeared only in *Boston Blackie* (1919), a collection of stories arranged as chapters, though the rogue detective was featured in radio and television series and numerous films. Boyle was a former newspaper editor who lost his job after becoming addicted to opium and ending up in prison for forgery and later for armed robbery. His first stories appeared under the byline of his prison identification number.

A writer who worried little about art, producing some 200 novels in various genres with remarkable craftsmanship for the pace at which he worked, was Frederick Faust. Publishing his first novel in 1919 (as far as anyone has determined) and subsequently writing under numerous pen names, Faust was publishing in the pulps before they became specialized. Faust is better known as the western writer Max Brand, but wrote ten detective and spy novels as Walter C. Butler, Max Brand and Frederick Frost. Most of these were published or serialized from 1935 to 1937 and four of them were published in book form for the first time in the middle seventies, nearly thirty years after Faust's death. All of the novels are readable today, but perhaps the most easily accessible are *Big Game* (1973), *Dead Man's Treasure* (1975) written as Max Brand, *The Bamboo Whistle* (1937), a spy novel written as Frederick Frost, and *The Night Flower*, written as Walter C. Butler.

1920s

For several decades beginning in the 1920s, detective fiction expanded and gained millions of readers. This Golden Age of detective fiction saw considerable experimentation and innovation with characters, situations, plots, and styles. The classic British story was easily recognized by its tight construction, upscale setting, and stilted style. It continued to gain popularity through the course of the decade, but the hard-boiled novel emerged in several forms, and the adventure mystery reemerged. It is not surprising that writers should grope for a style to express feelings about the predatory quality of society nor that they should be drawn to follow the lead of writers who expressed them in profitable ways. During the Depression this meant writing for the pulp magazines for a penny or so a word. Many of the pulp detective writers were soon forgotten and relatively few saw their work in hardcover editions. Some reached great fame as novelists as well as writers of detective fiction. Dashiell Hammett's work is probably most significant.

Charlotte Perkins Gilman's *Unpunished* (1997) portrays the male victim as deserving his fate because of the brutalization of his family, so that his feminist murderer deserves to remain free.[2] See Lillian S. Robinson, "Killing Patriarchy: Gilman, the Murder Mystery, and Post-feminist Propaganda" (1991); the novel is available as *Unpunished: A Mystery*, ed. with an afterword by Catherine J. Golden and Denise D. Knight (New York: Feminist Press, 1997); see also *The Charlotte Perkins Gilman Reader: The Yellow Wallpaper, and Other Fiction*, ed. and introduction by Ann J. Lane (New York: Pantheon Books, 1980).

Harry Stephen Keeler's intricate and bizarre mysteries set in Chicago began to appear with *The Voice of the Seven Sparrows* (1924) and continued through nearly fifty novels through the early 1950s. See Francis M. Nevins, Jr., "The Wild and Woolly World of Harry Stephen Keeler: 1" (1969).

Earl Derr Biggers began as a playwright, then achieved popularity as a mystery writer with *Seven Keys to Baldpate* (1913) but is best known for his six novels about Honolulu policeman Charlie Chan. Chan is an inverted image of the Oriental criminal mastermind popularized in the Fu Manchu figure created by Sax Rohmer in the first decade of the twentieth century. Chan appears in *The House without a Key* (1925), *Fifty Candles* (1926), *The Chinese Parrot* (1926), *Behind That Curtain* (1928), *The Black Camel* (1929), *Charlie Chan Carries On* (1930), and *The Keeper of the Keys* (1932), of which *Curtain* and *Chan Carries On* were best-sellers. Chan has been a controversial figure because like Harriet Beecher Stowe, Biggers created characters that became negative stereotypes as they became widely circulated. Through a host of nearly fifty films, several radio programs, a comic strip, comic books, and TV programs a small coterie of ethnic characters based on limited traits became popular with white audiences. As a novelty Chan would have disappeared, but as the character was reproduced, it became the sum of the depth of Chinese culture in the creations and most of what non-Chinese Americans experienced of Chinese culture. See William F. Wu, *The Yellow Peril: Chinese Americans in American Fiction, 1850–1940* (1982), Wayne Wang's film, *Chan Is Missing* (1982) and Frank Chin's novel, *Gunga Din Highway* (1994).

The middle-class dream of productive leisure woven into many classic detective stories received a powerful boost in the novels of Willard Huntington Wright, who wrote under the pen name of S. S. Van Dine. His detective, Philo Vance, first appeared in *The Benson Murder Case* in 1926, purportedly based on the Joseph Elwell murder case of 1920. Vance is a scholarly eccentric who carried out meticulously detailed investigations in a milieu of conspicuous consumption. Van Dine's success helped establish the convention of titles with six-letter catch phrases, using "Murder Case" for his dozen Philo Vance novels. Others in the series include *The Canary Murder Case* (1927); *The Greene Murder Case* (1928); *The Bishop Murder Case* (1929); *The Scarab Murder Case* (1930); *The Kennel Murder Case* (1933); *The Dragon Murder Case* (1933); *The Casino Murder Case* (1934); *The Kidnap Murder Case* (1936); and *The Gracie Allen Murder Case* (1938). An art critic and collaborator with H. L. Mencken and George Jean Nathan on other books, Van Dine established twenty rules for detective stories.[3] The success of his novels and the motion pictures based on them helped boost the popularity of detective fiction in the United States. Van Dine's phenomenal popular success influenced the creation of a number of detective figures with similar qualities, such as Ellery Queen, Nero Wolfe, and Thatcher Colt. See Jon Tuska's *Philo Vance: The Life and Times of S. S. Van Dine* (1971) and John Loughery's biography, *Alias S. S. Van Dine* (1992).

Though Van Dine dominated "classic" American detective fiction in the late 1920s and 1930s, Ellery Queen (pseudonym of first cousins Frederic Dannay and Manfred B. Lee) eventually surpassed Van Dine's popularity. With the publication of *The Roman Hat Mystery* (1929), the Queen machine got underway, leading to novels, short stories, plays, and radio, television and film scripts, *Ellery Queen's Mystery Magazine* (1941–present), dozens of collections of short stories, and much of the first bibliographical and critical work on American detective fiction. Ellery Queen scholars have divided the fiction into periods, from *The Roman Hat Mystery* through *The Spanish Cape Mystery* (1935), with Francis Nevins (1974) identifying *The Greek Coffin Mystery* (1932) and *The Egyptian Cross Mystery* (1932) as the best. The Hollywood years produced less polished, more sentimental fiction appropriate to film adaptation, of which the best is probably *The Four of Hearts* (1938), together with the beginning of the anthologies and the *Ellery Queen* radio program (1939–1948). Following this period, from about 1942, with the publication of *Calamity Town*, the writing is less in the classical puzzle form, with more attention given to character, setting, and atmosphere; the best of these novels include *Ten Days' Wonder* (1948), *Cat of Many Tails* (1949), *The Origin of Evil* (1951) and *The Glass Village* (1954), a satire on the paranoia of McCarthyism. Their planned last novel was *The Finishing Stroke* (1958), but a number of later novels were published under the byline. Writing as Barnaby Ross, the authors' other major character is the early Drury Lane, an actor who finds himself doing detective work. Dannay and Lee championed the fair-play rule, which gave the reader a reasonable chance to solve the mystery. All in all Lee and Dannay created a remarkable legacy of fiction, scholar-ship, and vehicles for the display of both new and established talent. See Anthony Boucher's pamphlet, *Ellery Queen: A Double Profile* (1951) and Francis M. Nevins' *Royal Bloodline: Ellery Queen, Author and Detective* (1974).

A writer who would capture more of the spirit of American violence and initiate a new tendency in detective fiction published his first novel, *The White Circle*, in 1926. Carroll John Daly, who many critics feel published the first story in the hard-boiled tradition, "The False Burton Combs," in *The Black Mask* in 1922, created Vee Brown, Satan Hall, and his most famous detective, Race Williams, who appeared in nearly twenty novels and a flood of short stories. His adventurer detectives, however, would be overshadowed by those of the more polished writers to come. Among his best novels are *The Snarl of the Beast* (1927) and *The Amateur Murderer* (1933).

1930s

Leslie Charteris is best known for his creation of Simon Templar, The Saint, who appeared first in England and then the United States in countless short stories, collections, and novels. An outlaw who is always ready to help someone in trouble while taking from the rich, The Saint began as a remarkable and enduring figure in the tradition of bandit stories through-out the world. The Saint aids the allies during World War II and softens his exploits after the war. *Meet the Tiger* (1928) marks the first appearance of The Saint in England, with *The Saint in New York* (1935) coinciding with the year of his arrival in the United States. Generally, Charteris's Brit-ish novels are the grittiest, with *The Saint Goes West* (1942), one of the best of the later works. See Burl Barer, *The Saint* (1993).

John Dickson Carr carried the puzzle story to its absurd conclusion in carefully constructed boxes through which no apparent murderer could have penetrated undetected. From *It Walks by Night* (1930) featuring the *juge d'instruction* of Paris, Henri Bencolin (soon replaced by Dr. Gideon Fell from *Hag's Nook* [1933] on), through novels written as Carter Dickson featuring Sir Henry Merrivale (*The Plague Court Murders* [1934]) and twenty or so more, Carr exploited most of the possibilities of the closed form. See also Joe R. Christopher, "The Social World in Dr. Gideon Fell's Shorter Cases" (1992), and Douglas G. Greene, *John Dickson Carr: The Man Who Explained Miracles* (1995).

Steven Gould Fisher, who wrote as Steve Fisher, Stephen Gould, and Grant Lane, began his nearly twenty suspense and mystery novels with *Spend the Night* (1935) and divided his time between fiction and screenplays.

Rudolph Fisher published *The Conjure Man Dies* (1932), a classic detective story with an all-black cast set in Harlem. While unspectacular in its use of the formula, it employs no less than three detective figures who cooperate in the solution of the mystery. Although it makes use of vaudeville stereotypes for two of the characters, the novel also presents a view of the black middle class, explores Africanness to some extent, and opens the possibility of alternatives to Western rationality.

C. Daly King was a psychologist who created detective stories with intricate plots, his Michael Lord assisting the New York Police Commissioner with the aid of a psychologist, Dr. L. Rees Pons. Critics cite his short story "The Episode of the Nail and the Requiem" (in the collection of stories, *The Curious Mr. Tarrant*, 1935) as one of the best locked-room stories ever written, with his novel, *Obelists Fly High* (1935), a minor classic of the genre among his six novels. Like Van Dine he included documents such as maps, timetables, and floor plans.

Writers who contributed classic and domestic detective novels during the 1930s include Phoebe Atwood Taylor, who wrote two series under her own name and as Alice Tilton. Asey Mayo appears in about two dozen novels, first in *The Cape Cod Mystery* (1931). Mayo is created in the spirit of Yankee dialect humor, an amateur sleuth who easily overmatches the local police. As Alice Tilton she created Leonidas Witherall, a closet thriller writer in a Boston suburb whose appearance resembles popular likenesses of Shakespeare; he first appears in *Beginning with a Bash* (1937) and continues through eight books. The detection in Taylor's stories is sometimes whimsical, and readers either loved the books or disposed of them half-read.

Mignon Good Eberhart early wrote a series of seven suspense novels in the manner of Mary Roberts Rinehart featuring middle-aged nurse Sarah Keate and detective Lance O'Leary, the best of which may be the first, *The Patient in Room 18* (1929). Susan Dare appeared in short stories, some of which are collected in *The Cases of Susan Dare* (1934). Eberhart also wrote four novels featuring policeman Jacob Wait. But with a shift away from series detectives to mystery and suspense novels, Eberhart was able to develop better atmosphere and more convincing psychological portrayal of her central characters. Emphasizing upscale settings and gothic moods, a wide range of novels cover historical and contemporary locales. Among her best works are *Five Passengers from Lisbon* (1946), *Man Missing* (1954), and *Message from Hong Kong* (1969).

Clayton Rawson, a magician himself, wrote a series of detective novels and stories featuring The Great Merlini, beginning with *Death from a Top Hat* (1938). Rawson's stories were, of course, puzzle stories.

In 1935 John P. Marquand, who is known for *The Late George Apley* (1937) and other mainstream novels, created a Japanese detective/investigator/agent, Mr. Moto, in *No Hero*. The six-novel series was broken only by World War II. Unlike Chan, Moto is more a man of action as well as an intellectual. See Richard Wires, *John P. Marquand and Mr. Moto* (1990).

An important novelist who helped create the criminal world in which police and detectives would operate is W. R. Burnett, who wrote numerous screenplays as well as novels. The novels, *Little Caesar* (1929), *High Sierra* (1940), and *The Asphalt Jungle* (1949), were highly successful motion pictures soon after they were off the press. Other novels of interest include *Dark Hazard* (1933) and *Vanity Row* (1952).

Dashiell Hammett, who for many brought the hard-boiled detective story to its most powerful form of expression, appeared in *The Black Mask* with his Continental Op during the 1920s and published *Red Harvest* (1929), *The Dain Curse* (1929), *The Maltese Falcon* (1930), *The Glass Key* (1931), *The Thin Man* (1934), *The Novels of Dashiell Hammett* (1966), *The Big Knockover* (stories, 1966) and other collections of stories under various titles. His work has been more or less available continuously since publication. Hammett continues to inspire writers and attract readers. Hammett is tough, uncompromising, and studiously experimental, with most of his work about the interminable play of power when the game is on the line. *Red Harvest* explores the power struggle of rival gangs over the town of Personville, during which the Continental Op gets caught up in the contagion of the violence. *The Dain Curse* employs gothic elements to explore the boundaries between crime and abnormal psychology, while *The Maltese Falcon* examines the limits of morality and ethics under the pressure of desire and greed. *The Glass Key* features a political operative rather than a detective in order to examine the relationships between power and wealth, while *The Thin Man* provides romantic byplay and comic relief featuring a married detective with a dog. Hammett's work has been linked to existentialism and other views on Prohibition, the Depression, and pre–

World War II anxiety. The hard-boiled style's detective and mystery form are found in Hammett's novels, first in *The Maltese Falcon*, where Bridgett O'Shaughnessy's plausible illusions waver like the summer air above an asphalt street, and *The Glass Key*, where Ned Beaumont balances an instrumental capitalistic self-interest and democratic honor. He is the precipitator of violence as he manipulates the illusions of others, but he does reveal a murderer and much deceit. See also Diane Johnson, *Dashiell Hammett* (1983), Steven Marcus's introduction to *The Continental Op* (1974) and the discussion in chapter 3 above; Jean-Pierre Deloux, *Dashiell Hammett* (1994); Dennis Dooley, *Dashiell Hammett* (1984); Carl Freedman and Christopher Kendrick, "Forms of Labor in Dashiell Hammett's *Red Harvest*" (1991); Sinda Gregory, *Private Investigations* (1984); Richard Layman, *Dashiell Hammett: A Descriptive Bibliography* (1979) and *Shadow Man: The Life of Dashiell Hammett* (1981); Edward Margolies, *Which Way Did He Go?* (1982); William Marling, *The American Roman Noir* (1995); William F. Nolan, *Dashiell Hammett: A Casebook* (1969) and *Hammett: A Life at the Edge* (1983); Paul Skenazy, *The New Wild West* (1982); Robert E. Skinner, *The Hard-Boiled Explicator: A Guide to the Study of Dashiell Hammett, Raymond Chandler and Ross Macdonald* (1985); Julian Symons, *Dashiell Hammett* (1985); Peter Wolfe, *Beams Falling* (1980); James Naremore, "Dashiell Hammett and the Poetics of Hard-Boiled Detection" (1984).

William Faulkner's Popeye in *Sanctuary* (1931) contrasts the cold-blooded thug with a flapper drawn to danger by a mindless need for stimulation. Purported to have been written as a potboiler, the novel nevertheless powerfully evokes current ideology about the dangerous edges of social norms of the time. Faulkner subsequently published a number of novels and stories involving mystery and detection, including *Intruder in the Dust* (1948) featuring an excellent mystery. Faulkner followed it with a collection of stories, *Knight's Gambit* (1949). While *Intruder in the Dust* is a fine novel, it is *Sanctuary* and the scraps of narrative throughout Faulkner's work that writers and readers best remember. Faulkner's characterization and the pathology he represents as the contemporary world are striking, memorable, and influential. See Andrew J. Wilson, "The Corruption in Looking: William Faulkner's 'Sanctuary' as a 'Detect'ive Novel'" (1994), who argues that the characters in *Sanctuary* live their lives as voyeurs whose observations of others substitute for their lack of inner lives. See also John T. Irwin, "Knight's Gambit: Poe, Faulkner, and the Tradition of the Detective Story" (1990); Wolfgang E. Schlepper, "William Faulkner's Detective Stories" (1985).

James M. Cain wrote naturalistic novels of unrelenting hard-boiled prose to describe the American Dream in visceral terms from the underside. Beginning with *The Postman Always Rings Twice* (1934), Cain wrote a number of novels that have entered into literature and film as expressions of 1930s pessimism in contrast to the upbeat films and escapist fantasy that became the fare of the media. Several of his novels, including *The Postman Always Rings Twice, Mildred Pierce* (1941), and *Double Indemnity* (1943), have become classics of film noir. Usually considered suspense novels, Cain's work nearly always involves crimes of one kind or another and are integral to understanding the development of hard-boiled crime fiction. See Roy Hoopes, ed., *Sixty Years of Journalism* (1985); William Marling, *The American Roman Noir* (1995); Paul Skenazy, *James M. Cain* (1989).

Gerald Kersh is known mostly for over 5,000 magazine articles and 3,000 stories, many flirting with the bizarre. Kersh also wrote a number of memorable mystery and suspense novels, however, including *Night and the City* (1938), *Fowler's End* (1957) and *Brock* (1969).

Erle Stanley Gardner is in a class by himself. One of the most prolific writers of detective fiction, his Perry Mason had become a household name in America by the late 1930s. Gardner's novels, *The Case of the Velvet Claws* (1933), *The Case of the Lucky Legs* (1933), *The Case of the Curious Bride* (1934), *The Case of the Counterfeit Eye* (1935), *The Case of the Caretaker's Cat* (1935), *The Case of the Stuttering Bishop* (1936), *The Case of the Dangerous Dowager* (1937), *The Case of the Lame Canary* (1937), and *The Case of the Substitute Face* (1938), were all among the decade's top sellers. Like other highly productive writers, Gardner picked up tricks of the trade early, found a character, theme, style, or gimmick, and developed them with enormous stamina and single-minded focus. Dorothy Hughes says that in his prime Gardner could dictate a Perry Mason, for which he is best remembered, in three and a half days, or four days if the time Gardner spent "thinking up the plot" (Hughes, 1978, 14) are counted. Gardner believed he had no talent as a writer, but he had determination, a good business sense, and learned the elements of his craft by studying the work of successful pulp writers, courses from the Home Correspondence School, and *Writer's Digest* publications. As his production increased, he wrote stories under such names as A. A. Fair, Kyle Corning, Grant Holiday, Robert Parr, Carleton Kendrake, Charles J. Kenny, Arthur Mann Sellers, Les Tillray, Dane Rigley, and Charles M. Stanton. When he left the law firm, he took three legal secretaries with him. In his letters to his publisher, he spoke frankly of himself as "a writing machine" working through a wholesaler (the publisher) to the consumer. Gardner demonstrated in the course of the eighty-two novels that the hard-boiled world could be softened by adopting some of the conventions of the classic detective story in the form of a courtroom drama. Mason's associates, his secretary, Della Street, and the detective, Paul Drake, provide casual flirtation and background detection, balancing respectively the effects of loose women and the police. The figure of Perry Mason was boosted by films, radio programs, and television. Gardner focused on dialogue and action, his sparse writing style and underdeveloped plots well suited to adaptation, but aside from this Gardner was simply a good storyteller whose readers enjoyed the yarns and the office byplay. Gardner also created, as A. A. Fair, the entertaining Bertha Cool and Donald Lam series, beginning with *The Bigger They Come* (1938). Gardner also wrote as Carleton Kendrake and Charles J. Kenny and created a range of likely and unlikely characters including Terry Clane, Sheriff Bill Eldon, and Gramps Wiggins. See also Alva Johnston's *The Case of Erle Stanley Gardner* (1947), Francis L. Fugate's *Secrets of the World's Best-Selling Writer: The Storytelling Techniques of Erle Stanley Gardner* (1980), Dorothy B. Hughes's *Erle Stanley Gardner: The Case of the Real Perry Mason* (1978), J. Kenneth Van Dover, *Murder in the Millions* (1984); J. Dennis Bounds's *Perry Mason: The Authorship & Reproduction of a Popular Hero* (1996).

Anthony Boucher (William Anthony Parker White), who also wrote as H. H. Holmes, was a widely respected reviewer, anthologist, critic, radio script writer, and friend to many fledgling and established writers of fantasy, science fiction, mystery, and other genres. Boucher also wrote mysteries and an occasional science fiction or dark fantasy story, usually involving intricate puzzles and an array of subterfuges. These appeared in a wide range of publications. Boucher's Fergus O'Breen, an Irish-American LAPD detective, and Lt. Jackson are brought into four cases, most notably *The Case of the Baker Street Irregulars* (1940), after the screenwriter of a Sherlock Holmes film is murdered. Boucher's first novel, *The Case of the Seven of Calvary* (1937), is a locked room mystery, as is *The Case of the Solid Key* (1941). Also of interest is *The Case of the Crumpled Knave* (1937). Boucher is one of the few writers to have an annual convention named after him (Bouchercon, 1970–present), though the honor is for his generosity and humanity as much as for his criticism and fiction. About a third of Boucher's sixty or so stories are collected in *Exeunt Murderers: The Best Mystery Stories of Anthony Boucher* (1983), and the best of Boucher's criticism is collected in *Multiplying Villainies: Selected Mystery Criticism, 1942–1968* (1973).

Rex Stout made his debut as a detective novelist with *Fer de Lance* in 1934, beginning one of the most widely known detective teams in the country in Nero Wolfe and Archie Goodwin. Wolfe is, in the manner of Dupin and Holmes, a masterful thinker with unusual habits and mannerisms, while Goodwin is a streetwise, updated, and sophisticated Watson figure and legman with investigative skills of his own. Stout's unique detective team joined the classic and hard-boiled detectives, giving his readers both the grand thinker in Nero Wolfe and something of the wisecracking, hard-boiled detective in Archie Goodwin. Together they make a remarkable team, with Goodwin serving as narrator with asides on Wolfe's vanity while he gathers evidence as would police in a classic detective story. In expanding Archie's role, Stout keeps the police on the periphery of the story, with Wolfe generally receiving all parties in his brownstone. Among his better than fifty detective novels, noteworthy are *League of Frightened Men* (1935); *Too Many Cooks* (1938); *Please Pass the Guilt* (1973); *The Rubber Band* (1936); *Over My Dead Body* (1940); *Where There's a Will* (1940); *Not Quite Dead Enough* (1944); *Too Many Women* (1948); *The Second Confession* (1949); *Murder by the Book* (1951); *Before Midnight* (1955); *Might as Well Be Dead* (1959); *The Doorbell Rang* (1965). He also wrote the Tecumseh Fox novels, *Bad for Business* (1940) and *The Broken Vase* (1941), and created women private detectives, Theodolinda 'Dol' Bonner and Sylvia Raffray in *The Hand in the Glove* (1937). Alphabet Hicks appears in *Alphabet Hicks* (1941); in paper as *The Sound of Murder* (1969 [Riley, 1965]). See Frederick Isaac's essay on Nero Wolfe in Mary Jean DeMarr's *In the Beginning* (1995); Bruce Beiderwell's "State Power and Self-Destruction: Rex Stout and the Romance of Justice" (1993); John McAleer, *Rex Stout: A Biography* (1977); J. Kenneth Van Dover, *At Wolfe's Door* (1991).

Jonathan Latimer wrote in a variety of subgenres, including among his novels a locked room story, *Headed for a Hearse* (1935), though most of his plots were uncomplicated; his style is hard boiled with witty repartee in the tradition of screwball comedy. His private detective, Bill Crane, has been compared to Hammett's Nick Charles and, interestingly, one of his screenplays was *The Glass Key* (1942). From 1960 to 1965 he wrote scripts for the *Perry Mason* television series. Among his best novels are *Murder in the Madhouse* (1934), his first, *The Lady in the Morgue* (1936), *The Dead Don't Care* (1938), and *Red Gardenias* (1939).

Patrick Quentin is the byline of Hugh Wheeler and, until 1952, Richard Webb. Wheeler and Webb also wrote under the names of Q. Patrick and Jonathan Stagge, creating several memorable characters including Peter Duluth, NYPD Lt. Timothy Trant, and Dr. Hugh Westlake. Duluth, an amateur, appears in a series of novels starting with *A Puzzle for Fools* (1936), through *Black Widow* (1952), which featured theatrical locations; in the first Duluth is drying out in a sanitarium after a successful stint as a Broadway producer. Under the Q. Patrick byline, Lt. Trant emerges as a witty, polished dandy, whose investigations are best performed in *Death and the Maiden* (1939).

Mabel Seeley set her suspense stories among the small towns of Minnesota and created through a combination of melodrama and romance some of the best had-I-but-known stories available. Her first novel, *The Listening House* (1938), is perhaps her best, though her work suffers from aspects made apparent in Ben Hecht's parody of *The Whistling Shadow* (1954), "The Whistling Corpse."[4]

Walter Gibson produced over 300 novels, mostly for *The Shadow Magazine* (1932–49) writing as Maxwell Grant, having created The Shadow for the magazine in 1932. A professional magician, Gibson wrote numerous books on magic, the occult, Eastern religion and the martial arts, gambling, strategies for table games, and so on. Writing one or two novels a month for *The Shadow Magazine*, he also wrote the Norgil series for *Crime Busters* (1941–47), apparently ghosted stories for Harry Houdini and others, and wrote *The Shadow* comic book. Gibson averaged about a million words, often about two dozen novels a year, of The Shadow alone. Considering the pace at which he wrote, Gibson had a remarkable gift for image and a craftsmanlike style. See J. Randolph Cox's *Man of Magic and Mystery* (1988).

Paul Cain (Peter Ruric) wrote stories for *The Black Mask* and other pulp magazines, producing one highly regarded novel, *Fast One* (1933), and a collection of stories, *Seven Slayers* (1946).

Also in the hard-boiled tradition in much of his fiction was Raoul Whitfield, who wrote about the Filipino private detective Jo Gar in a series of stories in *The Black Mask*. His ex-con detective figure Mal Ourney in *Green Ice* (1930), along with Jo Gar, are his best creations.

Lawrence Treat's *Run Far, Run Fast* (1937) began an interesting series of novels that shifted with *V as in Victim* (1945) to portray policemen who operate in the traditional manner of detectives in gathering evidence but who respond to other police matters and interact loosely as a team on a daily basis. Treat carried this form into the 1960s with *Lady, Drop Dead* (1960) and has been considered by most readers to be the founder of the police procedural.

George Harmon Coxe's fiction was widely read in the 1930s and 1940s, providing readers with a range of characters, mostly in the hard-boiled tradition. Kent Murdock is the first of his creations to appear in a novel, in *Murder with Pictures* (1935), adding Joyce Archer as wife in *Mrs. Murdock Takes a Case* (1941); the pair continued through nearly twenty novels. Flash Casey, a Boston crime photographer, appeared first in *Silent Are the Dead* (1942). Casey is a rougher version of Murdock, appearing in *Murder for Two* (1943), *Flash Casey, Detective* (stories, 1946), *Error of Judgment* (1961), *The Man Who Died Too Soon* (1962), and *Deadly Image* (1964). Coxe's series detective, Jack H. Fenner, a Boston private eye, is a natty former police detective, first appearing as a secondary character in *Four Frightened Women* (1939), then initially as the lead with Murdock as secondary character in *Fenner* (1971).

Geoffrey Homes created two memorable characters in addition to creating sound effects and writing screenplays for such well-regarded films as *Invasion of the Body Snatchers* (1956) and *Out of the Past* (1947), based on his own novel, *Build My Gallows High* (1946). Humphrey Campbell, part Paiute Indian, is simply an investigator who is tough, honest, and large. Homes also created a brief suspense series dealing with the movie industry; see, for example, *The Hill of the Terrified Monk* (1943). *Build My Gallows High* (1946) is considered the capstone of a series of detective novels and a classic of pulp fiction. Homes created another detective figure, Robin Bishop, who is a reporter, and a Mexican policeman, Jose Manuel Madero, who appears in two novels.

Brett Halliday (Davis Dresser) began his Miami-based Michael Shayne detective series with *Divided on Death* (1939), creating a memorable character who would break into radio and film and eventually title a magazine. Dresser wrote some eighty novels, many of them original paperbacks, collaborating with other writers for more. He wrote under at least eight pseudonyms, producing Westerns, suspense stories, and romances, but Halliday is the best known, and Michael Shayne promises to survive many reprintings. The *Mike Shayne Mystery Magazine* listed Dresser as editor, though he probably was not active in the magazine's publication. See Sharon A. Russell on Mike Shayne in DeMarr's *In the Beginning* (1995).

In *The Mysterious Mickey Finn* (1939), Elliot Paul created his detective, Homer Evans, as a bizarre parody of Philo Vance. The book is set in Paris, but it achieved an immediate audience, and Paul obliged with nearly a dozen more, moving his setting to the United States at the outbreak of war.

Horace McCoy's hard-boiled suspense fiction explores the social naturalism of the Depression. McCoy's atmosphere, characters, settings, and situations are the stuff of hard-boiled survival. It could be argued that these are the most significant ingredients, but many suspense novels shade into mysteries without formal investigations. *They Shoot Horses, Don't They?* (1935) features a dance marathon as a metaphor for life during the Depression; *Kiss Tomorrow Goodbye* (1948) is a gangster novel, and *No Pockets in a Shroud* (1948) features a journalist.

Frederick Nebel's *Sleepers East* (1933) and *Fifty Roads to Town* (1936), together with his collection *Six Deadly Dames* (1950), provide an idea how other writers used a hard-boiled style to express their own visions of life in the 1930s. Nebel's detective, Ben Cardigan, and homicide officer, Steve MacBride, are tough, wisecracking, and streetwise.

One of the few blind private detectives appearing in fiction was created by Baynard Kendrick, first president of the Mystery Writers of America. His Captain Duncan Maclain appeared in *The Last Express* (1937) and other novels and probably influenced the creation of television's *Longstreet*

(1971). Maclain appeared in some thirteen novels and a collection of stories.

Beginning with *The Big Sleep* (1939), Raymond Chandler's novels capture almost perfectly the balance between the vulnerable mystery narrator in a predatory milieu and the detective who must assert his solution to the crime. Chandler's work is more often cited as epitomizing hard-boiled detective narratives than even Dashiell Hammett's. There is no question that Chandler's softened and romanticized detective has been a more popular way to relate to a hard-boiled milieu than Hammett's figures. No writer more successfully combined sentiment, a moral sensibility, scenes of places where violence lurks, and a detective's understated tension. Chandler has probably had more direct influence on subsequent American writers of detective fiction than any other, certainly more on contemporary writers who value the hard-boiled tale and aspire to its art, social criticism, and romance. Chandler mixed these ingredients, dipping into the American social psyche to paint its seamy exploitation, its squandering of innocence, its decay of desire into pathological need. After stories in *The Black Mask, Dime Detective*, and elsewhere, Chandler published *The Big Sleep* (1939), *Farewell, My Lovely* (1940), *The High Window* (1942), *The Lady in the Lake* (1943), *The Little Sister* (1949), *The Long Goodbye* (1953), and *Playback* (1958) among his collections of stories, screenplays, and short stories. Philip Marlowe is the series character in all his novels except *Playback* and in most of the short stories, some of which were cannibalized for the novels. *Poodle Springs* (1964) was unfinished at his death in 1959. See Winifred Crombie's "Raymond Chandler: Burlesque, Parody, Paradox" (1983), which examines Chandler's style by applying J. Beekman, J. Callow, and M.A.K. Halliday's descriptive categories to explore patterns of burlesque of crime styles and self-parody. She disagrees with Frank MacShane that Chandler tries to make *The Long Goodbye* the definitive Chandler but sees the social combined with "stylistic comedy" (Crombie, 1983, 162). See also Matthew J. Bruccoli, ed., *Raymond Chandler: A Checklist* (1968); Rick Lott, "A Matter of Style: Chandler's Hardboiled Disguise" (1989); Edward Margolies, *Which Way Did He Go?* (1982); William Marling, *The American Roman Noir* (1995); Bernard Sharratt's *Reading Relations* (1982), which contains a perceptive chapter on Chandler; Paul Skenazy, *The New Wild West* (1982); Robert E. Skinner, *The Hard-Boiled Explicator: A Guide to the Study of Dashiell Hammett, Raymond Chandler and Ross Macdonald* (1985); Jerry Speir, *Raymond Chandler* (1981); J. K. Van Dover, ed., *The Critical Response to Raymond Chandler* (1995); Charles Wasserburg, "Raymond Chandler's Great Wrong Place" (1989); Mary Wertheim, "Philip Marlowe, Knight in Blue Serge" (1988); Peter Wolfe, *Something More than Night* (1985); Leon Arden, "A

Knock at the Backdoor of Art: The Entrance of Raymond Chandler"
(1985); Nicholas Freeling's chapter in *Criminal Convictions* (1994).

Aaron Marc Stein, who writes mostly as George Bagby and Hampton
Stone, created his first mainstream novel in 1930, then after trying a romance, fell into detective fiction with *Murder at the Piano* (1935). He has
written over a hundred since that time. The Inspector Schmidt series, written as Bagby, is set in Manhattan and runs nearly fifty novels. His Tim
Mulligan and Elsie Mae Hunt series begins with *The Sun Is a Witness*
(1940) and runs nearly twenty novels, while his Matt Erridge series began
with *Sitting Up Dead* (1958) and has run about the same length; both deal
with travel and exotic settings, though Mulligan and Hunt are archaeolo-
gists and Erridge is a mining engineer. Stein's Jeremiah X. Gibson and Mac
novels, about twenty of them written as Stone, began with *The Corpse in
the Corner Saloon* (1948) and involve two assistant district attorneys.

Though his first crime novel, *Bombay Mail* (1934), involved Inspector
Leonidas Prike, Lawrence Blochman's best-known character is Dr. Daniel
Webster Coffee, a pathologist in a midwestern city who was born in India.
Coffee appears in only one novel, *Recipe for Homicide* (1952), a number
of short stories, some of which are collected in *Clues for Dr. Coffee* (1964),
and in the television program, *Diagnosis Unknown* (1960).

1940s

Richard Wright published *Native Son* (1940), which adapted Chicago
news stories of the Nixon and Hicks case, occurring as he was writing the
novel.

Stanley Ellin got the attention of mystery readers with his "Specialty of
the House"[5] in 1948 and has written a number of highly respected detective
and suspense novels since that time, including his first, *Dreadful Summit*
(1948); *The Eighth Circle* (1958); *The Key to Nicholas Street* (1952);
House of Cards (1967); *The Valentine Estate* (1968); *The Bind* (1970); *The
Luxembourg Run* (1977); *Star Light, Star Bright* (1979); and *The Dark
Fantastic* (1983). See his essay in H.R.F. Keating's *Whodunit?* (1982).

Frances and Richard Lockridge are best known for their Pam and Jerry
North series beginning with *The Norths Meet Murder* (1940) and running
for nearly forty novels through *Murder by the Book* (1963), during which
the couple often cooperate as naive but successful investigators with Wiegand and Mullins of the NYPD. Several figures who were later to be featured appear among these novels. Many of the novels were adapted as films
and also became successful on radio. A series character appearing in some
sixteen novels was Merton Heimrich of the New York State Police; these
were on the whole a more tightly plotted series than the escapades involving
the Norths, with Richard's byline given top billing. Richard alone was cred-

ited with about thirty novels in three series, beginning with *Death in the Mind* (1945), featuring, variously, Heimrich, Nathan Shapiro, and Bernard Simmons.

Zenith Brown is better known as Leslie Ford, creator of a range of detective figures appearing in novels set in a wide range of locales. Writing first under the name of David Frome and later as Brenda Conrad, Brown wrote of murder among the genteel set. Loosely plotted, the novels were strong on descriptive detail, and several were exceptional for their sensitivity to historical nuance, as in the Washington novel, *Washington Whispers Murder* (1953), with echoes of McCarthyism, and *Siren in the Night* (1943), which captured something of the attitudes toward Japanese Americans shortly after the beginning of World War II.

Judson Philips wrote radio and television plays and over seventy-five novels, mostly crime beginning with *Cancelled in Red* (as Hugh Pentecost, 1939), featuring Luke Bradley, an NYPD inspector. He wrote over a hundred mystery and suspense novels in the course of more than sixty years, through the posthumous *Pattern for Terror*, with George Crowder and his nephew Joey. Philips created a range of detective and police series as Hugh Pentecost, including the John Jericho series represented in *Sniper* (1966); Pierre Chambrun, first appearing in *The Cannibal Who Overate* (1962); Julian Quist, beginning with *Don't Drop Dead Tomorrow* (1971); and others. Under his own name he created, among other characters, reporter Peter Styles, first appearing in *The Laughter Trap* (1964). His forté became terrorism.

Helen McCloy (Worrell Clarkson), who also writes as Helen Clarkson, created Dr. Basil Willing in *Dance of Death* (1938), the first American psychiatrist detective and the first to use his training in his investigations. In her novels, which began as classic stories and slowly began to take on more suspense, leading in some cases to outright thrillers, she creates well-crafted novels drawing on many pockets of arcane knowledge. Her *Two-thirds of a Ghost* (1956) satirizes the publishing industry and her *Through a Glass, Darkly* (1951) deals with a double.

Helen MacInnes's first book in 1941, *Above Suspicion*, marked the beginning of a remarkably successful series of thrillers, many of which have been filmed. Her locales with their catalogues of descriptive detail, the wealth of subplots, clear good and bad characterization, simple ideological perspective, and the portrayal of attractive lifestyles are ready-made for Hollywood. Nevertheless, *The Venetian Affair* (1963), *The Salzburg Connection* (1968), and *Prelude to Terror* (1978) are representative of the contemporary spy thriller.

Dolores Hitchens wrote under her own name and as others in a variety of subgenres. Some remember her best under the byline of D. B. Olson, author of spinster detectives Rachael and Jennifer Murdock, appearing first in *The Cat Saw Murder* (1940), and Professor A. Pennyfeather, who began with *Bring the Bride a Shroud* (1945). With her husband, Bert, she wrote a series about railroad detectives, including *End of the Line* (1957), *Sleep with Strangers* (1955), *F.O.B. Murder* (1955), *One-Way Ticket* (1956), *The Man Who Followed Women* (1959), and *The Grudge* (1963). *Sleep with Slander* (1960) is an excellent private eye novel.

Paul Ryan, who wrote as Robert Finnegan and Mike Quin, created the excellent Dan Banion series, beginning with *The Lying Ladies* (1946) and continuing through *The Bandaged Nude* (1946), perhaps his best, and *Many a Monster* (1948).

Frank Gruber, one of the most prolific writers in American history by his own report, did little to advance the art of the mystery story, but much to entertain his numerous readers. Gruber claimed to have written over 400 stories, 53 novels, 65 feature screenplays, about 100 television scripts, and at least 150 articles. Others dispute his record keeping. Gruber created the team of Fletcher and Cragg, a pair of sometime drifters surviving on their wits, with Fletcher providing the brains and Cragg providing the brawn in over a dozen novels beginning with *The French Key* (1940). Another team, Otis Beagle, a large-sized dandy who wears a fake diamond, and his sidekick, Joe Peel, work out of Hollywood. Finally, Simon Lash is an intellectual detective in *Simon Lash, Private Detective* (1941).

Zelda Popkin wrote a series of novels shortly prior to and during World War II involving Mary Carner, a department store detective, before she turned to mainstream literature. These are stories of a bright young woman in a gritty world, the best of which is probably *So Much Blood* (1944).

Kenneth Fearing wrote seven detective novels, of which *The Big Clock* (1946), is generally considered his best, perhaps a major contribution to the genre of psychological suspense. Its setting in magazine publishing is characteristic of such other thematic plots centered on an artist's colony (*Dagger of the Mind*, 1941) and fund-raising organizations (*The Generous Heart*, 1954). Born in Chicago, Fearing was also a journalist and poet, but his suspense novels are better remembered.

Cleve Adams's fiction represents pre–World War II American sympathies with fascism. His novels and stories were packed with action and values that were to crop up again in the work of a few mystery writers in the late 1940s and early 1950s. From *Sabotage* (1940) his Rex McBride and John Rye bounced around in confused plots abounding in stereotypes, though Francis Nevins feels his work held out great promise, noting his handling of character and scene in his last novel, *Shady Lady* (1955).

Dorothy B. Hughes was well-known on the West Coast and in the Southwest as mystery reviewer for the *Los Angeles Times* and author of spy thrillers. She also wrote classical stories featuring Inspector Tobin, beginning with *The So Blue Marble* (1940), as well as other detective and suspense fiction. Often set in the Southwest, her work includes *Ride the Pink Horse* (1946), set in Santa Fe. This novel is considered important in the tradition of dark suspense in the 1940s. See also *In a Lonely Place* (1947), a character study of a psychopath that was filmed by Nicholas Ray in 1950. *The Expendable Man* (1963) features the entrapment of a black doctor. Hughes also wrote an affectionate biography of Erle Stanley Gardner— *Erle Stanley Gardner: The Case of the Real Perry Mason* (1978). See also Lawrence J. Oliver, Jr., "The Dark-Skinned 'Angels' of Dorothy B. Hughes's Thrillers" (1984).

John Canady, who wrote as Matthew Head, published his first mystery, *The Smell of Money* (1943) as a teacher of art history at the University of Virginia, then created his memorable detective, Dr. Mary Finney, in *The Devil in the Bush* (1945), set in Africa. His African series is one of the first to deal with the rise of black consciousness in Africa.

Leigh Brackett, in addition to writing science fiction, also wrote *No Good from a Corpse* (1944), which is often considered along with such novels as Dolores Hitchens's *Sleep with Slander* (1960) as the best hardboiled private eye novel written by a woman. Readers should also note the suspense novel *The Tiger Among Us* (1957) about the vigilante reaction of a man to violent youths, as well as *An Eye for an Eye* (1957) and *Silent Partner* (1969).

Hilda Lawrence created the Mark East series set in Manhattan with *Blood upon the Snow* (1944) through *Death of a Doll* (1947), perhaps her best. Her mysteries, *The Pavilion* (1946) and two novelettes collected in *Duet of Death* (1949), are also of interest.

Lillian de la Torre is best known for her collected stories of Samuel Johnson as a detective figure in *Dr. Sam Johnson, Detector* (1946) and *The Detections of Dr. Sam Johnson* (1960), which are narrated by James Boswell, of course. Her novels, *Elizabeth Is Missing* (1945), *The Heir of Douglas* (1952), and *The Truth about Belle Gunness* (1955), are also meticulously researched historical investigations.

Margaret Millar created one of the earliest psychiatrist detectives in Paul Prye, who appeared in her first mystery, *The Invisible Worm* (1941), as a comic figure. Prye appeared in two subsequent novels, but the author then shifted to two novels involving Inspector Sands of the Toronto Police Department. After this she dropped series characters and concentrated on creating mystery and suspense, as in *Beast in View* (1955). Her detective figures, with a few exceptions, are not professionals, but are drawn into mysteries. See her interview in Diana Cooper-Clark's *Designs of Darkness* (1983).

Charlotte Armstrong wrote about thirty novels of suspense, most of which were heavily laden with moralisms. Her brief series with MacDougal Duff, which began with *Lay On, Mac Duff* (1943), were light in tone; typical of her subsequent work is *The Better to Eat You* (1954) and *A Dram of Poison* (1956).

John Franklin Bardin, who also wrote as Douglas Ashe and Gregory Tree, produced several suspense novels in the 1940s that have received renewed interest in recent years: *The Deadly Percheron* (1946), *The Last of Philip Banter* (1947), and *Devil Take the Blue-tailed Fly* (1948).

Helen Eustis's *The Horizontal Man* (1946), which received general acclaim for its use of psychoanalysis when published, was followed by only one further mystery novel, *The Fool Killer* (1954), and a volume of short stories, *The Captains and the Kings Depart and Other Stories* (1949).

Howard Browne's hard-boiled Chicago-based Paul Pine series, beginning with *Halo in Blood* (1946), *Halo for Satan* (1948), and *Halo in Brass* (1949), were first published under the name of John Evans. After moving to Hollywood to work in television, he published a fourth, *The Taste of Ashes* (1957), under his own name. His well-crafted fiction is characterized by an imaginative range of characters and devices. See John A. Dinan's *Chicago Ain't No Sissy Town! The Regional Detective Fiction of Howard Browne* (1997).

Alfred B. Harbage, a Shakespeare scholar who wrote as Thomas Kyd, created Sam Phelan in a series of novels, beginning with *Blood Is a Beggar* (1946) and continuing through *Blood of Vintage* (1947) and *Blood on the Bosom Devine* (1948). Kyd's novels are unusual among academic detective fiction in that they involve a semitough police hierarchy, with Phelan an ex-boxer in the ranks.

Beginning with *Pick Your Victim* (1946), Patricia McGerr created more than a dozen mysteries, working first with the novel approach of naming the accused and withholding the name of the victim on the first page and trying other variations to avoid the classic English puzzle. After exhausting variants, she settled into a more conventional form with her remaining novels and short stories.

Fredric Brown, who also wrote some of the best science fiction of the 1950s, created the remarkable Chicago detectives, Ed and Ambrose Hunter, who appeared in about a third of his twenty-three detective novels. Brown's use of paradox in his work is found in *The Fabulous Clipjoint* (1947), his first crime novel, and is exploited through most of the rest of his work.

Jack Iams's entertaining series of comic mysteries begins with *The Body Missed the Boat* (1947) and continues through eight novels, ending with *A Corpse of the Old School* (1955), but his best, *Death Draws the Line*

(1949), set in a comic-strip establishment, mixes farce and mystery exceptionally well.

Henry Kane, who also writes as Anthony McCall, created Peter Chambers, a hard-boiled private detective, in his first novel, *A Halo for Nobody* (1947), and carried him through over thirty novels. Among the Chambers novels, beginning with *The Private Eyeful* (1959), Kane gave Maria Trent star billing and worked her into some of the Chambers novels. He also created several Inspector McGregor novels and other fiction.

Harold Masur, who wrote as Guy Fleming and Edward James, created his Scott Jordan, a lawyer-detective "somewhere between Perry Mason and Archie Goodwin" who is personally involved in his cases.[6] He was successful enough to feature Jordan in nearly a dozen novels and a collection of short stories, beginning with *Bury Me Deep* (1947). He also ghosted Helen Traubel's *The Metropolitan Opera Murders* (1951).

Robert Wade and Bill Miller, who, until Miller's death in 1961, cowrote stories and novels under such names as Wade Miller, Dale Wilmer, and Whit Masterson, created Max Thursday, a San Diego hotel detective who appears in half a dozen novels, overcoming his drinking problem to rise to whatever trouble he encounters. Thursday first appears in *Guilty Bystander* (1947), after the authors' first novel, *Deadly Weapon* (1946). As Whit Masterson they wrote *Badge of Evil* (1956), the basis for the Orson Welles film classic *A Touch of Evil* (1957).

Hillary Waugh, who also writes as H. Baldwin Taylor and Harry Walker, is best known for his police procedurals, but he has also written gothic romances as Elissa Grandower and other mystery novels. Police Chief Fred Fellows, the law in Stockford, Connecticut, first appears in *Sleep Long, My Love* (1959), while Frank Sessions, a Manhattan homicide detective first appears in *"30" Manhattan East* (1968). Private detective Sheridan Wesley appeared in three novels, beginning with Waugh's first, *Madam Will Not Dine Tonight* (1947). Waugh's best novel may well be *Last Seen Wearing . . .* (1952), a procedural that has received much acclaim as one of the best created to date. See his *Hillary Waugh's Guide to Mysteries & Mystery Writing* (1991); also Joan Y. Worley in Earl Bargainnier and George Dove, *Cops and Constables: American and British Fictional Policemen* (1986).

Ursula R. Curtiss blends suspense with mystery in some twenty novels, beginning with *Voice Out of Darkness* (1948). Her fiction involves ordinary people conducting ordinary lives who find themselves caught up in mystery or endangered from something out of their past or seeking revenge for some social outrage. *The Noonday Devil* (1951), *The Forbidden Garden* (1962), and *Out of the Dark* (1964) are among the best.

Ruth Fenisong specializes in the gothic mystery with romantic overtones in her Gridley Nelson series, beginning with *Murder Needs a Face* (1942).

Critics find *Widow's Plight* (1955) and *But Not Forgotten* (1960) among her best.

David Dodge wrote over a dozen mystery novels, many set in South and Central America, involving several series characters. *Death and Taxes* (1941) and four other novels featured a witty couple in the manner of the Charleses and the Norths. He also wrote the highly successful *To Catch a Thief* (1952). A series featuring John Abraham Lincoln began with *Hooligan* (1970).

Margaret Scherf wrote well over twenty crime novels, beginning with *The Corpse Grows a Beard* (1940). Scherf etched small-town Episcopalian life and characters with a touch of wry. Her Reverend Martin Buell, Emily and Henry Bryce, and Grace Severance are series characters, with Severance, a retired pathologist who is sharp witted and clever, the most memorable, particularly in *To Cache a Millionaire* (1972).

Mickey Spillane became one of the most notorious writers of crime and spy fiction and for several years the most popular, with the introduction of his private detective, Mike Hammer, in *I, the Jury* (1947) and spy, Tiger Mann, in *Day of the Guns* (1964). Spillane's rabid violence and the McCarthyesque anti-Communism of especially his early novels has met with widely divergent critical opinions of his accomplishments. From 1947 to 1951 his first seven novels were best-sellers and sold over 40 million copies. His phenomenal sales proved irresistible to many writers who tried to imitate the ingredients of his success, while others complained that his hero was actually a villain. Spillane has continued to write and perform and is best known today as a television personality found in beer ads. Notable among his novels are *Vengeance Is Mine* (1950), *My Gun Is Quick* (1950), *The Big Kill* (1951), *One Lonely Night* (1951), *Kiss Me, Deadly* (1952) and *The Deep* (1961). His most recent, much more modest, is *Black Alley* (1996). See J. Kenneth Van Dover, *Murder in the Millions* (1984); John G. Cawelti's "The Spillane Phenomenon" (1969); Max Allan Collins, *One Lonely Knight: Mickey Spillane's Mike Hammer* (1984).

Cornell Woolrich's dissembled world allowed for no series characters, little hope, and a great deal of fear and suspense. His *The Bride Wore Black* (1940) has gone through several editions and remains a minor classic of American literature, as Woolrich himself is something of a cult figure among readers of suspense and the modern gothic. His first novel led to a *Black* series, including *The Black Curtain* (1941), *The Black Angel* (1943), and *Rendezvous in Black* (1948). As George Hopley he wrote *Night Has a Thousand Eyes* (1945), and as William Irish he wrote *Phantom Lady* (1942) and others. Most of his short stories are collected in twenty volumes, usually set in the 1930s or something like it, among urban despair, loneliness, and night shadows. Francis Nevin has called Woolrich the Poe of the twentieth century.[7]

Elizabeth Daly set her classic detective stories in New York among an isolated collection of wealthy people. Daly's detective is the bibliophile Henry Gamadge, first developed in *Unexpected Night* (1940) and appearing in some sixteen novels. Gamadge seems to be modeled on golden age classic detectives but does not have their usual arcane quirks. Among the better novels are *Murders in Volume 2* (1941) and *The Book of the Lion* (1948).

Marie Rodell, literary editor and agent, who wrote as Marion Randolph, probably had more knowledge of the field than skill or time. She helped many writers master their craft. Her best work may be *Grim Grow the Lilacs* (1941), where she used a country setting to exceptional effectiveness to tell a classic tale with muted gothic overtones. Her *Mystery Fiction: Theory and Technique* (1943) is practical and thoughtful.

Willis Todhunter Ballard is another prolific writer of pulp stories, Westerns and mystery novels who wrote as Todhunter Ballard, P. D. Ballard, Neil MacNeil, John Hunter, Parker Bonner, Sam Bowie, Hunter D'Allard, Harrison Hunt, John Shepherd, Brian Agar, Willard Kilgore, John Grange, Nick Carter, and others. Beginning in 1942 with *Say Yes to Murder*, one of his best, he created the Bill Lennox (troubleshooter for a Hollywood studio) series, and with *Pretty Miss Murder* (1961), the Lt. Max Hunter novels under his own name. As Neil MacNeil he published from 1958 with *Death Takes an Option* through *The Spy Catchers* (1966); and as P. D. Ballard a series of three more crime novels. Most of his novels were published in hardback until the early 1950s, then appeared as original paperbacks. His mysteries are often set in Las Vegas and emphasize a medium-tough milieu.

Shirley Jackson's work falls between gothic and mystery fiction, often containing elements of both. From her first, *The Road Through the Wall* (1948), to her sixth and last, *We Have Always Lived in the Castle* (1963), Jackson maintained a tension between madness and sanity, the natural and supernatural, the influence of the past and struggles of the present.

Dorothy Salisbury Davis created more than a dozen suspense novels beginning with *The Judas Cat* (1949) and says her best are *A Gentle Murderer* (1951), *The Pale Betrayer* (1965), and *God Speed the Night* (with Jerome Ross, 1968), which involve known villains with police playing lesser roles (Davis, "Some of the Truth," 1986).

Bart Spicer created Carney Wilde, a Pennsylvania-based detective, in his first hard-boiled novel, *The Dark Light* (1949). Wilde continued to appear for a decade until *Exit, Running* (1959). Then, with *Act of Anger* (1962), Spicer shifted to suspense and an excellent spy novel, *The Burned Man* (1966). With his spouse, Betty Coe, together writing as Jay Barbette, he collaborated on four other mysteries.

Vera Caspary began as a playwright and screenwriter in the 1930s, then with *Laura* (1943) burst into a series of mystery and suspense novels. Caspary is a master of the witty dialogue of people who fail to see the world as it is—often threateningly brutal under the guise of charm and empty gestures.

Phyllis Whitney began her romantic mystery novels with *Red Is for Murder* (1943), after having written juveniles, which she continues to publish, mixing gothic and romance elements. Her novels usually focus on a young woman and often involve some conflict between mother and daughter.

C. Hugh Holman, best known as an American literary scholar, wrote perhaps six mystery and detective novels from 1942 through 1951, most featuring Sheriff Macready, the law in Abeton, South Carolina, a fictional college town.

James Norman wrote mysteries, juveniles, and nonfiction in addition to being a professor. Perhaps his best work is his first, *Murder, Chop Chop* (1942), which began a series featuring the giant Mexican investigator, Gimiendo Hernandez Quinto, set in China prior to and at the beginning of World War II.

David Goodis, a freelance writer and screenwriter, wrote hard-boiled suspense novels and stories, including *Dark Passage* (1946), made into the famous Bogart film; *Nightfall* (1947); *Behold This Woman* (1947); *Cassidy's Girl* (1951); *Of Tender Sin* (1952); *Streets of the Lost* (1952); *The Burglar* (1953); *The Moon in the Gutter* (1953); *Black Friday* (1954); *Street of No Return* (1954); *The Wounded and the Slain* (1955); *Down There* (1956), on which François Truffaut based his film *Shoot the Piano Player* (1960); *Fire in the Flesh* (1957); *Night Squad* (1961); *Somebody's Done For* (1967). His novels are characterized by pessimism and despair, though often within an existential perspective that relates his novels to film noir and to other paperback classics of the period. See James Sallis's "David Goodis" (1993).

William Lindsay Gresham's *Nightmare Alley* (1946), portraying carnival life, has the flavor of capitalist metaphor found in Horace McCoy's *They Shoot Horses, Don't They?* Gresham's lurid prose, psychodrama, and his eye for the seedy sharper helps him maintain an intensity that matches the world he portrays.

The Gordons, Mildred and Gordon Gordon, wrote twenty suspense and mystery novels, from *The Little Man Who Wasn't There* (1946) through their Undercover Cat novels, emphasizing humor.

William P. McGivern, who worked in the pulps and Hollywood, produced two dozen detective and mystery novels, from *But Death Rides Faster* (1948)—notable for its previous appearance in a pulp magazine—through *Night of the Juggler* (1975). Known for his work featuring police, his best-known novel is probably *The Big Heat* (1953). *Rogue Cop* (1954) and *Odds Against Tomorrow* (1957), a criminal procedural in which racial conflict among the criminals echoes that of the larger society, are very good.

James Atlee Phillips, better known as Philip Atlee, began his mystery novels with *The Case of the Shivering Chorus Girls* (1942) but hit his own stride with his Joe Gall thriller series, beginning with *The Green Wound* (1963), which soon picked up the key title word Contract.

1950s

Robert Bloch is best known for *Psycho* (1959), primarily because of Alfred Hitchcock's notorious film. The preoccupation with psychopathic suspense, however, began with *The Scarf* (1947), and Bloch's talents are much broader. He produced screenplays, teleplays, and radio scripts as well as numerous short stories and anthologies.

Thomas B. Dewey, who also writes as Tom Brandt and Cord Wainer, created several series characters in nearly forty novels and a number of short stories. His first novel, *Hue and Cry* (1944), introduced Singer Batts, then with *Prey for Me* (1954) he developed his longest series around Mac, a Chicago detective who is an ex-policeman. Dewey also created the series detective Pete Schofield.

Day Keene wrote radio soap operas, pulp stories, and nearly fifty original paperbacks and hardcover books, most of which were murder mysteries. *Framed in Guilt* (1950), his first novel, came after a decade of pulp and radio scripting and reflects a hard-won craft.

Merriam Modell, who writes most of her suspense novels as Evelyn Piper, is known for *Bunny Lake Is Missing* (1957) and *The Nanny* (1964), both of which were made into films. *The Innocent* (1949) began a series of eight chilling suspense stories.

Although she advised young writers to "keep as clear of the suspense label as possible," most of Patricia Highsmith's work does involve suspense and certainly does not suffer by it. From her first novel, *Strangers on a Train* (1950), through *Edith's Diary* (1977), her fiction is remarkably fresh and readable. *The Talented Mr. Ripley* (1955) may be something of a reworking of Henry James's theme in *The Ambassadors* (1903) but releases it from James's Victorian sensibilities in such a delightfully perverse way that Ripley returns for several more novels. She discusses her prison novel *The Glass Cell* (1964) in *Plotting and Writing Suspense Fiction* (1966). See also her essay in H.R.F. Keating's *Whodunit?* (1982) and interview in Diana Cooper-Clark's *Designs of Darkness* (1983).

Richard S. Prather's Shell Scott is a Los Angeles–based private detective who battles his way through nearly forty comic paperback novels from *The Case of the Vanishing Beauty* (1950) through *The Sure Thing* (1975).

Thomas Walsh wrote numerous short stories and nearly a dozen police novels, beginning with *Nightmare in Manhattan* (1950), set in Grand Central Station. His portrayal of New York street life is exceptional, and his development of suspense is very good.

Harry Whittington, who also wrote as Ashley Carter, Robert Hart Davis, Whit Harrison, Kel Holland, Harriet Kathryn Myers, Blaine Stevens, Clay Stuart, Harry White, and Hallam Whitney, began by writing Westerns, then expanded to sexploitation, erotic gothics, and mysteries, all in paperback. The mysteries, more than a third of some ninety paperback originals, begin with *Slay Ride for a Lady* (1950), are often set in Florida, and range from suspense to detection.

Evelyn Berckman wrote nearly thirty mysteries and gothics, beginning with *The Evil of Time* (1955), sometimes mixing threads of the supernatural.

William Wiegand has produced only two crime novels, *At Last, Mr. Tolliver* (1950), a character study, and *The Treatment Man* (1959), the story of a prison revolt told in parts by an inmate and prison employee. His work is nonetheless notable.

Leonard S. Zinberg, writing as Ed Lacy, created two African-American private detectives in the course of some thirty mystery novels, many having boxing themes. Toussaint Moore, a postal employee working on the side in *Room to Swing* (1957) and *Moment of Untruth* (1964), and Lee Hayes, a former boxer in *Harlem Underground* (1965) and *In Black and Whitey* (1967), are based on Zinberg's friends and acquaintances in New York.

Mary McMullen published over a dozen mystery novels, beginning with *Stranglehold* (1951). Her emphasis is on the manners and character of urban career people.

Charles Willeford's reputation was resuscitated in the 1980s with interest in Miami, leading to his representation in critical work on hard-boiled fiction and the republication of a number of his novels, including *New Hope for the Dead* (1985), *Sideswipe* (1987), *The Burnt Orange Heresy* (1971), *Cockfighter* (1972), *Pick-Up* (1955), *The Woman Chaser* (1960), *The Way We Die Now* (1989). Others include *High Priest of California* (1956), *Off the Wall: A True Life Novel* (1980), dealing with serial killer David Berkowitz, *Miami Blues* (1984), and *Kiss Your Ass Good-Bye* (1988). John Williams (1991) says Willeford refined the Florida psychopath.

Helen Nielsen has written nearly twenty mysteries in addition to television script writing, beginning with *The Kind Man* (1951). Her mysteries often involve people caught in murder situations or drawn into them by circumstances. Several of her novels center on the lawyer Simon Drake.

Charles Williams wrote mostly original paperback suspense novels set in the South or on the sea or beaches, the plots often turning on a mystery surrounding a young woman, as in *Hill Girl* (1951), his first. Among Williams's nearly two dozen novels *Big City Girl* (1951), *Scorpion Reef* (1955), *The Big Bite* (1956), *Operator* (1958), *Stain of Suspicion* (1958), and *Dead Calm* (1963), filmed by Phillip Noyce (1989), are readable and provide something of the climate of the late 1950s.

Kendell Foster Crossen, writing as M. E. Chaber, a prolific writer of radio and television scripts, wrote over a dozen Milo March insurance investigator/private detective novels, beginning with *Hangman's Harvest* (1952). As Christopher Monig he wrote a short series of mysteries about the adventures of Brian Brett, an insurance claims adjuster in Los Angeles, beginning with *The Burned Man* (1956).

Richard Martin Stern's paperback original mystery novels began with *The Bright Road to Fear* (1958), though he soon moved to hardcovers after numerous short stories in slick and pulp magazines.

Jim Thompson wrote numerous original paperback suspense novels, of which nearly a dozen were reprinted during the Ronald Reagan years. After four less-startling novels, *The Killer Inside Me* (1952) created a figure in Lou Ford that exploits the formal and thematic loopholes in the genre. Ford is the son of an M.D. who is a deputy sheriff as well as a clever psychopath. Like Herman Melville, Thompson was resuscitated from obscurity by a changing interpretive paradigm resulting in the reprinting of his novels. Other works include *Heed the Thunder* (1946), *Nothing More than Murder* (1949), *Cropper's Cabin* (1952), *The Alcoholics* (1953), *Bad Boy* (1953), *The Criminal* (1953), *Recoil* (1953), *Savage Night* (1953), *A Swell-Looking Babe* (1954), *The Golden Gizmo* (1954), *A Hell of a Woman* (1954), *The Nothing Man* (1954), *Roughneck* (1954), *After Dark, My Sweet* (1954), *The Kill-Off* (1957), *Wild Town* (1957), *The Getaway* (1959), filmed by Sam Peckinpah (1972), *The Transgressors* (1961), *The Grifters* (1963), *Pop. 1280* (1964), *Texas by the Tail* (1965), *Ironside* (1967, novelization), *Child of Rage* (1972), *King Blood* (1973), *More Hardcore* (1987). See also *Fireworks, the Lost Writings of Jim Thompson*, edited and introduced by Robert Polito and Michael McCauley (New York: D. I. Fine, 1988); Max Allan Collins's essay in Jon Breen and Martin Henry Greenberg's *Murder Off the Rack* (1989); Gay Brewer's *Laughing Like Hell: The Harrowing Satires of Jim Thompson* (1996).

Nedra Tyre wrote half a dozen novels and a host of short stories involving suspense and detection, including a classic girls' reformatory novel, *Hall of Death* (1960). Her stories draw on her experiences with elderly and disadvantaged people, as well as her knowledge of the mystery field, evidenced in the short story "Murder at the Poe Shrine" (1955) and in such novels as *Mouse in Eternity* (1952).

Walter Tevis wrote few novels, but the suspense novels *The Hustler* (1959), filmed by Robert Rossen, and *The Color of Money* (1984), filmed by Martin Scorsese, are masterpieces of pool hustling.

Michael Avallone, Jr., wrote over a hundred novels, mostly original paperbacks in half a dozen genres, including mysteries, suspense, and detective fiction beginning in 1953 with *The Spitting Image* and *The Tall Dolores*. Both novels feature Ed Noone, a private detective who appeared in some forty of Avallone's nearly sixty mysteries.

Lionel White wrote over thirty-five crime novels, beginning with *The Snatchers* (1953), a criminal procedural like *The Big Caper* (1955) and others. He set other suspense novels in small towns, particularly in the South.

Joseph Hayes is best known as a playwright and for his first novel, *The Desperate Hours* (1954; television, 1955; film dir. by William Wyler, 1955), though he wrote nine other suspense novels.

Milton Lesser, who is better known by readers as Stephen Marlowe, also wrote as Andrew Frazer, Jason Ridgway, and C. H. Thames. After establishing himself as a science fiction author under his own name, Lesser published his first mystery as Stephen Marlowe, *Catch the Brass Ring* (1954). He published two other novels, then launched into his Chester Drum series, which constitute nearly half of his forty suspense, spy, and mystery novels. After his first three attempts, Marlowe hit upon the catch phrase for his Drum titles, such as *Murder Is My Dish* (1957) and *Peril Is My Pay* (1960). As Jason Ridgway he created five other suspense novels.

William Campbell Gault began his mystery fiction with *Don't Cry for Me* (1952), but is better known for his two series characters, Brock Callahan, who began in *Ring Around Rosa* (1955), and Joe Puma, who first appeared in *End of a Call Girl* (1958). Gault's settings are usually in Southern California. Callahan is an ex–football player.

Gloria and Forrest Fickling, who write as G. G. Fickling, created Honey West, who appeared in a Fawcett original paperback, *This Girl for Hire* (1957). West was moved from California, where she worked as a private detective, to New York, where she worked for the CIA as well. She also appeared on television for a season.

Carolyn Keene, pseudonym for several writers including Edward Stratemeyer and his daughter, Harriet Adams, produced the Nancy Drew series featuring the plucky girl detective, who Craig and Cadogan say "crystallizes spirit, optimism and adventurousness" (Craig and Cadogan, 1981, 245). Nancy Drew first appeared in *The Secret of the Old Clock* (1929). See Carolyn Stewart Dyer and Nancy Tillman Romalov, eds., *Rediscovering Nancy Drew* (1995); Bobbie Ann Mason's *The Girl Sleuth* (1975) is an early feminist critique of Nancy Drew and other mysteries; Margery

Fisher's *The Bright Face of Danger* (1986) is primarily concerned with adventure novels for children and contains a chapter on juvenile series detectives; see also David Farah, *Farah's Guide to the Nancy Drew Mystery Series* (1987).

Evan Hunter has written Westerns and science fiction and has assumed a number of names for his novels, but he is almost synonymous with Ed McBain, author of the 87th Precinct novels. His first novel appears to have been *The Big Fix* (1952), two years before his celebrated *The Blackboard Jungle* (1954). The 87th Precinct series of police procedurals by Ed McBain began with *Cop Hater* (1956) and has run to over thirty novels and a collection of short stories. Matthew Hope is the central figure in such novels as *There Was a Little Girl* (1994), set in and around a circus in Florida. See also McBain's essay, "The 87th Precinct" in Otto Penzler's *The Great Detectives* (1978). McBain explains why the composite protagonist won't work: the public wants individual heroes; the precinct is like a family with rank as father (Lt. Byrnes), older brother (Carella), and black sheep (Roger Haviland). See also George N. Dove's *The Boys from Grover Avenue* (1985) and his short version in Mary Jean DeMarr's *In the Beginning* (1995).

Gore Vidal has written a wide range of novels and sparkles in the contemporary literary limelight as acerbic wit and political gadfly, but less known are his three satirical detective novels, written as Edgar Box: *Death in the Fifth Position* (1952), *Death Before Bedtime* (1953), and *Death Likes It Hot* (1954). These are collected in *Three by Box: The Complete Mysteries of Edgar Box* (1978).

Talmage Powell writes in both his own name and as Jack McCready, creating the Tampa private detective Ed Rivers, formerly a New Jersey policeman, beginning with *The Killer Is Mine* (1959).

Henry Slesar, who also writes as O. H. Leslie, has written in a wide range of media, including advertising copy, radio, television, and film. His numerous short stories have appeared in digest magazines, and his occasional novels have mixed elements of suspense, psychological horror, mystery, and romance, from *The Gray Flannel Shroud* (1959) through *The Thing at the Door* (1974).

John B. West's Rocky Steele novels began with *An Eye for an Eye* (1959) to combine adventure with mystery in a fast-paced series. Steele is an ex-boxer whose fists often come into play. See Darwin T. Turner's "The Rocky Steele Novels of John B. West," in Larry Landrum, Pat Browne, and Ray B. Browne, eds., *Dimensions of Detective Fiction* (1976).

Richard Condon made his mark on suspense fiction with *The Manchurian Candidate* (1959) and has followed this with nearly a dozen further novels dealing with various aspects of crime.

Lester Dent, the prolific author of over 150 Doc Savage novels, also wrote half a dozen novels of suspense and detection.

Richard Matheson, who went on to focus on speculative fiction, wrote *Someone Is Bleeding* (1953) in the tradition of hard-boiled pathology.

Chester Himes began his career in literary crime and suspense with the publication of *If He Hollers Let Him Go* (1946), a tough black life novel honed on his prison experience. After moving to France in 1953 in part as a relief from racism in the United States, Himes gained a literary reputation and at the urging of his editor began the comic Coffin Ed Johnson and Grave Digger Jones series. *For Love of Imabelle* (1957; aka *A Rage in Harlem*) was followed by a series that included *The Crazy Kill* (1959), *The Real Cool Killers* (1959), *All Shot Up* (1960), *The Big Gold Dream* (1960), *Cotton Comes to Harlem* (1965), *The Heat's On* (1966), and ending with *Blind Man with a Pistol* (1969). See also his autobiographical work, *The Quality of Hurt* (1972) and *My Life of Absurdity* (1976). Himes is a major figure in the disputed ground of late modernism as well as a popular artist. Like Ishmael Reed, his parodic relationship to formula, culture, and commerce is of particular interest. See biographies and studies including James Lundquist's *Chester Himes* (1976), Stephen Milliken's *Chester Himes* (1976), Gilbert H. Muller's *Chester Himes* (1985) and Robert E. Skinner, *Two Guns from Harlem* (1989). See also John M. Reilly's "Chester Himes' Harlem Tough Guys" (1976); Henry Louis Gates's chapter in *Signifying Monkey* (1988); the chapter in Stephen Soitos's *The Blues Detective* (1996); Michael Denning, "Topographies of Violence: Chester Himes' Harlem Domestic Novels" (1988); Peter Freese, *The Ethnic Detective* (1992); Edward Margolies, *Which Way Did He Go?* (1982); Raymond Nelson, "Domestic Harlem: The Detective Fiction of Chester Himes" (1976); Robert P. Smith, Jr., "Chester Himes in France and the Legacy of the *Roman Policier*" (1981).

Peter Rabe's *Dig My Grave Deep* (1956) introduces a man who gets out of the mob to become a freelance operator with some similarities to John D. MacDonald's Travis McGee. See also *Kill the Boss Goodbye* (1956). See Donald E. Westlake's essay in Breen and Greenberg, *Murder off the Rack* (1989).

1960s

The influential Ross Macdonald (Kenneth Millar) developed another variation of the detective. After *The Dark Tunnel* (1944), a college novel mixed with Nazi intrigues, and *Blue City* (1947), which has similarities to Hammett's *Red Harvest* (1929), his novels turn to greater subtlety in which his detective, Lew Archer, is conscientiously developed as an extension of the author's moral sensibilities. Archer was introduced in *The Moving Tar-*

get (1949; written as John Macdonald), a figure not unlike Chandler's Philip Marlowe, though Chandler was critical of the book. As the series evolves through *The Drowning Pool* (1950), *The Way Some People Die* (1951), and *The Ivory Grin* (1959), the novels coalesce around the crime as a social pathology that is manifested in fiction as metaphor and the representation of broken families. In *On Crime Writing* (1973) Macdonald includes an essay on the writing of *The Galton Case* (1959), which he saw as a pivotal turn in his work toward the conflation of psychological and narrative revelation. See the interview in Diana Cooper-Clark's *Designs of Darkness* (1983); Sam L. Grogg's interview and Elmer Pry's "Lew Archer's 'Moral Landscape,' " in Landrum, Browne, and Browne's *Dimensions of Detective Fiction* (1976); Leonard W. Engel, "Locked Up: A Close Look at Ross Macdonald's 'The Underground Man' " (1987); L. L. Lee, "The Art of Ross Macdonald" (1986); Dennis Lynds, "Expanding the Roman Noir: Ross Macdonald's Legacy to Mystery/Detective Authors" (1986); Jeffrey H. Mahan, *A Long Way from Solving That One: Psycho/Social and Ethical Implications of Ross Macdonald's Lew Archer Tales* (1990); Edward Margolies, *Which Way Did He Go?* (1982); Paul Skenazy, "Bringing It All Back Home: Ross Macdonald's Lost Father" (1986); "Spheres of Influence: Personal and Social Stories in Ross Macdonald" (1986); Robert E. Skinner, *The Hard-Boiled Explicator: A Guide to the Study of Dashiell Hammett, Raymond Chandler and Ross Macdonald* (1985); Jerry Speir, *Ross Macdonald* (1979); T. R. Steiner, "The Mind of the Hardboiled: Ross Macdonald and the Roles of Criticism" (1986); Mary S. Weinkauf, *Hard-Boiled Heretic* (1986); Peter Wolfe, *Dreamers Who Live Their Dreams* (1977).

Elizabeth Linington publishes simultaneously and frequently as Dell Shannon, Lesley Egan, Egan O'Neill, and Anne Blaisdell as well as Linington. Linington says readers' interest in her police procedurals is in the police and their personal lives, though she often bases her novels on real crimes.[8] As Dell Shannon she began the Lieutenant Luis Mendoza series with *Case Pending* (1960); as Anne Blaisdell, she began the Sergeant Ivor Maddox series with *Nightmare* (1961). She then switched to Elizabeth Linington for the rest of the series, and as Lesley Egan she began her Jesse Falkenstein and Vic Varallo series with *A Case for Appeal* (1961). See Mary Jean DeMarr's essay in Bargainnier and Dove, *Cops and Constables* (1980).

Marvin Albert created Tony Rome, an ex-policeman based in Miami from *Miami Mayhem* (1960) through two other novels, *Lady in Cement* (1962) and *My Kind of Game* (1962), as well as other suspense novels.

Kin Platt, who wrote and illustrated comic strips from the late 1940s to the early 1960s and is known for his theatrical caricatures, also wrote numerous juvenile mysteries and crime novels, often with a moral emphasis, and adult mysteries. His *Sinbad and Me* (1966) has been acclaimed. His

Max Roper series, beginning with *The Pushbutton Butterfly* (1970), features sports settings and a detective working for a government-associated private intelligence and espionage service.

In addition to work in radio, theater, and film, Lucille Fletcher has written five excellent suspense novels, from *Blindfold* (1960) to *Eighty Dollars to Stamford* (1975), but these are overshadowed by the fame of *Sorry, Wrong Number*, a radio drama in 1944 that appeared on stage and film.

Ira Levin, perhaps best known for *Rosemary's Baby* (1967), *The Stepford Wives* (1972), and *The Boys from Brazil* (1976), created a range of novels, including the excellent *A Kiss Before Dying* (1953), which shifts from criminal procedural to detection to suspense, and *Sliver* (1991), assembled as a mainstream contemporary thriller.

John Jakes's reputation rests on his historical fiction, but among his hundred or so novels he also created the Johnny Havoc series, which express many of the same sentiments found in his novels of American history. Havoc works without a license because, as he says in *Johnny Havoc* (1961), it restricts his freedom as "an exponent of free enterprise."[9]

Cornelius Hirschberg's only suspense novel is *Florentine Finish* (1963), notable for its details on the New York jewelry business.

John Iannuzzi's novels, beginning with *What's Happening?* (1963), are strong on the workings of the courts and police in New York City, beginning with *Sicilian Defense* (1972), a gangster novel.

John Ball's *In the Heat of the Night* (1964) broke new ground in the police procedural with its use of an actual Pasadena, California police detective as the model for Virgil Tibbs. Ball's attention to authentic detail and his interest in informing his readers as well as entertaining them gives his work a seriousness in a subgenre often given to uncritical promotion of police or glorification of violence. See George N. Dove's essay in Bargainnier and Dove's *Cops and Constables* (1980).

Carolyn G. Heilbrun, writing as Amanda Cross, has created a series of academic mysteries featuring Kate Fansler, beginning with *In the Last Analysis* (1964). Her mysteries are decidedly murder stories that seek P. D. James's wit and incisiveness in a more sedate and mannered world. See the interview in Diana Cooper-Clark's *Designs of Darkness* (1983), the essay by Lois A. Marchino on Kate Fansler in DeMarr's *In the Beginning* (1995), and Julia B. Boken's *Carolyn G. Heilbrun* (1996).

Thomas Pynchon published *V* (1963), which includes Herbert Stencil, who searches for the anarchist woman spy who is named, variously, Venus, Virgin, and Void. *The Crying of Lot 49* (1966) centers on the investigations of Oedipa Maas as she reads clues in the investigation of a will. *Gravity's Rainbow* (1973) follows Lieutenant Tyrone Slothrop as he tracks Lieutenant Weissman (disguised as American Captain Blicero), the Nazi villain who attempts to create havoc. See also *Vineland* (1990) and *Mason & Dixon* (1997).

Clarence L. Cooper's *Black! Three Short Novels* (1997) appeared, which includes *The Dark Messenger, Yet Princes Follow*, and *Not We Many*, first published in the 1960s.

Robert L. Fish, who also writes as Robert L. Pike and Lawrence Roberts, has been entertaining readers since his *The Fugitive* (1962), when he introduced José da Silva of the Rio de Janeiro police. Other characters include Kek Huuygens, a Brazilian smuggler. As Pike, Fish created Lieutenant Clancy of Manhattan's 52nd Precinct (*Mute Witness*, 1963, which became the movie *Bullitt*, 1988), in which Lieutenant Jim Reardon operates in San Francisco. His collections of short stories include the Sherlock Holmes parodies *The Incredible Schlock Homes* (1966) and *The Memoirs of Schlock Homes* (1974). See Otto Penzler's interview with Fish in *The Great Detectives* (1978).

Joseph Harrington's Francis X. Kerrigan and Jane Boardman procedurals, beginning with *The Last Known Address* (1965), offer realistic portrayals of police work in New York City. See Martha Alderson and Neysa Chouteau in Bargainnier and Dove, *Cops and Constables* (1980).

George Baxt, who has written a number of screenplays, originated Pharoah Love in *A Queer Kind of Love* (1967), the first of a series of Love mysteries, notable for its portrayal of the New York gay subculture. See also *The Talking Pictures Murder Case* (1990).

Noel Behn's *The Kremlin Letter* (1966) and *The Shadowboxer* (1970) are marked by their early portrayal of the cynicism of espionage establishments.

As E. V. Cunningham, the prolific Howard Fast created nearly twenty crime novels including, most recently, those involving Masao Masuto, a Japanese-American Beverly Hills police detective, first appearing in *Samantha* (1967).

Charlotte MacLeod has published a range of mysteries for children and nostalgic adults from *Mystery of the White Knight* (1964) through several series characters featured in cheerful cozies organized around wealthy Boston families and small town Canada, often with holiday themes.

Clark Howard's *The Arm* (1967) is a suspense novel involving a professional crap shooter.

Michael Crichton is probably best known for his speculative suspense novels, such as *The Andromeda Strain* (1969), *The Terminal Man* (1972), *Westworld* (1975), *Congo* (1980), and *Rising Sun* (1992), but has also written a series of suspense novels as John Lange. Crichton's work is usually set in the near future or the high-tech present, sharing territory with the medical thrillers and quasi-horror in the spaces between contemporary thrillers and cyberpunk science fiction. See Elizabeth A. Trembley's *Michael Crichton: A Critical Companion* (1996).

Joe Gores was known for his short stories until the publication of *A Time of Predators* (1969) but has since published the series involving Dan Kearney, procedurals based on the detective agency for which he formerly worked where he specialized in repossessing cars. His best-known novel is *Hammett* (1975), in which he re-creates the author drawn back into detection in San Francisco in 1928. *Dead Man* (1993) and *Menaced Assassins* (1994) deal with assassination.

E. Richard Johnson began publishing his crime novels from prison with *Silver Street* (1968) and has produced a collection of novels dealing with criminality, gangsters, police, and a range of street crime.

Lawrence Block, who also writes as Chip Harrison and Paul Kavanagh, has written over fifty original paperback and hardcover novels dealing with crime, suspense and espionage, beginning with *Death Pulls a Double Cross* (1961) at the age of twenty-three. His Evan Tanner spy novels are fast paced and often humorous, while his Bernie Rhodenbarr novels, such as *The Burglar Who Studied Spinoza* (1981), feature a professional thief. The Matt Scudder private eye novels, such as *A Ticket to the Boneyard* (1990), deal with hard-boiled crime. See Lawrence Block and Ernie Bulow's *After Hours: Conversations with Lawrence Block* (1995).

Edward Hoch, who also writes as Irwin Booth, Stephen Dentinger, Pat McMahon, R. L. Stevens, and Mr. X, prefers the classic short story, of which he has allegedly written over five hundred, but after *The Shattered Raven* (1969), he began the brief series of novels featuring Carl Crader and Earl Jazine, the best of which is *The Frankenstein Factory* (1975). Some of Hoch's best short stories are collected in *Leopold's Way: Detective Stories by Edward D. Hoch* (1985).

Jay Williams, writing as Michael Delving, published seven crime novels beginning with *Smiling, the Boy Fell Dead* (1967), bringing folklore and antiques into the mysteries.

Ron Goulart is a pulp writer in the age of paperbacks, being versatile, highly productive, numerously named, and competent in several genres. His brief John Easy series, originating with *If Dying Was All* (1968), is set in Hollywood amongst zanies. Goulart also writes the Avenger stories as Kenneth Robeson, the Phantom stories as Frank S. Shawn, with numerous other novels and short stories among these. His anthologies of the pulps stimulated the nostalgic revival of interest in the 1970s.

Velda Johnston mixes the exotic locations and characters of romance fiction with mystery in nearly forty novels from *Along a Dark Path* (1967).

Dorothy Gilman has written juveniles in addition to her novels of intrigue centering around Mrs. Pollifax, starting with *The Unexpected Mrs. Pollifax* (1966), and her suspense stories, usually involving young women. She carries the spirit and inspiration of her youth stories into adult fiction. About half of her nearly dozen adult novels feature Mrs. Pollifax, perhaps the best of which is *Mrs. Pollifax on Safari* (1977).

Dan J. Marlowe has written two memorable series of original paperback novels, one featuring Johnny Killian, a sometime private detective, and the Earl Drake series, which features a professional thief, beginning with *The Name of the Game Is Death* (1962). Editorial pressure changed Drake from a thief to an espionage agent.

Lillian O'Donnell's mystery novels began with *Death on the Grass* in 1960, but her better-known police detective Norah Mulcahaney series began with *The Phone Calls* (1972) and her Mici Anhalt series with *Aftershock* (1977). See DeMarr's essay in her critical anthology, *In the Beginning* (1995).

John D. MacDonald was one of the most widely read authors in the United States. His *Wine of the Dreamers* (1951) is a minor classic in American speculative fiction. Over twenty of his nearly seventy novels construct the legend of Travis McGee, Fort Lauderdale, Florida, "salvage expert"–detective living aboard the houseboat, the *Busted Flush*. Borrowing Frances Crane's device of titles with color names, MacDonald's "color" novels are characterized by well-constructed plots, vulnerable women, sexual therapeutics, social commentary, and McGee's friendship with his pal Meyer. The first-person series begins with *The Deep-Blue Goodbye* (1964) and continues through twenty-one novels. The author of a small host of suspense and criminal novels and the cleverly modeled disaster novel *Condominium* (1977), MacDonald is thoughtful and entertaining, though the byplay with women has dated rapidly for some readers. See also *The J.D.M. Bibliophile*; T. Frederick Keefer, "Albert Camus' American Disciple: John D. MacDonald's Existentialist Hero, Travis D. McGee" (1985); Sam Meyer, "Color and Cogency in Titles of John D. MacDonald's Travis McGee Series" (1988).

Donald E. Westlake has written nearly a hundred crime and spy novels under a number of bylines, including Richard Stark, Curt Clark, Tucker Coe, and Timothy J. Culver, and includes among his novels science fiction as well. Westlake created several series characters. *The Mercenaries* (1960), his first crime novel, deals with a criminal organization, and his paperback Parker series, written as Richard Stark and beginning with *The Hunter* (1962), involves a single criminal. As Tucker Coe, Westlake created ex-policeman Mitch Tobin, who first appears in *Kinds of Love, Kinds of Death* (1966) and who in the course of the series becomes a private detective. Westlake's novels are characterized by grim humor in such novels as

The Fugitive Pigeon (1965) and by sympathy for outsiders. See the interview by William L. DeAndrea, "The Many Faces of Donald E. Westlake" (1988).

Emma Lathen (Mary Latsis and Martha Hennissart), called by Keating the "only genuine five-star mystery writer to appear in the late twentieth century," created a series of novels featuring John Putnam Thatcher, a New York banker–amateur detective in *Banking on Death* (1961). All of the Thatcher novels play on some aspect of business finance with secondary themes often involving Thatcher's personal foibles or corporate manners. As R. B. Dominic, the authors created Ben Safford in *Murder Sunny Side Up* (1968). Thatcher's position allows him access to a wide range of business activities, and the authors are adept at sketching in minor and major characters. See William A. S. Sarjeant, "Crime on Wall Street" (1988).

Ray Russell, who has written sardonic screenplays and a host of brief fiction, began his mystery novels with *Unholy Trinity* in 1967. Most of his fiction involves mystery with touches of the occult.

Harry Kemelman began with *Friday the Rabbi Slept Late* (1964), an almost single-handed revival of the armchair detective found here in the persona of the Rabbi David Small, who uses Talmudic thought as a means of reasoning through his solutions to crime. See Peter Freese, *The Ethnic Detective* (1992).

William F. Nolan is not easy to categorize as a crime writer, since he has written a wide range of fiction and nonfiction as well as screen and television plays, but is well known among crime readers as the author of a private eye novel set in the future, *Space for Hire* (1971), as well as *Logan's Run* (1967) and the sequel featuring a future policeman.

Barbara Mertz writes her detective fiction as Elizabeth Peters, her gothics as Barbara Michaels, and archaeological history under her own name. Beginning with *The Jackal's Head* (1968), she has written over a dozen mysteries, often with gothic overtones.

Robert L. Duncan, writing as James Hall Roberts, combines suspense, the search for faith, and a knowledge of archaeological history in *The Q Document* (1964), *The Burning Sky* (1966), and *The February Plan* (1967).

Dorothy Uhnak began her half dozen police novels with *The Bait* (1968), though she had earlier drawn on her experience as a detective with the New York City Transit Police Department to write the nonfiction work *Policewoman: A Young Woman's Initiation into the Realities of Justice* (1964).

Richard O'Connor, writing as Patrick Wayland, created several spy novels featuring Lloyd Nicholson, beginning with *Counterstroke* (1964). As Frank Archer he wrote the Joe Delaney series and several others beginning with *The Naked Crusader* (1964).

Under a variety of bylines, Dennis Lynds continued *The Shadow* series and the Dan Fortune series beginning with *Act of Fear* (1967). As William Arden he wrote the Kane Jackson books that began with *A Dark Power* (1968), and as Mark Sadler the Paul Shaw series beginning with *The Falling Man* (1970). He wrote another half dozen crime novels as John Crowe, and as another incarnation of Nick Carter wrote several Carter adventures.

Stanton Forbes, who also writes as De Forbes, Forbes Rydell (when writing with Helen Rydell), and Tobias Wells, has written a wide range of mystery and suspense novels, usually set in small towns or limited communities, as in *Grieve for the Past* (1963), which Dorothy B. Hughes calls "one of the finest mysteries of the sixties," though she is probably best known for her Knute Severson series, written as Tobias Wells.[10]

Ross Thomas began his political thrillers with *The Cold War Swap* (1966) and as Oliver Bleeck initiated the Philip St. Ives series with *The Brass Go-Between* (1969). *Briarpatch* (1984) has affinities with Hammett's *The Glass Key*. The novel won an Edgar for best novel and is considered by many readers to be his best book.

Collin Wilcox began his mystery writing with *The Black Door* (1967), in which a clairvoyant news reporter solves crimes, but with *The Lonely Hunter* (1969) he started his successful series featuring Lieutenant Frank Hastings of the San Francisco Homicide Squad. See Frederick Isaac in Bargainnier and Dove's *Cops and Constables* (1980).

Arthur Maling has published a dozen crime novels beginning with *Decoy* (1969), several of which have featured Brock Potter, a Wall Street brokerage analyst. Arthur Maling won the MWA Best Novel award for *The Rheingold Route* (1979).

Don Pendleton first wrote his crime novels as Stephan Gregory with *Frame Up* (1960), then under his own name, with *War Against the Mafia* (1969), he began The Executioner series that has continued through some forty novels, with scores more written under the name of Don Pendleton.

1970s

Joseph Hansen, who also writes as Rose Brock and James Colton, began his Dave Brandstetter series with *Fadeout* (1970) and continues it through a half dozen novels to date. His gay detective has the usual problems private detectives encounter with their domestic arrangements, but his access to gay subcultures opens new perspectives in a traditionally homophobic genre. See his "The Mystery Novel as Serious Business" (1984); also Landon Burns's essay on Dave Brandstetter in DeMarr's *In the Beginning* (1995).

Percy Spurlark Parker, who is well-known for his short stories, has also published *Good Girls Don't Get Murdered* (1974), featuring his series detective Big Bull Benson, African American owner of a Chicago hotel and bar. See his comments in Frankie Y. Bailey, *Out of the Woodpile* (1991).

Paul Erdman's first novel, *The Billion Dollar Sure Thing* (1972), partly written in prison after his conviction following the Swiss collapse of the First Bank of New York, won an MWA Best First Novel. Erdman's second novel, *The Silver Bears* (1974), also centered on banking in Switzerland and concerned a man who ends up in prison without criminal intent, while his third novel, *The Crash of '79* (1976), portrayed the collapse of the international banking system, and, subsequently, modern civilization.

Tony Hillerman's Joe Leaphorn, a Navajo tribal policeman, appears in *The Blessing Way* (1970) and after three novels alternates with Jim Chee, a younger Indian who is drawn to tradition but remains a police officer. Hillerman weaves a non-Indian view of Navajo and Zuñi culture into the series. Hillerman shifts "from writing romance-as-entertainment into writing novels-that-entertain," corresponding to his shift from featuring Leaphorn in the first three novels to featuring both Leaphorn and Jim Chee in the next three, to featuring Chee in the following three, through *Coyote Waits* (1990). Hillerman won the MWA Edgar Allan Poe award in 1974 after the publication of *Dance Hall of the Dead* (1973). Other novels include *A Thief of Time: A Novel* (1988), *Sacred Clowns* (1993), *The Joe Leaphorn Mysteries* (1992), and *Listening Woman* (1994 [1978]). See Leonard Engel's "Landscape and Place in Tony Hillerman's Mysteries" (1993) and Ellen Strenski and Robley Evens's "Ritual and Murder in Tony Hillerman's Detective Novels" (1981). Comments and interviews are found in *The Tony Hillerman Companion* (1994); his "Making Mysteries with Navajo Materials" (1989); interviews in John Williams's *Into the Badlands* (1991); Hillerman and Ernie Bulow, *Talking Mysteries: A Conversation with Tony Hillerman* (1991). See also Rosemary Herbert, *The Fatal Art of Entertainment* (1994); Ward Churchill, "Hi Ho, Hillerman . . . (Away): Unmasking the Role of Detective Fiction in Indian Country" (1992); Fred Erisman's "Hillerman's Uses of the Southwest" (1989) and "Tony Hillerman's Jim Chee and the Shaman's Dilemma" (1992); Peter Freese, *The Ethnic Detective* (1992); Michael Parfit, "Weaving Mysteries That Tell of Life Among the Navajos" (1990); Jack W. Schneider, "Crime and Navajo Punishment: Tony Hillerman's Novels of Detection" (1982); Jane S. Bakerman in Bargainnier and Dove, *Cops and Constables* (1980); John M. Reilly's *Tony Hillerman: A Critical Companion* (1996).

George V. Higgins began his criminal and police novels with *The Friends of Eddie Coyle* (1972); *Cogan's Trade* (1974); *The Friends of Richard*

Nixon (1975); *The Patriot Game* (1982). *Dreamland* (1977) centers the viewpoint in the consciousness of a pathological liar, *A Choice of Enemies* (1984) is an astute political novel on Boston politics. Others include *The Rat On Fire* (1981), *Outlaws* (1987), *Trust* (1989), and *Bomber's Law: A Novel* (1993). See also *George V. Higgins on Writing* (1990) and his interview in John Williams's *Into the Badlands* (1991).

Diane Johnson plays with the conventions of the nineteenth-century detective story in *The Shadow Knows* (1974).

Max Allan Collins began as a writer of paperback originals, beginning with *Bait Money* (1973), featuring ex-thief Nolan. A series involving a hired killer, Quarry, began in 1976 and continues through several novels. The hardback Mallory series, beginning with *The Baby Blue Rip-Off* (1973), features a Vietnam veteran ex-cop in Iowa. Collins has also written a book on Mickey Spillane and has written the *Dick Tracy* comic strip since 1977. Robert Baker and Michael Nietzel (1985) think his *True Detective* (1983) the best historical detective novel ever written.

Donald Goines was not the first writer to begin a career from within prison, nor the first African American, but few have translated street life so directly into the novel. He began with *Dopefiend: The Story of a Black Junkie* (1971), *Whoreson: The Story of a Ghetto Pimp* (1972), and *Street Players* (1973) and wrote at a torrid pace until his death in 1974. He is probably best known for *Daddy Cool* (1974) and *Never Die Alone* (1974). See also *Crime Partners* (1978). See Eddie Stone's biography, *Donald Writes No More* (1974).

Andrew L. Bergman's *The Big Kiss-Off of 1944* (1974) brought out Jack LeVine, a 1940s Hollywood detective in the manner, if not the features, of Raymond Chandler's Marlowe, and his *Hollywood and LeVine* (1975) includes Humphrey Bogart as a character and works in ex-President Nixon's early years. See David Geherin, *Sons of Sam Spade* (1980).

Jackson F. Burke's black detective, Sam Kelly, first appears in *Location Shots* (1974) in his New York City milieu.

Warwick Downing's detective, Joe Reddman, who was raised by a Cheyenne Indian woman, is a private investigator in Denver, starting with *The Player* (1974). Other novels include *A Clear Case of Murder* (1990) and *Choice of Evil* (1994).

Elinore Denniston was an accomplished writer of romantic suspense novels, beginning with *No Tears for the Dead* (1948) through nearly fifty novels written as Rae Foley and Dennis Allan, one of the best being *The Brownstone House* (1974).

Andrew Coburn writes suspense novels, beginning with *The Trespassers* (1974), as well as a series of police novels featuring Rita Gardella O'Dea, who first appears in *Sweetheart* (1985).

Jerome Charyn's *The Isaac Quartet* (1984), which kills off Manfred Coen, a cop, then features Isaac Sidel, a deputy police commissioner in New York; the collection includes *Blue Eyes* (1975), *Marilyn the Wild* (1976), *The Education of Patrick Silver* (1976) and *Secret Isaac* (1978). Later novels—*The Good Policeman* (1990) through *El Bronx* (1996)— enlarge on the figure. Charyn's New York is fragmented into ethnic territories and flamboyant characters. See the Jerome Charyn issue of the *Review of Contemporary Fiction* (1992) and David Madden's "The Isaac Quintet: Jerome Charyn's Metaphysics of Law and Disorder" (1992).

Richard Brautigan is better known as a poet, but his parodies of detective and mystery fiction include *Dreaming of Babylon: A Private Eye Novel 1942* (1977) and *Willard and His Bowling Trophies: A Perverse Mystery* (1975).

Dean R. Koontz has written in a broad range of popular genres under a variety of nom de plumes. His crime publications began in the mid-1970s with *Strike Deep* (as Anthony North, 1974) and have moved toward mainstream suspense, such as the closet terror in the recent *Intensity* (1995). His *Writing Popular Fiction* (1973) and *How to Write Best-Selling Fiction* (1981) are standard guides for writers of popular fiction. See also Martin H. Greenberg, Ed Gorman, and Bill Munster, eds., *The Dean Koontz Companion* (1994) and Bill Munster, ed., *Discovering Dean Koontz: Essays on America's Bestselling Writer of Suspense and Horror Fiction* (2nd ed., 1995).

Robert Irvine created two series set in his home state of Utah after a career in Los Angeles in TV news. Bob Christopher is a news reporter for an L.A. TV station beginning with *Jump Cut* (1974), while *Baptism for the Dead* (1988) introduces Moroni Traveler, an ex–professional football player.

Rex Burns [Raoul Stephen Schler] is creator of Gabriel Wager, a Chicano detective working out of the Denver Police Department. The character first appears in *The Alvarez Journal* (1975), which received the MWA award for the best first novel.

Thomas Harris has published only three novels and their screenplays, but all hit jackpots. *Black Sunday* (1975) mixed the enthusiasm for professional football with paranoia about Middle East terrorism after the oil crisis, and *Red Dragon* (1981) and *The Silence of the Lambs* (1988) capitalized on the fear of serial killers by mixing thriller, suspense and procedural elements.

James Crumley began his detective novels with *The Wrong Case* (1975), followed by *The Last Good Kiss* (1978) and *Dancing Bear* (1983), set in Montana and thereabouts. *The Last Good Kiss* (1978) develops a vision of the wasteland that goes beyond Chandler and Hammett. See *The Mexican Tree Duck* (1993). Keith Newlin argues in "C. W. Sughrue's Whiskey Visions" (1983) that the quest motif and whiskey as a visionary source combine "to reflect the detective's preoccupation with distinguishing true from false visions and values while elucidating truth," and that Crumley uses parody of the mission and detective role (Newlin, 1983, 546). See also Charles L. P. Silet's "Drugs, Cash and Automatic Weapons: An Interview with James Crumley" (1994).

Thomas Gifford began his mystery novels with *The Wind Chill Factor* (1975) and has published several since that time, including the nonfiction novel *The Man from Lisbon* (1977).

Peter Israel created the B. F. Cage series of suspense novels, beginning with *Hush Money* (1974). Cage is a Richard Nixon–era dirty tricks specialist. Israel sets most of his novels in France, where, beginning with *The Stiff Upper Lip* (1978), Cage sets up his operations, both legitimate and illegitimate, with attention to an upscale lifestyle.

Stephen Dobyns, known for his poetry as well as crime fiction, began his private eye Charlie Bradshaw "Saratoga" series with *Saratoga Longshot* (1976), set in a small community in New York. The series is sprinkled with quotation and arcane knowledge.

Thomas Berger has written several mystery parodies, such as *Who Is Teddy Villanova?* (1977), which involve New York City private detective Russel Wren. Another novel, *Killing Time* (1977), undermines the detective novel's epistemology.

William Hjortsberg produced the postmodern novel *Falling Angel* (1978), which overlays the premises of a hard-boiled detective story with the occult to produce a paradox of the self. *Nevermore* (1994) recreates the 1920s with the help of time, characters, and events from other decades and centuries. In his work Arthur Conan Doyle and Harry Houdini attempt to solve murders modeled on Poe's stories.

Ishmael Reed, whose foray through popular genres includes the postmodern Western, *Yellow-Back Radio Broke Down* (1969), does similar riot to the formula of detective fiction with *Mumbo Jumbo* (1972) and *The Last Days of Louisiana Red* (1974), where PaPa LaBas investigates crimes and attempts to come to grips with good and evil, the revision of history, subverting of stereotypes, white/black fantasies, and other themes. See Stephen Soitos's *The Blues Detective* (1996); Henry Louis Gates's *The Signifying Monkey* (1988); Michael Boccia's "Ishmael Reed's *Mumbo Jumbo*: Form of the Mystery" (1987); Lizabeth Paravisini, "*Mumbo Jumbo* and the Uses of Parody" (1986); Joe Weixlmann, "Culture Clash, Survival, and Trans-Formation: A Study of Some Innovative Afro-American Novels of Detection" (1994).

Kenn Davis featured his black San Francisco detective, Carver Bascombe (the author is not African American), in such novels as *The Dark Side* (1976), *The Fooza Trap* (1979), and *Words Can Kill* (1984). Others include *Melting Point* (1984) and *Blood of Poets* (1990).

James Gunn, who is also known for his science fiction and criticism, has written a detective novel featuring a magician's convention and the occult in *The Magicians* (1976).

George C. Chesbro, author of *King's Gambit* (1975), has created a series of novels involving Dr. Robert "Mongo" Frederickson, a dwarf private investigator who is interested in the occult and who often becomes involved in political intrigue. Mongo appeared in a series of magazine stories, then in such novels as *Shadow of a Broken Man* (1977).

John Gregory Dunne has published a number of novels with crime themes, such as *Dutch Shea* (1982), but is best known for a detailed novel on the moral struggle of police/priest brothers in *True Confessions* (1977).

Ralph McInerny's Father Roger Dowling first appeared in *Her Death of Cold* (1977) and has continued through nearly a dozen novels, while Mother Mary Teresa first appeared in *Not a Blessed Thing* (1981). His numerous publications develop strong religious themes, and titles play cleverly on catch phrases throughout.

Jules Feiffer's *Ackroyd* (1977) is a parody of both private detective fiction and Agatha Christie's *The Murder of Roger Ackroyd* (1926).

Robin Cook has written numerous medical thrillers, usually with topical social themes dramatized as investigations with speculative scenarios. These include *Coma* (1977), *Brain* (1981), *Fever* (1982), *Mindbend* (1985), *Outbreak* (1987), *Mortal Fear* (1988), *Vital Signs* (1991), and *Terminal* (1993). See Lorena L. Stookey, *Robin Cook* (1996).

Paula Gosling's *A Running Duck* (1978, retitled *Fair Game* for the 1978 American edition) began a series of mysteries featuring ordinary men who when threatened become capable of cunning and violence before settling into a love relationship.

Stephen Greenleaf published his first mystery novel, *Grave Error*, in 1979. Featuring former San Francisco lawyer Marshall Tanner, the novels evoke characters' pasts to discover relationships that have become tragic. Baker and Nietzel (1985) believe that Greenleaf's prose is more intelligent and engaging than that of any other contemporary private eye writer.

Carolyn Weston began her mystery novels in 1954, but it was not until her police series, featuring Casey Kellogg and Al Krug, appeared in *Poor, Poor Ophelia* (1972) that she began to attract considerable attention, with the novel forming the basis for the television program *Streets of San Francisco* (1972).

Richard North Patterson won the MWA's Best First Novel for *The Lasko Tangent* (1979).

James Patterson's *The Thomas Berryman Number* was judged Best First Novel (1976) by MWA.

Warren Kiefer won the MWA's Best Novel award with *The Lingala Code* (1972) and has published *The Pontius Pilate Papers* (1976) and *The Kidnappers* (1977).

R. H. Shimer won the MWA's Best First Novel with *Squaw Point* (1972), a study of Alaskan island life as well as a detective novel.

William Hallahan published *The Dead of Winter* (1972), then won the MWA's Best Novel for *Catch Me, Kill Me* in 1977; other imaginative works include *Foxcatcher* (1986) and *Tripletrap* (1989).

Charles Alverson's *Fighting Back* (1973) was followed in 1975 by the Joe Goodey series, beginning with *Goodey's Last Stand* (1975).

K. C. Constantine began the saga of his small-town Pennsylvania Sheriff Mario Balzic with *The Rocksburg Railroad Murders* (1972) and has continued it through nearly a dozen more. While the setup is similar to that mastered by Hillary Waugh, the novels are less concerned with police procedures than the manners and customs of rural Pennsylvania. Constantine has been lauded for capturing the nuances of speech that sharply differentiates his prose from that of similar crime fiction. See also his "Writing about Balzic" (1986).

James Jones, better known for such war novels as *From Here to Eternity* (1951), created a very heavy detective in *A Touch of Danger* (1973).

Warren Murphy published *Subways Are for Killing* (1973) and others before introducing Julian "Digger" Burroughs, an Irish-Jewish private detective specializing in fraud in Las Vegas in a series of novels published from 1982, including *Smoked Out*. In 1983 he introduced another Las Vegas detective, Devlin Tracy, in *Trace*.

Gardner Dozois and George Effinger published *Nightmare Blue* (1975), about the last private detective on Earth.

Mary Higgins Clark published her best-selling *Where Are the Children?* (1975), followed by further novels featuring terrorized women and children. See Linda C. Pelzer's *Mary Higgins Clark: A Critical Companion* (1995).

Brian Garfield [Francis Wynne] published a range of suspense novels, as well as Westerns and other fiction. He is probably best known for *Death Wish* (1972), a revenge novel that filmmakers turned into a series of vehicles for actor Charles Bronson. He won the MWA's Best Novel award for *Hopscotch* (1975).

Stuart M. Kaminsky was well established as a film professor and reviewer who had written one of the first books on film genres before branching out to detective fiction. Beginning with *Bullet for a Star* (1977), set in the 1940s and featuring Toby Peters, Kaminsky made his reputation with *Murder on the Yellow Brick Road* (1978). Peters continues to evoke 1940s nostalgia, but with *Rostnikov's Corpse* (1981) Kaminsky began a series with a Moscow detective and with *Lieberman's Folly* (1990) began a third series featuring an aging detective in Chicago, where Kaminsky has spent much of his life. Other novels include *Hard Currency* (1995).

Mike Jahn won MWA Best Paperback for *The Quark Maneuver* (1977), featuring a relationship between white cop Bill Donovan and Marcie Barnes, a black woman. Other novels include *Night Rituals* (1982), which adds subordinate Thomas Jefferson Lincoln; *Death Games* (1987); *City of God* (1992); and *Murder at the Museum of Natural History* (1995). See Jahn's comments in Bailey's *Out of the Woodpile* (1991).

William L. DeAndrea won the MWA's Best First Novel for *Killed in the Ratings* (1978), featuring Matt Cobb, a TV network troubleshooter, in a Golden Age–style plot and followed this with seven more television theme novels centered on Cobb. DeAndrea has also produced a series featuring Niccolo Benedetti and a brief spy series. He also produced the reference book *Encyclopedia Mysteriosa* (1994).

William Kienzle's Father Bob Koesler mysteries, set in Detroit, appeared first with *The Rosary Murders* (1979). Kienzle was a priest and editor of a Catholic newsletter before publishing fiction, which features Detroit settings and classic puzzle form.

Lawrence Sanders began his crime novels with *The Anderson Tapes* (1970), weaving themes of contemporary surveillance practices, out of touch criminals, and conflicting agendas among law enforcement agencies as revealed largely through documents. The book was quickly picked up for filming by Sidney Lumet (1972) and established Sanders's reputation. His second book, *The First Deadly Sin* (1973), features NYPD Captain Edward X. Delaney and plays on the procedural form and sensational crime to produce the ingredients for a best-seller. The series picked up on the success of Frederick Forsyth's formula for alternating the perspectives of criminal and pursuer. A third series features Archy McNally.

Martin Cruz Smith is best known for *Gorky Park* (1981) but began his crime fiction a decade earlier with *Gypsy in Amber* (1970), which includes a gypsy theme. *Gorky Park*'s protagonist is Arkady Renko, who also appears in *Polar Star* (1989) and *Red Square* (1992). He also produced a number of early novels as Nick Carter and Simon Quinn.

Ernest Tidyman is best known for his *Shaft* (1970) series, featuring black policeman John Shaft, but this white author has also written *Line of Duty* (1974), about a crooked cop, and *Dummy* (1974), focusing on a brain-damaged thug. The Shaft series—*Among the Jews* (1972), *Shaft's Big Score* (1972), *Shaft Has a Ball* (1973), *Goodbye, Mr. Shaft* (1973), *Shaft's Carnival of Killers* (1974) and *The Last Shaft* (1975)—led to the popularity of "blaxploitation."

Los Angeles Detective Sergeant Joseph Wambaugh appeared on the fictional crime scene with police procedurals *The New Centurions* (1970), *The Blue Knight* (1972), *The Choirboys* (1975), and a dozen subsequent books. *The Onion Field* (1973) portrays police as victims. He left the LAPD in 1974 and has consulted and written scripts for TV programs such as *Police Story* and *The Blue Knight*. His most recent novel is *Floaters* (1996).

Michael Z. Lewin began his detective fiction with *Ask the Right Question* (1971) and has written half a dozen novels featuring Indianapolis detective Albert Samson, whose distinguishing features are that he doesn't carry weapons and is nonviolent. Another series character is Lt. Leroy Powder, also of Indianapolis.

Robert Ludlum specializes in best-selling political thrillers, which he began with *The Scarlatti Inheritance* (1971). Ludlum's thrillers are thematic treatments of a wide range of post–John LeCarré tales of secrecy, insiders, and high stakes. Notable are *The Gemini Contenders* (1976), *The Bourne Identity* (1980), through *The Apocalypse* (1995). See *The Robert Ludlum Companion*, edited by Martin H. Greenberg (1993).

Bill Pronzini, prolific short story writer, novelist, and anthologist, began his criminal suspense novels with *The Stalker* (1971), along with his unnamed private eye series with *The Snatch* (1971); as Jack Foxx he writes the Dan Connell series. Pronzini is widely known for his anthologies and his columns in *Armchair Detective*.

Writing as Trevanian, Rodney Whitaker is best known for *The Eiger Sanction* (1972), a political thriller, and *The Main* (1976), a police procedural.

Nicholas Meyer has been widely praised and narrowly condemned for *The Seven-Per-Cent Solution: Being a Reprint from the Reminiscences of John H. Watson, M.D.* (1974), featuring Sherlock Holmes. The novel's popular success led to other attempts to play on the theme. Meyer followed the novel with *The West End Horror* (1976) and other novels such as *Target Practice* (1974).

Robert B. Parker has become one of the most successful private detective novelists with his Spenser series, set in Boston beginning with *The Godwulf Manuscript* (1973). Parker's work is self-consciously allusionist, referencing classic British literature and, of course, Raymond Chandler; with such characters as Tallboy he borrows from Dorothy L. Sayers as well. Parker extends Hammett, Chandler, and Ross Macdonald and employs a less coherent "jock" ethical code, which is not always successful. Parker won the MWA Best Novel award for *Promised Land* (1976). Other novels include *God Save the Child* (1973) and *Looking for Rachael Wallace* (1980), which garnered him feminist attention for its portrayal of a lesbian author to whom Spenser is assigned as a bodyguard, through over twenty other novels in the series. See Parker's essay in Robin Winks, *Colloquium on Crime* (1986); also Donald Greiser, "Robert B. Parker and the Jock of the Mean Streets" (1984); David Geherin, *Sons of Sam Spade* (1980); John W. Presley, "Theory into Practice: Robert Parker's Re-Interpretation of the American Tradition" (1989).

Roger L. Simon began his series of novels featuring Moses Wine, a Southern California private detective, in *The Big Fix* (1973), which won the MWA best first novel and has since published *California Roll* (1985). See David Geherin, *Sons of Sam Spade* (1980).

Elmore Leonard began his suspense and criminal novels with *The Big Bounce* (1969) and became popular with *Cat Chaser* in 1974 after a successful series of Westerns. *52 Pick-Up* (1974) is his first thriller set in Detroit; *Swag* (1976) features Frank and Stick, everyone's favorite villains; *The Hunted* (1977); *Stick* (1983) is set in Florida; *The Switch* (1978) features a strong woman at the center of the novel. Others include *Glitz* (1985), *Freaky Deaky* (1988), *Get Shorty* (1990) and *Out of Sight* (1996). See David Geherin, *Elmore Leonard* (1989), and Glenn Most, "Elmore Leonard: Splitting Images" (1988).

Arthur Lyons's Jacob Asch series set in Southern California began with *The Dead Are Discreet* (1974) and has continued through a dozen novels, each picking up a theme such as religion—*All God's Children* (1975)—or law and medicine, as in *At the Hands of Another* (1983). One novel, *Unnatural Causes* (1988), is coauthored with Thomas Noguchi, formerly the chief medical examiner of Los Angeles.

Clarence Major published *Reflex and Bone Structure* (1975), a postmodern foray into the genre. See Soitos's discussion in *The Blues Detective* (1996).

Martha Grimes has published a number of updated classic detective novels set in England, beginning with *The Man with a Load of Mischief* (1981). Her thematic material includes a fondness for children and pets, with a lighthearted tone and nostalgia for imaginative histories of artifacts. See Ray B. Browne, "Christie Tea or Chandler Beer" (1985); Susan L. Clark, "Murder Is Her Cup of Tea" (1988).

Gregory McDonald began his Fletch series, oriented to the information passing through a large newspaper office and featuring investigative reporter Irwin Maurice Fletcher. The series began with *Fletch* (1974), which won the MWA award for the Best First Novel. Fletch's appeal to the counterculture—young, witty, irreverent, wearing a T-shirt and blue jeans—was lost in the Reagan era. The most recent contribution is *Fletch Won* (1986). See his essay in H.R.F. Keating's *Whodunit?* (1982).

Vern E. Smith published *The Jones Men* (1974, reprinted 1976) based on his award-winning news story about the heroin subculture in Detroit. See Frankie Y. Bailey, *Out of the Woodpile* (1991).

John Lutz is best known as a writer of short stories, but his occasional novels, beginning with *The Truth of the Matter* (1971), set in the Ozarks, are well worth the reader's time. His Alo Nudger series includes *Buyer Beware* (1976) and *Nightlines* (1985). Another series features ex-cop Orlando PI Fred Carver in *Tropical Heat* (1986), *Scorcher* (1987), *Kiss* (1988), *Flame* (1990), *Bloodfire* (1991), *Hot* (1992), *Torch* (1994) and *Burn* (1995).

Ross Spencer's satirical private detective Chance Purdue of Chicago appears in *The Dada Caper* (1978), and comic detective Rip Deston of Saddleback Knob, Ohio, appears in *Echoes of Zero* (1981). Other novels include *The Missing Bishop* (1985), *Monastery Nightmare* (1986), *Kirby's Last Circus* (1987), *Death Wore Gloves* (1988), *The Fifth Script* (1989), *The Devereaux File* (1990), *The Fedorovich File* (1991).

Joe L. Hensley published *The Color of Hate* (1960; new edition, *Color Him Guilty*, 1987) on racism in the legal system, then created Donald Robak, a criminal lawyer who takes cases of outsiders in *Deliver Us to Evil* (1971) and others, such as *A Killing in Gold* (1978), *Robak's Cross* (1985), and *Fort's Law* (1987). Hensley is an African American judge.

1980s

Leonard Tourney introduced Matthew Stock as a sheriff in sixteenth-century England in *The Players' Boy Is Dead* (1980) and appears in a new novel about every other year.

After publishing her first four novels featuring actor Michael Spraggue, Linda Barnes discovered Carlotta Carlyle—formerly married ex-cop—for *A Trouble of Fools* (1987), *The Snake Tattoo* (1989), *Coyote* (1990), *Steel Guitar* (1991), *Hardware* (1994), and others.

Carl Hiassen began his Miami crime novels with *Powder Burn* (1981; the first of three with William D. Montalbano) to become one of several novelists to help fill the Florida void left by the death of the formidable John D. MacDonald in 1986. Hiaasen's novels, however, become progressively more contemporary and themes more bizarre. *Tourist Season* (1986), features a hurricane; *Double Whammy* (1987), professional bass fishing; *Skin Tight* (1989), plastic surgery; *Strip Tease* (1993), strippers; and *Native Tongue* (1991), theme parks. Others include *Stormy Weather* (1995). See the interview in John Williams's *Into the Badlands* (1991). See also Peter Jordan's "Carl Hiaasen's Environmental Thrillers: Crime Fiction in Search of Green Peace" (1990).

Norman Mailer is, of course, best known for his war novel, *The Naked and the Dead* (1948), as well as extended essays on American subjects such as "The Armies of the Night" (1968). He has also published the controversial *An American Dream* (1965), written in the manner of a suspense novel, and *Tough Guys Don't Dance* (1984), which can be read as a suspense novel that exploits realism to show the inadequacy of the detective formula to achieve closure. See Robert Merrill, "Mailer's Tough Guys Don't Dance and the Detective Tradition" (1993).

Richard Hoyt's John Denson and his Native American companion Willie Prettybird emerge in *Decoys* (1980) and continue through to the present.

Faye Kellerman superimposes the Jewish religious orthodoxy on the highly orthodox form of the detective novel in *The Ritual Bath* (1986). In *Justice* (1995), her ninth novel, she deals with the culture around the murder of a prom queen. See Ellen Serlen Uffen, "The Orthodox Novels of Faye Kellerman" (1992).

Andrew Greeley began writing crime novels with *Death in April* (1980), and with *Happy Are the Meek* (1985) originated the happy series featuring Monsignor John Blackwood Ryan. Greeley has published an enormous range of materials in religious sociology and inspirational fiction.

Marcia Muller began her Sharon McCone San Francisco private detective novels with *Edwin of the Iron Shoes* (1977), five years earlier than Paretsky and Grafton, but did not return to the character until 1982 with *Ask the Cards a Question*. She has mixed these with brief series of Elena Oliverez in *The Tree of Death* (1986) and Joanna Stark in *The Cavalier in White* (1986). See especially *Pennies on a Dead Woman's Eyes* (1992) and *Till the Butchers Cut Him Down* (1994).

Paul Auster published *Squeeze Play* (1982) and the postmodern *City of Glass* (1985), *Ghosts* (1986) and *The Locked Room* (1987), collected as *The New York Trilogy* (1987, 1990). See Barry Lewis, "The Strange Case of Paul Auster" (1994); Norma Rowen, "The Detective in Search of the Lost Tongue of Adam: Paul Auster's *City of Glass*" (1991); Alison Russell, "Deconstructing *The New York Trilogy*: Paul Auster's Anti-Detective Fiction" (1990); Oscar De Los Santos, "Auster vs. Chandler; Or, Cracking the Case of the Postmodern Mystery" (1994); and Robert Creeley's "Austerities" (1994).

Joyce Harrington is primarily known as a short story writer, but she has published several crime novels including the notable *Family Reunion* (1981), which draws on gothic imagery to broaden suspense.

Gerald Petievich has created Treasury agents Charlie Carr and Jack Kelley in a series beginning with *Money Men* (1981), but his best known novel is *To Live and Die in L.A.* (1984).

Joyce Carol Oates's extensive work includes many novels and stories that involve mysteries and crimes of various sorts. Her pseudonymous (as Rosamond Smith) novels, *Lives of the Twins* (1988), *Soul Mate* (1989), *Nemesis* (1990), and *Snake Eyes* (1992), are notable. Others include *Mysteries of Winterthurn: A Novel* (1984), which plays on the conventions of the nineteenth-century detective novel, as in Diane Johnson's *The Shadow Knows* (1974), but carries the practice much further by incorporating several genres and a wide range of themes. *Mysteries of Winterthurn* is split into three tales, all of which involve crimes against women. Cara Chill's "Un-Tricking the Eye: Joyce Carol Oates and the Feminist Ghost Story" (1985) discusses Oates's period mysteries.

Andrew H. Vachss's varied experiences in social services and law in New York and elsewhere have contributed to his unusual novels on crime. Each includes an imaginative mixture of stark realism and an unlikely group of specialists on the order of a street version of the cast of *Mission: Impossible*. The strongest themes involve child victimization. See *Flood* (1985), *Strega* (1987), *Blue Belle* (1988), *Hard Candy* (1989), *Blossom* (1990), *Sacrifice* (1991), *Shella* (1993), about adult child abuse victims. *Down in the Zero* (1994) deals with child pornography; other novels include *Batman: The Ultimate Evil* (1995), *Footsteps of the Hawk* (1995), and *False Allegations* (1996).

James Ellroy's Fritz Brown is an ex-cop Los Angeles private detective whose specialty is auto repossessions; see *Brown's Requiem* (1981), which is followed by *Clandestine* (1982), a thinly veiled novel of his mother's murder that features Fred Underhill of the LAPD. From that point things become somewhat more morbid and strange. Ace LAPD detective Lloyd Hopkins is the central character in *Blood on the Moon* (1984), *Because the Night* (1985), and *Suicide Hill* (1986). His L.A. Quartet includes *The Black Dahlia* (1987), which reconstructs the famous 1947 case; *The Big Nowhere* (1988), with the theme of the Red Scare of the 1950s; *L.A. Confidential* (1990), set in the mid-1950s; and *White Jazz* (1992), dealing with the turn of the decade. See the interview in Williams (1991).

Sue Grafton wrote for television before discovering Kinsey Millhone, detective fiction, and Santa Teresa, California (Ross Macdonald's imaginary town). Along with Sara Paretsky and Marcia Muller, Grafton created one of the first women private eyes. Her breezy Kinsey Millhone alphabet novels begin with *"A" is for Alibi* (1982) and have won numerous awards from various crime organizations here and abroad; she has served as past president of Mystery Writers of America and Private Eye Writers of America. Note her edited *Writing Mysteries: A Handbook* (1992); an interview is included in Rosemary Herbert, *The Fatal Art of Entertainment* (1994). See also Patricia E. Johnson, "Sex and Betrayal in the Detective Fiction of Sue Grafton and Sara Paretsky" (1994).

Loren D. Estleman is best known for over twenty hard-boiled novels set in Detroit, many featuring Amos Walker. He has written Westerns as well as other novels at a pace of two or three books a year, about half of which deal with crime. The first Walker novel is *Motor City Blue* (1980), and the best may be *Sugartown* (1984). He also has a short series of novels featuring Peter Masklin, a contract killer. See the interview by Keith Kroll, "The Man from Motor City" (1991).

Jonathan Valin began his mystery fiction with *The Lime Pit* (1980) and *Final Notice* (1980). His Cincinnati private eye is Harry Stoner, who gets involved in cases featuring the disintegration of cohesion in families or the workplace. *Fire Lake* (1987) features the reappearance of "the tragic mulatto" (Bailey, 1991, 107). Leanne is victimized by her well-meaning parents and tries to kill her white husband, but the police shoot her. See also *Missing: A Harry Stoner Novel* (1995).

Dolores Komo created *Clio Browne: Private Investigator* (1988), which features "the first private investigator in St. Louis" (Bailey, 1991, 111). Browne is African American, though Komo is not. See Bailey (1991).

Sara Paretsky introduced tough woman Chicago private detective V. I. Warshawski in *Indemnity Only* in 1982, the major theme of which was the insurance industry. This was followed by *Deadlock* (1984), which features a ride on a lake freighter. Paretsky says *Bitter Medicine* is about "the extent to which running medicine as a profit-based industry is in the long-term interests of virtually nobody" (quoted in Williams, 1991, 158). Other novels with strong themes include *Burn Marks* (1990) and *Tunnel Vision* (1994), about tunnel flooding and homeless persons; Paretsky edited the collection *A Woman's Eye* (1992). See also Kate Brandt and Paula Lichtenberg, "On the Case with V. I. and Kinsey" (1994); Patricia E. Johnson's "Sex and Betrayal in the Detective Fiction of Sue Grafton and Sara Paretsky" (1994); an interview in John Williams's *Into the Badlands* (1991); Linda S. Wells, "Popular Literature and Postmodernism: Sara Paretsky's Hard-Boiled Feminist" (1989).

William Caunitz, a Long Island police lieutenant, hit the best-seller lists with *One Police Plaza* (1984), after which he retired from the force. He followed the novel with *Suspect* (1986), *Bleak Sand* (1989), and other police novels. See interview by Waka Tsunoda, "On the Beat with William Caunitz" (1989).

Margaret Maron's series feature Lieutenant Sigrid Harad of the New York Police Department who first appears in the classic detective novel, *One Coffee With* (1982), and amateur North Carolina detective Judge Deborah Knott who makes her entrance in *Bootlegger's Daughter* (1992).

Julie Smith has created several series characters including San Francisco lawyer Rebecca Schwartz who appears first in *Death Turns a Trick* (1982), Paul McDonald, a San Francisco mystery writer who first appears in *True-Life Adventure* (1985), and a New Orleans series featuring policewoman Skip Langdon who appears in *New Orleans Mourning* (1990).

Aaron Elkins's main series features much-traveled physical anthropologist professor Gideon Oliver, who first appeared in *Fellowship of Fear* (1982) and has continued through half a dozen novels.

J. S. Borthwick mixes romance and amateur detection in nearly ten novels from *The Case of the Hook-Billed Kites* (1982).

Herbert Resnicow resuscitated the puzzle story in *The Gold Solution* (1983) and it has survived in various manifestations through nearly twenty novels.

Eric Sauter created private eye Robert Lee Hunter in *Hunter* (1983), a series that often features an hallucinatory style. The series includes the best-seller *Predators* (1988).

Jane Dentinger's cozy New York theater world mystery-romances beginning with *Murder on Cue* (1983) feature Jocelyn O'Roarke, whose wit and breezy style carry her through a range of professional and personal encounters.

K. K. Beck has written historical mysteries in the manner of early twentieth-century writers in such novels as *Death in a Deckchair* (1984) and *Young Mrs. Cavendish and the Kaiser's Men* (1987), and explored other variations such as the closet thriller *Unwanted Attentions* (1988).

Teri White began an unusual series of buddy novels featuring Blue Maguire and Spaceman Kowalski as a pair of Los Angeles cops in *Bleeding Hearts* (1984).

Richard Rosen introduced Providence, Rhode Island baseball player and amateur sleuth Harvey Blissberg in *Strike Three You're Dead* (1984). Blissberg soon becomes ex-baseball player and current private detective investigating murder in sports and TV.

Susan Dunlap has written a series of Jill Smith police procedurals set in Berkeley, California, beginning with *Karma* (1984) through *Sudden Exposure* (1996), together with private eye Kiernan O'Shaughnessy who first appears in *Pious Deception* (1989) and a series featuring electric meter-reading amateur detective Vejay Haskell.

Sister Carol Anne O'Marie's aging Sister Mary Helen of a small college in San Francisco first appears in *A Novena for Murder* (1984).

Sharyn McCrumb introduced Elizabeth MacPherson, who is studying forensic anthropology in North Carolina in *Sick of Shadows* (1984), and in *Bimbos of the Death Sun* (1987), created science fiction author sleuth Jay Omega and satirizes science fiction fandom. Finally, she created a suspense series drawing on lines from traditional ballads beginning with *If I Ever Return, Pretty Peggy-O* (1990).

Barbara Paul created her Marian Larch series with *The Renewable Virgin* (1984) and a historical series set among the cast of the Metropolitan Opera during the heyday of Enrico Caruso.

Nancy Pickard introduced her amateur sleuth Jenny Cain in *Generous Death* (1984) and continues her exploits through some dozen novels that raise social issues in an otherwise fairly cozy world. See Jeffrey Marks's interview (1993).

Orania Papazoglou began her mystery novels with *Sweet, Savage Death* (1984), about murder in romance publishing. A series followed featuring Pay McKenna, a romance writer. As Jane Haddam she also created the Gregor Demarkian series from *Not a Creature Was Stirring* (1990), set in Philadelphia. The series motif is holidays, as when *Bleeding Hearts* (1994) features a Valentine's Day theme.

Eric Zencey's *Panama* (1995) features the historical figure Henry Adams as detective during the bankruptcy in 1892 Paris of the company building the Panama Canal.

Jonathan Kellerman's *When the Bough Breaks* (1985) initiates Alex Delaware's investigative consultations. A child psychologist, Delaware is drawn into a series that continues through *Blood Test* (1986), *Over the Edge* (1987), *Silent Partner* (1989)—perhaps his best—along with *Time Bomb* (1990), *Private Eyes* (1991), *Devil's Waltz* (1992), *Bad Love* (1994), *Self-Defense* (1994), and *The Web* (1996). See Catherine M. Nelson's interview (1993).

Earl W. Emerson's private eye Thomas Black first appeared in *The Rainy City* (1985) and has continued in over half a dozen novels set in Seattle, Washington.

James Lee Burke began his Dave Robicheaux (Cajun ex-cop from New Iberia, Louisiana) novels with *The Neon Rain* (1987) and has continued them at a pace of about one a year ever since to *Cadillac Jukebox* (1996). The novels are a strange mixture of the sentimental, gothic, and pathological, as in *In the Electric Mist with Confederate Dead* (1993). See the interview in John Williams's *Into the Badlands* (1991).

J. A. Jance created J. P. Beaumont, inspired by John D. MacDonald's fiction, as a Seattle police detective in *Until Proven Guilty* (1985). Jance's *Desert Heat* (1993) features Joanna Brady, who becomes sheriff of a small town in Arizona. Her *Hour of the Hunter* (1991) is set on the Papago Reservation and weaves legend and myth into mystery.

Edward Gorman has produced an enormous amount of crime fiction and other work since the mid-1980s. His series characters include ex-cop Jack Dwyer in half a dozen novels from *Rough Cut* (1985) and a historical series reminiscent of dime novel settings featuring bounty hunter Leo Guild in *Guild* (1987).

John T. Lescroart's first detective novel, *Son of Holmes* (1986), features Auguste Lupa, a British agent whose name is a play on Poe's Auguste Dupin. Lupa appears again in *Rasputin's Revenge* (1987), then *Dead Irish* (1989) introduces private eye Dismus Hardy, an ex–San Francisco Police Department cop.

Marilyn Wallace created Oakland, California police sergeants Jay Goldstein and Carlos Cruz for *A Case of Loyalties* (1986), and has also created several suspense novels.

Former country and western performer [Richard] "Kinky" Friedman has produced nearly a dozen crime novels with his Kinky Friedman persona as central figure in settings in and around Greenwich Village. Beginning with *Greenwich Killing Time* (1986), the novels incorporate a prose somewhere between the later George V. Higgins and Hunter S. Thompson.

Bill Crider is a versatile writer in several genres with Texas Sheriff Dan Rhodes featured in a series beginning with *Too Late to Die* (1986) and amateur Carl Burns, English professor in a small Texas college that begins with *One Dead Dean* (1988).

Carolyn G. Hart writes mysteries in the classic manner in addition to children's stories and other work. Her series characters include Annie Lawrence and Max Darling in the classic tradition of Christie and Phoebe Atwood Taylor beginning with *Death on Demand* (1987) and Henrie O (Henrietta O'Dwyer Collins), a retired journalist who first appears in *Dead Man's Island* (1993).

Robert Crais has based a series of private eye novels on wisecracking Elvis Cole and Vietnam veteran ex-cop Joe Pike, beginning with *The Monkey's Raincoat* (1987).

Parnell Hall has written two series characters. The first is a private detective named Stanley Hastings who appears in a dozen novels from *Detective* (1987) and a smaller series written as J. P. Hailey featuring a Perry Mason–type lawyer, Steve Winslow, practicing in New York in *The Baxter House* (1988) and others.

Gillian Roberts (Judith Greber) created Philadelphia prep school English teacher Amanda Pepper in *Caught Dead in Philadelphia* (1987) and continues her mixture of romance, amateur detection and social issues such as battered women through half a dozen novels.

Mary Wings created a lively San Francisco milieu for Emma Victor, who begins as an amateur detective in *She Came Too Late* (1987; 1986 in England). Victor turns professional in the third novel of this "She Came" series, *She Came By the Book* (1996; 1995 in England). Wings has also written graphic novels and produced other work.

Lia Matera introduced two series featuring San Francisco law student Willa Janson in *Where Lawyers Fear to Tread* (1987) and tough corporate attorney Laura Di Palma in *The Smart Money* (1988).

Les Roberts is author of two series, including Cleveland private eye Milan Jacovich appearing in *Pepper Pike* (1988) and Saxon, a Los Angeles private eye, first appearing in *An Infinite Number of Monkeys* (1987).

Archer Mayor's police lieutenant Joe Gunther procedurals set in a Vermont city began with *Open Season* (1988).

Walter Satterthwait introduced Santa Fe private eye Joshua Croft in *Wall of Glass* (1988), along with two earlier novels centering on drugs and a brief series of historical mysteries.

Elizabeth George writes British-style detective novels in the manner of Dorothy L. Sayers, featuring aristocratic Inspector Thomas Lynley and unaristocratic but spunky Sergeant Barbara Havers, beginning with *A Great Deliverance* (1988).

Susan Rogers Cooper writes small town police stories beginning with *The Man in the Green Chevy* (1988), a series featuring Deputy Sheriff Milton Kovac of Prophecy County, Oklahoma. Other series invoke an amateur detective, E. J. Pugh, and Kemmey Kruse, a stand-up comic.

Robert J. Randisi has published some fifty novels, including his Henry Po series, featuring a New York racing club detective in *The Disappearance of Penny* (1980). Randisi founded the Private Eye Writers of America in 1982.

Karen Kijewski's Kat-title private eye series featuring Kat Colorado begins with *Katwalk* (1989) and mixes romance with a Sacramento locale.

African-American writer Clifford Mason features fifty-year-old private eye Joe Cuiquez in *The Case of Ashanti Gold* (1985) and he returns in *Jamaica Run* (1987), in which Cuiquez's Jamaican landlady is murdered.

1990s

Gar Anthony Haywood wrote *Fear of the Dark* (1988), *Not Long for This World* (1990), *Bad News Travels Fast* (1995), *Going Nowhere Fast* (1994), *You Can Die Trying* (1993), and *It's Not a Pretty Sight* (1996). Aaron Gunner, his series PI, is a sort of anti–John Shaft private eye— "older, shorter, balder and generally unhealthier than his creator" (Williams, 1991, 99). Haywood observes that "Law and order is definitely more of a grey area for black people, especially the underprivileged, than for the rest of us" (Williams, 1991, 100). See the interview in John Williams, *Into the Badlands* (1991).

Barbara D'Amato has written a series of novels featuring free-lance Chicago investigator Cat Marsala among a collection of fiction and non-fiction books. The series, centering on hard social issues, appropriately incorporate "hard" in the title, beginning with *Hardball* (1990).

Alan Russell created San Francisco private eye Stuart Winter in *No Sign of Murder* (1990), which takes place amidst animal research.

African-American writer Nikki Baker wrote African-American lesbian detective Virginia Kelly into her *In the Game* (1991), followed by *The Lavender House Murder* (1992), set in Provincetown, Massachusetts; see also *The Long Goodbyes* (1993) and *The Ultimate Exit Strategy* (1995).

Steven Saylor began his series featuring Gordianus the Finder located in the first century B.C. Rome in *Roman Blood* (1991).

Pulitzer Prize–winning reporter Michael Connelly's first police procedural *The Black Echo* (1992) featured Harry Bosch, a Vietnam veteran who works for the Los Angeles Police Department.

Eleanor Taylor Bland wrote *Dead Time* (1992), set in Chicago, Illinois, with a homeless children theme. *Slow Burn* (1993), *Gone Quiet* (1994), *Done Wrong* (1995), and *Keep Still* (1996) feature series policewoman Marti MacAlister. Both author and detective are African American.

Gary Phillips visits Los Angeles racial tensions in *Violent Spring* (1994), featuring an African-American private eye, Ivan Monk.

Rita Mae Brown's *Wish You Were Here* (1990), *Rest in Pieces* (1992), and *Murder at Monticello* (1994) feature a significant pet, nostalgia, a small isolated community to which murder intrudes, and the rest of the ingredients of a cozy; but the cat coauthors the book, and things are not altogether as idyllic as they appear.

Patricia Daniels Cornwell achieved success with her series featuring medical examiner Dr. Kay Scarpetta in *Postmortem* (1990), and eight successive novels, including *Body of Evidence* (1991), *All That Remains* (1992), and *Cruel & Unusual: A Novel* (1993). Cornwell's strength is in shifting violence away from action to suspense through the emphasis on forensic investigation and lurking psychopaths. In *The Body Farm: A Novel* (1994) Scarpetta reconstructs profiles of murderers from physical evidence; the body farm refers to a test site where bodies are buried to test the rate and status of decomposition. See an interview in Rosemary Herbert, *The Fatal Art of Entertainment* (1994).

Nancy Taylor Rosenberg has, beginning with *Mitigating Circumstances* (1993), published several novels focussing on legal themes and the problems of women in the criminal justice system.

Kate Ross introduced aristocrat and amateur sleuth Julian Kestrel in the historical mystery *Cut to the Quick* (1993), set in England in the 1820s.

Abigail Padgett created Bo Bradley, an investigator for San Diego's Child Protective Service who suffers from acknowledged manic-depressive cycles, in *Child of Silence* (1993). Themes emerging in the brief series include mental abnormalities and American Indian mythology.

D.J.H. Jones published *Murder at the MLA* (1993) and *Murder in the New Age* (1997), featuring Chaucer scholar and amateur sleuth Nancy Cook, with significant other PI Boaz Dixon.

Laurie R. King has begun two series, one in which Mary Russell is an amateur detective who befriends Sherlock Holmes in a series beginning with *The Beekeeper's Apprentice* (1994). The other series starts with *To Play the Fool* (1995) and introduces Kate Martinelli of the San Francisco Police Department.

Carol O'Connell introduced NYPD computer expert Kathleen Mallory in *Mallory's Oracle* (1994) in a brief series that quickly finds Mallory setting up a private eye business.

Janice Steinberg published *Death of a Postmodernist* (1995), *Death Crosses the Border* (1995), *Death-Fires Dance* (1996) and *The Dead Man and the Sea* (1997) featuring Margo Simon, a San Diego amateur detective who works at a public radio station.

T. J. Phillips published *Dance of the Mongoose* (1995), called a mystery in St. Thomas, and *Woman in the Dark* (1997) featuring Greenwich Village writer Joe Wilder.

Sherry Lewis published *No Place for Death* (1996) featuring amateur detective Fred Vickery, a senior citizen in the small town of Cutler, Colorado. Others include *No Place for Secrets* (1995), *No Place Like Home* (1996), *No Place for Sin* (1997), and *No Place for Tears* (1997).

Barbara Neely, also known for her non-mystery work, began the publication of the highly acclaimed series of investigations by Blanche White, an angry, overweight black domestic, in *Blanche on the Lam* (1992), followed by *Blanche Among the Talented Tenth* (1994) and *Blanche in the 'Hood* (1996). See an interview in Rosemary Herbert, *The Fatal Art of Entertainment* (1994).

John Sandford published a series of "prey" thrillers, including *Rules of Prey* (1989), *Shadow Prey* (1990), *Eyes of Prey* (1991), *Silent Prey* (1992), *Winter Prey* (1993), *Night Prey* (1994), *Mind Prey* (1995), *Sudden Prey* (1996).

Nora Deloach's *Mama Traps a Killer* (1995), *Mama Stalks the Past* (1997), and *Mama Stands Accused* (1998) mark the emergence of another African American talent.

Hugh Holton's *Presumed Dead* (1994), *Windy City* (1995), *Violent Crimes* (1997), and *Chicago Blues* (1996) add another name to the writers of imaginative Chicago crime. See Carolyn Tillery, "The Fiction of Black Crime" (1997).

Valerie Wilson Wesley's *When Death Comes Stealing* (1994), *Devil's Gonna Get Him* (1995), *Where Evil Sleeps* (1996), and *No Hiding Place* (1997) feature Tamara Hayle, an African-American woman private detective in Newark, New Jersey.

Judith Van Gieson publishes a series of ecology-sensitive novels with *North of the Border* (1988), featuring Neil Hamel, an Albuquerque lawyer. Others include *Raptor* (1989), *The Other Side of Death* (1990), *The Wolf*

Path (1992), *The Lies That Bind* (1993), *Parrot Blues* (1995), and *Hotshots* (1996).

Tamar Myers published *Too Many Crooks Spoil the Broth: A Pennsylvania-Dutch Mystery with Recipes* (1994), *Gilt By Association* (1996), *No Use Dying over Spilled Milk* (1995), *Parsley, Sage, Rosemary, and Crime* (1995). The novels feature as sleuth either Magdalena Yoder of an Amish-Mennonite community or Abigail Timberlake, owner of an antique shop.

Robert O. Greer's *The Devil's Hatband* (1996) featured an African-American detective and was set in Denver. It was followed by *The Devil's Red Nickel* (1997) and *Devil's Backbone* (1998).

Gary Hardwick's Detroit novel, *Cold Medina* (1996) appeared, featuring African-American police and city gangs, followed by *Double Dead* (1997).

In addition to her speculative fiction, Kate Wilhelm published, among many others, *The Hamlet Trap* (1987), *Smart House* (1989), *Sweet, Sweet Poison* (1990), and *Death Qualified* (1991), featuring attorney Barbara Holloway, with a sequel, *The Best Defense* (1994). Others include *Justice for Some* (1993) and *Malice Prepense* (1996).

Mary Willis Walker's acclaimed novels begin with *Zero at the Bone* (1991), involving amateur detective Katherine Driscoll, who investigates the death of her father. A series featuring Molly Cates, an Austin-based crime reporter, begins with *The Red Scream* (1994), dealing with a serial killer, with a sequel, *Under the Beetle's Cellar* (1995).

Barbara Wilson has published six mysteries in two series among more than a dozen novels and short story collections, beginning with *Murder in the Collective* (1984) and *Sisters of the Road* (1986). The first series features printer Pam Nilsen and the second featuring translator Cassandra Reilly begins with *Gaudi Afternoon* (1990). Both series involve the lesbian subculture of Seattle and draw on Wilson's background in publishing and translation. See Liahna Babener's essay in Kathleen Gregory Klein's *Women Times Three* (1995).

Walter Mosley's Easy Rawlins series set in Los Angeles from the 1940s to more modern times begins with the award-winning *Devil in a Blue Dress* (1990) and has gained enormous popularity. Mosley's color motif extends through *A Red Death* (1991), *White Butterfly* (1992), *Black Betty* (1994), and *A Little Yellow Dog* (1996), all of which deal with the responsibilities of fatherhood and the dilemmas of ethical decisions. Mosley makes a statement about literary realism in *Black Betty* when he has Rawlins say, "my memory of Huckleberry wasn't one of racism. I remembered Jim and Huck as friends out on the river. I could have been either one of them" (1994, 13). Theodore O. Mason, Jr.'s, "Walter Mosley's Easy Rawlins: The Detective and Afro-American Fiction" (1992) argues that Mosley's novel is concerned with borders between races and genders. African American "sites" are those where black identity is defined in contrast to white—as in Joppy Shag's bar where the character of DeWitt Albright is defined. Mason finds Georg Lukács and M. M. Bakhtin helpful.

Louis Owens published *The Sharpest Sight* (1992); *Bone Game* (1994); and *Nightland* (1996). Owens is one of the most versatile of contemporary writers, having published important work on American literature, particularly on John Steinbeck's vision and American Indian literature. He has also produced other creative work. The mystery novels, in addition to being entertaining, provide sobering and thoughtful rememories of the past that are also experimental forays into realism.

John Grisham's fame skyrocketed with his second novel, *The Firm* (1992), and has continued to rise through *The Pelican Brief* (1992), *The Client* (1993), *The Chamber* (1994), *The Rainmaker* (1995), and *The Runaway Jury* (1996). Capturing with perfect pitch the obsession with money and power that began in the early 1980s and the paranoia of the 1990s, Grisham's legal thrillers tap into several different audiences.

Scott Turow has published only legal thrillers to this point—*Presumed Innocent* (1987), *The Burden of Proof* (1990), *Pleading Guilty* (1993), and *Laws of Our Fathers* (1996)—but all have received a good deal of attention. All are legal thrillers that draw on Turow's experience in a Chicago law firm.

Dana Stabenow began her series of mysteries featuring Kate Shugak, a tough independent Aleut working in the Anchorage district attorney's office, with *A Cold Day for Murder* (1992), followed by *A Fatal Thaw* (1992), *Dead in the Water* (1993), *A Cold-blooded Business* (1994), *Play with Fire* (1995), *Blood Will Tell* (1996), and *Breakup* (1997).

Ronald B. Querry published *The Death of Bernadette Lefthand: A Novel* (1993) set in and around Santa Fe among Jicarilla and Navajo Indians.

ANTHOLOGIES OF AUTHOR CRITICISM

Kathleen Klein, ed., *Women Times Three* (1995) includes ten essays discussing the reader as author, category of reader, and reading requirements and capacities. All facets are women-oriented and employ to varying degrees feminist theory and practices. Of particular interest are Klein's suggestive observations on the relation of the first women's movement to Golden Age mysteries. Other essays include Margaret Kinsman on Joan Hess; Lois A. Marchino on Katherine V. Forrest; Priscilla L. Walton on

Sue Grafton; Paula M. Woods on D. R. Meredith; Mary P. Freier on Mary Roberts Rinehart's Hilda Adams; and Liahna Babener on Barbara Wilson.

Maxim Jakubowsky's *100 Great Detectives* (1991) contains very brief essays by mystery writers on detectives created by British and American writers. Americans include William Hjortsberg, Ross Macdonald, Andrew Vachss, William S. Burroughs, Ed McBain, Earl Derr Biggers, Dashiell Hammett, Phoebe Atwood Taylor, Jonathan Latimer, Edgar Allan Poe, John Dickson Carr, Elizabeth Daly, Fredric Brown, William McIlvanney, Tony Hillerman, Liza Cody, Marcia Muller, James Crumley, Sue Grafton, Ed Lacy, Charles Willeford, Bill Pronzini, Dorothy Gilman, Loren D. Estleman, Ellery Queen, James Lee Burke, Edward Mathis, Leslie Charteris, Julie Smith, Charlotte MacLeod, Jerome Charyn, James Ellroy, Robert B. Parker, Emma Lathen, Sara Paretsky, Charles Burns, Thomas Harris, Robert Irvine, Marc Behm, Haughton Murphy, Seymour Shubin, and Rex Stout.

Mary Jean DeMarr's *In the Beginning* (1995) includes essays by Frederick Isaac on Rex Stout's Nero Wolfe, Sharon A. Russell on Mike Shayne, George N. Dove on Ed McBain's 87th Precinct novels, Mary Jane DeMarr on Elizabeth Linington, Lois A. Marchino on Kate Fansler, and Landon Burns on Dave Brandstetter. Isaac says *Fer-de-Lance* seemed "destined" to be created; cites John McAleer's biography of Stout; Stout succeeds in merging the two traditions of the hard-boiled and classic. Russell employs Robin Wood's ideological analysis[11] to show that the series does provide some variants to the hard-boiled genre. For example, his professionalism leads to conflicts between the desire for success and ethics that include a suspicion of the corrupting power of money; he sleeps with clients and though a woman, Phyllis, seems a permanent fixture at one point she dies in childbirth to preserve the genre's "enduring image of the tough, lone male" (Russell, 1995, 104). George Dove focuses on *Cop Hater* (1956). The novel was planned as the first of a series (which had grown to some forty-five novels by Dove's writing). Lawrence Treat had shown two aspects of police methods: the plodding interviews, leg work, and intimidation; and laboratory work. Stoolie Danny Gimp is Steve Carella's informer. The series is highly accurate on forensic and lab details. McBain portrays family problems of the police officers. Each book employs a new strategy of which *Cop Hater* sets a "tone" resulting from the "slightly tilted geography and chronology" of the series (Dove, 1995, 108). There is a disclaimer that the book is not set in New York, but its geography could be superimposed over a map of the city. The police routines are not specific to one city. Dates do not correspond to the 1956 calendar. Meyer Meyer is always thirty-seven years old and the others age at varying speeds, so the book is not naturalistic. Carella is killed and later resurrected. There is no "ideological platform" (Dove, 1995, 111). The dialogue is good, but the book is stylistically "anemic" (Dove, 1995, 112). The reproduced documents appear authentic. The "Nut" role is consistent in the series and is played by a variety of characters; here a woman says the Cockroach Men are killing cops. Carella increasingly speaks for McBain. De Marr sees Elizabeth Linington's procedurals as predictable, but with unpredictable elements; plots are predictably interlinked, but officers are all expendable. *Case Pending* (1960) began the Luis Mendoza series under the Dell Shannon byline, with the same formula used in the Ivor Maddox and Sue Carstairs series begun with *Greenmask* (1964), published under her own name. As Lesley Egan she created a "slightly more complex" group beginning with *A Case for Appeal* (1961), starring attorney Jesse Falkenstein and officer Vic Varallo. Later novels lose the freshness of the earlier ones, although the numerous story lines and different events in the personal lives of officers make up for a similarity in the cases. Lois Marchino argues that Amanda Cross's [Carolyn Heilbrun] Kate Fansler series, beginning with *In the Last Analysis* (1964), becomes more and more metafiction that questions the grounding of truth in narrative. *In the Last Analysis* is "prone to charming digression and learned allusion. This makes for very doubtful verisimilitude but provides a sustained cleverness in the prose, in the witty dialogue and in the narrative voice" (Marchino, 1995, 158). But all characters sound a bit alike. Reed Amhearst is the love interest. By *The Players Come Again* (1990), Kate's age has changed from late thirties to midforties. Maureen T. Reddy has argued that Fansler's friendships with women are "ephemeral at best" and in *A Trap for Fools* (1989) Kate is concerned about distance between white and black women, but "blames black women as a group for making her uncomfortable" (Marchino, 1995, 159–160).[12] Landon Barnes focuses on Dave Brandstetter, who is a nationally known claims investigator. He is gay, and beginning with *Fadeout* (1970) his steady companion is Rod Fleming.

Diana Cooper-Clark's *Designs of Darkness: Interviews with Detective Novelists* (1983) contains interviews with P. D. James, Jean Stubbs, Peter Lovesey, Margaret Millar, Ross Macdonald, Howard Engel, Ruth Rendell, Janwillem van de Wetering, Patricia Highsmith, Julian Symons, Amanda Cross, Anne Perry, and Dick Francis. Cooper-Clark's introduction ranges over her training in traditional literary sensibilities and conversion to the recognition that detective fiction is respectable reading.

Jon L. Breen and Martin Harry Greenberg's anthology, *Murder Off the Rack: Critical Studies of Ten Paperback Masters* (1989), includes an introduction by Breen, with essays on Harry Whittington by Bill Crider, Ed Lacy by Marvin Lachman, Jim Thompson by Max Allan Collins, Vin Packer by Breen, Marvin H. Albert by George Kelley, Charles Williams by Ed Gorman, Donald Hamilton by Loren D. Estleman, Peter Rabe by Donald E.

Westlake, Don Pendleton by Will Murray, Warren Murphy by Dick Lochte.

H.R.F. Keating's *Crime & Mystery: The 100 Best Books* (1987) provides thumbnail sketches of a book or so by each of about forty American authors, including Mary Roberts Rinehart's *The Circular Staircase*, Melville Davisson Post's *Uncle Abner*, Dashiell Hammett's *Red Harvest* and *The Maltese Falcon*, Erle Stanley Gardner's *The Case of the Sulky Girl*, James M. Cain's *The Postman Always Rings Twice*, Rex Stout's *The League of Frightened Men*, Cornell Woolrich's *The Bride Wore Black*, Ellery Queen's *Calamity Town*, Raymond Chandler's *The High Window* and *The Long Goodbye*, Helen Eustis's *The Horizontal Man*, Fredric Brown's *The Fabulous Clipjoint*, W. R. Burnett's *The Asphalt Jungle*, Hillary Waugh's *Last Seen Wearing . . .*, Margaret Millar's *Beast in View* and *Beyond this Point Are Monsters*, Stanley Ellin's *Mystery Stories* and *Mirror, Mirror on the Wall*, Jim Thompson's *Pop. 1280*, M. G. Eberhart's *R.S.V.P. Murder*, Emma Lathen's *Murder Against the Grain*, Helen McCloy's *Mr. Splitfoot*, Patricia Highsmith's *The Tremor of Forgery*, Chester Himes's *Blind Man with a Pistol*, Ed McBain's *Sadie When She Died*, George V. Higgins's *The Friends of Eddie Coyle*, Tony Hillerman's *Dance Hall of the Dead*, Gregory McDonald's *Fletch*, Ross Macdonald's *The Blue Hammer*, Dorothy Salisbury Davis's *A Death in the Life*, Dorothy Uhnak's *The Investigation*, William McIlvanney's *Laidlaw*, Donald E. Westlake's *Nobody's Perfect*, Joseph Hansen's *Skinflick*, John D. MacDonald's *The Green Ripper*, Amanda Cross's *Death in a Tenured Position*, and Joseph Wambaugh's *The Glitter Dome*.

Robert E. Skinner's *The New Hard-Boiled Dicks: A Personal Checklist* (1987) provides a brief history of hard-boiled fiction, then provides sketches of Andrew Bergman, James Crumley, Loren D. Estleman, Stephen Greenleaf, Donald Hamilton, Chester Himes, Stuart Kaminsky, Elmore Leonard, Robert B. Parker, Richard Stark (Westlake), Jim Steranko, and Ernest Tidyman; special mention is given to Max Byrd, Max Allan Collins, John Gregory Dunne, Joe Gores, John D. MacDonald, L. A. Morse, Sara Paretsky, Bill Pronzini, Roger L. Simon, and Chris Wiltz.

Art Bourgeau's *The Mystery Lover's Companion* (1986) provides from ten or fifteen to a couple of hundred words on about 3,000 novels divided into American mysteries, English mysteries, thrillers and police procedurals, rated with from one to five daggers. Mandy Hicken and Ray Prytherch's *Now Read On: A Guide to Contemporary Popular Fiction* (1994) contains brief sketches and checklists for hundreds of British and American authors in twenty fiction categories, with appendices of literary prizes, together with indexes to authors, series, and recurring characters. Americans included in detective fiction are Lillian Jackson Braun, Elizabeth George, and Martha Grimes; under police work, Anne Blaisdell, Lesley Egan, Ed McBain, and

Dell Shannon; under spy stories, William F. Buckley and Helen MacInnes; under thrillers, Tom Clancy, Jonathan Kellerman, Robert Ludlum, Gregory McDonald, David Morrell; under women detectives, Amanda Cross, Marcia Muller, and Sara Paretsky.

David Geherin's *The American Private Eye* (1985) traces the career of the private eye through representative writers, including Carroll John Daly, Dashiell Hammett, Raoul Whitfield, Frederick Nebel, George Harmon Coxe, John K. Butler, Norbert Davis, Robert Leslie Bellem, Jonathan Latimer, Raymond Chandler, Cleve Adams, Brett Halliday, Howard Browne, Wade Miller, Bart Spicer, Richard S. Prather, Mickey Spillane, Ross Macdonald, Thomas B. Dewey, William Campbell Gault, Michael Collins, Robert Parker, Bill Pronzini, Michael L. Lewin, Joseph Hansen, Arthur Lyons, and Lawrence Block and offers reasons for the survival of the genre. Robert E. Skinner's *The Hard-boiled Explicator* (1985) provides reference and other information for study of Dashiell Hammett, Raymond Chandler, and Ross Macdonald.

Rosemary Herbert's *The Fatal Art of Entertainment: Interviews with Mystery Writers* (1994) includes interviews with Americans Sue Grafton, Tony Hillerman, Patricia D. Cornwell, Jane Langton, Jeremiah Healy, and Barbara Neely as well as English authors. H.R.F. Keating's *Whodunit? A Guide to Crime, Suspense, and Spy Fiction* (1982) contains essays on why they write by Stanley Ellin, P. D. James, Desmond Bagley, Dorothy Eden, Patricia Highsmith, Gregory McDonald, Lionel Davidson, Len Deighton, Eric Ambler, and himself.

NOTES

1. The chronology is rough because writers often produce work over a long period of time and the idiosyncrasies of a life's work may lead to gaps, periods of unusual productivity, or temporary work in other areas. Another anomaly of this arrangement is that writers that might be thought of as contemporaries may appear in different periods. Alphabetical organization of authors can be found in any of the excellent encyclopedias noted in the reference section.

2. Gilman's manuscript was finished in 1929 but unpublished during her lifetime. See the afterword to *Unpunished: A Mystery*, ed. and afterword by Catherine J. Golden and Daniel D. Knight (New York: The Feminist Press, 1997), 213–33.

3. See Van Dine's introduction to *The Great Detective Stories: A Chronological Anthology* (New York: Scribner's, 1927).

4. Collected in Howard Haycraft's *The Art of the Mystery Story* (1946).

5. First collected in his *Mystery Stories* (1956).

6. Quoted from Masur's comment in *St. James Guide to Crime and Mystery Writers* (1996), 209.

7. See Nevins's critical essay in *St. James Guide to Crime and Mystery Writers* (1996), 1076–77.

8. Comment in *St. James Guide to Crime and Mystery Writers* (1996), 649.

9. Quoted from Robert Baker and Michael Nietzel, *Private Eyes* (1985), 161.

10. See Hughes's comment in Reilly's *Twentieth Century* (1980), 594.

11. "Ideology, Genre, Auteur," in Barry Keith Grant, ed., *Film Genre Reader* (Austin: University of Texas Press, 1986), 59–73.

12. See "The Feminist Counter-Tradition in Crime: Cross, Grafton, Paretsky, and Wilson," in Ronald G. Walker and June M. Frazer, eds., *The Cunning Craft: Original Essays on Detective Fiction and Contemporary Literary Theory* (1990).

CHAPTER 5

REFERENCE

This chapter consists of two parts. The first provides information about reference works and the second about research collections.

REFERENCE WORKS

Authors

Allen J. Hubin's *Crime Fiction, 1749–1980: A Comprehensive Bibliography* (1984) and *1981–1985 Supplement to Crime Fiction, 1749–1980* (1994) are at this time the standard sources for author checklists and pseudonyms, covering some 60,000 books published in England, the United States, Japan, and Europe through date of publication. They include indexes to settings, series characters, and other useful information. Less comprehensive, but with a greater variety of information, the *St. James Guide to Crime & Mystery Writers*, edited by Jay B. Pederson, preface by Kathleen Gregory Klein (1996), is the retitled and revised edition of *Twentieth-Century Crime and Mystery Writers* (1980, 1985, 1991). This 1,264-page St. James volume is very useful. It is especially strong on American and British writers, with more coverage of the former British colonies than the earlier editions. Coverage of European, Asian, and African writers is thin. The volume contains biographical data including pseudonyms, author checklists, brief critical essays of various lengths on some 650 authors and often checklists of secondary sources. Some authors who appeared in earlier editions have been dropped from this one, and the attempt to match essay length to importance of the author appears to have been discarded. Ordean Hagen's *Who Done It?: A Guide to Detective, Mystery and Suspense Fiction* (1969) provided the initial data for subsequent author checklists but has been superseded by Hubin. In its final edition it includes some 20,000 titles identified as mystery, detective, or suspense novels. Included in the volume are a subject guide, sections on film adaptations, plays, lists of anthologies and collections, checklists of settings and awards, a character list of some 100 pages, and a title index. Frank N. Magill's *Critical Survey of Mystery and Detective Fiction* (1988) includes four volumes of biographical and bibliographical information, together with some indication of series characters for about 280 writers; it contains glossary and indexed designations of types, characters, authors, titles, and author nationality. J. Randolph Cox's *Masters of Mystery and Detective Fiction* (1989) is also useful for 74 writers. *The Crown Crime Companion* (1995) compiles and annotates a list of 100 writers considered to be the best by respondents of the Mystery Writers of America, perhaps an answer to a similar volume published in England. Albert Johannsen's *The House of Beadle and Adams* (1950) provides extensive treatment of the major dime novel publisher. This is a carefully researched two-volume listing of the publisher's production, together with biographical sketches of the authors.

Many other guides to authors and their varied works can be found in such books as Melvyn Barnes's *Best Detective Fiction: A Guide from Godwin to the Present* (1975), updated by *Murder in Print* (1986). The first volume is a lively annotated bibliography of some 250 authors who have written classic puzzle stories and whose work centers around the "how" or "why" of murder. More a series of reader's impressions and plot summaries than a formally annotated bibliography, this work is most useful to the casual reader. Julian Symons's *The Hundred Best Crime Stories* (1959) is based in part on a survey of critics and writers. H.R.F. Keating's *Crime & Mystery* (1987) provides a selective checklist of 100 mostly English and American books. Michael L. Cook's *Murder by Mail: Inside the Mystery Book Clubs, with Complete Checklist* (1979) provides information on the mass circulation of authors. Information on works published prior to the twentieth century can be found in Lyle Wright's three volumes, *American Fiction* (1965, 1966, 1969).

Two encyclopedias supplement author information with a broader coverage of themes, movie and TV tie-ins, character entries, and other kinds of information. Chris Steinbrunner and Otto Penzler's *Encyclopedia of Mystery and Detection* (1976) contains entries on most aspects of mystery and detective fiction. This illustrated volume is useful for its concise, accurate entries on authors, major works, central characters, and a wealth of other information on media treatments of the genre. More recently, similar updated coverage is included in William DeAndrea's *Encyclopedia Mysteriosa: A Comprehensive Guide to the Art of Detection in Print, Film, Radio, and Television* (1994). Dilys Winn's *Murder Ink: The Mystery Reader's Companion* (1977) and *Murderess Ink: The Better Half of the Mystery* (1979) contain a potpourri of information that is mainly for fun. Francis Lacassin's *Mythologie du Roman Policier* (1974) contains brief backgrounds on Poe, Biggers, Hammett, Chandler, Brown, Fearing, and Himes and for the appearances of these authors' works in several media.

Other specialized volumes organize data according to theme. Victoria Nichols's *Silk Stalkings: When Women Write of Murder; A Survey of Series Characters Created by Women Authors in Crime and Mystery Fiction* (1988) is an attempt to provide a comprehensive source of information on writers (women, teams, males creating women detectives) and their chief characters. The book is divided into five sections: (1) providing about one page, but often more, on authors and their work; (2) a "Master List" identifying autonyms, single and team pseudonyms, series character, publication date, alternate titles, and short story designations; (3) an appendix chronology noting span of series character appearances with number of books; (4) brief appendix matching pseudonyms to autonyms; (5) appendix matching series character to author. The book covers about 600 characters and more than 3,000 titles. Bernard A. Drew's *Heroines* (1989) lists women series characters in mystery, espionage, action, science fiction, fantasy, horror, Western, romance, and juvenile novels. Frances A. DellaCava and Madeline H. Engel's *Female Detectives in American Novels* (1993) provides a bibliography and analysis of woman and girl series detectives. See also Anthony Slide's *Gay and Lesbian Characters and Themes in Mystery Novels* (1993), which references over 500 British and American novels and stories, and *The Gay and Lesbian Detective* (1993), which provides a brief topical and critical history of the genre.

Tasha Mackler's *Murder . . . By Category* (1991) provides listings by topical and regional categories with brief plot summaries of novels in print. Otto Penzler, Chris Steinbrunner, and Marvin Lachman's *Detectionary: A Biographical Dictionary of Leading Characters in Detective and Mystery Fiction, Including Famous and Little-Known Sleuths, Their Helpers, Rogues, Both Heroic and Sinister, and Some of Their Most Memorable Adventures, as Recounted in Novels, Short Stories, and Films* (1971, 1977, 1980) is dated now but was at the time of publication the best source for fictional characters in mystery and detective stories. Steven Olderr's *Mystery Index* (1987) covers detectives and settings, as well as topical information for some 10,000 novels. Albert J. Menendez's *The Subject Is Murder* (1985; II, 1990) lists several thousand novels organized according to rather hard thematic categories: advertising, archaeology, art, circuses and carnivals, department stores, gardening, colleges, boats, religion, hotels and inns, literary people, radio and TV, film, Christmas, music, politics,

news, bookshops and libraries, trains, medicine, sports, supernatural, theater, weddings and honeymoons, and amnesia in the first volume, together
with a list of specialty bookshops; volume 2 also includes antiques, cook-
ing, fashion, and Halloween, along with a statistical breakdown of the
categories. On one of these topics see John E. Kramer, Jr., with John E.
Kramer III, *College Mystery Novels: An Annotated Bibliography Including
a Guide to Professorial Series-Character Sleuths* (1983). Jon Breen's *Novel
Verdicts* (1984) identifies novels dealing with courtroom fiction. James Sandoe's *Murder: Plain and Fanciful with Some Milder Malefactions* (1948)
contains a list of some 200 short stories and novels based on actual crimes
or criminals. R. A. Adey's *Locked Room Murders and Other Impossible
Crimes: A Comprehensive Bibliography* (1991) is exhaustive. Gary Lovisi's
Science Fiction Detective Tales (1986) surveys paperback novels.

Reviews

Current reviews of detective fiction are widely available in major newspapers, such as the *New York Times*, as well as local newspapers. A broad
spectrum of journals such as *The Wilson Library Bulletin* and *Library Journal* are alert to mystery and detective novels. Retrospective as well as current reviews can be found in the *Armchair Detective, Clues,* and other
journals of popular fiction, as well as fan magazines. William F. Deeck and
Steven A. Stilwell's *The Armchair Detective Index* (1992) indexes the magazine from its beginning in 1967 through 1987. Jacques Barzun and Wendell Hertig Taylor's *A Catalogue of Crime* (1971; rev. and enl., 1989) is
an annotated bibliography of novels and collections arranged by author,
together with an annotated critical bibliography and varied miscellaneous
information. Each author entry is accompanied by a two- or three-line
impression of the work, while the bibliography is useful for unusual items.
Emphasis in this volume is on the classic narrative; there is also a slight
coverage of American hard-boiled fiction. Robert E. Briney and Francis M.
Nevins, Jr. collected Anthony Boucher's reviews and other pieces in *Multiplying Villainies: Selected Mystery Criticism, 1942–1968, by Anthony
Boucher* (1973).

Bibliographies of Criticism

The second revised edition of Walter Albert's *Detective and Mystery Fiction: An International Bibliography of Secondary Sources* (1997) is the
most complete listing of information on detective fiction currently available.
Albert's volume is especially useful for information in fanzines and other
publications not noted in standard reference sources. The annotations are
often suspicious of contemporary critical approaches. Recurrent critical
bibliography is found in Albert's "Bibliography of Secondary Sources," be-

ginning in *Armchair Detective* in 1972. Similar coverage is provided in Jon L. Breen's more rancorous *What About Murder? A Guide to Mystery and Detective Fiction* (1981), which contains brief annotations of 239 items in categories designated as General Histories, Reference Books, Special Subjects, Collected Essays and Reviews, Technical Manuals, Coffee-Table Books, and New Editions and Supplements. Annotations tend to be longer than Albert's, though coverage is not as extensive. A further volume by Breen is *What about Murder? 1981–1991: A Guide to Books about Mystery and Detective Fiction* (1993), which adds 565 annotated items with the category of Coffee-Table Books deleted and Anthologies added. Breen claims to reveal "just how wrong [other bibliographers] have gotten things" (1993, viii), but he also claims his own volume "totals 640 pages, and includes a 115-page index" (1993, vii), when it is actually about 376 pages, with a considerably shorter index. See also Timothy W. Johnson and Julia Johnson's *Crime Fiction Criticism: An Annotated Bibliography* (1981). Marvin Lachman's *A Reader's Guide to the American Novel of Detection* (1993) identifies settings, plots and characters for over 160 authors. See also Gary Warren Niebuhr's *A Reader's Guide to the Private Eye Novel* (1993).

"Detective Fiction" often appears as a subsection of *American Literary Scholarship* (annual); otherwise look for it under headings such as "Themes, Topics and Criticism"; the subject index is keyed to names of authors. Standard sources of critical bibliography such as the *MLA Bibliography* should be consulted for scholarly articles, since these are not always included in fan bibliographies. On-line services such as ACAD are useful for selected popular magazine and scholarly journal articles on crime fiction but should be considered a starting point. Heta Pyrhönen's *Murder from an Academic Angle: An Introduction to the Study of the Detective Narrative* (1994) is a very good primer on critical trends within the limits the author sets. Pyrhönen argues that critical perspectives on detective fiction are inscribed in the narratives themselves, and this allows critical perspectives to be evaluated with reference to selected critical emphases on plot structure, sequence and causality, temporal displacement, delay, devices of suspense, generic elements, and truth as well as moral, epistemological, and psychological interpretations and social contexts (Pyrhönen, 1994, 2).

Articles

Critical articles can be found in a number of magazines and journals devoted to mystery and detective fiction. Since 1967 *The Armchair Detective* has been a prominent source of bibliography, interviews, reviews of books and conventions, miscellaneous articles, information for collectors, checklists, and other material. Critical commentary, reviews, and interviews were provided by *The Mystery Reader's Newsletter* between 1967 and 1974, and files of this publication are still useful. *Ellery Queen's Mystery Magazine* (1941–present) since 1975 has included "The Ellery Queen Mystery Newsletter." *Clues: A Journal of Detection* began semiannual publication in the spring of 1980 and continues to contribute critical essays on the genre. *Dime Novel Roundup* (1931–32, 1933–present) includes a wide range of articles and miscellaneous information on authors, titles, and topics; Michael L. Cook's *Dime Novel Roundup* (1983) provides an index of the journal through 1981. *The Mystery Fancier* publishes general information and author criticism on current writing.

Literary Contexts

The popularity of detective and mystery fiction in relation to other kinds of best-selling fiction and nonfiction can be inferred from Frank Luther Mott's *Golden Multitudes* (1947), James D. Hart's *The Popular Book* (1950), and Alice Payne Hackett and James Henry Burke's *80 Years of Best Sellers, 1895–1975* (1977). More recent best-sellers are discussed in Karen and Barbara Hinckley's *American Best Sellers: A Reader's Guide to Popular Fiction* (1987), based on the *World Almanac*'s listing of the top 20–30 sellers from 1965 to 1985; brief synopses are provided for 216 authors and 468 books. *Beacham's Popular Fiction* (1987) covers the period from 1950 to 1985 and provides publication information, biographical sketches, and reception; notes on novels identify social concerns, themes, characters, techniques and antecedents, and relation to previous work when relevant; an *Update* (1991) revises information on some 146 authors and includes 35 not covered in the original volume. Thomas M. McDade's *The Annals of Murder: A Bibliography of Books and Pamphlets on American Murders from Colonial Times to 1900* (1961) lists books and pamphlets on murders through about 1900. Memoirs of actual detectives are often noted, as are descriptions of real crimes that have provided inspiration for fiction. Mandy Hicken and Ray Prytherch's *Now Read On* (1994) suggests reading that follows up on a variety of authors and themes.

SPECIALIZED INFORMATION

John Cooper's *Detective Fiction* (1994) provides descriptive and pricing information on books considered to be collectable. Sources of pseudonyms other than those mentioned above include Susannah Bates's *The Pendex: An Index of Pen Names and House Names in Fantastic, Thriller, and Series Literature* (1981) and Lenore S. Gribbin's *Who's Whodunit: A List of 3218 Detective Story Writers and Their 1100 Pseudonyms* (1968).

Journals and Magazines

The Armchair Detective.

Clues: A Journal of Detection.

The Mystery Fancier.

RESEARCH COLLECTIONS

Manuscripts and papers of many mystery and detective novelists are available for research, and a number of libraries are building collections for the study of the genre. Listings in Lee Ash's *Subject Collections* (7th ed., 1993), the *National Union Catalog of Manuscript Collections* and *Special Collections in College and University Libraries* suggest that a number of libraries have strong holdings in the manuscripts of detective writers, but these are often not cataloged or the catalogs are not easily available. Ash identifies Columbia University Libraries Rare Book & Manuscript Library as having the largest mystery and detective manuscript collection. The Special Collections Department of the University of Pittsburgh libraries lists 415 cataloged manuscripts, Boston University's Division of Special Collections in the Mugar Memorial Library holds some 15,000 manuscripts representing over 100 authors (for which a list is available). Among those represented are Martha Albrand, Charlotte Armstrong, Michael Avallone, John Ball, William Ballinger, George Baxt, Evelyn Berckman, Leslie Charteris, Richard Condon, Ken Crossen, Ursula Curtiss, Jay Williams, Thomas Dewey, Doris Miles Disney, Mignon Eberhart, Stanley Ellin, Elizabeth Fenwick, Robert L. Fish, Deloris Stanton Forbes, Dorothy Gilman, Gordon and Mildred Gordon, Joseph Harrington, Evan Hunter, E. Richard Johnson, Frank Kane, Leonard S. Zinberg, Elizabeth Linington, Helen McCloy, Gregory McDonald, William P. McGivern, Arthur Maling, Helen Nielsen, Lillian O'Donnell, Dolores Hitchens, Barbara Mertz, Merrian Modell, Bill Pronzini, Kelley Roos, Richard Martin Stern, Phoebe Atwood Taylor, Dorothy Uhnak, Jack Vance, Donald E. Westlake, Phyllis Whitney, and Collin Wilcox.

The University of Oregon Library holds manuscripts and/or papers for Willis Todhunter Ballard, Francis Wynne, Frederick Nebel, Lenore Glen Offord, Margaret Scherf, Frank Ramsay Adams, Charles Alexander, Robert Wallace Grange, Mary Garden Collins, Thomas Albert Curry, John Hawkins, Jay Kalez, Jacquin L. Lait, and Louis Preston Trimble. The University of Oregon Library also holds the records of Renown Publications for 1955–72, which published the *Girl from U.N.C.L.E. Magazine* and *The Mike Shayne Mystery Magazine*. The University of California at Los Angeles holds manuscripts of Robert Leslie Bellem, Raymond Chandler, and others. Robert Bloch's manuscripts are at the University of Wyoming, as are those of Lawrence G. Blochman, Ray Russell, and others. George Harmon Coxe's manuscripts are held by the Beinecke Rare Book and Manuscript Library, Yale University. Dorothy Salisbury Davis's manuscripts are at Brooklyn College Library, Amber Dean's manuscripts are at the University of Rochester Library, while those of August Derleth are at the State Historical Society of Wisconsin Library. The University of Pennsylvania Library holds Howard Fast's manuscripts, St. Johns College, Annapolis, holds Leslie Ford's, and Indiana University holds the manuscripts of Joseph Hayes and Don Pendleton. The Humanities Research Center at the University of Texas-Austin holds the vast Ellery Queen collection, and includes Dashiell Hammett and Erle Stanley Gardner manuscripts. The University of Pittsburgh owns the Mary Roberts Rinehart materials. Aaron Marc Stein's manuscripts are at the Firestone Library, Princeton University, as are Willard Huntington Wright's Scribner's correspondence and the papers of Samuel McCoy, Raymond Holden, Jack Iams, and Robert Bernard Martin. Richard O'Connor's papers are at the University of Maine. Most of John D. MacDonald's papers are located at the University of Florida, although the University of Colorado boasts over a thousand volumes, including audiocassettes of his work. Rex Stout's library and personal papers are at Boston College. Listings for other writers can be found in the *St. James Guide to Crime and Mystery Writers* and other standard reference works.

Individual libraries also contain variant editions of authors' works and many contain specialized collections of popular writers. The Ira Wolff Collection at the University of California-San Diego contains some 2,500 Erle Stanley Gardner novels in many languages, as well as a large collection of Chandler and Hammett. A collection of Chandler's works can be found at the Kent State University Libraries at Kent, Ohio. Los Angeles's Occidental College contains the Guyman collection of first editions of mystery and detective fiction, including some 18,000 volumes through 1975. The Queen Collection at the University of Texas, the Sandoe Collection at Brigham Young University, the Jacques Barzun and Wendell Hertig Taylor Collection of first editions at the University of North Carolina (Chapel Hill), the Popular Culture Collection at Bowling Green State University and others are notable. The University of North Carolina (Greensboro) features detective works by women or featuring women from the late nineteenth to mid-twentieth century. The Russel B. Nye Collection at Michigan State University holds some 3,500 detective and mystery novels and runs of some 28 pulp titles; and the University of Wisconsin reports some 4,000 titles, mostly of British Golden Age novels. Princeton also reports strong holdings in Samuel Hopkins Adams, James M. Cain, Raymond Chandler, Erle Stanley Gardner, Ellery Queen, and Cornell Woolrich. Providence Athenaeum reports 4,000 volumes of American and British detective novels, including many translations. Most libraries will hold many more volumes than is at first apparent, because titles may not be adequately identified in subject catalogs or separated into defined collections. Collections of detective fiction can be found in all public libraries when these have not been forced to abandon them for lack of space, and more specialized collections can often be found in university libraries, especially those that have received gifts of or purchased large private collections.

The media for the development of much popular mystery and detective fiction—the dime novels and story papers of the nineteenth century and the pulps and paperbacks of the twentieth century—have not until recently been sought by research libraries. Now numerous libraries have attempted to collect such materials, and excellent collections are available in several locations in the United States. Ash (1993) remarks that the Johannsen Collection of 1,100 volumes at Northern Illinois University's Founders' Memorial Library "probably the most extensive collection [of dime novels] there is." The Library of Congress's twenty thousand issues of uncatalogued dime novels in 270 series must rank as one of the most comprehensive collections, though it remains nearly unusable. The New York Public Libraries' collection is identified in its *Bulletin* (1922). Other major repositories of dime novels can be found in the Popular Library Department of the Cleveland Public Library (1,300 issues), the Huntington Library (over 2,000), Yale University Libraries, the George H. Hess Collection of 4,000 dime novels and other books at the University of Minnesota libraries, and Oberlin College Library's 2,200 issues of eighty-nine series.

Because pulp magazines date only from about 1895 and were printed on high acid content paper and because they were considered subliterature, collections of them are less accessible than dime novel collections. Many pulps are in such delicate condition that libraries should refuse to copy them with any process that generates heat; certainly care should be taken in handling the now-brittle and yellowed paper where access is permitted. The University of California at Los Angeles reports 12,500 issues in four hundred titles, Harvard University libraries house an extensive collection, and numerous other libraries have samples or partial collections. The Lilly Library at Indiana University has strong holdings in pulp magazines. The Swen Franklin Parson Library at Northern Illinois University, for example, houses the Western Pulp Magazine Collection of six hundred magazine titles, and the David Mullins Library at the University of Arkansas contains the Gerald J. McIntosh Dime Novel Collection. The San Francisco Academy of Comic Art claims the largest collection of pulp magazines available, together with 1 million comic strips, 22,000 comics and some 12,500 hardcover detective and mystery novels.

BIBLIOGRAPHY

Adams, Donald K., ed. *The Mystery and Detection Annual*. Beverly Hills, CA: Donald Adams, 1972–73.

Adey, R. A. *Locked Room Murders and Other Impossible Crimes: A Comprehensive Bibliography*. Minneapolis: Crossover Press, 1991.

Agassi, Joseph. "The Detective Novel and Scientific Method." *Poetics Today* 3 (Winter 1982): 99–108.

Aisenberg, N. A. *A Common Spring*. Bowling Green, OH: Bowling Green State University Popular Culture Center, 1979.

Albert, Walter. "Bibliography of Secondary Sources." *Armchair Detective*, 1972– .

———, ed. *Detective and Mystery Fiction: An International Bibliography of Secondary Sources*. 1985. San Bernardino, CA: Brownstone Books, 1997. Rev. and enl. ed.

Alcott, Louisa May. *The Lost Stories of Louisa May Alcott*. Ed. by Madeleine B. Stern and Daniel Shealy. Secaucus, NJ: Carol Publishing Group, 1995.

———. *Louisa May Alcott Unmasked: Collected Thrillers*. Ed. and introduction by Madeleine Stern. Boston: Northeastern University Press, 1995.

Alderson, Martha, and Neysa Chouteau. "Joseph Harrington's Francis X. Kerrigan." In Earl F. Bargainnier and George N. Dove, eds., *Cops and Constables: American and British Fictional Policemen*. Bowling Green, OH: Bowling Green State University Popular Press, 1986, 33–42.

Alewyn, Richard. "Ursprung des Detektivromans." *Probleme und Gestalten: Essays*. Insel: Verlag, 1974, 341–349. Trans. as "The Origin of the Detective Novel" and repr. in Glen W. Most and William W. Stowe, eds., *The Poetics of Murder: Detective Fiction and Literary Theory*. New York: Harcourt Brace Jovanovich, 1983, 62–78.

Allen, Dick, and David Chacko, eds. *Detective Fiction: Crime and Compromise*. New York: Harcourt Brace Jovanovich, 1974.

American Literary Scholarship. Durham, NC: Duke University Press (annual).

Anderson, David. *Rex Stout*. New York: Ungar, 1984.

Arden, Leon. "A Knock at the Backdoor of Art: The Entrance of Raymond Chandler." In Bernard Benstock, ed., *Art in Crime Writing*. New York: St. Martin's Press, 1985.

The Armchair Detective. Midland, MN, 1967–present. The journal is being reprinted: Madison, IN: Brownstone Books, 1981– .

The Armchair Detective Book of Lists. Ed. by Kate Stine. New York: O. Penzler Books, 1995.

Ash, Lee. *Subject Collections: A Guide to Special Book Collections and Subject Emphases as Reported by University, College, Public, and Special Libraries and Museums in the United States and Canada*. Compiled by Lee Ash and William G. Miller, with the collaboration of Barry Scott, Kathleen Vickery, and Beverly McDonough. 7th ed. New Providence, NJ: R. R. Bowker, 1993.

Auden, W. H. "The Guilty Vicarage." In *The Dyer's Hand*. New York: Vintage Books, 1968. Often reprinted.

Aydelotte, W. O. "The Detective Story as a Historical Source." *Yale Review* 34 (Fall 1949): 76–95. Repr. In Larry Landrum, Pat Browne, and Ray B. Browne, eds., *Dimensions of Detective Fiction*. Bowling Green, OH: Popular Press, 1976.

Babener, Liahna. "Uncloseting Ideology in the Novels of Barbara Wilson." In Kathleen Gregory Klein, ed., *Women Times Three: Writers, Detectives, Readers*. Bowling Green, OH: Bowling Green State University Popular Press, 1995, 143–52.

Bailey, Frankie Y. *Out of the Woodpile: Black Characters in Crime and Detective Fiction*. Westport, CT: Greenwood Press, 1991.

Baker, Donald G. "The Lawyer in Popular Fiction." *Journal of Popular Culture* 3: 3 (Winter 1969): 493–516.

Baker, Robert, and Michael Nietzel. *Private Eyes: One Hundred and One Knights: A Survey of American Detective Fiction 1922–1984*. Bowling Green, OH: Bowling Green State University Popular Press, 1985.

———. "The Science Fiction Detective Story: Tomorrow's Private Eyes." *Armchair Detective* 18 (Spring 1985): 140–150.

Bakerman, Jane S. "Bloody Balaclava: Charlotte MacLeod's Campus Comedy Mysteries." *Mystery Fancier* 7 (Jan./Feb. 1983): 23–29.

———. "Cutting Both Ways: Race, Prejudice, and Motive in Tony Hillerman's Detective Fiction." *MELUS* 11 (Fall 1984): 17–25.

———. *10 Women of Mystery*. Bowling Green, OH: Bowling Green University Popular Culture Center, 1981.

———. "Tony Hillerman's Joe Leaphorn and Jim Chee." In Earl F. Bargainnier and George N. Dove, eds., *Cops and Constables: American and British Fic-*

tional Policemen. Bowling Green, OH: Bowling Green State University Popular Press, 1986, 98–112.

————, ed. *And Then There Were Nine—More Women of Mystery.* Bowling Green, OH: Bowling Green State University Popular Press, 1985.

Ball, Ian A., and Graham Daldry, eds. *Essays on Crime Fiction.* London: Macmillan, 1990.

Ball, John. "Cop Hater." In Mary Jean DeMarr, ed., *In the Beginning: First Novels in Mystery Series.* Bowling Green, OH: Bowling Green State University Popular Press, 1995.

————. "The Ethnic Detective." In John Ball, ed., *The Mystery Story.* San Diego: University of California Extension, 1976, 143–161.

————, ed. *The Mystery Story.* San Diego: University of California Extension, 1976.

Ballinger, John E. "Bibliomysteries." *American Book Collector* 3 (March-April 1982): 23–28.

Banks, R. Jeff. "Spillane's Anti-Establishmentarian Heroes." In Larry Landrum, Pat Browne, and Ray B. Browne, eds., *Dimensions of Detective Fiction.* Bowling Green, OH: Popular Press, 1976, 124–140.

Barer, Burl. *The Saint: A Complete History in Print, Radio, Film, and Television of Leslie Charteris' Robin Hood of Modern Crime, Simon Templar, 1928–1992.* Jefferson, NC: McFarland & Co., 1993.

Bargainnier, Earl F. *The Gentle Art of Murder.* Bowling Green, OH: Bowling Green University Popular Press, 1980.

Bargainnier, Earl F., and George N. Dove, eds. *Cops and Constables: American and British Fictional Policemen.* Bowling Green, OH: Bowling Green State University Popular Press, 1986.

Barnes, Melvyn. *Best Detective Fiction: A Guide from Godwin to the Present.* Hamden, CT: Linnet, 1975.

Barnes, Melvyn P. *Murder in Print: A Guide to Two Centuries of Crime Fiction.* London: Barn Owl Books, 1986.

Barthes, Roland. *S/Z: An Essay.* Trans. by Richard Miller; Preface by Richard Howard. New York: Hill and Wang, 1974. "Delay" and "The Hermeneutic Sentence" are included in Glenn W. Most and William W. Stowe, eds., *The Poetics of Murder: Detective Fiction and Literary Theory.* New York: Harcourt Brace Jovanovich, 1983.

Barzun, Jacques, ed. *The Delights of Detection.* New York: Criterion Books, 1961.

Barzun, Jacques, and Wendell Hertig Taylor. *A Book of Prefaces to Fifty Classics of Crime Fiction, 1900–50.* New York: Garland, 1976.

————. *A Catalogue of Crime.* New York: Harper, 1971; rev. and enl., 1989.

Bates, Susannah. *The Pendex: An Index of Pen Names and House Names in Fantastic, Thriller, and Series Literature.* New York: Garland, 1981.

Beacham's Popular Fiction, 1950–present. Ed. by Waltonzanne Niemeyer. Washington, DC: Beacham, 1987.

"The Beadle Collection." *Bulletin of the New York Public Library,* 22 (1922): 555–628.

Beekman, E. M. "Raymond Chandler and an American Genre." *Massachusetts Review* 14:1 (Winter 1973): 149–173.

Beiderwell, Bruce. "State Power and Self-Destruction: Rex Stout and the Romance of Justice." *Journal of Popular Culture* 27 (Summer 1993): 13–22.

Bell, Ian A. "Irony and Justice in Patricia Highsmith." In Ian A. Bell and Graham Daldry, eds., *Watching the Detectives: Essays on Crime Fiction*. London and New York: Macmillan, 1990, 1–17.

Bell, Ian A., and Graham Daldry, eds. *Watching the Detectives: Essays on Crime Fiction*. London and New York: Macmillan, 1990.

Bell, J., et al. *Crime in Good Company: Essays on Criminals and Crime-Writing*. London: Constable and Co., 1959.

Bendel, S. K. *Making Crime Pay*. Englewood Cliffs, NJ: Prentice-Hall, 1983.

Bennett, Maurice J. "The Detective Fiction of Poe and Borges." *Comparative Literature* 35 (Summer 1983): 266–275.

Benstock, Bernard, ed. *Art in Crime Writing*. New York: St. Martin's Press, 1985.

Bentley, Christopher. "Radical Anger: Dashiell Hammett's *Red Harvest*." In Brian Docherty, ed., *American Crime Fiction: Studies in the Genre*. New York: St. Martin's Press, 1988, 54–70.

Benvenuti, Stefano, and Gianni Rizzoni. *The Whodunit: An Informal History of Detective Fiction*. Trans. by Anthony Eyre, with "A Report on the Current Scene" by Edward D. Hoch. New York: Macmillan, 1982.

Bilker, Harvey L. *Writing Mysteries That Sell*. Chicago: Contemporary Books, 1982.

Binyon, T. J. *Murder Will Out: The Detective in Fiction*. Oxford and New York: Oxford University Press, 1989.

Birkhead, Edith. *The Tale of Terror: A Study of the Gothic Romance*. 1923. New York: Russell, 1963.

Black, Joel. *The Aesthetics of Murder: A Study in Romantic Literature and Contemporary Culture*. Baltimore, MD: Johns Hopkins University Press, 1991.

Block, Andrew. *The English Novel, 1740–1850*. London: Dawsons, 1962.

Block, Lawrence, and Ernie Bulow. *After Hours: Conversations with Lawrence Block*. Albuquerque, NM: University of New Mexico Press, 1995.

Bloom, Clive. *Twentieth-Century Suspense: The Thriller Comes of Age*. New York: St. Martin's Press, 1990.

Bloom, Clive, et al., eds. *Nineteenth Century Suspense from Poe to Conan Doyle*. Basingstoke: Macmillan, 1987.

Bloom, Harold, ed. *Classic Crime and Suspense Writers*. New York: Chelsea House, 1994.

Boccia, Michael. "Ishmael Reed's *Mumbo Jumbo*: Form of the Mystery." *Journal of Popular Literature* 3 (Spring–Summer 1987): 98–107.

Boileau, Pierre. *La Novela Policial*. Buenos Aires: Editorial Paidos, 1968.

Borowitz, Albert. *Innocence and Arsenic: Studies in Crime and Literature*. New York: Harper, 1977.

Boucher, Anthony. *Ellery Queen: A Double Profile*. Boston: Little, Brown, 1951.

———. *Multiplying Villainies: Selected Mystery Criticism, 1942–1968, by Anthony Boucher*. Ed. by R. E. Briney and Francis M. Nevins, Jr. Boston: Bouchercon, 1973.

Bounds, J. Dennis. *Perry Mason: The Authorship & Reproduction of a Popular Hero.* Westport, CT: Greenwood, 1996.

Bourgeau, Art. *The Mystery Lover's Companion.* New York: Crown Publishers, 1986.

Bradbury, Richard. "Sexuality, Guilt and Detection: Tension between History and Suspense." In Brian Docherty, ed., *American Crime Fiction: Studies in the Genre.* New York: St. Martin's Press, 1988, 88–99.

Brandt, Kate, and Paula Lichtenberg. "On the Case with V. I. and Kinsey." *Hot Wire: The Journal of Women's Music and Culture* 10 (Jan. 1994): 48–50.

Brazil, John R. "Murder Trials, Murder, and Twenties America." *American Quarterly* 33 (Summer 1981): 163–184.

Brean, Herbert, ed. *The Mystery Writers Handbook.* New York: Harper, 1956.

Breen, Jon L. *Novel Verdicts: A Guide to Courtroom Fiction.* Metuchen, NJ: Scarecrow, 1984.

———. *What About Murder? 1981–1991: A Guide to Books about Mystery and Detective Fiction.* Metuchen, NJ: Scarecrow Press, 1993.

———, ed. *What About Murder? A Guide to Mystery and Detective Fiction.* Metuchen, NJ: Scarecrow, 1981.

Breen, Jon L., and Martin Harry Greenberg, eds. *Murder off the Rack: Critical Studies of Ten Paperback Masters.* Metuchen, NJ: Scarecrow Press, 1989.

———, eds. *Synod of Sleuths: Essays on Judeo-Christian Detective Fiction.* Metuchen, NJ: Scarecrow Press, 1990.

Brewer, Gay. *A Detective in Distress: Philip Marlowe's Domestic Dream.* San Bernardino, CA: Borgo Press, 1989.

———. *Laughing Like Hell: The Harrowing Satires of Jim Thompson.* San Bernardino, CA: Borgo Press, 1996.

Briney, Robert E. "Death Rays, Demons, and Worms Unknown to Science." In John Ball, ed., *The Mystery Story.* San Diego: University of California Extension, 1976, 235–289.

Brophy, Brigid. *Don't Never Forget.* New York: Holt, 1966.

Browne, Ray B. "Christie Tea or Chandler Beer: The Novels of Martha Grimes." *Armchair Detective* 18 (Summer 1985): 262–266.

———. *Detective Fiction and Culture.* Bowling Green, OH: Bowling Green State University Popular Press, 1986.

———. *Heroes and Humanities: Detective Fiction and Culture.* Bowling Green, OH: Bowling Green State University Popular Press, 1986.

Brubaker, Bill. *The Detective Fiction of Jonathan Latimer.* Bowling Green, OH: Bowling Green State University Popular Press, 1993.

Bruccoli, Matthew J., ed. *Kenneth Millar/Ross Macdonald: A Checklist.* Detroit, MI: Gale, 1971.

———, ed. *Raymond Chandler: A Checklist.* Kent, OH: Kent State University Press, 1968.

Bruccoli, Matthew, and Richard Layman, eds. *Hardboiled Mystery Writers.* Detroit, MI: Gale, 1989.

Budd, Elaine. *13 Mistresses of Murder.* New York: Ungar, 1986.

Burack, A. S., ed. *Writing Detective and Mystery Fiction.* Boston: The Writer, 1945; suspense edition, 1967.

Burack, Sylvia K., ed. *How to Write and Sell Mystery Fiction.* Boston: Writer, 1990.

Burns, Landon. "Fadeout: Brandstetter's First Case." In Mary Jean DeMarr, ed., *In the Beginning: First Novels in Mystery Series.* Bowling Green, OH: Bowling Green State University Popular Press, 1995, 171–84.

Burns, Rex. "The Mirrored Badge." In Robin W. Winks, ed., *Colloquium on Crime: Eleven Renowned Mystery Writers Discuss Their Work.* New York: Charles Scribner's Sons, 1986, 23–40.

Butler, William Vivian. *The Durable Desperadoes.* London: Macmillan, 1973.

Caillois, Roger. *The Mystery Novel.* Trans. by Roberto Yahni and A. W. Sadler. Bronxville, NY: Laughing Buddha Press, 1984. Partially reprinted in Glenn W. Most and William Stowe, eds., *The Poetics of Murder: Detective Fiction and Literary Theory.* New York: Harcourt Brace Jovanovich, 1983.

Cambiaire, Celestin P. *The Influence of Edgar Allan Poe in France.* New York: G. E. Stewart, 1927.

Carby, Hazel V. Introduction. *The Magazine Novels of Pauline Hopkins.* New York: Oxford, 1988.

Carlisle, Charles R. "Strangers Within, Enemies Without: Alienation in Popular Mafia Fiction." In Larry Landrum, Pat Browne, and Ray B. Browne, eds., *Dimensions of Detective Fiction.* Bowling Green, OH: Popular Press, 1976, 192–201.

Carlson, Marvin A. *Deathtraps: The Postmodern Comedy Thriller.* Bloomington: Indiana University Press, 1993.

Carr, John C. *The Craft of Crime: Conversations with Crime Writers.* Boston: Houghton Mifflin, 1983.

Carter, Steven R. "Ishmael Reed's Neo-Hoodoo Detection." in Larry Landrum, Pat Browne and Ray B. Browne, eds., *Dimensions of Detective Fiction.* Bowling Green, OH: Popular Press, 1976, 265–274.

Cassiday, Bruce, comp. and ed. *Modern Mystery, Fantasy and Science Fiction Writers.* New York: Continuum, 1993.

———, ed. *Roots of Detection: The Art of Deduction Before Sherlock Holmes.* New York: Ungar, 1983.

Cawelti, John G. *Adventure, Mystery, and Romance: Formula Stories as Art and Popular Culture.* Chicago: University of Chicago Press, 1976.

———. "The Spillane Phenomenon." *Journal of Popular Culture* 3 (Summer 1969): 9–22.

Cawelti, John G., and Bruce A. Rosenberg. *The Spy Story.* Chicago: University of Chicago Press, 1987.

Champigny, Robert. *What Will Have Happened: A Philosophical and Technical Essay on Mystery Stories.* Bloomington: Indiana University Press, 1977.

Chandler, F. W. "The Literature of Crime Detection." In *The Literature of Roguery.* Boston: Houghton, Mifflin, 1907.

Chandler, Raymond. *The Simple Art of Murder.* Boston: Houghton, 1950.

Charney, Hanna. *The Detective Novel of Manners: Hedonism, Morality and the Life of Reason.* Rutherford, NJ: Fairleigh Dickinson University Press, 1981.

Chell, Cara. "Untricking the Eye: Joyce Carol Oates and the Feminist Ghost Story." *Arizona Quarterly* 41 (Spring 1983): 5–23.

Chimera. 5:4 (Summer 1947). Special issue on detective fiction.

Christianson, Scott. "Tough Talk and Wisecracks: Language as Power in American Detective Fiction." In Glenwood Irons, ed., *Gender, Language, and Myth:*

Essays on Popular Narrative. Toronto: University of Toronto Press, 1992, 142–56.

———. "Tough Talk and Wisecracks: Language as Power in American Detective Fiction." *Journal of Popular Culture* 23 (Fall 1989): 151–162.

Christopher, Joe R. "The Social World in Dr. Gideon Fell's Shorter Cases." *Mystery Fancier* 13 (Summer 1992): 3–22.

Churchill, Ward. "Hi Ho, Hillerman . . . (Away): Unmasking the Role of Detective Fiction in Indian Country." *Fantasies of the Master Race: Literature, Cinema and the Colonization of American Indians.* Monroe, ME: Common Courage Press, 1992, 249–288.

Clark, Susan L. "Murder Is Her Cup of Tea." *Armchair Detective* 21 (Spring 1988): 117–127.

Clover, Carol J. "Her Body, Himself: Gender in the Slasher Film." In Glenwood Irons, ed., *Gender, Language, and Myth: Essays on Popular Narrative.* Toronto: University of Toronto Press, 1992, 252–302.

Clues: A Journal of Detection. Bowling Green, OH, 1980– .

Cobb, Irvin S. *A Plea for Old Cap Collier.* New York: George H. Doran Co., 1921.

Cohen, R. "Private Eyes and Public Critics." *Partisan Review* 24:2 (Spring 1957): 235–243.

Cohn, Jan. *Improbable Fiction: The Life of Mary Roberts Rinehart.* Pittsburgh: University of Pittsburgh Press, 1980.

———. "Mary Roberts Rinehart." In Earl F. Bargainnier, ed., *10 Women of Mystery.* Bowling Green, OH: Bowling Green State University Popular Press, 1981.

Collins, Max Allan. *One Lonely Knight: Mickey Spillane's Mike Hammer.* Bowling Green, OH: Bowling Green University Popular Press, 1984.

Conquest, John. *Trouble Is Their Business: Private Eyes in Fiction, Film and Television, 1927–1988.* New York: Garland, 1990.

Constantine, K. C. "Writing About Balzic." In Robin W. Winks, ed., *Colloquium on Crime: Eleven Renowned Mystery Writers Discuss Their Work.* New York: Scribner's, 1986, 41–61.

Cook, Michael L. *Dime Novel Roundup: Annotated Index, 1931–1981.* Bowling Green, OH: Bowling Green University Press, 1983.

———. *Murder by Mail: Inside the Mystery Book Clubs, with Complete Checklist.* Evansville, IN: Cook, 1979; rev. and expanded ed., Bowling Green, OH: Popular Press, 1983.

———. *Mystery, Detective, and Espionage Magazines.* Westport, CT: Greenwood, 1983.

———. *Mystery Fanfare: A Composite Annotated Index to Mystery and Related Fanzines, 1963–1981.* Bowling Green, OH: Popular Press, 1983.

Cook, Michael L., and Stephen T. Miller. *Mystery, Detective, and Espionage Fiction: A Checklist of Fiction in U.S. Pulp Magazines, 1915–1974, I and II.* New York: Garland, 1988.

Cooper, [Robert] John. *Detective Fiction: The Collector's Guide.* Aldershot, Hants, UK; Brookfield, VT: Scholar Press, 1994.

Cooper-Clark, Diana. *Designs of Darkness: Interviews with Detective Novelists.* Bowling Green, OH: Bowling Green University Popular Press, 1983.

Corvasce, Mauro V., and Joseph R. Paglino. *Modus Operandi: A Writer's Guide to How Criminals Work*. Cincinnati, OH: Writer's Digest Books, 1995.

Cox, J. Randolph. "The Dime Novel Detective and His Elusive Trail: Twenty Years of Dime Novel Research." *Dime Novel Roundup* 54 (Dec. 1985): 90–94.

―――. *Man of Magic and Mystery: A Guide to the Work of Walter B. Gibson*. Metuchen, NJ: Scarecrow Press, 1988.

―――. *Masters of Mystery and Detective Fiction: An Annotated Bibliography*. Pasadena, CA: Salem Press, 1989.

Craig, Patricia, and Mary Cadogan. *The Lady Investigates: Women Detectives and Spies in Fiction*. New York: St. Martin's Press, 1981.

Craigie, Dorothy, and Graham Greene. *Victorian Detective Fiction: A Catalogue of the Collection Made by Dorothy Glover and Graham Greene*. Arranged by Eric Osborne, introduced by John Carter and preface by Graham Greene. London: Bodley Head, 1966.

Crider, Allen B. "Race Williams—Private Investigator." In Larry Landrum, Pat Browne, and Ray B. Browne, eds., *Dimensions of Detective Fiction*. Bowling Green, OH: Popular Press, 1976.

Crombie, Winifred. "Raymond Chandler: Burlesque, Parody, Paradox." *Language and Style* 16 (Spring 1983): 151–168.

The Crown Crime Companion: The Top 100 Mystery Novels of All Time. Selected by the Mystery Writers of America, annotated by Otto Penzler, compiled by Mickey Friedman. New York: Crown Trade Paperbacks, 1995.

Daldry, Graham. "The Voices of George V. Higgins." In Ian A. Bell and Graham Daldry, eds., *Watching the Detectives: Essays on Crime Fiction*. New York: Macmillan, 1990, 37–47.

Davis, David Brion. *Homicide in American Fiction, 1798–1860: A Study in Social Values*. Ithaca, NY: Cornell University Press, 1957.

Davis, Dorothy Salisbury. "Some of the Truth." In Robin W. Winks, ed., *Colloquium on Crime: Eleven Renowned Mystery Writers Discuss Their Work*. New York: Charles Scribner's Sons, 1986, 63–78.

Day, Gary. "Investigating the Investigator: Hammett's Continental Op." In Brian Docherty, ed., *American Crime Fiction: Studies in the Genre*. New York: St. Martin's Press, 1988, 39–53.

DeAndrea, William L. *Encyclopedia Mysteriosa: A Comprehensive Guide to the Art of Detection in Print, Film, Radio, and Television*. Englewood Cliffs, NJ: Prentice-Hall, 1994.

―――. "The Many Faces of Donald E. Westlake." *Armchair Detective* 21 (Fall 1988): 341–60.

Deeck, William F., and Steven A. Stilwell. *The Armchair Detective Index: Volumes 1–20, 1967–1987*. New York: Armchair Detective Library, 1992.

DeLamotte, Eugenia C. *Perils of the Night: A Feminist Study of Nineteenth-Century Gothic*. New York: Oxford University Press, 1990.

DellaCava, Frances A., and Madeline H. Engel. *Female Detectives in American Novels: A Bibliography and Analysis of Serialized Female Sleuths*. New York: Garland, 1993.

Dellon, Hope. "Editing the Mystery Novel." In Gerald Gross, ed., *Editors on Editing*. New York: Harper, 1985, 213–220.

Deloux, Jean-Pierre. *Dashiell Hammett: Underworld USA*. Monaco: Rocher, 1994.

DeMarr, Mary Jean, ed. *In the Beginning: First Novels in Mystery Series*. Bowling Green, OH: Bowling Green State University Popular Press, 1995.

Denning, Michael. *Mechanic Accents: Dime Novels and Working-Class Culture in America*. London/New York: Verso, 1987.

———. "Topographies of Violence: Chester Himes' Harlem Domestic Novels." *Critical Texts: A Review of Theory and Criticism* 5 (1988): 10–18.

Dentith, Simon. " 'This Shitty Urban Machine Humanised': The Urban Crime Novel and the Novels of William McIlvanney." In Ian A. Bell and Graham Daldry, eds., *Watching the Detectives: Essays on Crime Fiction*. New York: Macmillan, 1990, 18–36.

De Quincey, Thomas. "On Murder Considered as One of the Fine Arts." In *The Collected Writings of Thomas De Quincey*, ed. by David Masson. London: A. & C. Black, 1897, 9–124.

De Vries, P. H. *Poe and After: The Detective Story Investigated*. Amsterdam: Bakker, 1956.

Dinan, John A. *Chicago Ain't No Sissy Town! The Regional Detective Fiction of Howard Browne*. San Bernardino, CA: Borgo Press, 1997.

Docherty, Brian, ed. *American Crime Fiction: Studies in the Genre*. New York: St. Martin's Press, 1988.

Donaldson, Betty, and Norman Donaldson. *How Did They Die?* New York: St. Martin's Press, 1979.

Dooley, Dennis. *Dashiell Hammett*. New York: Ungar, 1984.

Dove, George N. *The Boys from Grover Avenue: Ed McBain's 87th Precinct Novels*. Bowling Green, OH: Bowling Green State University Popular Press, 1985.

———. *The Police Procedural*. Bowling Green, OH: Bowling Green University Popular Press, 1982.

———. *The Reader & the Detective Story*. Bowling Green, OH: Bowling Green University Popular Press, 1997.

———. *Suspense in the Formula Story*. Bowling Green, OH: Bowling Green State University Popular Press, 1989.

Dow, Paul E. *Criminology in Literature*. New York: Longman, 1980.

Drew, Bernard A. *Heroines: A Bibliography of Women Series Characters in Mystery, Espionage, Action, Science Fiction, Fantasy, Horror, Western, Romance, and Juvenile Novels*. New York: Garland, 1989.

Dyer, Carolyn Stewart, and Nancy Tillman Romalov, eds. *Rediscovering Nancy Drew*. Urbana: University of Illinois Press, 1995.

Eames, Hugh. *Sleuths, Inc.: Studies of Problem Solvers, Doyle, Simenon, Hammett, Ambler, Chandler*. Philadelphia: Lippincott, 1980.

Eco, Umberto, and Thomas A. Sebeok. *The Sign of Three: Dupin, Holmes, Peirce*. Bloomington: Indiana University Press, 1984.

Eden, Rick A. "Detective Fiction as Satire." *Genre* 16 (Fall 1983): 279–295.

Edenbaum, Robert I. "The Poetics of the Private-Eye: The Novels of Dashiell Hammett." In David Madden, ed., *Tough Guy Writers of the Thirties*. Carbondale: Southern Illinois University Press, 1968, 80–103.

Engel, Leonard W. "Landscape and Place in Tony Hillerman's Mysteries." *Western American Literature* 28 (Aug. 1993): 111–122.

————. "Locked Up: A Close Look at Ross Macdonald's 'The Underground Man.'" *Armchair Detective* 20 (Spring 1987): 183–185.

Erisman, Fred. "Hillerman's Uses of the Southwest." *Roundup* 1 (Summer 1989): 9–18.

————. "Tony Hillerman's Jim Chee and the Shaman's Dilemma." *Lamar Journal of the Humanities* 17 (Spring 1992): 5–16.

Evans, Odette L'Henry. "Towards a Semiotic Reading of Mickey Spillane." In Brian Docherty, ed., *American Crime Fiction: Studies in the Genre*. New York: St. Martin's Press, 1988, 100–114.

Faller, Lincoln B. "Criminal Opportunities in the Eighteenth Century: The 'Ready-Made' Contexts of the Popular Literature of Crime." *Comparative Literature Studies* 24 (1987): 120–145.

Farah, David. *Farah's Guide to the Nancy Drew Mystery Series*. Grand Blanc, MI: Farah's Books, 1987.

Fisher, Margery. *The Bright Face of Danger*. Boston: Horn Book, 1986.

————. "The Sleuth: Then and Now." *Quarterly Journal of the Library of Congress* 38 (Fall 1981): 276–284.

Flack, Jerry D. *Mystery and Detection: Thinking and Problem Solving with the Sleuths*. Englewood, CO: Teacher Ideas Press, 1990.

Fleenor, Juliann Evans, ed. *The Female Gothic*. Montreal; London: Eden Press, 1983.

Foucault, Michel. *Discipline and Punish*. 1975. New York: Vintage Books, 1979.

Franklin, H. Bruce. *Prison Literature in America: The Victim as Criminal and Artist*. New York: Oxford University Press, 1989.

Fraser, Howard M. *In the Presence of Mystery: Modernist Fiction and the Occult*. Chapel Hill: University of North Carolina Department of Romance Languages, 1992.

Freedman, Carl, and Christopher Kendrick. "Forms of Labor in Dashiell Hammett's *Red Harvest*." *PMLA* 106 (March 1991): 209–221.

Freeling, Nicolas. *Criminal Convictions: Errant Essays on Perpetrators of Literary License*. Boston: D. R. Godine, 1994.

Freeman, Lucy. *The Murder Mystique: Crime Writers on Their Art*. New York: Ungar, 1982.

Freese, Peter. *The Ethnic Detective: Chester Himes, Harry Kemelman, Tony Hillerman*. Essen: Verlag Die Blaue Eule, 1992.

Friedland, M. L., ed. *Rough Justice: Essays on Crime in Literature*. Toronto, Buffalo: University of Toronto Press, 1991.

Frye, Northrop. *The Anatomy of Criticism*. Princeton, NJ: Princeton University Press, 1957.

Fugate, Francis L. *Secrets of the World's Best-selling Writer: The Storytelling Techniques of Erle Stanley Gardner*. New York: W. Morrow, 1980.

Gardner, John. "The Espionage Novel." In H.R.F. Keating, ed., *Whodunit? A Guide to Crime, Suspense and Spy Fiction*. New York: Van Nostrand Reinhold, 1982, 70–80.

Gates, Henry Louis. *The Signifying Monkey*. New York: Oxford University Press, 1988.

The Gay and Lesbian Detective. Berkeley, CA: Mystery Readers International, 1993.

Geherin, David. *The American Private Eye: The Image in Fiction.* New York: Ungar, 1985.

———. *Elmore Leonard.* New York: Continuum, 1989.

———. *Sons of Sam Spade: The Private-Eye Novel in the 70s: Robert B. Parker, Roger L. Simon, Andrew Bergman.* New York: Ungar, 1980.

Gidley, Mick. "Elements of the Detective Story in William Faulkner's Fiction." In Larry Landrum, Pat Browne, and Ray B. Browne, eds., *Dimensions of Detective Fiction.* Bowling Green, OH: Popular Press, 1976, 228–246.

Gilbert, Elliot L. "McWatters' Law: The Best Kept Secret of the Secret Service." In Larry Landrum, Pat Browne, and Ray B. Browne, eds., *Dimensions of Detective Fiction.* Bowling Green, OH: Popular Press, 1976, 22–36.

Gilbert, Michael. "The Spy in Fact and Fiction." In John Ball, ed. *The Mystery Story.* San Diego: University of California Extension, 1976, 205–221.

Glassman, Steve, and Maurice O'Sullivan, eds. *Crime Fiction and Film in the Sunshine State: Florida Noir.* Bowling Green, OH: Bowling Green State University Popular Press, 1997.

Glover, Dorothy, and Graham Greene. *Victorian Detective Fiction: A Catalogue.* London: Bodley Head, 1977.

Godden, Richard. "Edgar Allan Poe and the Detection of Riot." *Literature and History* 8 (Autumn 1982): 206–231, 272.

Goodstone, Tony, ed. *The Pulps: Fifty Years of American Pop Culture.* New York: Bonanza Books, 1971.

Goulart, Ron. *Cheap Thrills: An Informal History of the Pulp Magazines.* New Rochelle, NY: Arlington House, 1972.

———. *The Dime Detectives.* New York: Mysterious Press, 1988.

———, ed. Introduction to *The Hard-Boiled Dicks: An Anthology and Study of Pulp Detective Fiction.* Los Angeles: Sherbourne Press, 1965; New York: Pocket Books, 1965.

Grafton, Sue, ed. *Writing Mysteries: A Handbook.* Cincinnati, OH: Writer's Digest Books, 1992.

Green, Martin. *Seven Types of Adventure Tale: An Etiology of a Major Genre.* University Park: Pennsylvania State University Press, 1991.

Greenberg, Martin H., Ed Gorman, and Bill Munster, eds. *The Dean Koontz Companion.* New York: Berkley, 1994.

Greene, Douglas G. *John Dickson Carr: The Man Who Explained Miracles.* New York: Otto Penzler, 1995.

Gregory, Sinda. *Private Investigations: The Novels of Dashiell Hammett.* Carbondale: Southern Illinois University Press, 1984.

Greiser, Donald. "Robert B. Parker and the Jock of the Mean Streets." *Critique* 26 (Fall 1984): 36–44.

Grella, George. "Murder and Manners: The Formal Detective Novel." *Novel: A Forum on Fiction* 4 (Fall 1970): 30–48. Reprinted in Larry Landrum, Pat Browne, and Ray B. Browne, eds., *Dimensions of Detective Fiction.* Bowling Green, OH: Popular Press, 1976, 37–57.

———. "Murder and the Mean Streets: The Hard-boiled Detective Novel." *Contempora: A Literary Magazine* 1 (March 1970): 6–15.

Gribbin, Lenore S. *Who's Whodunit: A List of 3218 Detective Story Writers and*

Their 1100 Pseudonyms. Chapel Hill: University of North Carolina Library, 1968.

Grimes, Larry E. "Stepsons of Sam: Re-Visions of the Hard-boiled Detective Formula in Recent American Fiction." *Modern Fiction Studies* 29 (Autumn 1983): 535–544.

Grisham, John. "The Rise of the Legal Thriller: Why Lawyers Are Throwing the Books at Us." *New York Times Book Review* (October 18, 1992), 33ff.

Grogg, Sam L., Jr. "Interview with Ross Macdonald." In Larry Landrum, Pat Browne, and Ray B. Browne, eds., *Dimensions of Detective Fiction.* Bowling Green, OH: Popular Press, 1976, 182–192.

Gross, Louis S. *Redefining the American Gothic: From Wieland to Day of the Dead.* Ann Arbor, MI: UMI Research Press, 1989.

Grossvogel, David A. *Mystery and Its Fictions: From Oedipus to Agatha Christie.* Baltimore, MD: Johns Hopkins University Press, 1979.

Gruber, Frank. *The Pulp Jungle.* Los Angeles: Sherbourne Press, 1967.

Guetti, James. "Aggressive Reading: Detective Fiction and Realistic Narrative." *Raritan* 2 (Summer 1982): 133–154.

Guyman, E. T., Jr. "Why Do We Read This Stuff?" In John Ball, ed. *The Mystery Story.* San Diego: University of California Extension, 1976, 361–364.

Hackett, Alice Payne, and James Henry Burke. *80 Years of Best Sellers, 1895–1975.* New York: Bowker, 1977.

Hagen, Ordean. *Who Done It?: A Guide to Detective, Mystery and Suspense Fiction.* New York: Bowker, 1969.

Haining, Peter, comp. *Detective Fiction: An Illustrated History of Crime and Detective Fiction.* Designed by Christopher Scott. London: Souvenir Press, 1977.

———. *Mystery!* London: Souvenir Press, 1977.

———. *The Penny Dreadful.* London: Gollancz, 1975.

———, ed. *The Fantastic Pulps.* London: Gollancz; New York: St. Martin's Press, 1975.

Hale, Virginia S. "Mark Twain, Detective." *Connecticut Review* 14 (Spring 1992): 79–84.

Hamilton, Cynthia S. *Western and Hard-Boiled Formula Fiction in America: From High Noon to Midnight.* Iowa City: University of Iowa Press, 1987.

Hamilton, Donald. "Shut Up and Write." In Robin W. Winks, ed., *Colloquium on Crime: Eleven Renowned Mystery Writers Discuss Their Work.* New York: Charles Scribner's Sons, 1986, 99–110.

Hancer, Kevin B. *The Paperback Price Guide.* Cleveland, TN: Overstreet Publications. Distributed by Harmony Books/Crown, 1980.

Hansen, Joseph. "Matters Grave and Gay." In Robin W. Winks, ed., *Colloquium on Crime: Eleven Renowned Mystery Writers Discuss Their Work.* New York: Charles Scribner's Sons, 1986, 111–26.

———. "The Mystery Novel as Serious Business." *Armchair Detective* 17 (Summer 1984): 250–254.

Harper, Ralph. *The World of the Thriller.* Cleveland, OH: Press of Case Western Reserve University, 1969.

Hart, James D. *The Popular Book: A History of America's Literary Taste.* New York: Oxford University Press, 1950.

Hartman, Geoffrey H. "Literature High and Low: The Case of the Mystery Story." In *The Fate of Reading and Other Essays*. Chicago: University of Chicago Press, 1975. Reprinted in Glenn W. Most and William W. Stowe eds., *The Poetics of Murder: Detective Fiction and Literary Theory*. New York: Harcourt Brace Jovanovich, 1983.

Haut, Woody. *Pulp Culture: Hardboiled Fiction and the Cold War*. London, New York: Serpent's Tail, 1995.

Haycraft, Howard. *The Art of the Mystery Story*. 1946. New York: Carroll & Graf Publishers, 1992.

———. *Murder for Pleasure: The Life and Times of the Detective Story*. 1941. New York: Biblo and Tannen, 1968. New material reprinted from *Ellery Queen's Mystery Magazine*, October 1951. New York: Carroll & Graf, 1984.

Hayes, Michael J. "Very Nearly GBH: Savouring the Texts of George V. Higgins." In Brian Docherty, ed., *American Crime Fiction: Studies in the Genre*. New York: St. Martin's Press, 1988, 115–30.

Hayne, Barrie. "Anna Katharine Green." In Earl F. Bargainnier, ed. *10 Women of Mystery*. Bowling Green, OH: Bowling Green State University Popular Press, 1981, 150–178.

Heissenbüttel, Helmut. "Rules of the Game of the Crime Novel." 1963. In Glenn W. Most and William W. Stowe, eds. *The Poetics of Murder: Detective Fiction and Literary Theory*. New York: Harcourt Brace Jovanovich, 1983.

Herbert, Rosemary. *The Fatal Art of Entertainment: Interviews with Mystery Writers*. Foreword by Antonia Fraser. New York: G. K. Hall; Toronto: Maxwell Macmillan Canada; New York: Maxwell Macmillan International, 1994.

Herron, Don. *Dashiell Hammett Tour*. San Francisco: Dawn Herron Press, 1982.

Hersey, Harold. *Pulpwood Editor: The Fabulous World of the Thriller Magazines Revealed by a Veteran Editor and Publisher*. New York: Stokes, 1937.

Hicken, Mandy, and Ray Prytherch. *Now Read On: A Guide to Contemporary Popular Fiction*. Hants/Brookfield, VT: Scholar Press/Ashgate Publishing Company, 1994.

Higgins, George V. *On Writing: Advice to Those Who Write to Publish (or Would Like To)*. New York: Holt, 1990.

Highsmith, Patricia. *Plotting and Writing Suspense Fiction*. 1966. Boston: The Writer, 1990.

Hilfer, Anthony Channell. *The Crime Novel: A Deviant Genre*. Austin: University of Texas Press, 1990.

Hillerman, Tony. "Making Mysteries with Navajo Materials." In Philip Dennis and Wendell Aycock, eds., *Literature and Anthropology*. Lubbock: Texas Tech University Press, 1989, 5–13.

———. "Mystery, Country Boys, and the Big Reservation." In Robin W. Winks, ed., *Colloquium on Crime: Eleven Renowned Mystery Writers Discuss Their Work*. New York: Charles Scribner's Sons, 1986, 127–48.

———. *The Tony Hillerman Companion: A Comprehensive Guide to His Life and Work*. Ed. by Martin Greenberg. New York: HarperCollins Publishers, 1994.

Hillerman, Tony, and Ernie Bulow. *Talking Mysteries: A Conversation with Tony Hillerman*. Albuquerque: University of New Mexico Press, 1991.

Hinckley, Karen, and Barbara Hinckley. *American Best Sellers: A Reader's Guide to Popular Fiction*. Bloomington: Indiana University Press, 1989.

Hochbruck, Wolfgang. "Mystery Novels to Choctaw Pageant: Todd Downing and Native American Literature(s)." In Arnold Krupat, ed., *New Voices in Native American Literary Criticism*. Washington, DC: Smithsonian Institution Press, 1993.

Hoffman, Nancy Y. "Mistresses of Malfeasance." In Larry Landrum, Pat Browne, and Ray B. Browne, eds., *Dimensions of Detective Fiction*. Bowling Green, OH: Popular Press, 1976, 97–101.

Hogarth, Basil. *Writing Thrillers for Profit: A Practical Guide*. London: Black, 1936.

Holman, C. Hugh. "Detective Fiction as American Realism." In James C. Austin and Donald A. Koch, eds., *Popular Literature in America: A Symposium in Honor of Lyon N. Richardson*. Bowling Green, OH: Bowling Green State University Popular Press, 1972.

Holquist, Michael. "The Mystery of Detective Fiction." *Meanjin* 40 (July 1981): 186–192.

———. "Whodunit and Other Questions: Metaphysical Detective Stories in Postwar Fiction." *New Literary History* 3 (Autumn 1971): 135–156. Repr. in Glenn W. Most and William W. Stowe, eds., *The Poetics of Murder: Detective Fiction and Literary Theory*. New York: Harcourt Brace Jovanovich, 1983.

Hoopes, Roy, ed. *Sixty Years of Journalism: James M. Cain*. Bowling Green, OH: Bowling Green State University Popular Press, 1985.

Hoppenstand, Gary. *The Dime Novel Detective*. Bowling Green, OH: Bowling Green University Popular Press, 1982.

———. *In Search of the Paper Tiger: A Sociological Perspective of Myth, Formula and the Mystery Genre in the Entertainment Print Press Medium*. Pref. by Ray B. Browne. Bowling Green, OH: Popular Press, 1987.

Hoveyda, Fereydoun. *Histoire du roman policier*. Préf. dialoguée de Jean-Louis Bory et Cecil Saint-Laurent. Paris: Editions du Pavillon, 1966.

Howells, Coral Ann. *Love, Mystery, and Misery: Feeling in Gothic Fiction*. London: Athlone Press, 1978.

Hubin, Allen J. *Crime Fiction II: A Comprehensive Bibliography, 1749–1980*. 1979. New York: Garland Publishing, 1984. Rev. and updated ed.

———. *1981–1985 Supplement to Crime Fiction, 1749–1980*. 1988. New York: Garland, 1994. Rev. ed., 2 vols.

———. "Patterns in Mystery Fiction: The Durable Series Character." In John Ball, ed. *The Mystery Story*. San Diego: University of California Extension, 1976, 291–319.

Hughes, Dorothy. *Erle Stanley Gardner: The Case of the Real Perry Mason*. New York: William Morrow, 1978.

Hühn, Peter. "The Detective as Reader: Narrativity and Reading Concepts in Detective Fiction." *Modern Fiction Studies* 33 (Autumn 1987): 451–466.

Humm, Peter. "Camera Eye/Private Eye." In Brian Docherty, ed., *American Crime Fiction: Studies in the Genre*. New York: St. Martin's Press, 1988, 23–38.

Ireland, Richard W. "The Phantom at the Limits of Criminology." In Ian A. Bell and Graham Daldry, eds., *Watching the Detectives: Essays on Crime Fiction*. New York: Macmillan, 1990, 68–83.

Irons, Glenwood. "New Women Detectives: G Is for Gender-Bending." In Glenwood Irons, ed., *Gender, Language, and Myth: Essays on Popular Narrative.* Toronto: University of Toronto Press, 1992, 127–41.

———, ed. *Feminism in Women's Detective Fiction.* Toronto, Buffalo: University of Toronto Press, 1995.

———, ed. *Gender, Language, and Myth: Essays on Popular Narrative.* Toronto: University of Toronto Press, 1992.

Irwin, John T. "Knight's Gambit: Poe, Faulkner, and the Tradition of the Detective Story." *Arizona Quarterly* 46 (Winter 1990): 95–116.

———. "Mysteries We Reread, Mysteries of Rereading: Poe, Borges, and the Analytic Detective Story: Also Lacan, Derrida and Johnson." *Modern Language Notes* 101 (Dec. 1986): 1168–1215.

———. *The Mystery to a Solution: Poe, Borges, and the Analytic Detective Story.* Baltimore, MD: Johns Hopkins University Press, 1994.

Isaac, Frederick. "Enter the Fat Man: Rex Stout's *Fer-de-Lance.*" In Mary Jean DeMarr, ed., *In the Beginning: First Novels in Mystery Series.* Bowling Green, OH: Bowling Green State University Popular Press, 1995, 59–68.

Jakubowsky, Maxim, ed. *100 Great Detectives; or, the Detective Directory.* New York: Carroll & Graf, 1991.

Jameson, Fredric R. "On Raymond Chandler." *Southern Review* 6 (1970): 624–650. Reprinted in Glenn W. Most and William W. Stowe, eds., *The Poetics of Murder: Detective Fiction and Literary Theory.* New York: Harcourt Brace Jovanovich, 1983.

Johannsen, Albert. *The House of Beadle and Adams and Its Dime and Nickel Novels.* 2 vols. Norman: University of Oklahoma Press, 1950.

Johnson, Diane. *Dashiell Hammett: A Life.* New York: Random House, 1983.

Johnson, Patricia E. "Sex and Betrayal in the Detective Fiction of Sue Grafton and Sara Paretsky." *Journal of Popular Culture* 27 (Spring 1994): 97–106.

Johnson, Timothy W., and Julia Johnson, eds. *Crime Fiction Criticism: An Annotated Bibliography.* New York: Garland, 1981.

Johnston, Alva. *The Case of Erle Stanley Gardner.* New York: William Morrow and Co., 1947.

Jones, Robert Kenneth. *The Shudder Pulps: A History of the Weird Menace Magazines of the 1930's.* West Linn, OR: FAX, 1975.

Jordan, Peter. "Carl Hiaasen's Environmental Thrillers: Crime Fiction in Search of Green Peace." *Studies in Popular Culture* 13 (1990): 61–71.

Kaemmel, Ernst. "Literature Under the Table: The Detective Novel and Its Social Mission." 1962. In Glenn W. Most and William W. Stowe, eds., *The Poetics of Murder: Detective Fiction and Literary Theory.* New York: Harcourt Brace Jovanovich, 1983.

Kalikoff, Beth. *Murder and Moral Decay in Victorian Popular Literature.* Ann Arbor: UMI Research Press, 1986.

Kayman, Martin A. *From Bow Street to Baker Street: Mystery, Detection and Narrative.* New York: St. Martin's Press, 1992.

Keating, H.R.F. *Crime & Mystery: The 100 Best Books.* New York: Carroll & Graf, 1987.

———. *Murder Must Appetize.* London: Mysterious Press, Lemon Tree Press, 1981. Rev. ed.

————, ed. *Whodunit? A Guide to Crime, Suspense, and Spy Fiction.* New York: Van Nostrand Reinhold Co., 1982.

Keefer, T. Frederick. "Albert Camus' American Disciple: John D. MacDonald's Existentialist Hero, Travis D. McGee." *Journal of Popular Culture* 19 (Fall 1985): 33–48.

Kelly, R. Gordon. "The Precarious World of John D. MacDonald." In Larry Landrum, Pat Browne, and Ray B. Browne, eds., *Dimensions of Detective Fiction.* Bowling Green, OH: Popular Press, 1976, 149–161.

Kermode, Frank. "Novel and Narrative." In John Halperin, ed., *Theory of the Novel: New Essays.* New York: Oxford, 1974. Reprinted in Glenn W. Most and William W. Stowe, eds. *The Poetics of Murder: Detective Fiction and Literary Theory.* New York: Harcourt Brace Jovanovich, 1983.

Klein, Kathleen, ed. *Women Times Three: Writers, Detectives, Readers.* Bowling Green, OH: Bowling Green State University Popular Press, 1995.

Klein, Kathleen Gregory. *The Woman Detective: Gender & Genre.* 1988. Urbana: University of Illinois Press, 1995.

————, ed. *Great Women Mystery Writers: Classic to Contemporary.* Westport, CT: Greenwood Press, 1994.

Klein, Marcus. *Easterns, Westerns, and Private Eyes: American Matters, 1870–1900.* Madison: University of Wisconsin Press, 1994.

Knight, Stephen. *Form and Ideology in Crime Fiction.* London: Macmillan, 1980; Bloomington: Indiana University Press, 1980.

————. " 'A Hard Cheerfulness': An Introduction to Raymond Chandler." In Brian Docherty, ed., *American Crime Fiction: Studies in the Genre.* New York: St. Martin's Press, 1988, 71–87.

————. "Radical Thrillers." In Ian A. Bell and Graham Daldry, eds., *Watching the Detectives: Essays on Crime Fiction.* New York: Macmillan, 1990, 172–89.

Koontz, Dean. *How to Write Best-Selling Fiction.* Cincinnati, OH: Writer's Digest, 1981.

————. *Writing Popular Fiction.* Cincinnati, OH: Writer's Digest, 1973.

Kramer, John E., Jr., with John E. Kramer III. *College Mystery Novels: An Annotated Bibliography Including a Guide to Professorial Series-Character Sleuths.* New York: Garland, 1983.

Kroll, Keith. "The Man from Motor City." *Armchair Detective* 24 (Winter 1991): 4–11.

Lacan, Jacques. "Seminar on 'The Purloined Letter.' " 1966. *Yale French Studies* 48 (1972): 39–72.

Lacassin, Francis. *Mythologie du Roman Policier.* 2 vols. Paris: Union Generale d'Editions, 1974.

Lachman, Marvin. *A Reader's Guide to the American Novel of Detection.* New York: G. K. Hall; Toronto: Maxwell Macmillan Canada; New York: Maxwell Macmillan International, 1993.

LaCombe, Alain. *Le Roman Noir Américain.* Paris: 10/18, 1975.

LaCour, Tage, and Harald Mogensen. *The Murder Book: An Illustrated History of the Detective Story.* London: Allen and Unwin, 1971.

Lambert, Gavin. *The Dangerous Edge.* New York: Grossman, 1976.

Landrum, Larry N., Pat Browne, and Ray B. Browne, eds. *Dimensions of Detective Fiction.* Bowling Green, OH: Popular Press, 1976.

Lavender, William. "The Novel of Critical Engagement: Paul Auster's *City of Glass.*" *Contemporary Literature* (Summer 1993): 219–239.

Layman, R. *Shadow Man.* New York: Harcourt Brace Jovanovich, 1984.

Layman, Richard. *Dashiell Hammett: A Descriptive Bibliography.* Pittsburgh: University of Pittsburgh Press, 1979.

———. *Shadow Man: The Life of Dashiell Hammett.* New York: Harcourt Brace Jovanovich, 1981.

Leavis, Q. D. *Fiction and the Reading Public.* New York: Russell, 1965.

Lee, Billy C., and R. Reginald. *Murder Was Bad: Essays on Mystery and Detective Publishing from Paperback Quarterly.* San Bernardino, CA: Borgo Press, 1986.

Lee, L. L. "The Art of Ross Macdonald." *South Dakota Review* 24 (Spring 1986): 55–66.

Leitch, Thomas. "From Detective Story to Detective Novel." *Modern Fiction Studies* 29 (Autumn 1983): 475–484.

Lewis, Barry. "The Strange Case of Paul Auster." *Review of Contemporary Fiction* 14 (Spring 1994): 53–61.

Lewis, Ffragcon C. "Unravelling a Web: Writer versus Reader in Edgar Allan Poe's Tales of Detection." In Ian A. Bell and Graham Daldry, eds., *Watching the Detectives: Essays on Crime Fiction.* New York: Macmillan, 1990, 97–117.

Library of Congress. National Library Service for the Blind and Physically Handicapped. *More Mysteries.* Washington, DC: The Service, 1992.

Literary History of the United States. Ed. by Robert E. Spiller, Willard Thorp, Thomas H. Johnson, and Henry Seidel Canby. New York: Macmillan, 1953.

Littler, Alison. "Marele Day's 'Cold Hard Bitch': The Masculinist Imperatives of the Private-Eye Genre." *Journal of Narrative Technique* 21 (Winter 1991): 121–135.

Lock, Helen. *Detective Undercurrents in Recent African American Fiction.* New York: P. Lang, 1994.

Lofts, W.O.G., and Derek Adley. *The Men Behind Boy's Fiction.* London: Baker, 1970.

Logan, Michael F. "Detective Fiction as Urban Critique: Changing Perspectives of a Genre." *Journal of American Culture* 15 (Fall 1992): 89–97.

Lott, Rick. "A Matter of Style: Chandler's Hardboiled Disguise." *Journal of Popular Culture* 23 (Winter 1989): 65–75.

Loughery, John. *Alias S. S. Van Dine.* New York: Scribner's; Toronto: Maxwell Macmillan Canada; New York: Maxwell Macmillan International, 1992.

Lovisi, Gary. *Science Fiction Detective Tales: A Brief Overview of Futuristic Detective Fiction in Paperback.* Brooklyn, NY: Gryphon Books, 1986.

Lowery, Lawrence F. *Lowery's The Collector's Guide to Big Little Books and Similar Books.* Bowling Green, OH: Bowling Green State University Popular Press, 1981.

Lundquist, James. *Chester Himes.* New York: Ungar, 1976.

Lynds, Dennis. "Expanding the Roman Noir: Ross Macdonald's Legacy to Mystery/Detective Authors." *South Dakota Review* 24 (Spring 1986): 121–124.

McAleer, John. *Rex Stout: A Biography.* Boston: Little, Brown, 1977.

MacAndrew, Elizabeth. *The Gothic Tradition in Fiction.* New York: Columbia University Press, 1979.

McBain, Ed. "The 87th Precinct." In Otto Penzler, ed., *The Great Detectives*. Boston: Little, Brown, 1978, 87–98.

McCormick, Donald. *Who's Who in Spy Fiction*. New York: Taplinger, 1977.

McCormick, Donald, and Katy Fletcher. *Spy Fiction: A Connoisseur's Guide*. New York: Facts on File, 1990.

McDade, Thomas M. *The Annals of Murder: A Bibliography of Books and Pamphlets on American Murders from Colonial Times to 1900*. Norman: University of Oklahoma Press, 1961.

McDonald, Gregory. "On Getting Rid of an Idea." In H.R.F. Keating, ed., *Whodunit? A Guide to Crime, Suspense and Spy Fiction*. New York: Van Nostrand Reinhold, 1982, 94–96.

Macdonald, Ross. *On Crime Writing*. Santa Barbara, CA: Capra Press, 1973.

Macherey, Pierre. *Crime and Ideology*. New York: Columbia University Press, 1966.

Mackler, Tasha. *Murder . . . By Category: A Subject Guide to Mystery Fiction*. Metuchen, NJ: Scarecrow Press, 1991.

McLeish, Kenneth, and Valerie McLeish. *Bloomsbury Good Reading Guide to Murder Crime Fiction and Thrillers*. London: Bloomsbury Publishing, 1990.

McNutt, Dan J. *The Eighteenth-Century Gothic Novel: An Annotated Bibliography of Criticism and Selected Texts*. New York: Garland, 1975.

MacShane, Frank. *The Life of Raymond Chandler*. New York: Dutton, 1976.

McSherry, Frank D., Jr. *Studies in Scarlet: Essays on Mystery and Detective Fiction*. San Bernardino, CA: Borgo Press, 1986.

Madden, David. "The Isaac Quintet: Jerome Charyn's Metaphysics of Law and Disorder." *Review of Contemporary Fiction* 12 (Summer 1992): 164–172.

———, ed. *Tough Guy Writers of the Thirties*. Carbondale: Southern Illinois University Press, 1968; London: Feffer and Simons, 1979.

Magill, Frank N., ed. *Critical Survey of Mystery and Detective Fiction: Authors*. 4 vols. Pasadena, CA: Salem Press, 1988.

Mahan, Jeffrey H. *A Long Way from Solving That One: Psycho/Social and Ethical Implications of Ross Macdonald's Lew Archer Tales*. Lanham, MD: University Press of America, 1990.

Maida, Patricia D. *Mother of Detective Fiction: The Life and Works of Anna Katharine Green*. Bowling Green, OH: Bowling Green State University Popular Press, 1989.

Malin, Irving. *New American Gothic*. Preface by Harry T. Moore. Carbondale: Southern Illinois University Press, 1962.

Mandel, Ernest. *Delightful Murder: A Social History of the Crime Story*. 1984. Minneapolis: University of Minnesota Press, 1985.

Mann, Jessica. "The Suspense Novel." In H.R.F. Keating, ed., *Whodunit? A Guide to Crime, Suspense and Spy Fiction*. New York: Van Nostrand Reinhold, 1982, 56–60.

Marchino, Lois A. "The Professor Tells a Story: Kate Fansler." In Mary Jean DeMarr, ed., *In the Beginning: First Novels in Mystery Series*. Bowling Green, OH: Bowling Green State University Popular Press, 1995.

Marcus, Steven. "Introduction" to Dashiell Hammett's *The Continental Op*. New York: Random House, 1974. Reprinted as "Dashiell Hammett," in Glenn W. Most and William W. Stowe, eds., *The Poetics of Murder: Detective*

Fiction and Literary Theory. New York: Harcourt Brace Jovanovich, 1983, 198–209.

Margolies, Edward. "The American Detective Thriller and the Idea of Society." In Larry Landrum, Pat Browne, and Ray B. Browne, eds., *Dimensions of Detective Fiction*. Bowling Green, OH: Popular Press, 1976, 83–87.

———. *Which Way Did He Go? The Private Eye in Dashiell Hammett, Raymond Chandler, Chester Himes, and Ross Macdonald*. New York: Holmes and Meier, 1982.

Marks, Jeffrey. Interview with Nancy Pickard in *Armchair Detective* 26 (Spring 1993): 85–88.

Marling, William. *The American Roman Noir: Hammett, Cain, and Chandler*. Athens: University of Georgia Press, 1995.

Mason, Bobbie Ann. *The Girl Sleuth: A Feminist Guide*. Old Westbury, NY: Feminist Press, 1975.

Mason, Theodore O., Jr. "Walter Mosley's Easy Rawlins: The Detective and Afro-American Fiction." *Kenyon Review* 14 (Fall 1992): 173–183.

Masters, Anthony. *Literary Agents: The Novelist as Spy*. New York: B. Blackwell, 1987.

Matthews, Catlin, and John Matthews. *The Western Way: A Practical Guide to the Western Mystery Tradition*. London: Methuen, 1985.

Mead, David G. "Signs of Crime: Aspects of Structure in Science Fiction Detective Stories." *Extrapolation: A Journal of Science Fiction and Fantasy* 28 (Summer 1987): 140–147.

Melvin, David Skene, and Ann Skene Melvin, comps. *Detective, Espionage, Mystery, and Thriller Fiction & Film: A Comprehensive Bibliography of Critical Writing through 1979*. Westport, CT: Greenwood Press, 1980.

Menendez, Albert J. *The Subject Is Murder: A Selective Subject Guide to Mystery Fiction*. New York: Garland, 1985.

———. *The Subject Is Murder: A Selective Subject Guide to Mystery Fiction, II*. New York: Garland, 1990.

Merrill, Robert. "Mailer's Tough Guys Don't Dance and the Detective Traditions." *Critique: Studies in Contemporary Fiction* 34 (Summer 1993): 232–246.

Merry, Bruce. *Anatomy of the Spy Thriller*. Dublin: Gill and Macmillan, 1977.

Meyer, Sam. "Color and Cogency in Titles of John D. MacDonald's Travis McGee Series." *Rhetoric Society Quarterly* 18 (Summer-Fall 1988): 3–4, 259–260.

Miller, D. A. "Alibis of the Police." *L'Esprit Createur* 26 (Summer 1986): 37–47.

Milliken, Stephen. *Chester Himes*. Columbia: University of Missouri Press, 1976.

Mills, Maldwyn. "Chandler's Cannibalism." In Ian A. Bell and Graham Daldry, eds., *Watching the Detectives: Essays on Crime Fiction*. New York: Macmillan, 1990, 117–33.

Moore, Lewis D. *Meditations on America: John D. MacDonald's Travis McGee Series and Other Fiction*. Bowling Green, OH: Bowling Green State University Popular Press, 1994.

Most, Glenn. "Elmore Leonard: Splitting Images." In Barbara A. Rader and Howard G. Zettler, eds., *The Sleuth and the Scholar: Origins, Evolution, and Current Trends in Detective Fiction*. Westport, CT: Greenwood Press, 1988.

Most, Glenn W., and William W. Stowe, eds. *The Poetics of Murder: Detective Fiction and Literary Theory*. New York: Harcourt Brace Jovanovich, 1983.

Mott, Frank Luther. *Golden Multitudes: The Story of Best Sellers in the United States*. New York: Macmillan, 1947.

Mottram, Eric. "Ross Macdonald and the Past of a Formula." In Bernard Benstock, ed., *Essays on Detective Fiction*. New York: St. Martin's Press, 1984, 97–118.

Muller, Gilbert H. *Chester Himes*. Boston: Twain, 1989.

Muller, John P., and William J. Richardson, eds. *The Purloined Poe: Lacan, Derrida, and Psychoanalytic Reading*. Baltimore and London: Johns Hopkins University Press, 1988.

Munster, Bill, ed. *Discovering Dean Koontz: Essays on America's Bestselling Writer of Suspense and Horror Fiction*. 2nd. ed. San Bernardino, CA: Borgo, 1995.

Munt, Sally. *Murder by the Book? Feminism and the Crime Novel*. New York: Routledge, 1994.

Murch, A. E. *The Development of the Detective Novel*. New York: Philosophical Library, 1958.

Mussell, Kay. *Women's Gothic and Romantic Fiction: A Reference Guide*. Westport, CT: Greenwood Press, 1981.

Mystery Writers of America. *The Mystery Writer's Handbook: A Handbook on the Writing of Detective, Suspense, Mystery and Crime Stories*. Ed. by Herbert Brean. New York: Harper and Brothers, 1956.

Narcajac, Thomas. *Une Machine à Lire: Le Roman Policier*. Paris: Denoöl Gonthier, 1975.

Naremore, James. "Dashiell Hammett and the Poetics of Hard-boiled Detection." In Bernard Benstock, ed., *Art in Crime Writing*. New York: St. Martin's Press, 1983, 49–72.

National Union Catalog of Manuscript Collections and *Special Collections in College and University Libraries*.

Nelson, Catherine M. "A Criminal Mind: An Interview with Jonathan Kellerman." *Armchair Detective* 26 (Winter 1993): 11–15, 92–95.

Nelson, Raymond. "Domestic Harlem: The Detective Fiction of Chester Himes." In Larry Landrum, Pat Browne, and Ray B. Browne, eds., *Dimensions of Detective Fiction*. Bowling Green, OH: Popular Press, 1976, 162–173.

Nelson, William, and Nancy Avery. "Art Where You Least Expect It: Myth and Ritual in the Detective Series." *Modern Fiction Studies* 29 (Autumn 1983): 463–474.

Neuburg, Victor E. *The Popular Press Batsford Companion to Popular Literature*. Bowling Green, OH: Bowling Green State University Popular Press, 1983.

Nevins, Francis M., Jr. "Name Games: Mystery Writers and Their Pseudonyms." In John Ball, ed., *The Mystery Story*. San Diego: University of California Extension, 1976, 343–359.

———. *Royal Bloodline: Ellery Queen, Author and Detective*. Bowling Green, OH: Bowling Green State University Popular Press, 1974.

———. "The Wild and Woolly World of Harry Stephen Keeler: 1." *JPC* 3:4 (Winter 1969): 635–643.

———, ed. *The Mystery Writer's Art*. Bowling Green, OH: Popular Press, 1971.

Newlin, Keith. "C. W. Sughrue's Whiskey Visions." *Modern Fiction Studies* 29 (Autumn 1983): 545–55.

Nichols, Victoria. *Silk Stalkings: When Women Write of Murder; A Survey of Series*

Characters Created by Women Authors in Crime and Mystery Fiction. Berkeley, CA: Black Lizard Books, 1988.

Nickerson, Edward A. " 'Realistic' Crime Fiction: An Anatomy of Evil People." *Centennial Review* 25 (Spring 1981): 101–132.

Niebuhr, Gary Warren. *A Reader's Guide to the Private Eye Novel.* New York: G. K. Hall; Toronto: Maxwell Macmillan Canada; New York: Maxwell Macmillan International, 1993.

Noel, Mary. *Villains Galore: The Heyday of the Popular Story Weekly.* New York: Macmillan, 1954.

Nolan, William F. *The Black Mask Boys: Masters in the Hard-Boiled School of Detective Fiction.* New York: W. Morrow, 1985.

———. *Dashiell Hammett: A Casebook.* Introduction by Philip Durham. Santa Barbara, CA: McNally & Loftin, 1969.

———. *Hammett: A Life at the Edge.* New York: Congdon and Weed, 1983.

Norville, Barbara. *Writing the Modern Mystery.* Cincinnati, OH: Writer's Digest Books, 1986.

Nye, Russel B. *The Unembarrassed Muse: The Popular Arts in America.* New York: Dial Press, 1970.

O'Brien, Geoffrey. *Hardboiled America: The Lurid Years of Paperbacks.* New York: Van Nostrand Reinhold, 1981.

OCork, Shannon. "The Truth, More or Less, as Long as It Makes a Good Story." In Lucy Freeman, ed., *The Murder Mystique: Crime Writers on Their Art.* New York: Ungar, 1982.

Odell, Robin. *Jack the Ripper in Fact and Fiction.* London: Harrap, 1965.

Ogdon, Bethany. "Hard-boiled Ideology." *Critical Quarterly* 34 (Summer 1992): 71–87.

Olderr, Steven. *Mystery Index: Subjects, Settings, and Sleuths of 10,000 Titles.* Chicago: American Library Association, 1987.

Oliver, Lawrence J., Jr. "The Dark-skinned 'Angels' of Dorothy B. Hughes's Thrillers." *MELUS* 11 (Fall 1984): 27–39.

Palmer, Jerry. "The Thriller." In H.R.F. Keating, ed., *Whodunit? A Guide to Crime, Suspense and Spy Fiction.* New York: Van Nostrand Reinhold, 1982, 61–65.

———. *Thrillers.* 1978. New York: St. Martin's Press, 1979.

Panek, LeRoy Lad. *An Introduction to the Detective Story.* Bowling Green, OH: Popular Press, 1987.

———. *Probable Cause: Crime Fiction in America.* Bowling Green, OH: Bowling Green State University Popular Press, 1990.

Paravisini, Lizabeth. "*Mumbo Jumbo* and the Uses of Parody." *Obsidian II: Black Literature in Review* 1 (Spring-Summer 1986): 113–127.

Parfit, Michael. "Weaving Mysteries That Tell of Life among the Navajos." *Smithsonian* 21 (Dec. 1990): 92–105.

Parker, Robert B., and Anne Ponder. "What I Know about Writing Spenser Novels." In Robin W. Winks, ed., *Colloquium on Crime: Eleven Renowned Mystery Writers Discuss Their Work.* New York: Charles Scribner's Sons, 1986, 189–204.

Paul, Robert S. *Whatever Happened to Sherlock Holmes?: Detective Fiction, Popular Theology, and Society.* Carbondale: Southern Illinois University Press, 1991.

Pavett, Mike. "From the Golden Age to Mean Streets." In H.R.F. Keating, ed., *Crime Writers: Reflections on Crime Fiction by Reginald Hill, P. D. James, H.R.F. Keating, Troy Kennedy Martin, Maurice Richardson, Julian Symons, Colin Watson*. Additional material by Mike Pavett. London: British Broadcasting Corporation, 1978.

Pearsall, Jay. *Mystery and Crime: The New York Public Library Book of Answers: Intriguing and Entertaining Questions and Answers About the Who's Who and What's What of Whodunits*. New York: Simon & Schuster, 1995.

Peck, Harry Thurston. *Studies in Several Literatures*. 1909. Freeport, NY: Books for Libraries Press, 1968. Series: Essay index reprint series.

Pederson-Krag, Geraldine. "Detective Stories and the Primal Scene." Repr. in Larry Landrum, Pat Browne, and Ray B. Browne, eds., *Dimensions of Detective Fiction*. Bowling Green, OH: Popular Press, 1976, 58–63. Also in Glenn W. Most and William W. Stowe, eds., *The Poetics of Murder: Detective Fiction and Literary Theory*. New York: Harcourt Brace Jovanovich, 1983, 13–20.

Pelzer, Linda C. *Mary Higgins Clark: A Critical Companion*. Westport, CT: Greenwood, 1995.

Penzler, Otto. "The Amateur Detectives." In John Ball, ed., *The Mystery Story*. San Diego: University of California Extension, 1976, 83–109.

———. "The Great Crooks." In John Ball, ed., *The Mystery Story*. San Diego: University of California Extension, 1976, 321–341.

———. *The Private Lives of Private Eyes, Crime Fighters, and Other Good Guys*. New York: Grosset and Dunlap, 1977.

———, ed. *The Great Detectives*. Boston: Little, Brown, 1978.

Penzler, Otto, Chris Steinbrunner, and Marvin Lachman, eds. *Detectionary: A Biographical Dictionary of Leading Characters in Detective and Mystery Fiction, Including Famous and Little-known Sleuths, Their Helpers, Rogues, Both Heroic and Sinister, and Some of Their Most Memorable Adventures, as Recounted in Novels, Short Stories, and Films*. New York: Hammerhill Paper, 1971; Woodstock, NY: Overlook Press, 1977; revised and updated edition, New York: Ballantine, 1980.

Perez, Janet, and Genaro J. Perez. "The Hispanic Thriller." *Monographic Review/Revista Monografica* 3 (1987): 139–305.

———, eds. "Hispanic Science-Fiction/Fantasy and the Thriller." *Monographic Review/Revista Monografica* 3 (1987): 1–2.

Peterson, Audrey. *Victorian Masters of Mystery: From Wilkie Collins to Conan Doyle*. New York: Ungar, 1984.

Pierce, Hazel Beasley. *A Literary Symbiosis: Science Fiction/Fantasy Mystery*. Westport, CT: Greenwood, 1983.

Pierson, James C. "Mystery Literature and Ethnography: Fictional Detectives as Anthropologists." In Philip Dennis and Wendell Aycock, eds., *Literature and Anthropology*. Lubbock: Texas Tech University Press, 1989, 15–30.

Planells, Antonio. "El genero policiaco en Hispanoamerica." *Monographic Review/Revista Monografica* 3 (1987): 148–162.

Poe, Edgar Allan. "The Philosophy of Composition." 1846. In James A. Harrison, ed., *The Complete Works of Edgar Allan Poe*. Vol. 14. New York: Society of English and French Literature, 1902.

Pope-Hennessy, Una. *Edgar Allan Poe: A Critical Biography*. New York: Macmillan, 1934.

Porter, Dennis. *The Pursuit of Crime: Art and Ideology in Detective Fiction*. New Haven, CT: Yale University Press, 1981.

Powers, Richard Gid. *G-Men: Hoover's FBI in American Popular Culture*. Carbondale: Southern Illinois University Press, 1983.

———. "J. Edgar Hoover and the Detective Hero." In Larry Landrum, Pat Browne, and Ray B. Browne, eds., *Dimensions of Detective Fiction*. Bowling Green, OH: Popular Press, 1976, 203–227.

Prager, Arthur. *Rascals at Large; or The Clue in the Old Nostalgia*. New York: Doubleday, 1971.

Presley, John W. "Theory into Practice: Robert Parker's Re-Interpretation of the American Tradition." *Journal of American Culture* 12 (Fall 1989): 27–30.

Priestman, Martin. *Detective Fiction and Literature: The Figure on the Carpet*. New York: St. Martin's Press, 1991.

Pronzini, Bill. *Gun in Cheek: A Study of "Alternative" Crime Fiction*. New York: Coward, McCann & Geoghegan, 1982.

Pronzini, Bill, and Marcia Muller. *1001 Midnights: The Aficionado's Guide to Mystery and Detective Fiction*. New York: Arbor House, 1986.

Pry, Elmer. "Lew Archer's 'Moral Landscape.' " In Larry Landrum, Pat Browne, and Ray B. Browne, eds., *Dimensions of Detective Fiction*. Bowling Green, OH: Popular Press, 1976, 174–181.

Pykett, Lynn. "Investigating Women: The Female Sleuth after Feminism." In Ian A. Bell and Graham Daldry, eds., *Watching the Detectives: Essays on Crime Fiction*. New York: Macmillan, 1990, 48–67.

Pyrhönen, Heta. *Murder from an Academic Angle: An Introduction to the Study of the Detective Narrative*. Columbia, SC: Camden House, 1994.

Radcliffe, Elsa. *Gothic Novels of the Twentieth Century: An Annotated Bibliography*. Metuchen, NJ: Scarecrow Press, 1979.

Rader, Barbara A., and Howard G. Zettler, eds. *The Sleuth and the Scholar: Origins, Evolution, and Current Trends in Detective Fiction*. Westport, CT: Greenwood Press, 1988. Series: Contributions to the Study of Popular Culture, no. 19.

Radine, Serge. *Quelques Aspects du Roman policier psychologique*. Geneva: Editions du Mont-Blanc Geneve, 1960.

Raha, B. J. "Seeley Regester: America's First Detective Novelist." In Barbara A. Rader and Howard G. Zettler, eds., *The Sleuth and the Scholar: Origins, Evolution, and Current Trends in Detective Fiction*. Westport, CT: Greenwood Press, 1988.

Randisi, Robert J., ed. *Writing the Private Eye Novel: A Handbook by the Private Eye Writers of America*. Cincinnati, OH: Writer's Digest Books, 1997.

Rauber, D. F. "Sherlock Holmes and Nero Wolfe: The Role of the 'Great Detective' in Intellectual History." In Larry Landrum, Pat Browne and Ray B. Browne, eds., *Dimensions of Detective Fiction*. Bowling Green, OH: Popular Press, 1976, 89–96.

Reddy, Maureen T. *Sisters in Crime: Feminism and the Crime Novel*. New York: Continuum, 1988.

Redmond, Donald Aitcheson. *Sherlock Holmes Among the Pirates: Copyright and Conan Doyle in America, 1890–1930*. Westport, CT: Greenwood Press, 1990.

Reilly, John M. "Beneficient Roguery: The Detective in the Capitalist City." *Praxis* 3 1 (1976).

———. "Chester Himes' Harlem Tough Guys." *Journal of Popular Culture* 9 (1976): 935–947.

———. "The Politics of Tough Guy Mysteries." *University of Dayton Review* 10 (1973): 25–31.

———. *Tony Hillerman: A Critical Companion.* Westport, CT: Greenwood, 1996.

———, ed. *Twentieth-Century Crime and Mystery Writers.* New York: St. Martin's Press, 1980.

Review of Contemporary Fiction 12 (1992). Special Jerome Charyn issue.

Reynolds, Quentin. *The Fiction Factory; or, from Pulp Row to Quality Street: The Story of 100 Years of Publishing at Street and Smith.* New York: Random House, 1955.

Reynolds, William, and Elizabeth A. Trawley, eds. *It's a Print! Detective Fiction from Page to Screen.* Bowling Green, OH: Bowling Green State University Popular Press, 1994.

Ringe, Donald A. *American Gothic: Imagination and Reason in Nineteenth-century Fiction.* Lexington: University Press of Kentucky, 1982.

Roberts, Bette B. "The Strange Case of *Mary Reilly*." *Extrapolation* 34 (Spring 1993): 39–47.

Robinson, Lillian S. "Killing Patriarchy: Gilman, the Murder Mystery, and Post-feminist Propaganda." *Tulsa Studies in Women's Literature* 13 (Fall 1991): 273–286.

Rodell, Marie F. *Mystery Fiction: Theory and Technique.* New York: Duell, 1943. Rev. ed. New York: Hermitage House, 1952.

Rollason, Christopher. "The Detective Myth in Edgar Allan Poe's Dupin Trilogy." In Brian Docherty, ed., *American Crime Fiction: Studies in the Genre.* New York: St. Martin's Press, 1988, 4–22.

Rosenheim, Shawn. " 'The King of "Secret Readers" ': Edgar Poe, Cryptography, and the Origins of the Detective Story." *ELH* 56 (Summer 1989): 375–400.

Ross, Cheri L. "The First Feminist Detective: Anna Katharine Green's Amelia Butterworth." *Journal of Popular Culture* 25 (Fall 1991): 77–86.

Roth, Marty. *Foul and Fair Play: Reading Genre in Classic Detective Fiction.* Athens: University of Georgia Press, 1995.

Roucek, Joseph S. "The American Detective, Murder and Violent Novel in Its Sociological Aspects." *Indian Journal of Social Research* 5:2 (1964): 178–186.

Routley, Erik. *The Puritan Pleasures of the Detective Story: A Personal Monograph.* London: Gollancz, 1972.

Rowen, Norma. "The Detective in Search of the Lost Tongue of Adam: Paul Auster's *City of Glass*." *Critique: Studies in Contemporary Fiction* 32 (Summer 1991): 224–234.

Ruehlmann, William. *Saint with a Gun: The Unlawful American Private Eye.* New York: New York University Press, 1974.

Russell, Alison. "Deconstructing *The New York Trilogy*: Paul Auster's Anti-Detective Fiction." *Critique: Studies in Contemporary Fiction* 31 (Winter 1990): 71–84.

Russell, Sharon A. "Mike Shayne: A Series Starts and Restarts." In Mary Jean DeMarr, ed., *In the Beginning: First Novels in Mystery Series.* Bowling Green, OH: Bowling Green State University Popular Press, 1995, 91–104.

Rycroft, Charles. "A Detective Story." *Psychoanalytic Observations* 26 (1957): 229–245.

St. James Guide to Crime and Mystery Writers. Ed. by Jay B. Pederson, introduction by Kathleen Gregory Klein. Detroit: St. James Press, 1996.

Sallis, James. "David Goodis: Life in Black and White." *Armchair Detective* 26 (Spring 1993): 16–22, 96–100.

Sampson, Robert. *Yesterday's Faces: A Study of Series Characters in the Early Pulp Magazines, Vol. I.* Bowling Green, OH: Bowling Green State University Popular Press, 1983.

———. *Yesterday's Faces, Vol. II.* Bowling Green, OH: Bowling Green State University Popular Press, 1984.

Sandoe, James. *Murder: Plain and Fanciful with Some Milder Malefactions.* New York: Sheridan House, 1948.

———. "The Private Eye." In John Ball, ed., *The Mystery Story.* San Diego: University of California Extension, 1976, 111–123.

Santos, Oscar De Los. "Auster vs. Chandler; Or, Cracking the Case of the Postmodern Mystery." *Connecticut Review* 16 (Spring 1994): 75–80.

Sarjeant, William A. S. "Crime on Wall Street." *Armchair Detective* 21 (Spring 1988): 128–145.

Sayers, Dorothy L. "Introduction." *Omnibus of Crime.* New York: Payson and Clark, 1929.

Scarborough, Dorothy. *The Supernatural in Modern Fiction.* 1917. New York: Octagon Books, 1977.

Schlepper, Wolfgang E. "William Faulkner's Detective Stories." *Archiv fur das Studium der Neueren Sprachen und Literaturen* 222 (1985): 136–144.

Schneider, Jack W. "Crime and Navajo Punishment: Tony Hillerman's Novels of Detection." *Southwest Review* 67 (Spring 1982): 151–160.

Scott, Sutherland. *Blood in Their Ink: The March of the Modern Mystery Novel.* 1953. Folcroft, PA: Folcroft Editions, 1973.

Sharratt, Bernard. *Reading Relations: Structures of Literary Production: A Dialectical Text/Book.* Atlantic Highlands, NJ: Humanities Press, 1982.

Silet, Charles L. "Drugs, Cash and Automatic Weapons: An Interview with James Crumley." *Armchair Detective* 27 (Winter 1994): 8–15.

———. *The Hard Boiled Detective Novel.* New York: Scribner's Reference, 1997.

Simon, Reeva S. *The Middle East in Crime Fiction: Mysteries, Spy Novels and Thrillers from 1916 to the 1980s.* New York: L. Barber Press, 1989.

Simons, John. "*Real* Detectives and *Fictional* Criminals." In Ian A. Bell and Graham Daldry, eds., *Watching the Detectives: Essays on Crime Fiction.* New York: Macmillan, 1990, 84–97.

Skenazy, Paul. "Bringing It All Back Home: Ross Macdonald's Lost Father." *South Dakota Review* 24 (Spring 1986): 94–109.

———. *James M. Cain.* New York: Continuum, 1989.

———. *The New Wild West: The Urban Mysteries of Dashiell Hammett and Raymond Chandler.* Boise, ID: Boise State University, 1982.

———. "Spheres of Influence: Personal and Social Stories in Ross Macdonald." *South Dakota Review* 24 (Spring 1986): 72–93.

Skene, Melvin, David Skene, and Ann Skene Melvin, comps. *Crime, Detective, Es-*

pionage, Mystery and Thriller Fiction & Film: A Comprehensive Bibliography of Critical Writing Through 1979. Westport, CT: Greenwood, 1980.

Skinner, Robert E. *The Hard-boiled Explicator: A Guide to the Study of Dashiell Hammett, Raymond Chandler and Ross Macdonald.* Metuchen, NJ: Scarecrow, 1985.

———. *The New Hard-Boiled Dicks: A Personal Checklist.* Madison, IN: Brownstone Books, 1987.

———. *Two Guns from Harlem: The Detective Fiction of Chester Himes.* Bowling Green, OH: Bowling Green State University Popular Press, 1989.

Slide, Anthony. *Gay and Lesbian Characters and Themes in Mystery Novels: A Critical Guide to Over 500 Works in English.* Jefferson, NC: McFarland & Company, 1993.

Slung, Michele. "The Gothic." In H.R.F. Keating, ed., *Whodunit? A Guide to Crime, Suspense and Spy Fiction.* New York: Van Nostrand Reinhold, 1982, 65–69.

———. "Women in Detective Fiction." In John Ball, ed., *The Mystery Story.* San Diego: University of California Extension, 1976, 125–141.

Smith, Myron J., Jr. *Cloak-and-Dagger Bibliography: An Annotated Guide to Spy Fiction, 1937–1975.* Metuchen, NJ: Scarecrow Press, 1976.

Smith, Robert P., Jr. "Chester Himes in France and the Legacy of the *Roman Policier.*" *College Language Association Journal* 25 (Sept. 1981): 18–27.

Snodgrass, Richard. "Down These Streets, I Mean, a Man Must Go." *South Dakota Review* 24 (Spring 1986): 7–27.

Soitos, Stephen F. *The Blues Detective: A Study of African American Detective Fiction.* Amherst: University of Massachusetts Press, 1996.

———. "Crime and Mystery Writing." In William L. Andrews, Frances Smith Foster, and Trudier Harris, eds., *The Oxford Companion to African American Literature.* New York: Oxford University Press, 1997.

Speir, Jerry. *Raymond Chandler.* New York: Ungar, 1981.

———. *Ross Macdonald.* New York: Ungar, 1979.

Spencer, William David. *Mysterium and Mystery: The Clerical Crime Novel.* Ann Arbor: UMI Research Press, 1989.

Stafford, David. *The Silent Game: The Real World of Imaginary Spies.* Athens: University of Georgia Press, 1991.

Stasio, Marilyn. "Another Body, Another Show: Bravo for the Backstage Mystery." *New York Times Book Review*, Oct. 17, 1993, 44–45.

———. "Murder Least Foul: The Cozy, Soft-boiled Mystery." *New York Times Book Review*, Oct. 18, 1992, 42–43.

Steele, Timothy. "Matter and Mystery: Neglected Works and Background Materials of Detective Fiction." *Modern Fiction Studies* 29 (August 1983): 435–450.

———. "The Structure of the Detective Story: Classical or Modern?" *Modern Fiction Studies* 27 (Winter 1981–82): 555–570.

Stein, Aaron Marc. "The Mystery Story in Cultural Perspective." In John Ball, ed. *The Mystery Story.* San Diego: University of California Extension, 1976, 29–58.

Steinbrunner, Chris, and Otto Penzler, eds. *Encyclopedia of Mystery and Detection.* New York: McGraw-Hill, 1976.

Steiner, T. R. "The Mind of the Hardboiled: Ross Macdonald and the Roles of Criticism." *South Dakota Review* 24 (Spring 1986): 29–53.

Stern, Madeleine B., ed. *A Double Life: Newly Discovered Thrillers of Louisa May Alcott*. Boston: Little, Brown, 1988.

Stewart, R. F. *And Always a Detective: Chapters on the History of Detective Fiction*. North Pomfret, VT: Newton Abbot; David & Charles, 1980.

Stille, Alexander. "Fiction Follows Life in Novels of Turow." *National Law Journal* (July 9, 1990): 8.

Stone, Eddie. *Donald Writes No More: A Biography of Donald Goines*. Los Angeles: Holoway, 1974.

Stookey, Lorena L. *Robin Cook: A Critical Companion*. Westport, CT: Greenwood Press, 1996.

Strenski, Ellen, and Robley Evens. "Ritual and Murder in Tony Hillerman's Detective Novels." *Western American Literature* 16 (Nov. 1981): 205–216.

Suits, Bernard. "The Detective Story: A Case Study of Games in Literature." *Canadian Review of Comparative Literature/Revue Canadienne de Litterature Comparée* 12 (June 1985): 200–219.

Sullivan, Eleanor. "The Short Story." In H.R.F. Keating, ed., *Whodunit? A Guide to Crime, Suspense and Spy Fiction*. New York: Van Nostrand Reinhold, 1982, 51–55.

———. "Writers on Their Mysterious Calling." In Lucy Freeman, ed., *The Murder Mystique: Crime Writers on Their Art*. New York: Ungar, 1982, 118–125.

Summers, Montague. *Gothic Bibliography*. London: Fortune Press, 1941.

———. *The Gothic Quest: A History of the Gothic Novel*. 1938. New York: Russell and Russell, 1964.

Sutherland, Scott. *Blood in Their Ink*. London: Stanley Paul and Co., 1953.

Svoboda, Frederic. "The Snub-nosed Mystique: Observations on the American Detective Hero." *Modern Fiction Studies* 29 (Autumn 1983): 557–568.

Swanson, Jean R., and Dean James. *By a Woman's Hand: A Guide to Mystery Fiction by Women*. Preface by Nancy Pickard. New York: Berkley Books, 1994.

Swirski, Peter. "Literary Studies and Literary Pragmatics: The Case of 'The Purloined Letter.' " *SubStance* 25 (1996): 69–89.

Symons, Julian. *Criminal Practices: Symons on Crime Writing 60's to 90's*. London: Macmillan, 1994.

———. *Critical Occasions*. London: Hamish Hamilton, 1966.

———. *Dashiell Hammett*. New York: Harcourt Brace Jovanovich, 1985.

———. *The Hundred Best Crime Stories*. London: Sunday Times, 1959.

———. *Mortal Consequences: A History from the Detective Story to the Crime Novel*. New York: Harper & Row, 1972. Published in England as *Bloody Murder: From the Detective Story to the Crime Novel: A History*. London: Faber, 1972. Revised and published as *Bloody Murder: From the Detective Story to the Crime Novel: A History*. New York: Penguin, 1985; Viking, 1985; revised ed., London: Pan Books, 1992.

Talburt, Nancy Ellen. "Red Is the Color of My True Love's Blood: Fetishism in Mystery Fiction." In Ray B. Browne, ed. and intro., *Objects of Special Devotion: Fetishism in Popular Culture*. Bowling Green, OH: Popular Press, 1982, 69–88.

Tallack, Douglas G. "William Faulkner and the Tradition of Tough-Guy Fiction." In Larry Landrum, Pat Browne, and Ray B. Browne, eds., *Dimensions of Detective Fiction*. Bowling Green, OH: Popular Press, 247–264.

Tani, Stefano. *The Doomed Detective: The Contribution of the Detective Novel to Postmodern American and Italian Fiction*. Carbondale: Southern Illinois University Press, 1984.

Taylor, Bruce. "The Real McCone." *Armchair Detective* 23 (Summer 1990): 260–69.

Thompson, Gary Richard, ed. *The Gothic Imagination: Essays in Dark Romanticism*. Pullman: Washington State University Press, 1974.

Thompson, Jon. *Fiction, Crime, and Empire: Clues to Modernity and Postmodernism*. Urbana: University of Illinois Press, 1993.

Thomson, H. Douglas. *Masters of Mystery*. 1931. New York: Dover, 1978.

Tillery, Carolyn. "The Fiction of Black Crime: It's No Mystery." *American Visions* 12 (April-May 1997): 18–22.

Todorov, Tzvetan. "Typology of Detective Fiction." In *The Poetics of Prose*. Trans. by Richard Howard. Ithaca, NY: Cornell University Press, 1977, 42–52.

Trembley, Elizabeth A. *Michael Crichton: A Critical Companion*. Westport, CT: Greenwood Press, 1996.

Trotter, David. "Theory and Detective Fiction." *Critical Quarterly* 33 (Summer 1991): 66–77.

Tsunoda, Waka. "On the Beat with William Caunitz." *Armchair Detective* 22 (Spring 1989): 137–141.

Turner, Darwin T. "The Rocky Steele Novels of John B. West." In Larry Landrum, Pat Browne, and Ray B. Browne, eds. *Dimensions of Detective Fiction*. Bowling Green, OH: Popular Press, 1976, 140–148.

Turner, Robert. *Some of My Best Friends Are Writers, but I Wouldn't Want My Daughter to Marry One*. Los Angeles: Sherbourne Press, 1970.

Tuska, Jon. *The Detective in Hollywood*. Garden City, NY: Doubleday, 1978.

———. *Philo Vance: The Life and Times of S. S. Van Dine*. Bowling Green, OH: Bowling Green State University Press, 1971.

Twentieth-Century Crime and Mystery Writers. New York: St. James Press, 1980, 1985, 1991.

Twentieth-Century Romance and Gothic Writers, ed. by James Vinson; assoc. ed., D. L. Kirkpatrick. Preface by Kay Mussel. London: Macmillan, 1982.

Tysh, Chris. "From One Mirror to Another: The Rhetoric of Disaffiliation in *City of Glass*." *Review of Contemporary Fiction* 14 (Spring 1994): 46–52.

Van Dine, S. S. "Twenty Rules for Writing Detective Stories." *American Magazine* (1928). Reprinted in Howard Haycraft, ed., *The Art of the Mystery Story: A Collection of Critical Essays*. New York: Carrol and Graf, 1946, 189–93.

Van Dover, J. Kenneth. *At Wolfe's Door: The Nero Wolfe Novels of Rex Stout*. San Bernardino, CA: Borgo Press, 1991.

———. *Centurions, Knights & Other Cops: The Police Novels of Joseph Wambaugh*. San Bernardino, CA: Borgo Press, 1995.

———. *Murder in the Millions: Erle Stanley Gardner, Mickey Spillane, Ian Fleming*. New York: Ungar, 1984.

———. *You Know My Method: The Science of the Detective*. Bowling Green, OH: Bowling Green State University Popular Press, 1994.

———, ed. *The Critical Response to Raymond Chandler.* Westport, CT: Greenwood Press, 1995.

Van Meter, Jan R. "Sophocles and the Rest of the Boys in the Pulps: Myth and the Detective Novel." In Larry Landrum, Pat Browne, and Ray B. Browne, eds., *Dimensions of Detective Fiction.* Bowling Green, OH: Popular Press, 1976, 12–21.

Vicarel, Jo Ann. *A Reader's Guide to the Police Procedural.* New York: G. K. Hall, 1995.

Vollmer, August, and A. E. Parker. *Crime, Crooks and Cops.* New York: Funk and Wagnalls Co., 1937.

Walker, Ronald G., and June M. Frazer, eds. *The Cunning Craft: Original Essays on Detective Fiction and Contemporary Literary Theory.* Afterword by David R. Anderson. Macomb, IL: Western Illinois University Press, 1990.

Walsh, John. *Poe the Detective: The Curious Circumstances Behind "The Mystery of Marie Rogêt."* New Brunswick, NJ: Rutgers University Press, 1968.

Wark, Wesley K. *Spy Fiction, Spy Films, and Real Intelligence.* London and Portland, OR: F. Cass, 1991.

Wasserburg, Charles. "Raymond Chandler's Great Wrong Place." *Southwest Review* 74 (Autumn 1989): 534–545.

Watson, Colin. *Snobbery with Violence: Crime Stories and Their Audience.* London: Eyre and Spottiswoode, 1971; New York: St. Martin's Press, 1972; rev. ed. London: Eyre Methuen, 1979.

Waugh, Hillary. "The American Police Procedural." In H.R.F. Keating, ed., *Whodunit? A Guide to Crime, Suspense and Spy Fiction.* New York: Van Nostrand Reinhold, 1982, 43–46.

———. *Hillary Waugh's Guide to Mysteries & Mystery Writing.* Cincinnati, OH: Writer's Digest Books, 1991.

———. "The Mystery Versus the Novel." In John Ball, ed. *The Mystery Story.* San Diego: University of California Extension, 1976, 61–81.

———. "The Police Procedural." In John Ball, ed. *The Mystery Story.* San Diego: University of California Extension, 1976, 163–187.

Weibel, Kay. "Mickey Spillane as a Fifties Phenomenon." In Larry Landrum, Pat Browne, and Ray B. Browne, eds., *Dimensions of Detective Fiction.* Bowling Green, OH: Popular Press, 1976, 114–123.

Weinkauf, Mary S. *Hard-boiled Heretic: The Lew Archer Novels of Ross Macdonald.* San Bernardino, CA: Borgo Press, 1986.

Weisberg, Richard H. *The Failure of the Word: The Protagonist as Lawyer in Modern Fiction.* New Haven: Yale University Press, 1984.

Weixlmann, Joe. "Culture Clash, Survival, and Trans-Formation: A Study of Some Innovative Afro-American Novels of Detection." *Mississippi Quarterly* 38 (Winter 1984–85): 21–31.

Wells, Carolyn. *The Technique of the Mystery Story.* Springfield, MA: Home Correspondence School, 1913, rev. 1929.

Wells, Linda S. "Popular Literature and Postmodernism: Sara Paretsky's Hard-Boiled Feminist." *Proteus: A Journal of Ideas* 6 (Spring 1989): 51–56.

Wertheim, Mary. "Philip Marlowe, Knight in Blue Serge." *Columbia Library Columns* 37 (Feb. 1988): 13–22.

Whitley, John S. "Pudd'nhead Wilson: Mark Twain and the Limits of Detection."
    Journal of American Studies 21 (April 1987): 55–70.
Whitney, Phyllis. "Gothic Mysteries." In John Ball, ed. *The Mystery Story*. San
    Diego: University of California Extension, 1976, 223–233.
Williams, John. *Into the Badlands*. London: Paladin, 1991.
Willett, Ralph. *The Naked City: Urban Crime Fiction in the USA*. Manchester and
    New York: Manchester University Press; distributed in the U.S. and Canada
    by St. Martin's Press, 1996.
Wilson, Andrew J. "The Corruption in Looking: William Faulkner's 'Sanctuary' as
    a 'Detective Novel," *Mississippi Quarterly* 47 (Summer 1994): 441–461.
Winkler, John J. *Auctor & Actor: A Narratological Reading of Apuleius' Golden
    Ass*. Berkeley: University of California Press, 1985.
Winks, Robin. "American Detective Fiction." *American Studies International* 19
    (Autumn 1980): 3–16.
———. *Modus Operandi*. Boston: David R. Godine, 1982.
Winks, Robin, ed. *Colloquium on Crime: Eleven Renowned Mystery Writers Dis-
    cuss Their Work*. New York: Scribner's, 1986.
———, ed. *Detective Fiction: A Collection of Critical Essays*. Englewood Cliffs,
    NJ: Prentice-Hall, 1980.
Winn, Dilys, ed. *Murder Ink: The Mystery Reader's Companion*. New York: Work-
    man, 1977; rev. ed., 1984.
———. *Murderess Ink: The Better Half of the Mystery*. New York and London:
    Workman, 1979.
Winston, Robert Paul, and Nancy C. Mellerski. *The Public Eye: Ideology and the
    Police Procedural*. New York: St. Martin's Press, 1992.
Wires, Richard. *John P. Marquand and Mr. Moto: Spy Adventures and Detective
    Films*. Muncie, IN: Ball State University, 1990.
Woeller, Waltraud, and Bruce Cassiday. *The Literature of Crime and Detection:
    An Illustrated History from Antiquity to the Present*. 1984. New York: Un-
    gar, 1988.
Wolfe, Peter. *Beams Falling: The Art of Dashiell Hammett*. Bowling Green, OH:
    Bowling Green State University Popular Press, 1980.
———. "The Critics Did It: An Essay Review." *Modern Fiction Studies* 29 (Autumn
    1983): 389–433.
———. *Dreamers Who Live Their Dreams: The World of Ross Macdonald's Nov-
    els*. Bowling Green, OH: Bowling Green State University Popular Press,
    1977.
———. *Something More than Night: The Case of Raymond Chandler*. Bowling
    Green, OH: Bowling Green State University Popular Press, 1985.
Wolstenholme, Susan. *Gothic (Re)visions: Writing Women as Readers*. Albany:
    State University of New York Press, 1993. Series: SUNY series in feminist
    criticism and theory.
Woods, Paula L., ed. *Spooks, Spies, and Private Eyes: Black Mystery, Crime, and
    Suspense Fiction*. New York: Doubleday, 1995.
Woolf, Mike. "Exploding the Genre: The Crime Fiction of Jerome Charyn." In
    Brian Docherty, ed. *American Crime Fiction: Studies in the Genre*. New
    York: St. Martin's Press, 1988, 131–43.

Wright, Lyle. *American Fiction, 1774–1850*. San Marino, CA: Huntington Library, 1969.

———. *American Fiction, 1851–1875*. San Marino, CA: Huntington Library, 1965.

———. *American Fiction, 1876–1900*. San Marino, CA: Huntington Library, 1966.

Wrong, E. M., ed. *Crime and Detection*. 1921. New York: Oxford University Press, 1926.

Wu, William F. *The Yellow Peril: Chinese Americans in American Fiction, 1850–1940*. Hamden, CT: Archon (Shoestring Press), 1982.

Yates, Donald A. "Locked Rooms and Puzzles: A Critical Memoir." In John Ball, ed. *The Mystery Story*. San Diego: University of California Extension, 1976, 189–203.

Zizek, Slavoj. "The Detective and the Analyst." *Literature and Psychology* 36 (1990): 27–46.

INDEX OF NAMES

INDEX OF SUBJECTS AND TITLES

About the Author

LARRY LANDRUM is a professor of English at Michigan State University, where he teaches popular culture, multicultural literature, and film theory.

ISBN 0-313-21387-9

HARDCOVER BAR CODE